RUINED ALPHAS

THE POISONVERSE

AMY NOVA

D1727363

Because of Marie...

And Havoc.

CONTENT

HOLD UP! Is there anything I should be aware of as a reader?

Oh hi! First up, you know you're about to read a book written by an adult for adults, right? OK Cool, cool, let's get to it.

"Why choose" is the language I prefer to use when dealing with intimate relationships between multiple people, because, as I see it, everyone gets to choose love. Oh, and everyone is queer.

Great! I'm down! What else?

There's discussion about childhood trauma and abuse, violence against women, and abuse by high control groups, trafficking (these topics are discussed and explored with limited graphic depictions on page).

Discussion of food being withheld or used as punishment may be distressful if disordered eating is distressful for you.

There is a mass casualty event with limited graphic depictions.

No abuse happens between love interests on page.

Got it. Understood. Noted.

Other things that may be stressful... broken kneecaps, amnesia, concussions and broken ribs, waffle denial, pack brothers doing some fuckery for the greater good, really bad cocktails, ruthless sluts and a sunshine psychopath.

I am so ready! How's the spice?

For me, this is medium spicy. It's omegaverse so there is a heat scene and knots. IYKYK. And you caught the part about everyone being queer, right?

BRING IT ON! Oh and who is your favorite character?

Oh dear, you'll have to stalk me on social media to find out!

ONE

LUTHER SAINT

"Capture or kill?"

"They haven't issued a kill order. Yet." Talon handed me zip cuffs.

We were called in last minute for this job. Someone with a bigger paycheck than me didn't think New Oxford PD could handle one tiny suspected omega terrorist.

"We really doing this without Jackson?" I asked, snapping the cuffs to my utility belt and immediately regretting asking.

Talon's aura went all sharp and spiky. Cross just raised an eyebrow, scratching his short beard, and adjusted the MP5 across his shoulder. Talon could barely stand to be a mile apart from Jackson. Splitting up for two jobs in one night put the entire pack on edge.

"Our objective hasn't changed," Talon said, ignoring my question. "We want to get to her first. She's only wanted for questioning right now."

The system was not kind to misbehaving omegas.

And Ruin Winters was a very bad omega.

Ruin Winters was a social media starlet. Her signature jet black hair and black lips earned her the nickname "bombshell". Appropriate, since things were now blowing up around her.

She ran an omega mean girl tabloid blog. Some really nasty girl-on-girl violence. Outing people for affairs, plots to sabotage ball gowns, and other gossip taken to the extreme.

The higher-ups were convinced she was working with the Reset, the notorious beta-run organization hell bent on bringing down the Alpha Omega Institute. Cross agreed. Well, he believed, given the level of technological skill it took to hide a person's real identity on social media, that somebody with deep pockets was funding her. If Cross couldn't find you, money had to be involved.

We watched a huddle of men scurry across the parking lot of the warehouse facility. Talon pulled on gloves, balling his fists to get the fit right. He jutted his chin towards the men.

"Cross, you shadow PD command."

My turn to raise an eyebrow. That was usually Jackson's job. With his boy-next-door looks, people never saw Jackson as a threat. Cross, at 6'3" with shaggy beard, tattoos crawling up his hands and neck, was a walking billboard for the Gritch District's most wanted list.

"Luther, you take the south side. No cameras there."

I cracked my neck and resisted the urge to roll my eyes. We all knew that was a bad tactical decision given the state of my aura. So, I would be cooling my heels in the boondocks.

I turned and stalked off before Talon could get into pep talk mode.

"Hey," he shouted at me, "No Leroy Jenkins nonsense tonight." I rolled my eyes at the old gamer joke. I didn't want to admit I had the habit of throwing myself into situations where careful planning was the better option.

At least I had avoided a "buck up little camper" speech that wasn't going to help, anyway. Nothing was helping.

I pulled at the front of the flak jacket. I didn't mind vests. They were like nesting for alphaholes, all swaddled up and cozy in Kevlar, leather and ceramic ballistic plates. But I couldn't get comfortable in my own skin, so body armor was torture today.

Patting the front pocket of the vest, I tried some of that deep breathing shit. I stashed a picture of my sister in there, like it was a lucky rabbit's foot. The black-and-white printout of the pic was the only thing that made me feel remotely sane some days. It gave me hope. At least one of us might be OK after all we went through.

"This is Commander Treyfor. All sectors report."

A groan of disgust seeped into the pack bonds as the radio chatter began. On jobs like this, we could work in almost complete silence. We got more information through our pack bonds than we could with banter and shouted orders. When command got chatty on comms, the job would be a disaster.

The pack, all four of us, were the Gold Pack and Rogue Enforcement Agency's most effective strike force. Normally, we were running down rogue alphas, while working behind the scenes to right some wrongs in the GPRE.

We rarely hunted omegas. Society was quite effective at stamping out the rebellious ones. It didn't need our help.

Someone, somewhere, didn't have confidence that Commander WhatTheFuckWasHisName could get the job done. We were here to watch and overrule his jurisdiction with glee.

I ducked into the lonely warehouse on the outskirts of the facility. It was a ghost town of parade floats and storage containers. The bright fake flowers were eerie in the ambient security lighting.

I couldn't sit still and keep my aura together. It got worse when I was alone, unless I was running. I stalked the perimeter, weaving in and out of the ostentatious decorations that were rolled out once or twice a year and then forgotten about. Guess they ended up here.

A few months back, I blew up my aura when the old man died, and things went south for my sister. It left me feeling scattered and rough around the edges. I was duct taping myself back together ever since. Duo, our medic and boss, said it would get better.

It wasn't.

The really hard part was that I had to keep it all under wraps. Hiding things from your pack was tricky.

I ran my hand over my blond buzz cut and mentally went through my gear, touching each pocket and ticking off its contents. Anything to keep my thoughts out of danger zones like...

The pack.

Lying to the pack.

Being a rogue alpha and lying to the pack about it.

Being a rogue alpha, who hunts rogue alphas for a living, for an organization with the mission of eliminating rogue alphas...

And troublesome omegas.

Fuck.

My aura sizzled at the word "omega" tickling my brain.

All alphas had a protective and possessive streak, and that doubled when an omega bonded into your pack. Hunting an omega went against all our alpha instincts. You needed aura gymnastics to not go insane in the process.

That was precisely why our pack didn't have, and didn't want, an omega.

We spent far too much time on the dark side of bonded relationships, the ones that society didn't want to acknowledge. We existed to sweep it under the carpet, by eliminating rogues and pulling omegas out of bad situations.

Given what we've seen, we were all a little sensitive when it came to omegas. Even Cross, who didn't like anybody and seemed to barely tolerate the pack most days, had flattened more than one dive bar when someone got too handsy with an omega.

And this was all on top of Talon and Cross' history with omegas. Throw my gold pack omega sister into the mix? Yeah, we had omega-related trauma.

Instincts, as sucky as they were, ruled alphas and omegas. That's why I didn't buy it. This panic stirred up around a potential terrorist omega was political. It really wasn't in their nature. Someone was pulling her strings.

Ruin Winters made fun of omegas.

Ruin Winters wasn't strapped with machine guns running around blowing up buildings.

Sure, Winters' signature black lip prints were showing up at all sorts of disturbances, but really, that was totally easy to fake.

There was a boom and two soft pops.

I reached for the pack bonds. Something had happened, but it didn't feel like people were dying. I pulled my MP5 off my back, silent as a ghost.

A rusty door hinge screamed and then a soft thud as it shut. Footsteps? Two people? Maybe three?

I heard some muttered conversation that I couldn't make out through the tinny echoes. I put my back flat against one of the rusty containers and peered around the corner of a rose-encrusted float, confident the shadows would eat me up. Three figures filed past a gap in the clutter.

Well, well, well.

Let's just nip this in the bud right now. I could take down three betas, no problem. I was big enough that I could sit on all three of them until I got them in cuffs. *Capture not kill.*

I scaled to the top of a storage container, doing my best to keep from making noise. I was stashed out here because my aura was the problem, but my aura would help me bring in these three.

Two men and a woman, maybe? One was shorter and more slight.

Could be a dude, didn't want to be sexist.

Shock-and-awe was the way to go here. If you assert your authority hard and fast, most people comply, except for rogues, obviously.

"Good evening, ladies and gentlemen. I'll be in charge of your incarceration this evening. Would you be so kind as to get down on the ground and put your hands on your head?" My deep voice echoed and bounced off the metal walls.

OK. That was a terrible line. I would not be including that in my report, but I never got to grandstand and be all showy. That was normally Talon's thing.

Predictably, they halted and looked around.

"Up here, you dumb motherfuckers." That was a little better. I angled myself so they could see I had a weapon trained on them, even in the dim light. They didn't have to know I would not fire on them.

The tallest of the trio put his hands up, flashed me a "please hold" finger, and pulled something from his back pocket. I squinted... looked like a little black box the size of a deck of cards, with an antenna... oh fuck.

The BOOM sent me flying from the top of the steel container. The ballistic plates did nothing to absorb the impact when I hit the ground. Sharp pain split my head in two. Concussion. My vision dimmed. I shook my head, like that would get things in the right place, but it just blurred everything. I breathed in smoke and dust.

I scrambled to my feet. Training had me ignoring the pain in my head and side. I bit back the urge to retch. Panting, I kept the trio in my line of sight, just barely. One figure tore away from the other two and darted left.

That's the one I would grab.

High-pitched ringing cut off my hearing. I pulled on my aura for more speed and backup. The pack would come running now.

I caught up with alpha speed and snagged the back of his jacket. Hauled him to a stop, slammed him against the wall.

Not a *him*.

Her.

Ink black hair. Fair skin.

Black. Fucking. Lips.

Eyes like sea glass, blues and greens swirling in a face too pretty to be real even with heavy makeup.

I blinked furiously. I was seeing double. Everything had an unreal haze. Hard to get my eyes to focus. Hard to know what was real.

The gun in my face was real enough, even if there were two of them.

Ruin Winters pulled a gun on me.

Fair enough.

I had my gun to her head.

Her lips were moving. I couldn't hear with my ears still ringing from the explosion. I shook my head to get them working again.

"You're going to drop the gun." I hoped my voice was loud enough. Panic drenched her.

She did not drop the gun.

Her hand shook, eyes went wide when it hit both of us.

Her scent.

Creamsicles. Orange and vanilla. Sweet and sticky on a hot summer day at the playground. An omega's scent.

I panted. Lowered my gun.

"How?"

She was urgent. Lips, matte, black as sin, round and full, sweet as her scent, were moving, shouting maybe. She stepped back and then ran for it, taking her scent with her.

I was paralyzed.

By her scent.

I just watched her run away from me.

Something thudded into my back. If my ears hadn't been jacked, I would have heard the flashbang grenade roll away from me.

My last thought, before everything went black...

Ruin Winters, the terrorist I was assigned to capture, was my mate.

RUIN WINTERS

"I told you. I told you this was all wrong. If you listened..." The rest of my mutter was cut off with his fingers biting into my arm, hard enough to snap the bone. I choked back a scream, my knuckles going white on the prop gun they had given me.

"You did this, didn't you, you little fucking nester whore? Sabotaged the whole fucking thing." His grip on me was the only thing keeping me upright and moving.

We all stopped at the popping sounds before picking up the pace. They were half dragging me now. The impossible heels they put me in caught on the cracked pavement.

"How could I have..." they pushed me through the door of the warehouse.

It didn't matter, none of it mattered. It would be my fault no matter what I said or what actually happened. The car was on the other side. It was faster to go through the building than around before they blew it up. They wouldn't get their precious video now.

I snatched my arm away and struggled to keep up. He let me go, needing two hands to text.

"Fuck, Lance is down." Bennett said over his phone. Billy just grunted.

"It's fine. We continue with the mission. Drop the bitch off to establish an alibi. Some of the footage will still be usable."

Bennett stopped and reached for me again. I wasn't keeping up.

"Good evening, ladies and gentlemen..." the voice echoed through the warehouse, deep, rich, commanding. My breath caught... He was like an avenging angel, standing on top of a metal box, only his outline visible, his features all in shadow.

"Up here, you dumb motherfuckers."

A superhero sent to catch the villain.

Thank god.

I closed my eyes. Relief flooded me like the scent of cut grass.

I was caught.

It would all stop.

He would make it all safe.

I would be dead.

I smiled, waiting for his bullet.

I screamed. The explosion sent me to the ground, landing hard on my butt. Gravel and debris cutting into my palms.

I watched him fall.

No.

Smoke and grass swirled around me. It was wrong for explosions to smell this good.

Bennett wrenched me to my feet. I pulled free and bolted.

"We can't lose her!"

"Get the car. We'll catch her on the other side."

I ran as hard as I could.

I couldn't. I couldn't go back, not if he's...

Bennett. Bennett caught me. Grabbed me from behind. He yanked me back. I hit the wall. My gun came up on reflex. I knew it was a prop. They would never let me have bullets.

And then he stole my breath.

The superhero. My angel. Eyes the color of pine trees in late summer. Blond hair cut close to his head, creating a halo around him in the dim light. An alpha towering over me. A monster triple my size.

And the only one who could save me.

He looked at my gun and pressed his own to my temple.

"Please, do it. I can't. I can't go back. Please don't make me."

"You're going to drop the gun." His voice was like far off thunder, the promise of danger and relief.

And then his scent came for me.

He smelled like summer picnics when you were a kid, applewood smoke from the barbeque and cut grass. He wore the scent of perfect summer days, with playgrounds and swing sets flying so high, knowing someone will catch you. Life before you knew you were defective, and the world hated you.

He was beautiful, and he was mine. Always had been.

And they would kill him because of it.

I shook my head at the ridiculous thoughts. My eyes shot wide and fear clawed at my insides. Not for me. For him.

"How?" He lowered his gun, looking confused.

"Go. You have to go. Please. They can't find you. If they know, if they know you're... You have to go. Please. They'll hurt you like they hurt me. You have to go."

He wasn't listening. He didn't believe me. He didn't know. He didn't know what would happen.

I took a step back, and another. If he wouldn't leave, I would. Go back to them. It was the only way he'd be safe. I couldn't let them know. They couldn't know he was...

I ran. My heart exploding in my chest. I stumbled through a door. Outside, the pavement was smoother, easier to move on. Tires screeched.

The door of a white van opened, hands grabbed me, pulling me in.

I dropped the fake gun. It was useless. I was useless.

They were shouting, screaming. All I could hear was my heartbeat, like it pounded for *him*. The van jolted forward, sending me to the dirty floor. I protected my head, my face, from the blows that would come. It would be worse if I let them bruise my face.

I didn't care. It didn't matter as long as we were far away from *him* and he was safe.

TWO

LUTHER

The grass was cool against my back. Just grass and sky and shadows cast by her. Caged by her hair and her scent as she leaned over me. Her taste on my lips. Sweet. Dreamy.

My name shouted in the distance. Urgent.

Her lips trembled.
"Go." The word leaving her black lips.

"Step back. He's going to come up swinging."

The acrid bite of vinegar, but a thousand times worse, stole the citrus and sunshine.

"Fuck, no, her scent."

I struggled to my feet. Gagging, I spat, wiping at my nose, full of chemicals and bile. My vision swam, I couldn't see straight. I fell to my knees and barfed proper now.

A hand touched my back, I stumbled to two feet and swung, a big sloppy punch that only connected with air.

"Cross?" Three of him danced in front of me. I squinted one eye, so I only saw doubles now. He held the smelling salts capsule in front of me.

He hauled me back upright and pinned me to the wall with one big hand.

His lips moved. I shook my head. Closed my eyes and rubbed my ear. I felt his fingers turn my chin. He wiped something off my ear lobe.

"Where is she? Do you have her?"

"Luther, stay with me." His voice was muffled. I could barely hear. He snapped his fingers in front of my face. I saw it, but didn't hear it.

Talon's face in mine now. I jerked out of his hands. He was trying to pry my eyes open.

"Our mate, man." I mumbled, speech slurring as I slid down the wall, as the lights were turned out.

"No, no, no. Luther. Fuck. Luther."

On an ocean of grass now. A sea of blue and green. Salt on my lips, orange on hers. Pitch black clouds marring the sky.

"Come back to me, Luther." Talon was hauling me up by the vest. "I swear to fucking god, I will make you walk right into the clinic yourself if you don't snap out of this."

That got through loud and clear.

No doctors.

"OK, OK. I got this." I tried pulling out of his grasp.

"Do you know where you are?" Talon was still trying to check my pupils.

"In a fucking car, you asshole."

"SUV." Cross corrected from the driver's seat.

"You sure about that? A minute ago, you were telling me you were swimming in an ocean of grass with your mate."

"Where is she?" Panic gripped me.

"Fuck," Cross said.

"She who, Luther?"

"I... I don't know. Didn't you smell it, though?"

"Luther, you were in a warehouse that was rigged with explosives. You were not eating ice cream in a park."

"Talon?" Cross asked nervously.

"Pull your aura in, get a hold of yourself, or I will take you in."

I nodded and closed my eyes for a second. Everything hurt. The longer I was upright and thinking about it, the more the details just fell away.

"What happened?" I asked.

"The Reset." Cross said. "They rigged a few of the warehouses with explosives. Big and showy, no real damage. The parade is fucked, though." He chuckled.

I looked at Talon. He was texting and cursing. I put my hand on the headrest in front of me. The swaying of the car threatened to bring back the barfs. Talon put the phone to his ear. A robotic voice told him to leave a message.

"Pick up the fucking phone, Jackson." He said, before shoving it back in his pocket. I traded a glance in the rearview with Cross. Talon cursing at Jackson was a bad sign.

"Ruin." I muttered.

"Yeah, Jackson is ruining some shit tonight."

"No. Winters."

He pulled his phone out again, like he didn't just check it 2 seconds ago.

"No, Ruin Winters wasn't there. We told them their intel was wrong."

"But I..." What? What exactly had I seen? I saw her, black hair, black lips. No. That was a dream. No, that wasn't her in the dream. Not Ruin. My mate. Mate? In the warehouse? Fuck.

"Luther." Talon tapped me on the face a few times.

"OK. OK." I pulled away from him, blinking. I rubbed my temples and groaned. Pretty sure now that I broke a rib, moving hurt. I took a slow, deep breath. It hurt too much to make it make sense. Concussions fucking sucked.

JACKSON SERRANO

The leather creaked, giving up its cherry whiskey scent, as I rearranged the plates on the table. She'd go for the dessert first. Always did. Everything else could go home in a doggie bag. Whipped cream didn't travel.

I tugged the oversized leather coat down when the absurd synchronicity of this moment hit me. Fucking poetic justice.

Cross was wearing this exact leather jacket, sitting at this exact table at this exact diner 10 years ago, and I was buying him food he couldn't afford.

I was too pretty to be out after dark in the Gritch District. Not because I was afraid I'd get jumped. Half the time I hoped a motherfucker would. I got perverse glee out of someone underestimating me. It was a kink.

The problem was people wouldn't talk to me.

I fell in love with Cross the second I met him. But not in a romantic way. And certainly not in the desperate, fiery, all-consuming way I loved Talon.

That night, Cross was holding me up with a revolver, attempting to rob the pretty boy who was skulking around a back alley of some dive bar five or six blocks from here. I'd disarmed him with excessive force and gave him a hundred to walk into that bar and get the ID off a guy we were hunting down for suspected trafficking.

Twenty minutes later, he'd walked out with the ID, a split lip and a girl's number scrawled on a waxy bar napkin. From that moment on, I knew I loved him like pack. Pack was everything. And there wasn't a damn thing I could do about it then, except to buy him dinner and wait.

I checked my watch. It was heavy and comforting. This was cutting it close. I was running out of time. I'd run grannies down in the street to make it to the mall on time if I had to.

My foot was tapping under the table. It took more effort than usual to force it still. On a good day, being apart from Talon would put me on edge. I would crawl inside that man's skin if I could. Today was not a good day.

The rest of the pack, Talon, Cross, Luther, was working a job across town. It wasn't that I didn't trust their skill, I didn't trust New Oxford PD not to cock things up and get them all hurt. I turned my phone off and tucked it back in the inside pocket of the jacket. Talon wouldn't text again until the job was done.

The lack of actual information, all the noise coming through the pack bonds, and nerves about the mall meeting were going to send me over the edge. I nuzzled into the jacket, taking in Cross' faint scent that lingered like a memory. It was as close to touching them as I could get right now.

Bells on the door tinkled as Vex pushed her way into the diner and headed right for me. As usual, she was well put together, with a cream jacket, jeans, and giant bug-eyed sunglasses that she definitely couldn't afford. I flicked my glance out the window, it was already getting dark. You see, with glasses like that, you only think of one thing - covering up a black eye given to them by someone who claimed to love them.

I was 80% sure that was not the case here, but it still had my aura kicking out sparks. Yeah, we worked for the GPRE, but more than half our time was spent working against the GPRE, getting vulnerable people safe before they got on their radar.

That was the only thing that would pull me away from the pack when we were working.

She slid into the booth and immediately put a forkful of pie into her mouth. She pushed the sunglasses up on her head. I caught a flash of the gold ring around her eyes before she slammed them down again, remembering why she was wearing them.

"What's good?" I pitched my tone low and comforting. Whatever was going on with her, she didn't need overprotective alpha bullshit.

"Oh, you know, same old same old," she said around a bite.

I nodded, knowing that was an absolute lie.

"Whatchu got for me?" If I could get her talking, my pretty face and my yummy aura could probably get her to open up.

She picked up a french fry from my plate and an onion ring from hers, taking a bite of each.

"Was shaken down by NOPD for information about GPRE strike forces," she said around the mouthful.

"OK. Two things," I flashed her two fingers, "define 'shaken down' and how the fuck did that happen?"

She winced and tried to hide it, but I caught it.

"Well, I *may* have gotten myself into a situation where I *may* have told someone that my boyfriend was in the GPRE."

"Fuck, Vex."

That girl's penchant for lying was going to get her into trouble one day that she couldn't get out of. Her mouth routinely wrote checks that her little gold pack omega ass could not pay. She could be smart, but she made dumb, impulsive decisions. Talon and I were thinking about working on a plan to get her financially stable and out of New Oxford for good.

You didn't have to be a duchess to make it on your own as an omega, what with housing and income assistance and free health care. But Vex was gold pack, and couldn't claim any of those rights. Her only skill was masquerading as a beta, and it wasn't like you could make a career out of that.

"I know, I know, but I lost a contact. Things got carried away."

"What about the cop?"

She grimaced. "He pushed his way into my apartment the next day asking about my boyfriend and GPRE packs."

"And?"

"Aisha dealt with him." A smirk curled her lips up.

"Ugh, I hope she drew blood!" My smile was vicious and delighted.

Vex popped a french fry in her mouth, pride dripping off her.

First rule of the Gritch; if NOPD bites, you bite back.

"Got a name?"

"Ray?" She wrinkled up her brow. "Ford? Fordroy? Fordray? Reyferd?"

It didn't matter. The 'intel' Vex gave us never panned out. That's not why I was paying her. I needed a way to funnel her money that she didn't see as sus. She put on a good show, with expensive sunglasses and outfits, and *assuring* me kleptomania was an illness—*and had nothing to do with wealth*—but I knew better. And she was the last person who needed to be on the GPRE radar.

"You need me to follow Pinky this week?" she said, then drew in her brows like she made a mistake.

Even the silly nickname gave me butterflies.

I'd been trailing some asshole when it hit me and the scent locked in. I couldn't catch up, the street was too crowded and I couldn't lose my tail. I saw her go into a day spa.

Vex took advantage of my distraction, drooling over my omega, as an opportunity to try to pick my pocket, badly. I'd threatened to arrest her. Vex knew a gold pack in jail was a bad idea, so when I offered to pay her to go in that salon, get the girl's name, she'd jumped. She over performed too, and even got the girl's HeatMatch app screen name - PinkHairDontCare.

Vex had been doing small jobs for me since. Not that I needed her help. I could stalk Pinky and clone her phone all by myself like a big boy. But it was clear the girl did not catch my scent seeing as I was pumped full of scent blockers that day. She had no idea she'd accidentally run into her fated mate. And I wanted to keep it that way until I could warm the pack up to the idea of a scent matched omega.

It wasn't going well, and I couldn't wait anymore. I looked at my watch. I had to go.

I put a white box and an "aspirin" bottle on the table.

This is what she had called me for. If Vex knew how expensive these contacts lenses were, she'd have a heart attack. They were top of the line, undetectable. Your lover could be a centimeter from your face, staring into your soul and not see even a shimmer of gold in your eyes, the only dead giveaway that marked a gold pack omega.

"These are illegal." I tapped the pill bottle, even if it wasn't the first time we'd done this. "Don't get caught."

We had a stash of drugs that we swept up from crime scenes. Of course we had scent blockers provided by the GPRE. You couldn't go undercover smelling like an alpha. And we bought on the black market, too. Vex wanted scent blockers stronger than prescription. I'd give her anything she wanted to keep her on this side of a dark bond.

She nodded, stuffing the pill bottle in her bra.

"You sure you're good?" I stood and peeled five $100 bills from my money clip, tucking them under her pie plate.

"Yup."

She was lying. I knew it. She knew it. But not much I could do if she didn't ask for help. She didn't trust me, and that was fine.

I paid the tab on my way out and told them to box up all the food for Vex with an extra slice of pie.

Then, I was running to my car. The mall was halfway across town. It would be bad manners to show up late when meeting your scent matched omega.

THREE

RUBY FROST

My hands were dirty and scraped. I didn't know how I was going to lie about that one. I picked at a spot on the palm with my nail. It felt like a splinter under my skin.

I crouched in the back of the van, holding on as best I could. I had changed out of the black jeans and turtleneck, stuffing that and the wig in the backpack. I had to use dark red lipstick. The makeup wipes never took off all the cheap black stuff.

Bennett hit the brakes hard, knowing it would make me topple forward. I was going to show up filthy at this point.

"Look." Billy grabbed me by the shoulder, his dishwater blond hair lying limp on his forehead. "The timing is already fucked up. You have to make sure you're caught on all the cameras. You remember where they are?"

Of course I remembered. I wasn't dumb. I knew the layout of New Oxford Central Mall better than he did.

"Get coffee and pay with the card."

I rolled my eyes. Billy grabbed me by the throat and slammed me into the wall of the van.

"I am sick and tired of your shit."

"They'll see handprints on my neck." I said through gritted teeth.

Fear flashed in his eyes for a second before he let go.

They wanted to catfish this guy. He was supposed to be the son of someone important. Well connected, rich, special. They wanted to get to his pack. Typical alpha full of rage and hormones.

Only he wasn't.

He wasn't mean or gross like all the other guys I met online. Both as Ruby Frost and Ruin Winters. JJSeeks was sweet and charming. He asked what I thought about things. He didn't jump right to questions about heat.

They wanted to set him up, catch him stepping out on his pack, and then have Ruin Winters tear him to pieces for it with text message and video proof.

It was convenient that he could establish an alibi for us, too. There was no way a judge would believe we got from the warehouse to the mall for coffee and a first date in this short amount of time.

I braced myself for the light to change and the jerk forward. I already looked a mess. Ruby Frost was supposed to have more class than this. She was a sweet little omega who worked in a day spa and chatted about reality TV with rich omegas and betas all day.

I brushed at the conservative beige skirt and blouse. I looked boring and rumpled. Bennett had chosen this outfit, and it sucked.

I was so tired. So tired of it all. I closed my eyes and rested my head on my arm. And it was like *he* was waiting for me. I knew it was my imagination. It was all I had left.

He would never have chosen an outfit like this. *He* would have picked something pretty, with soft fabric and graceful lines. *He* wouldn't put his hands on me, not like that, not with disgust in *his* eyes.

We pulled to a jarring stop again, and I let go of *his* image like Billy and Bennett could see him too. That cop was there to kill me. I shouldn't be worried about *his* safety. I shouldn't be worried about *him* at all. There was just something... I couldn't shake the feeling that *he* was reaching out for me. That we were connected somehow. None of it made sense. I touched my lips like I could still taste smoke on my tongue.

Billy slid the door open and hopped out. I sighed and grabbed the cheap leather bag. All it had in it were scent dampening wipes, this ugly red lipstick, a wallet with one card and the phone. I hugged it to my side as he walked me into the building.

"Remember, you have to spend at least a half hour in the food court. You'll get a text and you'll say you have to go. Go out the main entrance so you get on all the cameras."

I just nodded with my head down. I didn't want to catch my reflection in any of the shop windows.

He handed me a slip of waxy paper, with the quarter-sized metal mesh sticker attached.

"Put it on his collar and don't fuck this up."

I slid the cheap GPS tracker into my bag.

I kind of hoped JJ didn't show. I knew this was all fake, but he was nice. I wanted to make it look like I cared, like I dressed up pretty for him before I ruined his life. I just wanted to pretend for a half an hour that I was normal.

Billy left so I could make my way to get coffee on my own. Waiting in line, I read all the items on the menu. It distracted me from thinking about the warehouse. I was only allowed black coffee, but it was nice to think about all the options.

"What can I get you, sweetie?" said the woman behind the counter.

She was a cute, older beta, with a flash of white in her hair. I narrowed my eyes. Maybe she wasn't a seer. Platinum blond was trendy right now. Ruin made fun of it all the time.

There was a picture of a green and white drink on a sign at the register. The green was summer bright, and it pulled at me.

"What's this?" I asked, pointing to the drink.

"Oh, matcha latte. They're great."

"What does it taste like?"

"A little hard to describe." She bit her lip, thinking of the right words. "It's creamy because of the milk, and on the sweet side. But matcha is a type of green tea, so it tastes floral and herby. Some people don't like it. They say it tastes like grass."

"Oh, I'll have that." My mood brightened instantly. Billy would probably knock me around when he checked the bank statement, but I shrugged it off. I'd survived worse. And he wasn't allowed to hit my face anymore.

I checked the dating app for messages from JJ. There was nothing new. I scrolled all the way to the beginning and read it for the millionth time while I waited for my drink.

He really was sweet. He told me about his pack, and his mom. The details were a little vague, but I was a stranger after all.

Yes, they made me fish for dirt, but I really wanted to know what growing up in a pack was like. I grew up with foster families. All betas. And betas didn't do packs.

They always said packs were oppressive and violent. If you didn't do what the pack lead said, you were beaten, or worse. And if you were an omega, they could make you do whatever they wanted.

Omegas could never say no.

I looked at his picture again. He was simply beautiful. Not hot, but beautiful. His hair fell across his forehead in that perfect wave. It was almost as black as Ruin's. He was squinting in this picture. His smile was so big, it crinkled up his eyes. They'd be warm and dark, and inviting. The kind of eyes that made you feel safe. And he smiled like a movie star. Dimples making him look younger than he was. I brushed my thumb over his picture, resisting even the wisp of hope that this might all be real.

He should be on the cover of magazines, going to balls and parties, not meeting a defective omega in a mall.

My drink was ready, and I made a little circuit of the food court while I waited for him, trying to find my resolve again. The purpose of the mission.

The Institute was corrupt and evil. It enslaved omegas and let dangerous alphas terrorize society. They controlled us with lies and propaganda, supported by the media, convincing us this was natural, normal. Alphas needed to be eliminated for society to flourish. Packs had to be destroyed.

I looked around at the handful of people having a late dinner. Any one of them could be an alpha. Any one of them could fly into a rage and level the whole place. I looked down at his picture again. Even as beautiful as he was, he could be that kind of dangerous alpha, too.

I had all the pamphlets memorized. I had written them out, word for word, as punishment a million times. I let the words wash over me. It was soothing, and brought my panic down.

I took a sip of the drink. It was a little too hot. I frowned. It didn't smell like *him* at all. It didn't even smell like grass.

I sighed and looked up.

He was there and everything shifted.

He was in a red sweater that made his tan skin glow, even in the ugly light of the food court. He had on a beat up leather jacket too, like he was trying to dress down. I could feel his smile all the way over here. He was beautiful.

We both took a step forward, then another, until we ate up the distance. His scent poured all over me. Black pepper and sandalwood, the expensive kind. Everything else in the world faded away, just him and his scent.

27

I felt like I shrank and doubled in size at the same time. Black pepper with lingering traces of smoke, and grass, and cherries, so thick I could taste it coating my tongue. My body hummed, my head emptied except for one word...

Mate.

"Hi." His voice was soft and wrapped around me like his scent until it became my everything. "I think you need to sit down." He nodded at the table next to us.

He held out a hand to lead me over. I put my hand in his, and sparkles exploded all over my body. My vision dimmed and my knees gave out. He stepped into me and caught me around the waist, grabbing my cup of tea before I dropped it.

"I got you."

Don't ever fucking let go.

I was dimly aware of him pulling my bag off my shoulder and placing it on the chair next to me. His hands, big, warm, sure, wrapped mine around the paper cup.

"Drink." He said. So I did. I would do anything he asked.

"Wha... What's happening?" My voice was a whisper, afraid to break this spell.

"I think this is what happens when you find your scent match."

The words took a while to settle into place. They were alien and more dangerous than sticking your hand into a snake pit.

"Scent match. I didn't think that was real." I whispered.

"Does this feel real?"

"Absolutely not."

His smile lit up his face, making him even more beautiful.

"I'm Jackson Serrano."

"Ruby Frost." I said robotically.

"Ruby," he closed his eyes and said my name like it was precious. "Your scent is amazing."

I flushed, and looked down at my hands. Tears suddenly stung my eyes. Words and memories flooded me. Since the day I perfumed, and it was known I was an omega, my smell had been offensive. I was banished from the house, and made to sleep on the porch, or worse, because no one could stand my stink.

"Your scent," he went on, "is like summer vacation. Oranges and vanilla ice cream. Like you just had the best day of your life and you're sitting in the sun hoping it never ends."

I tried. I tried every day to scrub it off. To not smell so bad, to give people one less reason to hate me. To prove I wasn't an animal, a thing ruled by smell like a dog.

"Hey," he tilted my chin up, wiping a tear off my cheek. "You OK?"

I shook my head. I couldn't speak. I was too afraid of what might come out. He took my hand in his and softly, rhythmically rubbed his thumb over my inner wrist. My heartbeat fluttered all over the place until it followed the pace he created.

Scent matches were a hoax. They weren't real. It was brain-washing by the Institute and traditionalist propaganda. Scent match was a lie they told omegas to keep them subjugated and compliant. This wasn't real. This couldn't be real.

"Jackson." I tried his name out on my tongue. It fit. It fit perfectly. I stole a look at his face, his beautiful face. His eyes caught me, held me, like everything was going to be OK.

He... he was... He was an alpha. Full of rage and domination. A monster, the only thing worse was a rogue. If he liked your scent, he would steal you away, give you to his pack, do... unspeakable things to you. Bite you. Bond you. Make you a slave. And the pack, the pack would tear you apart when your heat hit.

But... he wasn't, he wasn't any of that.

"Do you have a pack?" I blurted out.

His smile got even bigger, if that was possible.

"Yes, and they will fall in love with you too."

My heart started to pound. I should run, I should run in terror.

But all I wanted to do was fall into him, be small and warm, in his arms... in the pack's arms...

"Talon is pack lead. I've loved him forever." He glowed talking about his pack. "Luther will scoop you up and make you pancakes, as many as you want. And Cross. He's quiet, and strong, and smart. He'll fix anything that's broken."

Broken. I was broken. And there was no fixing me. That was the only thing I knew to be true.

"You're... you're not like anything I was told..." my voice was so soft, I wasn't sure I actually said that aloud.

His brow crinkled, like I wasn't making any sense. None of this made sense.

Mate.

The word circled around and around in my head, chasing down and eating up all the other thoughts.

I stood up, grabbed my bag, and willed myself not to fall down. Or fall into his arms.

"I... I have to go." And I braced myself. Because this was when he would attack. Grab me, throw me over this shoulder. Take me.

He stood. He towered over me. It should make me terrified. He was bigger, stronger. He was alpha. But I felt... safe.

And I couldn't handle that.

"I know this is a bit of a shock. When can I see you again?"

I stepped backwards. Just to see. A test. Would he let me leave? Would he let me go?

I turned and took three more steps before stopping. My body was screaming at me not to leave, but to jump into his arms, and never let go. It was wrong. It was a lie. Scent matches weren't real. Mates. They were not real.

I dug in my bag for the GPS chip and brought it out with my phone.

Remember the mission, Ruby.

Slowly, I met his eyes again. They were full of... I licked my lips. I couldn't even think the word. And he was just standing there, waiting for me.

"Your drink?" He said, holding the cup out to me.

I stepped back to him, the wafer thin chip on my fingertips. He drew a finger down my upper arm. Orange and pepper swirled between us. Holding my breath, I crumpled the chip in my fingers before dropping it in his pocket, hoping to damage it. Maybe the chip would never work and they'd forget all about him.

I swallowed, nodded once, and said "Monday".

His smile was so... loving... it threatened to knock me off my feet.

I fled the mall. I knew I was supposed to wait for a text. But I couldn't breathe with the taste of pepper on my tongue.

FOUR

LUTHER

Cross was hefting me to my room. A snarl twisted in my throat.

I braced myself on the door frame, preventing us from moving further. His arm was around my chest. He gave me a few soothing pats and a taste of his cool, collected aura. Cross might have been an asshole, but he was a nonjudgmental asshole. At least about this.

I couldn't have anyone in my room. All my bullshit alpha hormones had fixated on it. The second someone stepped into this space, territorial rage tore through me.

"Couch?" his voice was low in my ear.

I nodded and didn't fight him off like I normally would. I couldn't count the times he'd had to sit on me to do a medical assessment. Concussions were my jam, apparently.

Talon walked in, talking on his phone. He was debriefing with Duo, our handler at GPRE. His clipped responses were washing in and out of my brain. I really should have been paying attention.

I reached up to rip the Velcro at the shoulder of my vest. My fingers never made it, sharp pain stabbed my side, forcing a grunt out of me.

Cross crouched in front of me, pulling at his beard.

"Concussion and broken ribs, my man. You sure you don't want to go in?"

"Fuck you."

"That's what I thought." He reached up and started ripping at the strips on my vest. My ears were still ringing, and the Velcro tearing was deafening.

We worked together to get the vest off, I groaned at the loss of the comforting hug of the Kevlar. I sat back and took some shallow panting breaths.

Talon cut his call and tapped his phone on his palm. I could feel a speech coming on. I leaned my head back on the couch and groaned. My brain was trying to claw its way out.

A car door thudded shut. Jackson's aura seemed like it seeped under the door. Thank fuck. That would distract Talon.

Jackson stood in the doorway, his eyes fell on me first. He scanned me from head to toe and back again. I didn't know if this was how it worked for all packs, but with us, when one of us got hurt, that screamed in the bonds. And if you weren't there when the hurt happened, it was really uncomfortable. It was like you needed a physical confirmation before the bonds would let you be.

I flicked my eyes to Talon. He did that head-to-toe scan thing with Jackson too. It was probably where Jackson picked it up. If they were separated for more than five minutes, it was like Talon had to make sure Jackson was real and in one piece.

There was lingering tension between the two of them. Jackson left the pack bonds open all the time. He was raised in a world where pack was everything, and that was just what pack did.

They fought like any other mates, and Jackson would always take it a step too far. Not because he was being a dick, but because he was a slut. Tipping Talon into angry make-up sex was his favorite thing in the world. Talon would lie and tell you he didn't play along, but he totally did.

The last month or so? Even I could tell something had changed.

"Go fight or fuck, but can we get on with this?" Cross stood, beginning the process of ripping off his own gear.

I barked a laugh and pain stabbed me from eight places at once.

"What happened?" Jackson asked. He stood next to Talon, their shoulders just brushing. It was like the bonds groaned in relief. Mates were a thing.

Mates.

The word swirled around my brain. I sat up and rubbed my chest like a second heartbeat began to thump there.

"Nothing until shit blew up." Talon said.

"Those explosions were rigged for show, not for damage." Cross jutted his beard at me. "There was nothing in this sector but junk and parade stuff. Why blow that up?"

"Suspects?" Jackson asked.

"Duo said they scooped up a few teens, with beta IDs. PD says it was an elaborate prank."

"This all feels like a set up. A trap." Cross said.

"So, they stoked the Ruin Winters rumors for clout?" Jackson asked.

"Ruin?" I tried sitting up again, biting back the pain.

"Nah, the kids say she wasn't involved."

"But she was there. I saw her."

"Was that before or after you cracked your skull?" Cross muttered while stacking gear to put away. Talon frowned.

"I could have swore..." I touched my lips, like a taste was still there.

I had cracked my head and conjured up blue-green eyes. Not

the first time a phantom woman danced in my head when I had a concussion. Probably wouldn't be the last either.

I blinked and shook my head. The details faded, washing away like all dreams. Fuck me. The concussion was really bad this time.

"Luther?" My name landed on me like a ton of bricks. Talon only used that tone with me when I knew I had to get a grip. I pulled my unstable aura back in as best I could.

When I'd joined the pack, we'd made the decision not to tell Cross and Jackson I was a rogue. At least not at first. As time went on, I just couldn't do it. It would piss off Cross. He had a history with rogues.

It would break Jackson's heart.

Jackson had grown up in a traditionalist pack. That was more politically correct than the media would ever be. "Fundamentalist" was usually the term that got thrown around. Two packs merged to consolidate a business empire, creating a pack with a dozen alphas, four omegas in a sprawling compound in the Citrine Hills suburbs.

Rogues, only born to gold pack omega parents, were the biggest threat to the perfect life traditionalists advocated for. Rogues unbalanced everything. They could not be controlled by law or by pack bonds.

If Jackson knew he had a rogue in his pack? I didn't know if he could recover from that.

I shook my head. It took three attempts for me to shimmy to the edge of the couch.

"I'll be fine. I just need a shower and sleep." I answered Talon's aura, not his words.

Cross put his hand out to me. I grasped his forearm, and he hauled me to my feet. Stars sparkled on the edges of my vision.

"Alright, killer, let's get moving." He angled me down the hallway towards his room. "I don't know if I trust you to keep on your feet in the shower."

I leaned against the white tile in Cross' bathroom, panting. I managed to get the utility belt off all by myself, but Cross had to do the boots.

I tried to hook my thumb in the collar of my shirt to hoist it over my head, but got stuck. Cross' barking chuckle just poured salt in the wound.

"Up we go." I struggled to get my arms up so Cross could pull the tee over my head.

"Fuck off," I groaned, with no malice.

His fingertips skirted the edges of my abs, turning me to get a look at my back.

"Those are going to be impressive in the morning." He patted a sore spot a little too hard. "I think they're bruised, not broken. You want me to tape you up?" He stepped back to turn the shower on.

"Maybe later." I let my head hang back on the tile, gathering courage to move again.

He stepped close. I could feel the warmth of his body pouring off him. Pulling my eyelids down with his thumbs, his scowl told me he knew I was downplaying all this. But he'd give me just enough rope to hang myself with.

Cross yanked the tail of my belt and ripped it through the loops with just enough force to get barks of pain out of me. He hooked a finger in a belt loop and pulled me off the wall.

"What exactly is included in your nursemaid services?" I mumbled as he manhandled me into the shower.

I kicked my pants free from my legs.

"Are you going to fall if I let go?" He said, holding my head under the spray. I shook no, planted my hands on the walls and let the hot water loosen up all the muscles.

I rubbed at the ache in my chest that had nothing to do with my busted ribs. It was like suddenly something was missing, like I forgot my keys. No, not keys, something more precious.

I washed my face and skimmed the rest of my body with Cross' lemon scented soap. I wrinkled my nose. It smelled sour rather than fresh. Orange would be better.

I staggered out of the shower, snapping a towel off the bar and wrapping it around my hips. I was running a lot lately, and had lost some weight, my abs cast shadows now. The bruise licking my side was already magnificent.

Cross was sitting on the vanity, kicking his feet. I raised an eyebrow at the cigarette hanging from his lips. Talon hated it when he smoked in the house.

"Special circumstances." He grumbled and flicked the butt into the toilet.

He held out two pills in the palm of his hand. I shook my head, snatching another towel that I hoped was clean to drape over my shoulders.

"Just take them." The irritation in his voice was barely contained. "So help me god, Luther, I will kneel on your chest and force them down your throat."

He probably would, too. Like a big baby, I snatched the pills out of his hand and cupped some water from the sink to wash them down.

I followed him out to the bedroom. It was monotone gray. The only thing keeping it from looking like a prison cell were the black and white photography prints on the wall, and the ludicrous amount of books. He crossed his arms, and became an unmovable barrier when I headed for the door.

"You got two choices. The couch or..." he jutted his chin toward his bed. "I'm going to be checking on the concussion every hour or so. Do you want me barging into your room?"

The wisp of abject rage that fluttered through my aura answered the question for me. I didn't have the energy for all the delightful consequences of being a rogue in hiding. I rubbed my face and turned around. Rogues were prone to unstable auras. Rogues dealing with life stress and injuries? Fucked.

"I get to be the big spoon." I muttered, crawling into Cross' bed.

"Not a chance." He wandered around the room, flicking on every light he had. He knew I couldn't sleep if it was dark. "You want some food?" He asked from the door.

"Do we have orange juice?"

"I'll see."

I flung my arm over my eyes, and tried to find a comfortable position. Sleep stole in with memories of sunshine and playgrounds.

JACKSON

I thumbed through our conversation again. Every scrap of text from her was like a bite of cheesecake, but I was ravenous, starving. It was not enough. Meeting her, for real this time, was not enough. It wouldn't be enough until my teeth were on her neck. It probably still wouldn't be enough.

She was perfect.

The ache of not having her was going to drive me mad. I rolled my head on my neck to release some of the tension I was holding.

His scent stole into the room and filled me. Salt water and pine. The door closed softly behind him. His scent consumed me, always had, but now, it made the ache of missing part of myself sharp like broken glass.

His lips grazed the back of my neck. I twisted away from him, with a soundless grunt of effort.

"Oh, c'mon baby…"

"Don't *'c'mon baby'* me." I ducked from his grasping fingers.

"Jacks…" he sighed, tired.

"Luther is hurt." I stuffed the phone into my back pocket. "Cross's ankle still isn't right."

"That's 'cause he's dumb and won't do PT." He muttered as he sat on the edge of the bed to unlace his boots.

I forced his knees apart and knelt between them, batting his hands away, tugging at the laces.

I tossed one boot, then the other, into the bottom of our open closet. I ran my hands up his quads, massaging them. His head lolled back, and he breathed deep.

"Dumb or not, he'd be healing faster if we had an omega."

He leaned back on an elbow and looked down his body at me.

"All that shit going on with Luther? With his sister? His aura is all over the place. Thank god it's not aura sickness, but still."

Talon flicked the button of his pants open in invitation.

"The time is never going to be right. You have to make the time right. Isn't that what you said when you bit me and Cross and made us pack? My mother still hasn't forgiven you."

I leaned into him, my body pressing into his hardening cock.

"We need an omega."

I poured all my aching need into my voice. I needed him. On every level. My brain needed him, my body, my aura. Since the moment I met him when I was sixteen and he told me no. That need never stopped burning. Now, I needed her.

He threaded fingers in my hair and pulled me up for a kiss. It took all my strength to turn my head just slightly.

"No."

With a groan of denial, he flopped back on the bed. "No" was our safe word. It was a new game we were playing. He loved watching me writhe and struggle not to be bratty and coy and do the *'oh no, please, don't, not that'* thing. But 'no' actually meant 'no' in this house.

I sat back on my heels, even this much space was too much between us. He bent his knee, bringing his foot to the bed, and ripped the hidden knife sheath free from his ankle, tossing it away from the bed.

"How are you going to bring an omega home to this?"

This was the argument we'd been having for a month now. According to Talon, the life we led was not conducive to having a little puff ball of needy omega around.

"What are we going to do, teach her how to clean guns, and duck when bullets fly?"

I stood, my breath shaky. I put Cross' jacket back on.

"*I* need an omega."

"Are you going out or something?" He gave me a look like he was disappointed I was still fully dressed.

"Yeah, I'm angry and frustrated. And... Luther doesn't need more agitation in the pack bonds."

We both looked toward Luther's room, like we could see through walls.

I took a second in the hall to pump my fists. My fingers were shaking like a junkie. My aura felt the same. I didn't know if I could hold it together much longer.

I ducked into the kitchen to grab a bottle of water. Cross was leaning against the fridge eating ice cream right from the pint. Luther was taller than Cross, but his general menacing demeanor made it seem like he took up much more space.

"How is Luther?" I asked, cracking the top of a water bottle.

He shrugged, which told me physically Luther would be fine. All other sectors of wellness were questionable at this point. We knew something was wrong, seriously wrong, but we couldn't put a finger on it.

"He's got a concussion. I'll keep checking on him."

Cross was cold, abrasive, a total asshole, until one of us was injured. His bedside manner sucked balls, but he'd make sure you made it out alive.

"You're..." I said hesitantly, "going to go into his room?"

"No, he's sleeping in my bed." He put a spoonful of ice cream in his mouth.

I leaned on the island counter, a wicked grin spreading across my face.

"I would pay good money…"

"Slut," Cross barked what I was going to interpret as a laugh.

"Our favorite blond himbo and," I gave him an up and down look with a raised eyebrow, "motorcycle gang tough guy with a heart of gold? That's a walking fetish come alive. It has its own porn genre."

"I ain't got no heart, gold or otherwise." He put the pint back in the freezer. The dishwasher door creaked as he opened it to stow away the spoon.

"If the pack had an…" I didn't even get to the word "omega" before he spat out a "no" and stalked out of the kitchen.

I pinched the bridge of my nose in frustration. You couldn't even say the "O" word around Cross without him breaking things.

I collapsed onto the counter and banged my head a few times. I pulled my phone out of my back pocket and brought up the one selfie she had sent me.

There was no going back now. She'd met me. She knew we were a scent match. The rest of the pack was just going to have to get on board.

FIVE

RUBY

"Ruin." he said, anger coming out of him white hot like he was a beta with an aura.

"What?"

"You keep saying 'Ruby', not 'Ruin.' You're fucking it up." He stood right in front of me. I was almost too tired to tilt my head back to look at him.

Having a building blow up around you... an avenging angel not kill you... meeting your... *mate*... and then recording a few hours of video was exhausting.

"Oh," I said distantly. Ruby. Ruin. What did it matter? They didn't exist. Neither of them were real.

He whispered in my ear, prompting "The corrective action..." then punched me in the stomach. I doubled over, biting my tongue to keep in the scream.

"The corrective action..." He said again.

"Must match the misstep." I finished.

I nodded. I deserved this. It was appropriate. It was warranted.

I slammed my hand over my mouth and swallowed back the fried rice that threatened to come back up. I swallowed hard, again and again. I would not puke. The corrective action would be to lick it up off the floor. I didn't want to do that again.

"She would never say this." I muttered, dabbing at a tear that threatened all the careful contouring and liner.

"Just read the words. You can read, right? You're not a complete dumb fucking animal."

With the ring lights shining in my eyes, I couldn't see his face. It didn't matter. No matter how hard I tried to explain to them about the brand, content consistency, what worked, what didn't work, they never listened.

"This is the last one," he hit a bunch of keys, "And we're rolling. Read it."

I stared at the camera for a second to get into character. Ruin felt a million miles away after JJ. Jackson. And his scent that tickled my nose and warmed me all over.

"Read. It."

I blinked, looked at the camera, turned my shoulder in, angled my chin just like Ruin would.

"Oh no, did the pretty little pageant queens lose their pretty little parade floats? What ever will us omegas do without our Miss September celebration? Ruin Winters here to say… Boom."

I followed the instructions to blow a kiss at the camera.

It was terrible. Not blowing up the warehouse last night. That was smart. This video was terrible. They were trying too hard to make "boom" a catch phrase.

They didn't get it. They didn't get the symbolism of destroying one of the biggest omega events of the year. The balls and the September pageant were all most omegas ever talked about. They worked for years on the floats, the costumes. Taking that away from them would be a blow.

And nobody would get hurt. Nobody should have gotten hurt.

The plan was to rig a bunch of explosions in the warehouse where they stored the parade floats and film Ruin Winters, frolicking in the debris, gun in hand, to kick off the new phase of the plan. But law enforcement found out.

And then it all went wrong.

And then *him*. *He* came out of nowhere. *He* chased me down. *He* was huge. *His* shoulders were twice as wide as I was. An alpha. I could tell by *his* scent. *His* scent. *He* smelled... wonderful... Applewood smoke and cut grass. *His* scent wrapped around me. Covered me, filled me. Made me feel alive. I wanted to jump into *his* arms, have *his* big hands hold me, never let me go. Maybe *he* could keep the monsters away.

Bennett was replaying the video, making minor edits. It was the last one on the production list.

"Fuck," he said, picking up his phone when a text message dinged. "Mason says the chip we planted isn't working right."

I ducked my head. They wouldn't blame this on me. They were too cheap to get good equipment.

I got up and stretched before picking up the take-out container. I didn't want to eat it. But it might be the only food he'd bring home for the next few days. I took a spoonful and choked it down. I turned away from him to rub my stomach. This one didn't hurt that bad. Not yet, at least.

"Here." He threw a bit of red lace at me. I shook it out and narrowed my eyes at him. He stared me down. "What? Tits out. Hurry up."

I sighed and stripped out of the wig and turtleneck before putting on the red lace bra. I didn't even bother to check the mirror to make sure I got the wig back on straight. These videos were never on the production list.

I sat back down. At least the apartment was warm and I wouldn't shiver.

"Fuck." He said as he thundered around the folding table that he used as a desk. He moved the ring light and camera in closer. I tried not to smirk in satisfaction. It was really hard to color correct bruises in 4K video.

I looked down at my body. A purple ring circled my upper arm, both of them actually, other marks here and there. My cleavage was pristine. It would just be headshots tonight. Finally satisfied, he cued up new text on the teleprompter. These scripts... I... I read them. I didn't think about them. I never let the words stick in my brain. I said the words, but no one was there to listen.

He didn't listen.

I tried to tell *him*, the angel. I tried to tell *him* to run, to get safe, that I wasn't worth dying for. But *he* couldn't hear me. So, I ran instead.

Bennett sat back down, and took out his dick, stroked himself as I finished up the last few scripts. Neither of us cared if they were good. They were working for him, at least.

"Who needs an alpha when I have you?"

All the words blurred, just characters on a screen. They meant nothing. I meant nothing.

Bennett yelled cut.

He stood. His pants open.

Sometimes I just let it happen.

Sometimes it needed to happen.

It was the only thing that could prevent heat. The handbook was very clear - *"To prevent the onset of the abnormal rutting state of 'heat', the subject must go no more than two days between intercourse."*

It was medicinal. He had to do it. It was prescribed. It was to cut off the hormones, the hormones that made me an animal, a debased evil creature that harmed everyone and everything in society.

This would prevent heat. Heat killed omegas. Alphas ripped

omegas apart from the inside out in heat. The press, the media, were lying about it. Omegas died every day. And they covered it up. They showed me the pictures. I saw the proof, little girls, older women, bodies torn apart by alphas in rut.

This was the only way I could save myself. This wasn't for pleasure. This wasn't for enjoyment.

Sometimes I needed it to prevent heat.

Sometimes... sometimes I wanted it. And it was never enough. It was like putting out a fire with teaspoons of water. I always wanted more, needed more. Which was just proof I was the worst of them. The ultimate danger. An omega so bad I would be the source of destruction for everyone.

Sometimes... well, only once... I fought back. Maybe tonight I'd earn a matching scar for my left hip.

He snapped his fingers at me. I didn't move.

"Get the fuck up."

I shook my head. My mouth went dry. I pictured *him*, my warehouse angel, standing over Bennett's shoulder. *He* would help me fight.

Jackson's face materialized in my mind's eye. He could never see this. He could never see me, the real me.

Bennett took a step toward me.

"You have to. You fucking nester whore. If I don't fuck you, you'll go into heat. Your slick already gets everywhere. I don't want to clean that shit up."

I scrambled around the card table, scattering make-up tools and take-out containers. My fingers snagged the spoon he gave me to eat with. I wasn't allowed forks, knives; only plastic spoons, and paper plates.

I snapped the brittle plastic and held it like a threat, to my chest.

He laughed at me and took another step.

I dug it into my flesh and dragged it a stinging inch.

His eyes went wide. I could smell fear on him. I risked a look down. An ugly red scrape and a single drop of blood.

No visible marks.

That was a new rule.

After the black eye that forced Ruin off the air, they put Billy in the kennel for a week. The wimp cried after day two. I'd once done 32 days. Bennett wouldn't even survive one.

"Get in the fucking bathroom, you disgusting nester whore."

I walked backwards, feeling my way with my hands. I didn't blink. He slammed the door, and I heard the latch click.

Now, the panic set in. My whole body shook. I couldn't get enough air. I fumbled behind me for the knob and cranked the water to hot. There was no shower curtain, the shower head was angled tightly to the wall.

I'd shower for real later, with the industrial de-scenting soap. I just wanted the warmth and the noise to create a buffer zone.

I eyed the linen closet. It was the only closet that wasn't padlocked. I flicked my eyes to the door, to the handle. I licked my dry lips and tried to swallow.

I'd risk it. Just for a little while.

I pulled the door open and shifted the 8-pack of toilet paper. There was barely enough room. I had to pull my knees all the way to my chest and hug them. They didn't padlock this door because they didn't think I could fit. Nesting was a perverse indulgence, and it carried the most painful corrective action.

In the dark, I was squeezed tight, like a hug. Like Jackson's arms around me. In the dark, he couldn't see me.

In Jackson's lap, safe.

His hand around my throat, safe.

Warmth spreading through my body finally.

I closed my eyes and took one long, slow breath.

TALON SERRANO

I gave up on sleep hours ago. We kept the room cool, but it was freezing without Jackson next to me.

There was too much in my head. And my bed was empty.

I heard the doorknob turn. I stopped myself from smiling and pretended to be asleep. The door shut with a soft click and then lots of fabric rustling.

"I hope you're faking it and you've been hard for hours for me." Jackson said in a stage whisper.

I whipped the sheet back, my cock getting hard at just the sight of him.

He already had his pants off his hips, stroking himself slowly, squeezing just below the head, exactly how he liked it.

He was gorgeous like this, working himself over, getting ready for me. He was gorgeous always. Kicking off his pants, he crawled up my body, stretched out on top of me, his tongue doing dangerous things in my mouth. The friction between our cocks absolutely unsatisfying and perfect. We loved riding the line between frustration and bliss.

He pulled his tongue from my mouth and stared down at me.

"I have a new fantasy."

I groaned, flipping him over and grabbing a bottle of lube we kept on the nightstand.

He'd work for weeks on a fantasy, just to tell it to me in exquisite detail, and sear it into my brain while I fucked him slow, so I didn't mess up the storytelling. I'd then spend weeks planning out how to make it happen.

I pressed just the tip of my cock into him and held his hips so he couldn't rock back. He wanted hard and fast, and I'd make him work for that reward.

"The fantasy?" I prompted.

"This." He said around a pant. "You, taking me slow, just like this, when you know I want to be fucked stupid. Making me wait, maybe beg for it," we both moaned on my short pump in further, "while I'm..." he stopped, a full body shiver taking him as I pulled all the way out. I paused, hoping for a whimper of need.

"While you are?"

"While I'm about to knot the omega beneath me."

My whole body tightened, I dug my nails into his hips, sliding back in.

"You, telling her what a good little omega she is. Beautiful. Perfect."

I bit my lip, knowing my control was going to evaporate.

"You tell her she can't come, until she takes my knot."

I pushed all the way in, flattening him to the bed, holding him down by the wrists. My ear right by his lips, our hard breaths, or scents mingling together.

"You fuck me slowly," his voice a whisper caressing my brain, "my knot right at her entrance, not letting her have it until she screams your name."

And I lost it at that. I pulled him up by the hips and had him brace himself on the headboard. I fucked him hard and fast as he filled my senses with an image of the little omega, her scent, her taste, how she'd come on command, her slick, thick and delicious. Our auras mingling. Her, weak, spent, and a completely satisfied pool of jelly after our knots.

Finally, I was drenched in sweat and breathing like a freight train. I kissed his neck and pulled out. I was the weak one now. Jackson was energized. He kissed me roughly and bounced off the bed to shower.

I laid there for a minute, catching my breath before joining him. Letting myself live in the fantasy of having an omega in the pack. I squeezed my eyes shut on the regret.

Our life was just too dangerous to put a perfect little omega at risk like that. I was too dangerous to be given free rein over another person like that.

SIX

RUBY

"Charisma, this is too much," I whispered over the hundred-dollar bill that I was absolutely not going to let go of.

"Sweetie, I know how the spa industry works. You don't get a cut of the tips and without you, I'd never get into this place." She winked at me and folded my hand around the bill before sweeping out on a cloud of lavender and honey scented massage oil.

I pocketed the bill to take care of later and opened the spreadsheet on my phone. I entered the time and service, but there wasn't much to fill out in the notes section. She said she was running late because the Longwood pack were pitching a fit about the cost of dresses for the upcoming Institute ball. It was probably insignificant, but I logged it anyway. Charisma was one of the best fashion designers in the city and was a wealth of sources and leads.

I had woken up shaking and the only thing that had worked was not thinking about last night, and focusing on menial tasks. There was always something to neaten, straighten, arrange, or record in the spa. If I got desperate, I could fold laundry. I had to squeeze around Ansley and Belle to get back at my desk. They were leaning across the top of the reception desk, digging in the candy bowl for the sugar-free watermelon ones.

"What do you think, Ruby?" Asked Ansley.

"About what?" I plastered a smile on my face. This conversation could be about anything from potholes to Brazilian wax horror stories.

"About Ruin!? You did see all the posts last night, right? She's teasing something big."

"I agree with Romeo Knight. She's trash and we shouldn't be following her." Belle said smugly.

"You're full of it, Belle. I know you subscribe to all her channels."

"Whatever," Belle rolled her eyes.

"Well," my cheeks warmed, "She has made some good points."

"Like what?"

I hesitated, this was always dangerous waters. People showed their true colors when you pushed back against societal norms.

"Like the retroactive tax breaks packs can apply for when they have alpha offspring? Tanya Rice did that series on how it reduces omegas to baby making factories and encourages illegal drugs to boost fertility." It also devalued betas, the majority of society, and put into law discrimination policies. The poor treatment omegas could face was the easier side of the conversation. No one enjoyed talking about beta justice.

Belle groaned. "I don't know how you can sit through Tanya's show on Beta-Watch. That whole TV channel exists to hurt omegas."

"As betas," Ansley put a dramatic hand to her chest, "we know there are some omegas that need to be taken down a notch. Present company excluded, of course, Rubes." She flashed me a huge grin that I was pretty sure wasn't fake.

"Ansley! Gossiping about omegas gone wild is one thing, but promoting actual violence? Ruin Winters has taken things too far." Belle's voice got all squeaky.

I tucked a lock of my hair behind my ear and let them argue it out. It was too short. It was always getting in my eyes. I wished I could have it even a little bit longer. The sudden image of Jackson's hand in my hair, pulling, forced me to take a quick breath.

My phone buzzed again in my pocket. It had been going off all day. Each time, I flushed. I felt like I had to squeeze my legs together to stop it from spreading. At this rate, I'd be risking heat. I was going to have to let Bennett... I shivered, feeling grossed out.

The spa manager didn't like us checking our phones too often. It made us look like we weren't client focused. And I wasn't about to take it out in front of these two.

I wished I could set the vibration pattern to know if it was a HeatMatchApp message or one of the other ones. No one would bat an eye at a single omega using a dating app.

I kept busy the rest of the day. I rearranged the display of essential oils and scent enhancers a half a dozen times. It was apparently a skill to find a perfume to compliment your scent. Keeping my hands busy kept the creeping anxiety at bay. It was almost like last night had never happened.

I could pretend. I was good at pretending.

As usual, I was the last one to leave, even though my shift technically ended an hour ago. I let everyone keep thinking that I put in the extra time to gain brownie points. I stopped in the bathroom to spray myself down with scent blockers before heading out.

I had gotten a few other tips. Omegas just loved throwing around their alphas' money. I took the time to tuck the bills into the hidden pocket I had sewn into the hem of this skirt. I learned the hard way it was best to go home with empty pockets.

Setting the alarm at the back door, I double checked to make sure the alley was empty. Yes, it technically was a shortcut to get to the other side of the shopping district, but it also kept you away from prying eyes. I leaned against the side of the building to open the HeatMatch and reread the messages.

8:45am

> JJSeeks: Morning

> JJSeeks: Sad I have to drink this alone

He'd sent a pic of him behind the wheel of his car, a cup of coffee from BetaButter's waffle truck balanced on his knee. He took it from shoulder height, looking down his body, so all I got was his thighs that stretched his jeans and his hand. Long fingers wrapped around the paper cup. His sleeve pushed up his forearm, showing off muscles, and his watch. I zoomed in on his watch. It wasn't a showy brand like a Rolex or anything. It was like one of those divers' watches that had all sorts of dials on the watch face that did more things than just tell time.

3:12pm

> JJSeeks: Reminded me...

The next pic was him balancing a pale pink flower on his fingertips. It was zoomed in so you could see it was wet, water droplets clung to the petals and his fingers. If I wasn't a defective omega, I'd know what kind of flower it was. I touched my hair, wishing it was still pink. It was back to brown with warm red and gold highlights. The spa paid for it. They wanted their omega receptionist to properly represent their brand. And pastels were out this year.

3:52pm

JJSeeks: Monday?

I bit my lip and tapped the phone on my forehead. I had to stop this. For so many, many reasons. I couldn't go home smelling like a needy omega. I couldn't, I shouldn't be investing time in this pipe dream.

Agreeing to meet him was stupid. I had to stop thinking about him. Or the other one from last night. When they found out... I squeezed my eyes shut to try to wish the anxiety away. I tucked the phone in my bag and headed down the alley to cut through to the street behind.

I didn't even make it to the curb before all the disgusting omega needs and debased instincts swamped me and rooted me to the spot. I took some shallow breaths to push all of that down.

God damnit.

I did a full 360, looking in all directions to make sure no one was watching. I was alone with the brick walls and trash dumpsters. I pulled up my sleeve so my arm would be bare. Stepping up to the wall, I rested the back of my hand against the brick, palm facing me, with fingers relaxed and curled in just slightly. Just enough to show off my French manicure, also paid for by the spa. They let me keep it because I had to look the part.

I snapped the pic and sent it before I had second thoughts.

6:42pm

> PinkHairDontCare: Empty...

I attached the pic.

I tried to push away the image of his hand, the long fingers, the watch, the wet fingertips, pinning my wrist to the wall...

While *he* held my neck.

I wouldn't think of the other one either. *He* was huge, and *he* made me feel small, and I didn't understand why that made me feel good. I gave myself 30 seconds to enjoy the tingles racing through my body. I licked my lips, feeling the slick pool between my legs.

Taking a deep breath, I checked the time on my phone before shoving it back into my bag. I had just enough time to stop at the sandwich shop around the corner from my apartment to clean up with wet naps in the bathroom before going home. Disgusted, I hurried out onto the street, hating how my body always betrayed me like this.

SEVEN

LUTHER

The bastard took the keys to my bike. I had another bike up at the cabin, but he'd effectively stranded me. There was no way I'd be seen on Cross' Hound. It was a classic motorcycle that only old men rode. Apparently driving with a concussion was a "bitchass move" according to Cross. Whatever. Now, I was riding the *oh-shit* handle above the passenger door of his truck as we drove into the West Side. Being a passenger tweaked all my control issues.

I had woken up with a headache and a hard-on. Never a great combination. I dragged myself into my own bedroom, leaving Cross' bed, crawled into my fuzzy blue bathrobe, and got down to the hard work of wishing those two things away.

Every time I closed my eyes, my bruised brain coughed up a gorgeous woman with blue-green eyes. I was used to nightmares that haunted you even when you were awake. A sex goddess with plump lips was a new torture. I was starting to freak myself out, because I couldn't shake the images.

A few frustrating hours later, I pulled on my trainers and sweats. I needed a run, pound out some miles to shut my brain up. Cross blocked the door, and told me it was a bad idea with the concussion and ribs. He bet me that I couldn't touch my toes without crying.

I lost that bet and now I owed him waffles.

Cross was taking the long way around instead of cutting through the central shopping district on the West Side. If I asked him why, he'd tell me traffic sucked. I suspected there had been a pack meeting to lay down the law to keep me out of the neighborhood that my sister lived in. No one, myself included, wanted to see how an accidental meet up would go.

"What's it like..." the thought trailed off as I watched expensive looking people going to expensive looking places out the window of Cross' truck.

"What?" It was the only word he said the whole trip.

"Nothing."

"No, what?"

"What's it like, finding your scent match?"

It felt like the temp in the truck dropped 20 degrees. The pack bond wasn't just shut, he'd poured concrete on it.

"Sorry." I shouldn't have opened my big, dumb mouth.

He had discussed it exactly once, all detached, like he was reading the police report. Jackson had filled in all the details for me. It wasn't ever a topic we brought up.

"I'll treat you to waffles another day." I said, pretty sure I had killed his appetite.

"Nah, we're here."

We pulled into the parking lot of the Crimson Bullet and I had the door open, my feet on the ground, before the truck came to a full stop. I was on edge, and now running from the shame of the insensitive question. What the fuck was wrong with me? Cross caught up, and we headed to the back of the line.

Now, this was the kind of carbo loading I could get behind.

BetaButter's Waffles were literally better than sex. Just like their cheery signage said.

Hot, crispy, dripping with ooey, gooey goodness. Given the mileage I was clocking right now on my runs, this was basically calorie free.

I usually ordered a two-waffle sundae with as much chocolate as I could fit into the paper bowl.

I lingered on the menu. The scent of orange zest demanded my attention tonight. The menu read "Citrus Curd Brulee". What the fuck was a curd?

I flicked a glance at Cross, weirdly nervous he'd get all judgy about my dessert choice. But that wasn't his style. He did waffles with vanilla ice cream. Boring.

I licked a drop off the edge of the container as I followed him to a table. The citrus hit my tongue. It was sweet and tart, not my thing generally, but tonight? It was the only thing I could dream of sinking my teeth into.

A fat drop of melting whipped cream oozed over the edge and plopped right on to the toe of my Docs as we sat. Irritated, I set down my overflowing plate, grabbed a napkin to wipe my boot toe. I had just broken them in enough that they were like butter on my feet. I'd pounded 10k runs for a week in these boots to get them just right. If you couldn't run in your boots, then why bother?

"Fuck Ruin Winters man, I bet she's not even an omega."

Two alphas and a beta sat down next to us with their waffles, mid conversation. I nodded at the newcomers as they took up half of the picnic table. The chatty alpha, decked out in artfully torn designer jeans, rolled his eyes, licking caramel sauce off his finger. The woman, a beta, had platinum hair and looked bored already with her company for the evening.

"But she gets into aura-exclusive parties..."

"I've been telling you forever now..."

"Oh, here it comes. Who red pilled you, Tag? You gotta stop watching Romeo Knight fan boys," said the red-headed alpha. That was smart advice. Romeo Knight was mildly annoying as an evening talk show host, but his fans were rabid and generally gross.

"Look, if you've been following her from the beginning, the change is obvious."

Cross put a huge spoonful of ice cream in his mouth with a pointed look. He pulled out his phone and set it screen down on the table, obviously close to the threesome next to us. He was recording.

"It's the clothes. They totally changed. And well, obviously she's now reading off a teleprompter and doesn't sound like herself. She sounds like someone pretending to be Ruin Winters." Tag said.

"What about her clothes? They're not even medium-level slutty."

I rolled my eyes. Bashing a woman for enjoying fashion and her body was an idea that should have been left in the last century.

"Yeah, yeah, dude, that's the point. See, back when she started she had this like... What did you call it Amber?"

"Starving Model who can't get a gig chic." The beta girl said, blowing smoke in their faces. I smoothed the dollop of orange curd over the top of my waffles, making sure every square had some.

"Yeah, right, now it's like she has no sense of style."

"What does that have to do with anything?"

"And the weight loss?"

"Omega bitches lose weight all the time. The balls and pageants and shit are coming up."

I snorted and Cross suppressed a laugh. It was a pet peeve of the entire pack, this obsession some omegas had with thinness. It riled Jackson up to comical levels. If we had an omega, no doubt we'd come home one day and find that Jackson had tied her to a chair and fed her cupcakes. The beta chick rolled her eyes at me and lit another cigarette.

"Yeah, but Ruin is all 'anti' that, right? She's burning the world down. You think she cares about bikini contests?" Tag said.

"Whatever, man, you think too much about this shit."

"Oh, and don't forget the bruises." Said Amber.

"Right, right? The video was up for like an hour. One comment asking if she was OK cause it looked like she had a black eye. It came down, and she was off the air for a week."

I was listening and thinking, tapping my plastic fork on the edge of my plate. There was something I just couldn't shake about Ruin. Just trying to think about it sent ice pick pain through my head. Cross was thinking too, the pace of his fork slowed. We read the file on her, and none of this was mentioned.

I finally dug my fork in and got a big bite of waffle goodness ready to go.

"Dude, you gotta get over your omega obsession. Unless, of course, it's that little gold pack slut. Man, I would dark bond her in a heartbeat, then get her down on her knees. Her and Ruin? I would…"

"What the fuck did you say?" The fork stopped halfway to my mouth.

"Fuck off man, this is a private conversation."

"Luther…" Cross warned.

"Nah, nah, tell me again, my guy. Tell me how you'd turn a defenseless woman into a slave and rape her."

Dead silence washed over the parking lot. That's the thing no one ever said out loud about gold pack omegas. It was totally legal to bite them, dark bond them and do whatever the fuck you wanted to them.

"Not my fault she's fucked in the head, made some bad

choices and turned herself into filth." He flipped his red hair out of his eyes.

I stood up so fast, I sent the table cartwheeling over, splattering my uneaten waffle sundaes all over the douchebags.

"Say it again." My aura flooded the parking lot.

He froze like a cartoon stuck on pause. I saw Cross out of the corner of my eye, stand and circle us. His presence in my awareness gave me space to breathe. The crowd in line for waffles were all backing away.

I took one step. The ginger backed up a dozen. Tag, his buddy, no where to be seen. He tripped over one of the low benches and landed flat on his back, panting in terror. That was the thing with alphas, especially young alphas. They thought they're hot shit, unstoppable. Thought they could dominate any situation. They crumbled into nothing the second they learned there was someone else on the planet that could dominate them.

"Let's not pull a Leroy Jenkins tonight." Cross said, warning me not to go off half-cocked. His aura grumbly like his voice.

I put my boot on the kid's neck.

Cross stepped into me, wedging his body between me and the kid, a hand on my hip.

"Curb stomping this asshole will mess up your boots." It was almost a purr in my ear. That got through. I really liked these boots.

It took a lot of effort to pull my boot back and let him breathe again. If I didn't walk away right now, I might not be able to. If he ran, it would be all over.

Rage was dimming my vision and putting twinkling stars in the blackness around me.

Cross knew I was approaching a point of no return. He pulled me forward a step by my belt buckle. That gave me the ability to take the next one. He paced me, walking backwards, providing cover, making sure the ginger boy and his buddy didn't find some balls and decide to jump us. After a couple dozen feet, he turned, and we walked shoulder to shoulder.

We rounded the building into the alley behind the club. I pulled my fist back to punch the wall. Grunting, Cross caught my fist, shaking with the effort to prevent me from connecting with the wall.

"You don't need a broken hand and ribs in one week." Cross snarked.

He palmed the back of my neck. My vision was reduced to pinpricks and fuzzy, color fading.

I pushed at him, sending him flying back a few paces before he caught himself.

Cross didn't know.

He didn't know why I ran. Why I didn't drink. Why Talon sent me to the cabin alone. He didn't know why I was falling apart.

He didn't know I went rogue at six-years-old to protect a little girl from bullies, and killed people.

Then that crazy motherfucker took me in. The only one that would take a six-year-old killer. Experimenting on me with his nutty ideas about how to control auras.

And his daughter, who became my sister.

She became the only thing I cared about in the world.

He forced her to go gold pack.

Kept her ignorant, a prisoner, making a choice for her that would ruin her life.

Then he forced me out. Said he'd kill her himself, turn us both in. Give me to the Institute.

I had to. I had to leave her to save her. It broke me.

Cross didn't know.

Neither did Jackson.

Duo and Talon had been covering for my fucked-up aura for years now. And I didn't know how much longer I'd be able to keep it together.

EIGHT

RUBY

What was I doing? This was literally insane. I was only on that dumb app because Ruin Winters needed information on an omega that was cheating on his beta girlfriend.

"Can I help you?" The shop girl startled me and I dropped my phone. I blew out a breath, relieved the screen wasn't cracked. I wasn't sure if they'd give me a new one.

"I'm, um, meeting someone."

"Are you alright?" She followed my gaze across the street, lines wrinkling her forehead.

"Oh yes, thank you."

"If there's," she stepped forward and touched my arm, "someone bothering you…"

Like a girl who works in a shoe store could help me? I tried to give her a winning smile, a Ruin Winters smile.

"Well, you take all the time you need." She retreated a little, but kept an eye on me.

I shouldn't even be doing this. They'd kill me if they found out. My job was done. They had a chip on him. My stomach cramped thinking about what they were going to do with that information.

But I couldn't say no. And this went beyond the fact that omegas were physically incapable of saying no. I touched the shoe display next to me as my head swam. I had to see him again, to make sure this was all real.

I tapped my phone open once more. It was 1:58. I should just go. This was too dangerous. He wasn't here yet. I could just delete my profile and he'd never find me.

Then I saw him turn the corner. The same jacket he wore last time. He glowed. I was pulled forward and bumped right into one of the product displays, knocking over a handbag. All I could see was him. Everything else melted away.

The shop girl came up to straighten the wallets on the shelf next to me, giving me sidelong concerned looks. I gave her a weak smile.

She tapped my elbow and handed me a card. It read "Lucy's House: Shelter for omegas with unstable auras." I turned to give it back to her, but she was gone. She had retreated all the way into the back of the shop. I turned the card over in my fingers. I ripped it in half and stuck it in my bag.

The kind of trouble I was in… she couldn't help with. No one could help.

This was a quiet street, lined with little boutiques and restaurants. The spa was right around the corner, so I could make it back fast if I had to. Adelle, the spa manager, was out today. Belle said she'd cover the desk for as long as I needed since her massage client canceled. It was just a quick coffee. That's it.

He was sitting right across from the counter, a paper coffee cup in front of him and a pink flower on the table. He stood instantly when he saw me. I could feel his smile all the way over here. He was beautiful.

"Jackson." I breathed.

His scent wrapped around me and made me feel like I had slipped into a warm bath. His fingers twitched like he wanted to touch me.

"I'm so glad you let me see you today." His smile, the dimples, he made my knees shake.

I put my fingers on the table just in case the room started spinning. I tried not to frown at his word choice. *'Let me see you.'* He said it as if I was in control, like I could say no or something.

I licked my lips. I'd swear I could taste him. His scent was everywhere, sandalwood, like all the expensive soaps and lotions in the spa. He stepped up to me and put his hand on my back. It sent shivers through my body.

"How about we go for a walk?" he asked. "Scent matches can be a little overwhelming at first."

Nervously, I fiddled with my collar. He ushered me toward the door and held it open.

We strolled slowly down the street in silence for a while.

It was awkward, because it wasn't awkward. It was... nice. It was just nice being next to him.

"I have so many questions, but I'm all tongue tied."

I snorted. "I doubt that."

"Your scent just does things to me. I want to know everything about you, but your scent just scrambles my brains. And I'm just left following you like a puppy with his goofy smile on my face."

He turned and walked backwards in front of me, and pointed to his smile. His dark hair fell in front of his eyes and he brushed it back with casual movement. The dimples made him look just perfect.

"That's not goofy. That's beautiful." I said without thinking.

He shoved his hands in his pockets and returned to my side. I had questions too, but I couldn't think of a single one. I pulled my bag up on my shoulder. It was sunny, but chilly for April.

"Oh, here," he said, shrugging out of his jacket and putting it over my shoulders. I drowned in his scent. I closed my eyes, and it became my whole world. I swallowed because I also got very, very horny. It was like he was touching me everywhere. It was all I could do to stay on my feet and keep walking.

He maneuvered me into a tiny park. It wasn't much more than a patch of struggling grass and two benches. He held out his hand to help me sit down, like I was important or something. He sat too, his torso turned towards me. He moved a lock of hair out of my eyes. I wanted to lean into him and feel his hands on me, his body all over mine.

"This is beautiful," his eyes roamed all over my hair. "The pink hair in the pic you sent, absolutely adorable. This? The streaks of gold and amber? Stunning. You glow like sunrise." He hooked his arm over the back of the bench and put his ankle on his knee. He seemed happy just to be next to me.

"You," I had to clear my throat, the word squeaked out. "You said you had a pack?" He nodded and smiled huge, like he was delighted by the question. "What's that like?"

"Crazy," he rolled his eyes, "in the best possible way. It's like," He looked up to the sky to think for a minute, "You are 4 times bigger than yourself. You're never really alone. You can just reach out and feel that other person there, even if you're not in the same room. They know what you're feeling. It's amazing."

Terrifying more like it. "So, they can read your mind?"

He laughed. The sound rippled over my skin.

"Not at all. Let me think of an example. Oh, I know," he reached over and lightly stroked my ring finger. "Cross broke his finger, this finger, a few years back. We were in his shop, arguing. He was really mad at me," His eyes went wide and sparkled with delight.

"What did you do?" Anxiety spiked out of nowhere and was instantly soothed by his touch on my hand.

"I may have taken his bike in the rain and crashed it." He

didn't look sorry at all. "Anyway, I was trying to apologize. He was angry..."

"And he hit you?"

"No, of course not. He was trying to put a drill away, and it slipped off the shelf and crashed on his hand."

"Oh." I slid an inch towards him.

"Depending on what else is going on, if I feel that same emotion in the bond, it could mean he's mad at me for doing something I shouldn't have done, or it could mean he broke his finger again." His dimples flashed.

As he talked a bit about his pack brothers, he found ways to touch me. Taking a leaf out of my hair, pulling the jacket tighter, touching my knee for emphasis. People touched me all the time, but I had never wanted it, not like this. And it never did *this* to me. I felt calm, maybe even safe for the first time in a long time, and I wanted to be touched... everywhere. I just let his voice flow over me, washing everything away.

"So, what do you think?"

"Hmmm." His words dimly registered.

"Do you want to go meet them?"

"Sure," I sighed, content.

His smile erased all the darkness from the world. A wave of pure joy stole my breath. He stood and held out his hand to pull me to my feet. My bag slipped off my shoulder, threatening to disconnect us.

"May I?" he asked, gesturing to my bag. I gave a small nod, not really sure I knew what he was asking. It was just weird he was *asking* for permission. He took my bag gently from me with his free hand so he could hold mine.

He wanted to hold my hand.

I closed my eyes and let him pull me forward.

We walked for a short while, or for miles. I didn't care anymore, so long as he was holding my hand. He opened the car door and helped settle me in and set my bag at my feet. I shrank back in the seat when he leaned in and over, clicking the seatbelt into place.

"Safety first," Jackson said with a wink, adjusting the shoulder strap so it wouldn't choke me.

I put my hands to my cheeks. What the fuck was I doing? I had to get out of here.

His car door thunked gently, and the engine rumbled. He held his hand out to me. I looked at it, not knowing what he wanted.

"Please?" he asked. He asked… please. Nervously, I put my hand in his. Jackson snaked his fingers through mine so he could hold my hand and manipulate the stick shift at the same time.

Jackson pulled smoothly into traffic. His thumb stroked and soothed my index finger.

Fuck.

I was lost.

NINE

CROSS STIRLING

Firearms covered the boring beige carpet of the living room floor. We'd gotten a ready alert. We were officially on standby.

Duo would be calling with a full brief, but I was already deep in the chatter on some of the more nasty message boards. It was a good thing for us that criminals were morons.

The Reset was recruiting and there was talk of some splashy events to get the public on their side. Talon and I were being proactive, cleaning weapons, packing go bags. I had Luther's utility belt across my knees, trying to figure out a better configuration for the gear. I wanted the weight on his hips, not strung across his lower back.

"Explain the thing about Ruin again." Talon's voice rumbled over the sound of sliding metal as he reassembled a handgun.

"Yeah, weirdest thing. So, the dumb fucks are using all these code words. Tons of messages about "walks in the park", which I think is a stand in for the warehouse incident." I put Luther's belt aside, mostly satisfied with the gear placement. It would be better if he could put the extra magazines in his pocket, but that was not smart. "And the hot topic right now is a "pizza delivery" for today, this afternoon. There's a thing about "go karts" but that doesn't have a date. I haven't figured that one out yet."

"OK. So, what's Ruin's code word?"

"That's the thing. There isn't one. Any time they talk about Ruin Winters, they say "RUIN WINTERS", all spelled out, usually in all caps."

"I'm not following, Cross." Talon moved on to loading up magazines with ammo, the soft metallic clicks oddly soothing.

"They are all jazzed about their little special code words. Really hyped up on the super spy nature of it all. And she's the only element that's out in the open, emphasized even."

Talon frowned, running a thumbnail across his eyebrow. That was his tell that he was thinking. And I didn't need the bonds to tell me they were not good thoughts.

"You're saying it's an intentional set up?"

I shrugged.

"I have watched entirely too much of her content over the weekend. I feel confident I can now distinguish several brands of lipstick and scent boosters. But it's eerie. You can pinpoint the exact video where there is a shift in her content. It's subtle. I'd show it to you, but I don't think you'd see it unless you fanboy'ed over her. But she goes from your typical air headed omega being super fucking mean, to..." I struggled to put it into words. "Someone else is pulling the strings, and she's pissed about it. And that's about the same time the porn started."

"Porn?" Talon wiped his hands on a rag.

"Yeah, it's bizarre and gross. Most of it is soft core. Just her in a bra saying things a twisted beta with small dick energy would want to hear. 'You're much bigger than my alpha.' It's fucked up."

This was the most I'd talked all week. I swore Talon gave me all the research projects just to force the conversation out of me. I kept to the edges of the pack, kept the fucking bonds on lock down. I was a loner by nature. I should have never been in a fucking pack to begin with.

I finished packing the go bags, pulling the zippers with more force than necessary. There was something about the whole warehouse situation that didn't make sense. They hyped us up to catch the little terrorist and all that showed up were beta hooligans?

I rubbed my wrist across my forehead and blew out a breath to take the edge off my simmering anger. NOPD were not our friends. We weren't openly hostile to them, but fuck ups like this made it hard to respect them. In fact, their incompetence led to Luther getting hurt? That was going to sting for a while. He was not in a great place to begin with.

Even in his sleep, Luther's aura was a mess. I'd stayed up reading while he slept off his concussion. His aura had eventually chased me from my own god damn bedroom. My hands paused on checking the batteries of the flashlight I was tucking into the outer pocket of Luther's bag. His aura had been a mess for a long time. Way before his gold pack sister got thrown into Gavin's.

Smartest thing Talon ever did was banning him from seeing her. Gavin's wasn't a place you wanted your sister, or anyone you cared about.

Gavin's Treasures was barely a step above legal prostitution. It was where alphas with no standards or prospects could get the attention they so desperately craved from omegas who had no options left. It was fucked up on too many levels that Gavin's was his sister's best option. The place was full of gold packs and omegas kicked out of families and places like Berry Creek for being unfortunate enough to perfume.

I went a couple of times to see her. I sat at the bar like a patron, hoping I could bring back news that it wasn't as bad as he feared. And then she killed her alpha.

An extreme example, but all omegas were gods of chaos. You shouldn't have a thing in your life that you come to depend on for your sanity, your wellbeing. They'd engineered us this way, wedging us into this sick catch-22 where all of who you were craved the exact thing that was created to destroy you.

A car pulled into the drive, and a small private smile spread across Talon's face. I didn't think he was aware that he did that, that he smiled with a sense of relief every time Jackson came home.

We both picked our heads up and looked at the door at the same time. Jackson's aura felt 10 times bigger than it should have been.

He was happy to the point of stupidity.

Jackson was usually always happy. There were days where his aura was the only thing that got us all through. I'd had a normal shitty childhood with parents that cared more about booze and drama than the six kids they had and they had no fucking clue what to do with a teenaged alpha. Talon was on his own young, by choice. His mom left when he was a baby and his dad ran drugs. Luther went through the stuff of nightmares.

And then there was Jackson, privileged, wealthy boy-next-door, captain of the football team, youngest graduate of the academy. You name the glowing accolade and he had it. Yeah, his mom was overbearing, but that was really the only cross he had to bear. It was poor luck that he met Talon at sixteen and not some daughter of a duchess or one of the old families.

But there was something else, something new in Jackson's aura. Talon and I traded a look. He felt it too, and I was pretty sure he didn't know what it meant, either.

The digital lock on the door beeped, opening slowly. Jackson filled the doorway and backed into the room. He turned, a monstrously huge smile on his face. His dimples were craters in his plump cheeks.

He led a small woman in by the hand. Her hair was the color of expensive mahogany, but a touch lighter, polished to a blistering glow. It fell about her face in carefully controlled messy "beachy waves", a new term I learned in all my Ruin research. A purse hung off her bent elbow. A leather coat was over her shoulders, dwarfing her... My chest tightened, making it hard to breathe.

I looked at Talon, who was riveted, then back at Jackson, and tilted my head like a confused dog hearing the word "bork" for the first time.

And then sunshine exploded into my life.

Orange, like when your nails dig into the peel, the zest jumping right up to meet you and crème brûlée melting on your tongue, rich and sinful. I fell back on my ass, put a shaking hand to my mouth. I closed my eyes to take in her scent that wrote secret promises on my soul, claiming me instantly.

Fuck no.

Not again.

Not ever again.

TEN

TALON

She glowed in the doorway, ringed in a halo of bright spring sun. The light was not quite enough to chase away the darkness that clung to her edges. She was small, perfect, scared and wounded... I didn't know how or why, but I knew it as a fact, like water was wet.

And she was mine.

The sharpness of her orange scent cut by exotic vanilla, warm and sweet... Her scent covered me, flipped all my switches, the ones that should never be flipped.

I cut off a growl that attempted to claw its way out of me and destroy worlds for her. I wiped my mouth with the back of my hand, like the taste of blood already lingered there.

Jackson turned to me. More beautiful than he had ever been, stealing what breath remained.

Oh god.

He loved her.

He was already in love with her. I felt it in his aura, hot flames whipping out at us, ensnaring us and dragging us in.

He found our pack's scent match, and he was already burning for her.

He nudged her hand forward. An offering. A gift. He was giving that love to me if I wanted it. Pride and awe at finding this treasure rolled off him.

Her eyes were wide and her knuckles white with a tight grip on the lapel of the jacket. She was in his clothes, that ratty leather jacket. His scent, that rich spice I couldn't get enough of, would be all over her... marking her... I swallowed as the black pepper and orange hit my senses. What would I smell like... I forced the thought away with effort.

She took a sip of air, then her head got loose on her shoulders and a knee gave way. Instantly, we were all on our feet. Jackson had a sure grip on her waist, but she regained herself quickly after the scent match shock.

A scent match.

God damnit.

Her eyes darted around the room, unsure of where she was, until they landed on the stockpile of guns and gear on the floor. Her breathing caught, and she took a nervous step back. A smile, fake around the edges, emerged on her lips. It was well-practiced and would fool most.

She was fawning, buying her way out of danger with pretty smiles and words. It was a trauma response and we saw it in omegas every day, like people pleasing to the extreme.

Something in me twisted and rocked my soul so loud that it should have shaken the house. It reminded me...

Pack lead.

I was pack lead.

I looked at Jackson, my love, my life.

I was about to ruin him.

Scent match or no, I was snuffing this out right quick.

"I'm Talon." I said, hoping there was no growl in my voice.

Her eyes flicked to me and I held back a gasp. They reached for me. No. They reached for hope, and hope just happened to look like me.

"This is Cross." Cross was taking short breaths to even out the gymnastics going on in his aura. Not even Cross could clamp down the bond right now.

She looked up at Jackson like he was already her rock, a source of strength she could endlessly tap into. I watched the alpha in him bloom, like his aura was presenting fresh and new.

My god. She loved him already and didn't know it.

"This is Ruby Frost," he said. He did not have to add "our mate." He ran a knuckle down her cheek, making her eyes flutter.

I looked down at the arsenal on the floor. We needed to put a little order into the chaos.

"Cross, take Ruby," I paused, her name feeling right in my mouth, "out for a little stroll while Jackson and I tidy up."

Right. Tidy up. Like there was clean laundry to be sorted and not semi-legal weapons to store away.

"Cross." I said again. The air shook slightly with a growl. She shrank back. It was subtle, but I caught it. She looked at me for reassurance. And then the smile was back.

Cross' aura filled the space between them. It was sharp, almost ugly. It forced her back out onto the porch.

Jackson's fingers lingered on the door, like he could touch her through it, then he twirled around.

He fucking twirled, biting his lip, the joy of endless possibilities spinning him around. He was absolutely in love and absolutely stunning. I was torn between wanting to fuck him on the spot or strangle him to death.

I knelt and started roughly packing gear haphazardly.

"She's perfect, isn't she? Ugh, I just want to bite her and eat her up."

"What the fuck are you thinking, Jackson?"

JACKSON

I closed my eyes and took a deep breath. Ruby's scent in this house just did things to me. Her orange and vanilla brightening everything up, bringing it all together. Making the dark, rich, broody scents of my pack all the more sexy.

I beamed a smile at Talon. And then I went cold.

He locked down the pack bonds. It was like chopping off one of my legs, making me unstable. I hated when he did that. It always felt personal. Like he didn't trust me. He wanted me close, but only so close.

He gestured to the pile of weapons that could supply a small army. I shrugged. So what?

"She's terrified, and you walk her into the middle of a war zone?"

I cocked my head and looked at him. I heard all his words, but they weren't making sense.

"She's... she's our..."

"She's in danger now. You just put that girl's life on the line for what?"

"For you. For Luther. For all of us."

Talon knelt and started stacking up gear on the old towel he used to protect the carpets.

"Did you even stop to think for one goddamn second how you fucked with the lives of 5 people?"

I joined him, going to one knee, my hands moved automatically... doing whatever the fuck Talon was doing. I didn't notice. I didn't care. The complete absence of his aura against mine was numbing.

"When I caught her scent..." Why didn't he see? Why didn't he get it?

"No, you didn't. You are so used to getting everything you

want, without working for it, without thinking how it impacts others..."

"Talon..." He was making it hard to breathe. I felt like he was throwing me into a deep dark hole and piling dirt on with every word.

"Not to mention that we talked about this. As a pack. We talked and agreed. We did not want an omega. You have just made a set of choices selfishly that impacts all of us."

"This isn't any omega. It's not like I brought a gold pack home from Gavin's for a night of fun and a quickie dark bond. Talon, she's our scent match." I followed him blindly into the laundry room where the gun safes were. Muscle memory had me clearing and stowing the firearms without a thought. Talon's rules - no gun play or unsecured weapons in the house.

"Scent match or not, we are not making her pack."

I was choking. I couldn't get a breath in.

"Talon, I want..."

"It's not about you, Jackson. Did you even discuss this with her? Or just slobber all over her with your golden retriever boy energy? And she's just along for the ride, high on alpha vibes? Did you push your aura on her? Get her to comply? You did, didn't you? For fuck's sake, Jackson."

He shoved our go bags into a corner next to the couch and roughly stacked the tactical vests. His face was a mask of betrayal, anger carving lines into his sharp, beautiful features.

"She's our scent match." The words got tangled up in my throat. I had to choke them out.

Talon became an immovable force. He let his aura out, just a little. It was thick like pudding, putting a wall between us. Panic beat at my chest. It seemed so... permanent...

"You disobeyed..."

Hot, stinging anger crashed into me, bursting out through my aura.

"Disobeyed? Did you just fucking say that? Disobeyed?"

Lava poured into the crack between us, rocking Talon back a step. I wouldn't even give him that much space.

"I am your fucking mate, your partner. Pack. I am alpha. I don't *obey* you. I am not your submissive or..."

The door lock beeped. Cross' big hand pushed the door open.

Ruby flooded in. Her scent, her aura, soothing, fortifying.

And it was the only thing I wanted now.

RUBY

They were huge. Gigantic. Massive. Alphas.

All the stories from my childhood resurfaced. The uncontrollable rage. The aggression. The lust. How they used and abused women and omegas.

I should be terrified. I should run screaming. But I was just confused. I didn't feel scared. I felt... safe.

Until I looked at Cross.

That was his name, right? *Cross... Talon...*

I took a step back, trapping myself in a corner of the porch. He didn't move, but he kept coming at me. His aura?

I've been kept away from alphas. They were too dangerous to associate with. Cross looked every bit of the killer he was. A beard hid his face, except for his eyes. They were... compelling. Dark blue with flecks of black, like an angry midnight sky. A black t-shirt stretched across his chest. He was broad, thick, and his hands were huge. They could break me in half.

And his scent... whisky and cherries. Sweet and stinging.

He nodded his head down the stairs and out to the front lawn.

I pulled my bag up my shoulder, using it like a shield across my body, somehow convincing myself that the cheap leather could protect me when he attacked.

I managed to get down the short steps without giving him my back, practically twisting to keep him in sight.

He stayed exactly one step behind me, herding me down the path to the sidewalk.

I looked up and down the street. It was deserted. The house was on a dead end. Thick woods rolled out from behind.

We were alone. No one would hear me... Not even Jackson could get here fast enough if...

I flicked my eyes back toward the house, willing Jackson to come out and save me from... my mate?

I looked down, tucking hair behind my ear.

Mates. Scent matches. I...

But it was all a lie. Propaganda and media hype. Endless stories, movies, and books that promised if you were a good little omega, you'd live out a fairytale of money and fashion and people doting on you. While behind the scenes, alphas used your body like a drug to keep themselves calm and productive members of society.

Cross' aura pressed into me. It was going to swallow me whole. Even in the light breeze, his scent wrapped around me. I glanced up at the house again and squinted. There was a pink ceramic frog tucked under a bush next to the steps. I frowned, like it was mocking me.

"Mmm hmm." It felt like purr or growl vibrating the air around me. "Not even Jackson could help you now, little one." He circled me with slow, careful steps.

My emotions swirled in a dangerous mix of fear and... lust.

How fucked up was it that I was lusting after my... mate?

No.

He was a stranger. A dangerous killing machine, ruled by his hormones, no better than an animal. Like me.

I rubbed the center of my chest. A stupid attempt to get my insides to calm down. I suddenly remembered the cut there. I had put it there while *he* watched. The warehouse angel. I closed my eyes and pulled *him* out of my imagination. *He* was big enough. *He* could push Cross away.

They both circled me now.

I licked my lips and swallowed. I needed... Ruin.

I pretended to be her every night. Ruin Winters was what omegas were supposed to be. Sexy, mean, and she always got her way.

Could I be her now? Be Ruin not Ruby? Ruby was worthless, nothing, but Ruin commanded attention.

I squared my shoulders, tossed my hair out of my face and looked at Cross directly.

He stopped his prowl, tilted his head. His lips turned up in an evil smirk.

"What's happening in there?" I asked putting a hand on my hip.

"They're fighting. Can't you feel it?" He wedged his hands in his back pockets like nothing mattered.

"About me?" His gaze on me was too direct, it made my insides shake.

"Yes."

I tore my eyes from him and stared down the front door.

"No one wants an omega." His voice was hushed and sharp. "We don't want you."

He started circling me again.

"You walked into our living room and ruined four lives."

I flicked my eyes to him nervously.

"Talon will make him choose. You. Or the pack. Either choice fucks us." His circle got tighter, closer to me.

"If he chooses the pack, he'll pine. Our bond will start to disintegrate with Jackson feeling incomplete."

His scent filled my space, making my eyes water.

"If he chooses you, that will shatter our pack bonds, leaving us all broken and useless. Worse, it destroys the scent match, too."

"What do you mean?" The question tumbled out of me.

Cross was silent until he was standing right in front of me.

"You scent match to a pack, not an individual. If a pack shatters, if the bonds are broken, the scent match dies. He'll lose his love, Talon, his brothers, the pack, and his scent match. Everything. We will all suffer."

Jackson was sweet, perfect, beautiful. A new feeling of protectiveness pushed down the fear. With that and Ruin, I could do anything.

It had me standing in front of the door before I even registered that I had moved.

I was stopped by a keypad on the door that I didn't know how to operate. I slid my eyes to Cross, who was right next to me. I gave him one of Ruin's "how dare you" looks and nodded to the keypad.

His grin was cruel. He knew only bad things were behind that door.

He reached across me and punched in the number, the beeps sounding cheery and bright, then he pushed the door open.

Dread swamped me. Talon and Jackson were standing inches apart. Talon had his arms crossed, looking defiant. Jackson had a finger in Talon's face. I backed up a step, right into Cross.

I was dead.

I was so dead.

They were going to take this out on me.

ELEVEN

RUBY

Ruin not Ruby.

    Ruin not Ruby.

    Ruin not Ruby.

If I could sit in front of a camera all night and pretend I was wealthy and powerful, a star with 1.2 million followers while trying not to throw up fried rice, then I could make small talk with three alphas.

Correction... *Mates. Alpha mates. Pack mates. Scent matches.*

What did that even mean? They told me that was a myth. It was a pipe dream meant to keep omegas in line. They told me it was drugs and brainwashing, media propaganda.

But... I felt it. Like when you've been sick and your ears finally pop and you notice you couldn't actually hear anything for the longest time and now you can.

Don't trust this. You can't trust this.

Alphas were dangerous and aggressive, no matter how sweet they seemed.

Jackson looked... awful. His sun-kissed skin was too pale to be healthy, his face crumpled with anger and pain... that I caused. He saw me and his breath caught. I watched him carefully rearrange his body language and expression.

Guns. The room had been covered in guns. These were not sweet, cuddly men. They were dangerous. And they were programmed to think that you, as an omega, a mate, were their property.

A quick chat, to make everything right with Jackson, and then I needed to leave and never see them again.

If they let you leave...

An ache set up in my chest and began to spread. I blinked slowly and conjured the image of my avenging angel, the killer, all in black from the warehouse. *He* would be a wall between us. *He* could push them all away. I could be safe behind *him*.

I raised my head and angled my shoulder forward like Ruin did on every video, and loosened my grip on my bag. I could do this.

The living room was pretty boring, to be honest. Nothing like the pack houses they showed on Westside Omegas, that reality TV show the girls at work were obsessed with. There were three couches, deep blue, arranged in a U shape. And no coffee table.

That was weird. Right? You should have a coffee table in a living room.

There was a framed abstract painting on the wall. It looked like it was picked only because it matched the couch. Hallways branched to the left and right, and there was an archway that led into a dining room with a big table that could sit a dozen people. Everything was tidy and boring. That couldn't be said about the men in the room.

Cross was huge. It felt like he was a foot taller than me. The sides of his head were shaved, and his long hair was pulled back in an elastic. I could tell it would be wavy when he let it down, when I ran my fingers through it. I blinked to get rid of that image. Tattoos peeked out of his shirt on his arms and neck. My brain wanted to linger on where else he might be tattooed.

I looked at Jackson to wipe away those images, but that was no better. Jackson was beautiful even if his face still held tension. He looked like he should be in a tux, dodging photographers with a duchess on his arm. His soft brown eyes sparkled and held me, making me want to fade away to where there was nothing but him. His eyes roamed over me like fingertips, burning everywhere he touched.

Cross stepped around me and further into the room to shut the door behind us. There was something final about that. Closing the door on some chapter of my life.

Their scents.

No one prepared me for the whole scent thing. Their scents were hitting me from all sides, mingling and swirling together into something that felt... right. It tugged me in all different directions, making me feel calm and safe and agitated and horny and scared and complete all at the same time. It was too much sensory input. I wanted to cover my ears, like that would somehow calm things down.

Ruin not Ruby.

I had to get a hold of myself and get out of here.

I put my hand on my hip and let my bag rest in the crook of my elbow. I took on that haughty, privileged stance like clients at the spa, like Charisma, when they were about to demand the world like it was their birthright.

A soft electronic trill broke the silence. Talon took out his phone, frowned and tucked it away again.

"Good guys or bad guys?" I asked with a raised eyebrow.

"I'm sorry?" Talon turned more directly to me, squaring off.

I gestured to the room that was now empty of guns, but I could see gear tucked behind the edge of the sofa.

"When you walk into someone's living room and there are

91

weapons everywhere, 'good guys or bad guys' is a natural question that might pop into my pretty little head, don't you think?" I gave him my best *You're An Idiot* look.

"Good guys." Jackson beamed at me.

"We're law enforcement." Talon countered.

"Law enforcement?" My tone was disbelieving. "What kind of 'law enforcement' keeps their weaponry in their living room and not at a police station?"

Worry creeped into Jackson's face and he shot a glance at Talon, who didn't respond, just cocked his head at me, like it was a ridiculous question he wasn't going to demean himself to answer.

"Why... Why don't we sit and chat for a minute?" Jackson gestured to the couches.

They each claimed one for themselves, leaving me to choose. Jackson was overwhelming me, like he was tugging me in with his aura, while Talon was pushing me out, down and away, but that was no less magnetic in its own way.

I chose Cross, but sat as far from him as possible, resisting the urge to lean into his cherry whiskey scent that held the promise of things that I couldn't have. Crazy that the most dangerous looking one felt the safest. He was honest. He wanted me gone. I wanted to be gone. We could be teammates at least.

Awkward silence filled the space like it had an aura of its own. All of their scents intensified, making me feel drunk, now. Dark, sensual, spicy, with something clean tying it all together. I tried not to, but I took a deep breath to draw the scents in.

Talon was directly across from me, scowling. But even that was somehow mesmerizing. He was tall, but not as tall as Cross. There was something... something I had never felt before, like he could tell me to stand right here, and the building could burn around me before I would move. His face was all hard angles, sharp cheekbones and jaw. He eased back into the cushions, legs spread wide, taking up space. An elbow rested on the arm of the couch, and he pinched his bottom lip while contemplating me. He smelled like ocean forests, sea salt and pine.

My insides shivered. All I could think about was kneeling between his legs, caged by his body, his hands in my hair, feeling... safe.

I needed to look away. No, *Ruby* needed to look away. *Ruby* needed to run and hide from whatever this was, but *Ruin* could hold his stare.

Talon leaned forward, rested his forearms on his knees, like he had made a decision.

"Scent match or no," he started, with no expression on his face, "as a pack, we decided we would never take on an omega."

That detonated like a bomb in all the auras in the room.

TWELVE

LUTHER

I put my head between my knees and panted it out.

It'd been a long time since I had vomited from a run. Sweat followed gravity and dripped off my nose as I concentrated on not barfing. When I started distance running as a kid, I spewed every run. The Old Man would give me shit about it. 'Wasting perfectly good food.' Food was his favorite weapon. Kids were easy to control when you messed with their food.

I walked my hands up my thighs to get to an upright position. A drastic change in blood flow would not help the situation. I'd love to just lie out flat in the parking lot. But it was gravel. Not only would that shit hurt, some drunk ass leaving happy hour a little too happy was liable to run right over me.

And Moxie hated dead people in her parking lot.

I ran a hand across my bare torso. Everything was still sore to the touch. I needed to cool off and not be so sweaty before going in for a drink. My size alone would have me sticking out in this dive bar on the edge of suburbia. Being half naked and sweaty, covered in bruises, was not the vibe of the Delta Lounge.

I groaned when I finally pulled the shirt on and walked in. My usual spot at the end of the bar was open. Didn't matter, Mox would bully anyone out of it. I liked having my back to the wall. I guessed that was the main reason we didn't do fine dining as a pack. None of us felt terribly comfortable being exposed, and it was just weird if we all lined up on one side of the table.

"What are we doing here?" I gestured at her wig as I sat. She had stark white hair. It branded her a seer. She said it was bad for business, so she had a vast collection of wigs.

"Luther, my dove, you wouldn't know stylish if it hit you with a truck." She put her fingertips to her chin and batted her eyes, turning her head to show off the style. "Ruin Winters has the 1950s bombshell look back in style."

Some unnamed emotion clawed at my gut to get out. She would be a dead ringer for Ruin, minus the black lips.

She cracked open a bottle of water for me and then put her forearms on the bar. She ran her eyes up and down me. "You have been hit by a truck," was her professional assessment.

"Explosion." I corrected her, paused and added "and I think a grenade. That part is unclear."

"Hm, no, that's not it."

"Listen woman, I was there. I totally got blown up. You want to see the bruises?" I hiked the corner of my shirt up.

"Luther, we've discussed this. You're not allowed to flash your beautiful abs unless you're going to use them. And we decided no fucking, remember?"

"Yeah, why did we do that?"

"I honestly don't know. But off topic, something is…" the rest of her thought didn't come out as she pulled cocktail ingredients to her.

Moxie was a seer. She was born with white hair, a red eye, and the ability to see auras. Freaky, yes, but didn't mean she was a bad person. She could just read you like a book, and then read you to filth for the fucked up things you did to your aura.

We got friendly years back when she was about to get jumped in her own damn bar, and I, like the fucking gentleman I was, disarmed everyone, handed her a baseball bat and let her go to town. And I unlocked a new kink that day - watching omegas beat the shit out of people.

I always stopped in for a drink if I was out on a run on this side of the preserve behind the house. If I took the paved road that ringed the preserve, it was just under 10 miles. Running through, on the trails, it was about 4. So, a good halfway point for long or short runs.

And Mox made the best cocktails. She used to work at The Valkyrie as a mixologist, but then life happened, one bad boyfriend too many and she gave it all up and opened up this place. She loved that I didn't drink so she could work that much harder to make a delicious concoction. And there was always an umbrella in it. Mostly because she hoped one day, a regular would pop off about a manly man drinking girlie drinks, and she'd get to sit back while some forceful reeducation about gender norms happened.

She stood with her hands on her hips, staring at her bar tools.

"Did you forget how to pour?" I said, shifting on the bar stool. Running did not agree with the cracked ribs. Cross was fucking right. Of course he was.

"You know that I like to make you drinks based on your aura, and this is what your aura is doing, you fucking weirdo."

She put a cherry in the bottom of short fat glass, then added exactly 4 pieces of ice. She filled it with two shots of whipped cream flavored vodka.

I cocked my head, puzzled. She never made me a drink with booze. Even before I told her why I didn't drink, she knew. The aura shit, duh. She added a few pumps of that liquid coffee sweet syrup stuff to a cocktail shaker with a splash of cream, shook it until it wasn't quite whipped cream but close, and floated it on top of the liquor. She picked up a lemon and contemplated it, tossing it a few times in her hand. She put it down, and her fingers found an orange instead.

"Peel that." She said, putting it on the bar in front of me.

"All right, some audience participation. You know how I like to watch though." I dug my fingers into it, the sharp bite of citrus getting loosed into the air. I pulled off a few bits of the skin and stacked them in a neat pile.

She grabbed some of the peel and carved the gross white part off and cut them into thin strips. She rimmed the glass with some of the peel and dropped the rest of the twists on top of the cream.

She set it in front of me and we both stared at it.

"I highly recommend you don't drink that. It's going to be terrible."

"Then why the fuck did you make it?"

"*Then why the fuck did you make it?*" she mocked back at me. "I don't know, Luther, you tell me. Why is your aura like this?" She made a messy gesture like she was finger painting in the air.

We both stared down at the glass like it was a test. I still had at least a four-mile run back to the house and a shot would make that a barfy run for sure.

"I think I'm seeing things." I said to the drink.

"Things?" Mox drummed her fingers on the bar.

"A woman."

"Hmmm."

"Well?" It wasn't like her not to give her two cents.

"I'm not a doctor. Or an arkologist."

"But you are a…" I gave her an exaggerated wink.

"Fine. Look, there's nothing technically wrong with your aura. I've told you before, under normal circumstances, even a seer wouldn't be able to tell you were a..." now it was her turn to wink. We didn't like saying "seer," or "rogue" in mixed company.

"Whenever someone has a traumatic experience, their auras can cycle."

"Cycle?"

"Not a technical term, just my word for it. It's like your aura gets turned up to 11 and then gradually comes back down. Your aura is doing that. All the time. And has been for months. I frankly don't know how you're still on your feet."

Good fucking question.

"But right now? It's like... I don't know. It's like it is looking for car keys. That pause before the frantic moment before you flip the fuck out." She shrugged and swiped all the orange peel off the bar.

I put my nose in the glass, the sweet orange and vanilla pulled at me. A dull ache erupted behind my eyes, like someone was digging in there to pull out a memory.

Every time I closed my eyes I saw this woman. The details were fuzzy, like she was a memory of a memory. My brain was trying to remember a hallucination it kicked out from a brain injury. Maybe I should go get checked over for TBIs.

"Who does this smell like to you?" I tilted the glass towards Mox.

"Rancid knotters and nesters."

We both whipped our heads around to the douche throwing slurs from the other end of the bar.

He was sitting with a few beta buddies. All of them decked out in fatigues, total weekend warrior style, going to knock their dicks around in a paintball field or something.

"Do you want me to?" I raised an eyebrow at Moxie.

"Pfft," she blew out a puff of air. "I got this."

She sauntered down the bar, upping all that omega magnetism

so that a beta could even feel it. She leaned across the bar suggestively.

"Talk nice," she purred, and put a finger to his lips to hush him. "The last man that used his dirty mouth like that ended the evening crawling across my floor in lingerie saying 'sorry mommy' while I fucked his wife."

I raised both eyebrows at that. Moxie sure did know how to push the right buttons.

"Fucking whore." He spat on the ground.

I stood. Mox casually drew up the baseball bat she kept out of sight under the bar. The dumbass corralled his buddies. My size alone herded them towards the door.

I snagged him by the back of his jacket with a little shake.

"Pay your bartender." I growled.

He dug in his pocket for his money clip. He flipped through some bills to get to a 20. I pinched the lone hundy that was sticking up, slid it out.

"Now say thank you, mommy." The dude sputtered, unable to get the words out. I rolled my eyes and pushed him to the door. Somehow, he managed to get out of the building without crawling.

I handed her the bill, and she stuffed it in the tip jar.

I wiggled my finger toward the parking lot. "I'm just gonna, you know…"

"If you're going to kill him, drag him to the woods. I am not hosing blood off my parking lot again."

"Yes, ma'am," I said with a little salute.

Ducking out the door, I put my back flat against the building. They had parked their white van facing out, right next to the building. I had clocked it as a delivery van. I wasn't actually going to kill the assholes, but I did want to make sure they vacated the premises properly.

"Fucking whore." The tough guy spat again.

"We've only got five minutes left to kill, anyway." I heard the van doors slide open and closed, the engine turned over. Windows must have been down because I still heard every word.

"Should we…" a voice trailed off.

"No, we don't need to synchronize our watches again, Bennett," the tough guy said snidely.

"Let's just go over it one last time." I could hear them rummaging through things in the van, some dull thuds, some glass clinking sounds, barely audible above the engine.

"A Team will approach from the street and cover the front door."

My ears perked up, this was not paintball chit chat.

"We'll come up through the woods and ram the back patio door. It's bullet proof, so we probably won't bust it. This will force those four fucking knotters out the side door where we can just pick them off."

I froze. My vision dimmed. All the energy leached from my aura, rooting me in place. They squealed out of the parking lot and turned on the road that went the long way around the preserve.

There was only one house that had bullet proof patio doors.

They were coming for the pack.

TALON

I rejected this girl. Jackson's aura collapsed in on itself, just as something bulldozed through the pack bonds.

I shared a look with Cross. I couldn't bring myself to look at Jackson just yet.

Something was very wrong.

Luther was running.

And not the "hey, let's go for a jog" kind of run. He was running for his life. Cross felt it, too. He was panic breathing, short panting breaths to fill his bloodstream with oxygen, giving him fuel to move. We all avoided looking at Ruby.

Cross pulled out his phone and sent a text. We all turned toward the kitchen when we heard Luther's phone ding. Fuck. I was going to duct tape that thing to his body. He never took it with him on a run.

My phone buzzed.

"Duo," I said as I stood, reading the pop-up on my phone, so they would know it wasn't Luther. The pack bonds were practically vibrating and getting worse with each heartbeat.

"Excuse me," I said with a nod to Ruby, who was twisting her fingers nervously in her lap. Even an idiot beta could pick up on the vibes of the room.

I tapped the call button on my phone before I even made it out of the room.

"Loco." Duo said as the call connected. I froze and turned back to my pack. "Loco." Duo repeated, a frantic edge to his voice.

Loco was our bug out code word. Established long ago and practiced like fire drills. It meant shit had hit the fan in a way we could not rectify.

"What?" I said in a hush. Jackson and Cross were both on their feet now.

"Tell Cross the pizza delivery is you. It's you. Loco. Get the fuck out."

The call cut.

I looked at Cross, the phone still to my ear. Three heartbeats passed. I shot a look at Ruby, and Cross nodded. And then we were all in movement, Jackson and I hit the gun safe, emptying it and slinging MP5s over our shoulders.

Back in the living room, Cross had our fire and bullet proof bag that held all our passports and IDs, his computer and other valuables we couldn't abandon. He had Ruby in the center of the room, pulling a ballistic vest over her head. It would be far too big, but it was something.

"What is happening?" Ruby's voice didn't shake, but terror and confusion leaked off of her, making her citrus scent sting.

Seeing Ruby, a defenseless, vulnerable civilian omega wrapped in Kevlar was half my nightmares come true.

The second half of my nightmares were the protective rage surging through my soul.

RUBY

Loco.

Our code word in the foster home was *Blitz*. It meant the same thing. Bad people were coming to do bad things.

Every family in Berry Creek practiced. We were always prepared for the government to raid us or for roaming packs of alphas to steal our little brothers and sisters.

Talon, Cross, and Jackson were more serious than we were. These drills always had a sense of excited anticipation, like we were about to fulfill our destiny or something.

But they were doing it wrong.

All wrong.

They were getting things to leave. We should be barricading ourselves in. We should be moving the youngest towards the windows. Alphas were less likely to hurt children. We should be hunkering down, not preparing to run.

I found myself alone in the circle of couches. I could just go, just walk away, like none of this happened. I closed my eyes, and the scents of this house rooted me to the spot. Dark and spicy, but fresh.

For the second time in a week, I was standing on the edge of danger and death.

I had stared past *his* gun in the warehouse, into *his* bright eyes, and asked *him* to pull the trigger. That same resolve and peace settled on me, the anticipation of an end much like the glee of those attack drills.

Except... Jackson. That end could find him, too.

Cross appeared in the archway leading to the back of the house. He pulled up short, almost like he forgot I was here.

All that peace and calm evaporated, burned away at a fierce protectiveness. He was mine and I wouldn't let anything happen to him.

He slung his bag over his shoulder and dug for something in a pile of gear next to the couch. He stepped to me and settled a bullet-proof vest over my head. He went down on one knee in front of me to adjust the straps around the sides. The sound of ripping Velcro was deafening in the calm before the storm.

His hands grazed me here and there as he tried to get the fit right. It was clinical and efficient but fire burned under his light touch. He rested a hand on my hip, naturally, casually, like he'd been doing it his whole life.

He scrubbed his face with his hand, like the thought he was having was too big for his skull to contain. I tucked my hands behind my back and knotted my fingers together. I was desperate to touch him, to run my fingers through his hair. That would be... wrong.

He exhaled a hard, short breath, like a decision had been made, and a course decided upon. He grabbed the hem of my skirt and tore it to my hip. I gasped, desire flaring in me.

"In case we have to run." Cross said in explanation as he stood and looked down at me. My heart was racing, but not from fear. I almost laughed. I had the crazy thought that nothing bad could happen so long as we were together.

A boom shook the entire house. Cross curled his immense body around mine.

"Breach. They rammed the fucking back porch." Talon was

suddenly there, guns and gear slung over him. He passed off weapons to Cross.

Something fast moving caught my attention out of the corner of my eye. I turned and looked out the bay windows in the front of the house.

It was *him.* My warehouse angel.

And then *he* was gone, consumed by shattering glass and flame.

THIRTEEN

LUTHER

I took the crow fly path through the preserve, a straight line to the house, not the meandering trails and footpaths. They had 10 miles to drive. I had 3 miles, maybe, to run through the woods. On a paved track I could do it, I could beat them. Through brush and over downed logs, it would be close.

I tore into my aura and the pack bonds. They should feel it, they had better feel it.

Fuck me for leaving the house without my phone.

My size was a disadvantage. Branches and brambles snagged at my clothes, but I was moving too fast for it to matter much. I had to get there first. I had to get them out. The last part was straight uphill. My lungs were burning, competing with my quads for attention.

That edge was there, right there, that cliff I couldn't fall off. That line between me and insanity, the power and promise of being a rogue, was right there. All I had to do was reach for it. And then nothing would stop me. Rogues weren't bound by any law of the universe. We could defy physics if we were really determined.

I came out of the woods at full speed. I heard the crash; they hit the back of the house. It was steel and concrete reinforced, it would hold. It better hold. The other van crept down the street. We were an equal distance to the house now.

A chubby guy got out of the van, something in his hands. He was paying attention to that, fiddling with it, and took no notice of the lunatic running like a bat out of hell.

Light flared between his hands, fire dangling off the end of a cloth stuffed in a bottle. He finally looked up when he heard my foot pound on the first porch step. I took the rest of the steps in one go.

And my world shattered to a halt.

She was there. In my living room.

The Molotov cocktail smashed against the front door, pulling a curtain of fire around me. I flung myself off the porch, landing hard on my back, sparks bursting in my vision. Sightless, I lunged for the fat man who was back pedaling from the burst of heat and throat punched him until his delight broke into gagging breaths.

My vision went gray, like my aura stole the color from the world.

Gun fire popped from behind the house.

Two sharp taps of my fist and I obliterated the guy's kneecaps. Even if his buddies picked him up off my lawn, he'd never walk right again.

I heard my bike rev, that distinct grumbling purr. Blinking furiously to get my eyes working, I stumbled around the corner of the house, just in time to catch Cross, sitting up high on my bike, not crouched over, kicking up dust and grass as he hit the tree line. It would be a bitch on the dirt path, but it was the fastest way out, and Cross was better on a bike than I was.

The distinct TAT-TAT-TAT-TAT of an MP5 pulled my attention

back to the house. Jackson was crouched low to the ground, firing blindly around the corner of the house, giving cover to Cross's escape. Talon saw me, nodded to the woods as he loaded a fresh magazine.

"*Loco*. Jackson. Go." Talon's voice boomed over crackling fire and shotgun blasts. There were dirt bikes and ATVs stashed in the woods, just for this reason. Jackson and Talon froze, consuming each other for what might be the last time, before they both snapped back to action. Talon sprayed the backyard with gunfire to make a path for Jackson, walking right into whatever mess was going on behind the house, like he was bulletproof.

"Don't make me raise my voice, Luther," Talon said, in a raised voice. Tires squealed behind me. The white van bounced over the curb and b-lined for the woods to run Cross down.

Abso-fucking-lutely not.

It took thirty seconds for me to catch up to the van and dive for the back door handle. It wrenched open, and I felt the sting of road rash on my shin. I pulled myself into the back of the van.

I broke the nose of the passenger, a thin wiry beta. Pulled the gun from his hip holster, I double tapped the driver, his blood spraying the windshield. I somehow managed to drag him out of the bucket seat, the van slowing enough for me to move the dead-weight out of the way, and get one hand on the steering wheel, slowing to a safe stop.

Once I had the car under control, I strained to hear gunfire or any ruckus at the house.

"I'm trying to listen here," I said absently to the groaning man while I wiped my brow with shaking hands. I stepped over the bodies to close the back doors of the van. There were only two cars at the scene. I had high confidence the other vehicle wouldn't be coming this way. Talon would make sure of that.

We were obviously in a *Loco* protocol. Bug out, get safe, lose tails and get to the cabin after 24 hours.

A plan we put in place years ago and never thought we'd have to use. I hauled the broken beta up to a sitting position. He was spitting blood and moaning. Broken noses sucked. Too bad.

I still had the gun in my hand. I nudged his head back with the barrel, so he'd look up at me.

"So, you want to tell me what this is about?"

"Fuck off." He said, leaning over to spit out blood.

"Not the right answer, man." I said as my vision went out.

Smell came back first. The sharp sting of gun smoke was like a slap in the face. It took me a second to piece together that the pile of mush on the floor of the van was the guy's face. The gun was still in my grip, fingers cramping around the trigger. I wiped brain matter and bone chips off my cheek with the back of my hand.

Blacking out was a bad sign. A very bad sign.

CROSS

I hit the kickstand and wiped my mouth with the back of my hand, resisting the urge to spit. I fanned my fingers out in front of me. They were shaking. I balled them into fists.

Swinging a leg over the back of the bike, I pulled her off in a rough movement, letting go of her immediately. She wobbled and reached out for the bike to steady herself.

I had pulled over to check for a tail and to get away from her fucking scent.

I'd skidded a street bike over miles of dirt foot trails, did 90 in a 45, left my pack to fend for themselves and all I could think about was the taste of orange and cream on my lips. And her warm body fitting perfectly under my protective shell.

She tugged at the Kevlar vest and smoothed out her torn skirt. A tantalizing hint of her thigh flashed as she shifted her weight and looked around. There was something so wrong about that. I shouldn't have torn her skirt. I had known we'd have to run and then escape on the bike. A tight-fitting skirt would have made that impossible. But tearing her skirt felt like a violation, like an act of violence.

Every time I saw a scrap of flesh emerge from the brutalized skirt, it turned me on and that was fucking with me, in ways that I could not manage being fucked with.

I slid my eyes away and focused on the bend in the road. If we had a tail, that curve in the road would show them, and keep us hidden. The last thing we needed was an ambush at the cabin.

I had to work hard to detach the name 'Jackson Serrano' and 'Jackson Albright' from any paperwork leading to the cabin. Serrano was easy because Talon was a nobody. When Talon registered the pack, Jackson insisted on taking Talon's last name. That did not wipe out the fact that he was an Albright, and the Albrights, his birth pack, were newsworthy. He did his best to keep a low profile, but on a slow news day, if Jackson spilled a coffee in public, someone would write about it. Jackson was our biggest security risk.

It was a terrible decision to go directly to the cabin. I knew that, but I had limited options.

I cracked my neck, adjusting the shoulder strap of the messenger bag and gun, hoping to relax enough to open the pack bonds fully. I knew they weren't dead. Nothing on this earth felt like those bonds shattering when your pack died. I wanted general feedback on their physical state.

I could tell Jackson was agitated and hyper. He might still be running. Talon was agitated and angry. I could sense a faint ache between the two of them, which told me they weren't together. And Luther was... cold. Alive for sure, but his emotions were flatlined. That couldn't be good.

The sound of Velcro tearing had me spinning back to Ruby.

"What are you doing?" Her hand paused on the second strap at my question.

"I thought..." She dropped her hands and changed what she was going to say. "You need this more than me, don't you?"

I heard the words. They entered my brain. I could rattle off the definition of each word. But I still wouldn't have been able to comprehend what she said.

"You're important. I'm not." She said by way of explanation with a heavy dose of "duh" in her voice.

If you were an alpha, you could be President with Ruin Winters throwing hand grenades at you and you'd still fight off your bodyguards to protect the omega in the room. That is, unless you were a rogue or psychopath. I'd never known an omega not to understand that on a fundamental level and accept it without question.

This alpha and omega bullshit was instinctual, not logical.

She dropped her hands and twisted her fingers in knots. The look on my face must have given her the answer she needed.

I wiped my mouth again. I couldn't get rid of her taste.

The road remained empty. A tail would have caught up by now.

I swung my leg over the bike. "Get on," I said, nodding behind me.

"Um," she bit her lip, and I was momentarily frozen. "How do I get on?"

"Put your right foot here and swing your left leg over the bike." I had to run my hand down her calf to guide her foot to the right place. Her skin was soft and smooth. She gasped at my touch and my heartbeat responded immediately, pounding at my rib cage.

I reached for one of her arms and pulled it around me, resting her fingers on my belt.

"There's no sissy bar, so you're going to have to lean into me and hold on."

Her hands splayed across my belly, looking for the best place to rest.

This was a bad idea. Her touching me like this, her touching me at all, might be worse than being overwhelmed with her citrus and vanilla scent.

I kicked the engine on and she jumped, squeezing me tight.

Fuck.

Think about danger, think about people chasing you, think about anything except her hands on your body. Think about Luther.

TALON

The hinges on the door of the ancient Winnebago screamed as I pried it open. Ivy had claimed half the rusted behemoths, and I had to push vines out of the way to duck in. This old farm was halfway between the city and the cabin. They raised alpaca instead of cows now. The owners knew I used this place from time to time. I had gotten one of their kids into rehab years ago. This was their repayment.

Each of us had a bolt hole, somewhere we could hide out if necessary. We'd only had to run like this once. And that was a false alarm. Bad intel about Riot sent everyone at the GPRE into a panic. The fucker probably planted the rumor himself just to fuck with us.

I pulled out my phone and started taking notes. I had to keep my brain occupied. The ache of not having Jackson with me set me on edge.

I got as far as partial license plates and the name "Billy" before the absence of information in the pack bonds ratcheted up my irritation. I couldn't even pace in the cramped RV. They were all alive. That I knew for sure. And they were all safe. Safe being a relative concept at this point.

Luther, though, I couldn't parse. I kept getting the sense that he was covered in blood, but he was uninjured.

He was close to losing it. Completely. His control, given everything he was put through, was greater than the average alpha, but dredging up his past, his sister, the old man dying, he was on a razor's edge. With a concussion, scrambling his brains and a direct threat to his pack? He needed more than I could give him. He needed an...

Omega.

A Mate.

Fuck.

FOURTEEN

CROSS

"Fuck." Ruby blurted as she stubbed her toe on something in the dark room.

I stifled a smirk. She seemed so prim and proper, haughty almost, not the kind of girl that cursed.

The cabin would be dark and cold until I got the generators going.

"You can take that thing off," I said, turning, as we stepped into the mudroom. I tapped on the battery-operated lantern we kept here.

She nearly collided with me and back pedaled. I reached for her to help get her out of the vest. She shied away, like she didn't want me to touch her.

That was fine. She was a big girl, she could figure it out herself. I leaned against the washing machine and crossed my arms, watching her struggle.

Tact vests were not rocket science, but it did take finesse to get them off. The velcro strips had a tendency to flop back in place and reattach with the slightest movement.

Her hair, wind whipped and messy, got caught up in velcro hooks. She tugged at it with increasing aggression, little sounds of frustration coming for her. She fought with it well past the point a normal person would have asked for help.

"Let me ..." I said. She backed away from me even further, pulling harder. It finally gave with a slight pop of her head.

I narrowed my eyes at her, which she refused to meet. She laid the vest on top of the dryer, smoothing the velcro back into place. A few dozen of her hairs clung to the shoulder strap.

A perverse anger simmered in me. I couldn't quite name the source of it, but it made my skin crawl. I grabbed her by the upper arm and pulled her into the kitchen. Her body was hot and soft under my fingers. I let go the second I realized I was manhandling her for no good reason.

Why should I care that she pulled out her own hair out of stubbornness?

I had about an hour's worth of work to get the cabin running. We hadn't expected to be back for a few months, so the furniture was covered with drop cloths, and the solar batteries and generators needed to be checked and started.

She wasn't pack. She didn't belong here. I didn't want her making herself at home. Where should I put her?

Your bed, asshole.

The thought screamed in my head. I pinched the bridge of my nose.

Fucking alpha hormones. Making you want things you didn't actually want.

The cabin had a pack bedroom. A huge room with a huge bed. I thought it was a waste of space. Jackson insisted on it. It was neutral territory, a demilitarized zone that was sometimes necessary for alphas living in close quarters. It was tradition in his birth pack. They actually had a whole house just for heat and ruts, with big open spaces, pillows everywhere, packed with everything cozy and satisfying. So, Jackson insisted on a pack bedroom, which was never used and would never be used.

Fucking Jackson.

That son of a bitch always got his way, eventually. No one saw how ruthless he was at the crunchy center of his fuckboy exterior.

He'd lied, cheated, and bribed his way through the academy. On the morning of the last PT test, he spiked the coffee of his biggest competitor with laxatives, knocking the kid out of the race for the number one spot. Jackson had to come out on top because only the valedictorian got to pick their assignment. And Jackson wanted on Talon's team.

Then Jackson needed a pack.

Of course, he didn't cause the events that happened, but he was right there to capitalize on it. And how did he accomplish this miraculous feat? By genuinely being exactly the kind of brother, pack or birth, that I had always wanted, that I didn't find in my first pack. He made Talon's bond the answer to every problem that I ever had and would ever have. The asshole.

I swept Ruby with some side eye.

I was not doing this again.

Jackson would have to deal with disappointment for the first time in his life.

There was a tiny spare bedroom for guests we never had. It was on Luther's side of the cabin. I had the north side. Talon and Jackson were upstairs. Talon occasionally slept in the spare room when he was mad at Jackson and wanted to prove a point. They always woke up in the same bed, though.

I led her right to the plain white boxy room with a tall bed. I thought it was supposed to be a canopy bed at some point, but there were no curtains around it. I pushed the door wide and guided her in. The bed, like all the furniture in the house, was covered in a huge white sheet to keep the dust off when we weren't here. I rolled it up, revealing the white duvet and fluffy pillows. The bed would be the perfect height to have her stretched across it as I stood at the foot of the bed and...

Fuck.

I cringed and took a deep breath before balling up the dust cover and tossing it into the hall.

"Stay here. I have some work to do." That was more gruff than I intended.

I looked back at her as I pulled the door shut from the hall. She was looking at the bed like she'd never seen one before. A hint of her thigh flashed in her ruined skirt.

This was adrenaline, fight or flight teaming up with stupid hormones I had no control over.

I did not want to fuck her.

She was not getting bitten into the pack.

I would never have another mate again.

I snatched the drop cloth off the floor and stormed down the hall to kick on the generators and get the satellite up and running.

FIFTEEN

JACKSON

I patted the douche's chest, like we were sharing a joke after walking off the back nine at the Club. I needed the distraction to hide the fact that I was stealing his jacket off the back of the bar stool. I faked a laugh, gave him a wink like we were old chums, before sliding past him to the exit.

Smiling prettily, I held the door open for a giggling clutch of betas who piled into the crowded bar just in time for last call. Once I hit the street, I pulled the jacket on, popping the collar, walking faster than all the drunks around me.

I had been ducking in and out of East Side bars for the past couple of hours. Easiest way to lose a tail is to make them squeeze through a space packed with people. I ditched the dirt bike in Centennial Park. Didn't matter who found it. All the VIN numbers were filed off.

Flipping through my phone, I leaned against the call buttons in the vestibule. Someone would be along to open the door. Worst case? I'd order take-out and make her buzz us in.

I pulled up Ruby's selfie to destroy the image seared in my

brain. My omega, my mate, standing in my living room in a flak jacket with flames exploding around her.

And then Talon, a gun in each hand, leaving him behind. I closed my eyes, trying to force my heart rate to slow.

Cross on that bike. Ruby under him.

Luther.

I didn't even get a last look at Luther. I was already in the woods when Talon yelled at him to go.

Everyone was alive. That's what mattered. The rest we could fix.

A woman pulled open the street doors. She was pretty, a beta obviously, with curves in all the right places. She gave me an appraising look, pausing before stepping into the tight space with me.

"Lost my key. Again. Do you mind? My girlfriend will kill me if she finds out I lost them."

She softened up at the word "girlfriend". Alphas and omegas didn't use that word. So, I was fine, safe, one of them, despite what I might smell like. My dimpled smile and the pathetic look I was wearing probably didn't hurt either.

She tucked her bangs behind her ear, turned her key in the lock, and let me hold the door open for her. I hung back as she pressed the button for the elevator.

When it dinged its arrival, I faked a phone call.

"You go, I'm going to take this…" I made a show of covering the receiver, giving her a wink as she stepped into the elevator. "Yeah, sorry about that, Carl. Look, I know it's late, but you have my spare keys, right?"

The doors slid shut. I kept up the fake conversation as the machinery whirled her away with grinding sounds. My agitated state could be felt by a corpse. No need to make yet another woman fear for her life today.

Pacing in tight circles, I tried to organize what happened. Line it all up like I was writing a report. Of course there'd be no paper trail on this attack. But it gave my thoughts a framework to latch on to. I stopped and rubbed my face. We did leave bodies, though. At least one. That might be tricky.

Six suspects, probably. At least two hit the front of the house.

Luther put one down. Probably not fatal. He wasn't armed. Not that he needed a gun to kill people. At least three people in the back. They had a similar look, related maybe. One slighter than the other.

Two vans, not identical, similar makes, different models. Generic white passenger vans.

A partial plate. A42. I'd kept repeating it as I ran through the woods. Over and over. A plate would help us get the fuckers. We had done more with less information.

Once we were all back together, we'd fill in the gaps and go hunting.

The elevator dinged, and I slid in, feeling slightly calmer. Plotting vengeance was soothing to the soul. I got off on the fourth floor.

The hallway smelled stale and dingy. I tried my best to talk Jonquil out of moving in here. She was insistent. I ran a background check on all of her neighbors. Minor drug violations and one DV case were the only thing to come up. This wasn't the Gritch District, but it wasn't West Side either. And it certainly wasn't the gated community we grew up in.

I leaned on the doorbell with exactly two taps, smiling to myself. One long, one short. It was code for the pack kids. "Let me in. Hide me. I'm breaking curfew. The dads are gonna beat my ass." She'd get its meaning.

Sure enough, when she opened the door, her face was screwed up in confused concern. I grabbed her face and kissed her forehead as she stepped back to let me in.

"Jonnie, I need a shower and your car."

"Who dragged you through the gutter? Oh my god. Are you fighting with Tal?"

"No, it's all good, just..."

"Work." She finished for me.

I smirked. The birth pack knew I worked for the GPRE. Everyone thought it was a desk job. Jonnie figured out that was sus years ago.

She was in an oversized Omegas of Bradley Hill t-shirt with her sandy blond hair piled in a messy bun.

"And I'm not giving you my car," she said, pulling towels out of a cardboard box. We had just moved her in here last week. She hadn't made a ton of progress unpacking. "I had to beg dad for it. I'm not giving it up."

"Which dad?" I ducked my head out of the bathroom. This was bound to be juicy gossip.

"Xavier," she said, adding an eye roll.

He was everyone's least favorite dad and because of that he bought big splashy gifts. When we were being extra mean to each other growing up, we'd taunt each other with, "Xavier is your daddy." Most of us were conceived in heat, so it was impossible to know which one of the alphas' DNA you were actually working with. Not that it mattered. Pack was pack.

I stepped in under the shower spray and frowned. The water pressure was shit. I'd have Cross come by and put in a new shower head for her. I needed about an hour under the hot water to have any hope of easing away my tension. Anxiety wouldn't loosen its grip on me until I could touch the pack and know they were OK.

"You're still taking me to the Perfume and the Alphabeta's concert, right?" Jonnie said from the other side of the shower curtain.

"Jonnie, you're not sixteen. You don't need your pack mate to get you into concerts anymore. You're an adult with registered ID and everything." I finished washing up with the bougie eucalyptus soap I had gotten her for Christmas. I had gotten Jared in the Secret Santa draw, but Jonquil was my favorite pack mate, despite the 10 year age gap. I always got her a gift. And I was an asshole. I didn't care who knew she was my favorite.

"Yeah, but it's a dumb beta ID. That's not going to get me backstage."

She meant it as a joke, but I heard the sting of disappointment in her voice.

Our branch of the Albright pack was unusually huge. There were a dozen alphas and four omegas. This generation had 14 kids and two of the omegas were not done having babies yet.

Jonnie's 20th birthday had come and gone with no perfume. Which meant she was off to start her own life outside the pack. She could be a late bloomer, but the odds were really low. Our little sister, Juniper, perfumed last year, and was being a cunt about it.

"Of course we will go to the concert together. But you have to get the tickets. I'm not standing in line. I'll bring..." I said, stepping out of the shower and wrapping a towel around my waist when butterflies erupted in my stomach.

I'll bring Ruby.

They would love each other. A huge grin spread across my face.

"Cool," she said, dumping out the contents of a box and sorting through the messy pile. "They're having a meet and greet downtown for when the tickets go on sale. And you know Perfume and Zenith are going to do something batshit. Ester, you know Ester from the Frasier Pack, right? She's camping out for tickets, so I'm going to join her after work."

"Excellent. You need money?"

She stood and snapped a shirt out of the pile.

"No." She said it in that tone that did mean she needed money. I dug my phone out of the pile of discarded clothes and transferred a thousand into her account with a few taps.

"Oh, I need to borrow some spare clothes. Jeans, some leggings, a couple tops."

"For you?" She raised an eyebrow at me.

"No, a girl in a tough spot we're trying to help out. Just some stuff to get through a couple of days."

She shrugged and tore open a cardboard box.

"You think Luther would make me a batch of pancakes for the freezer? You know, a housewarming gift?" She said as she packed an old gym bag with a few items.

I slicked my hair back. It would dry on its own, and I stepped back into my jeans. A men's dress shirt dangled from her outstretched fingers. I gave her a questioning look.

"It's yours, asshole," she said, rolling her eyes. "Remember? The September Pageant like three years ago? Alester Dunhill ripped my dress? You stomped him into the ground and broke his kneecap? Made me wear the shirt home?"

"Oh right, how's he doing?" I pulled the shirt on and buttoned it up.

"Disabled."

We both looked at each other and laughed. The world just needed to learn the hard way, never to touch what's mine.

She leaned against the archway that separated the miniscule kitchen from the living area of the studio apartment. The look she gave me was calculating. She knew the secret ins and outs of my bullshit. We didn't have bonds. She couldn't feel my aura. But she could read me crystal clear.

"You sure you're OK?"

"Yes, and I'll be even better very, very soon." I beamed at her.

Just the thought of biting Ruby into the pack was going to make the rest of this night bearable.

"The keys are on the hook." She nodded towards the door.

"Ugh," I said, squeezing her in a rough hug, "you are the best. We're up at the cabin for a while, but we'll have you over for dinner when we get back."

"Oh, and don't forget…"

"Luther's pancakes." I finished for her as I stepped out the door, blowing her a kiss.

SIXTEEN

RUBY

They are all going to die.

Bennett and Billy were shooting at my... pack.

I rubbed my face. Cross' scent was all over me. Cherries and whisky, sweet and stinging. It smelled... wonderful. Now that the wind wasn't whipping at me, his scent was everywhere, making me... hot and wet. It made me feel drunk. I had only been drunk once... and that was before... before all this.

My body didn't move. I stood still where he left me. But my insides were running, screaming, shouting.

They were all going to die. What was I thinking? Letting Jackson pull me here. I lead them to the pack... *my pack.*

No.

They weren't mine. I couldn't have them. Look what I've already done to them. When they found out, when they knew what I did, who I was ... Oh my god. They were law enforcement. Wasn't that what Talon said? All the guns?

They had attacked the police.

I had to get out of here. I had to find my way back to Berry

Creek. Come up with some bigger plan for Ruin Winters that they could get excited about. Make them forget about Jackson and the pack. I didn't even know where I was, but I had to go.

Oh god.

I was alone with a pack of alphas.

They'd smell my omega slick and lose control. Alphas always did. They'd never let me go. They'd force me into heat. Then bite me, dark bond me, trap me, keep me.

Nausea rose. I skidded on the shiny white tile of the bathroom as I ran for the toilet. How would they punish me if I threw up on the floor? It would be worse than licking it off the floor.

Alphas had no mercy. They were all violence and aggression. I hadn't eaten in a day, maybe two. Nothing would come up.

Sweat broke out on my forehead. I wiped at it. Sweat would make my stench worse. The room was too big, there was too much space, they'd find me... and...

I crawled across the tile to the skinny tall linen closet door and ripped it open. No padlock on this one, either.

It was mostly empty, spare towels, sheets. I made space on the floor, stashing spare rolls of toilet paper on a higher shelf. There was just enough room. I scrambled in and pulled my knees in close, wedging my fingers under the door to pull it closed as best I could.

In the dark, I rested my head on my knees, closed my eyes and tried to take a deep breath.

CROSS

I washed soot and ash off my hands at the kitchen sink. The solar-powered radiant heat floors would take a while to warm. I started a fire in the living room to take the chill off. Wood smoke calmed my nerves somewhat.

I gripped the edge of the sink and hung my head. My aura

rubbed against me like sandpaper, made worse by the fact that the pack wasn't here. I was pretty certain now Luther was injured. But I couldn't tell how. Not dead, but not well.

They would all hunker down for the next 24 hours before making their way here. I shouldn't have come directly here either. It was a bad tactical move to lead people right to your safe house, but I didn't have a lot of choices. Being on the run with an omega strapped to your back was less than ideal.

This plan, the *Loco* plan, was the right thing to do from a safety standpoint, but it did not take into consideration how pack bonds and our auras would fuck with our mental state. And every hour would get increasingly shitty with the lack of information.

Pulling open the pantry, my hands were jerky and clumsy, sorting through the supplies to find something passable for a meal. There was stuff in the freezer in the garage, but I wasn't touching that.

I grabbed a collection of peanut butter, crackers, some fruit snacks, protein bars and tiny chip bags. Luther and Jackson ate like toddlers. I grabbed a bottle of tequila and jammed it in the crook of my arm, carrying the haul to the counter.

My fingers stilled while twisting off the cap to the booze. Numbing out would be great, but did I really want to lower my inhibitions right now?

Yes, the fuck you do.

I took a few breaths until it wasn't shaky anymore and put the booze back. Instead, I tore open a pack of fruit snacks, popping a few in my mouth as I made my way down the hall. I grimaced at the excessive sweetness.

I pushed the door open before I remembered I should have some fucking manners.

"Ru…"

The room was empty. The bed was untouched. I pretty much figured she'd curl up and do the nesting thing. Granted, we didn't have the required pillows and blankies for that, but that's what omegas did, right? Cocooned up in bed when stressed?

I backed out of the room and checked the rest of the house, even the pack bedroom.

She wasn't here.

An echo of that awful panic, that awful day, started chiming through me.

I double checked the house, upstairs, the walk-ins. All the bathrooms. I circled my way back to her room.

I stepped into her bath, my hand stilling on the shower curtain. I held my breath for courage and swept it back. The stark white tile was unblemished and blinding.

I raked a hand through my hair, ripping the elastic out, like my brain couldn't handle even that much extra pressure. My own hair clung to it, like hers had clung to the velcro.

I turned it over in my hands, demanding my attention to stay on the elastic, the hair, its texture and not stray to the dangerous past. It slipped through my shaking fingers, silently bouncing once on the hard floor. I bent to pick it up.

A scrap of pink fabric was caught up in the crack of the closet door, out of place in the mostly empty room. I fingered it, Ruby's skirt, the edges were rough from where I'd ripped it.

I squeezed my eyes shut, struggling for sips of air. This is how I found *her* too, nine years ago.

I knew instantly. His rage, her pain. His aura blew, unrecognizable, alien and oily. Stella wasn't here, she wasn't anywhere in the house. I checked and double checked. But I could feel her still, and it was more than just her lingering cinnamon scent. Red spots on the white linoleum led me to the garage. The only thing out of place... a streamer of long red hair escaping from the standing freezer.

·   ·   ·

I blinked away the memory of Stella in the freezer. I could not blink away abject fear and rage.

I tore the flimsy closet door off the hinges, blindly reaching in and pulling Ruby out by her arm. Her eyes were wide and wild. Blue green. Not brown. Her hair, short and messy. Not long and red.

Not Stella.

It was Ruby. The omega who'd walked into my living room and destroyed my pack only hours ago. This wasn't *my* omega smelling of burned cinnamon and blood. *My* omega, who died in my arms.

I turned Ruby roughly in my hands looking for entry and exit wounds I knew wouldn't be there. Her clothes were rumpled but otherwise perfect save for the gash I'd torn in it hours ago.

She struggled silently in my hands, not fighting back, just trying to pull free. I set her down on her feet and let go. She bolted from the bathroom, never turning her back on me, putting herself in a corner.

"What the fuck were you doing?" My voice almost slurred from anger and flashback memories.

"Nothing."

"Nothing? What the fuck do you mean?"

"Nothing." Ruby said, lifting her chin. Not in defiance, but in denial.

"Were... were you nesting?"

"No."

I stared at her like I was losing my mind. I looked back over my shoulder, back into the bathroom.

I *had* ripped the door off. She *had* been in the closet.

Right?

"That would be wrong." Her voice was cold with absolute conviction, like she was repeating a rule.

The space wasn't more than 2 foot by 3 foot. If she wasn't nesting, what the fuck was she doing? Nesting was a perfectly natural and healthy instinct. Why deny it like this?

My thoughts stalled out, ground to a halt. Something was happening here that I didn't understand.

Too much had already happened to process. The attack. The pack bonds. Luther. The flashback. Ruby. Her sour orange scent clouded everything.

My aura was pushing the limits of what my psyche could tolerate. Conflicting instincts were pulling me apart.

The alpha drive to protect what's yours. The pounding instinct to destroy any threat.

She was both.

The thing to protect and the threat to my pack.

This scent matched omega, was backed into a corner, and frozen in terror.

She needed protection. From me. I was the threat. Only... I felt like *I* needed protection from *her.*

It was an effort to drag in a breath while my aura and instincts warred. Like last time. Then, when my pack bonds shattered and my aura began to untether, I felt lost in inky space, not even a star to anchor to.

Now, I was at the bottom of an ocean, the pressure all around, too great. It would force an internal collapse. Crumpled like a sheet of paper.

"Don't fucking do that again."

"I'm not doing anything."

Her tone was flat, so much so that I couldn't tell if that was a promise or a denial.

Either response would have made me angry. I wasn't her alpha. She wasn't my omega. She didn't have to obey me. That would have pissed me off as much as a lie. This? The fact I couldn't tell anything from her body language? That was unsettling.

"Stay in this room." I stalked towards the door and pulled it open.

I waited three heartbeats for a response and none came. She shifted her weight from foot to foot. That flash of thigh from her torn skirt chased me from the room. I eased the door shut behind me with excessive caution. I already broke one door tonight, and I needed a solid barrier between us.

SEVENTEEN

LUTHER

I struggled to squeeze into the bottom of the closet and yank at the bald, demented baby doll that we'd nailed to the board. The thing was still creepy. Even more creepy now that I was an adult and had a better understanding of what it meant when old men gave gifts to little girls.

Lhevus had an "associate" over. Some big wig from Berry Creek would pop by to discuss experimental drugs and the old man's theories about aura development and management.

What was the dude's name? Something pompous, like Wotherton. I snapped my fingers when I remembered it was Forthright. Mason Forthright.

He brought my sister gifts every time. When he gave her this baby doll, she sat right in the middle of the living room and chopped its hair off and dyed the stubby fuzz pink with a highlighter.

He stopped bringing gifts after that.

We'd cracked up as we nailed it inside her closet, saying its ghost would protect her hidey hole. After Havoc perfumed, he was here all the time, practically begging Lhevus to let him take her to the "reeducation" school he was building. I throat punched him after that and he never came back.

I fished around inside and, by touch alone, identified the box of glow sticks. I'd stolen them for her from the gas station down the road. Prize in hand, I leaned against the doorjamb.

Her room hadn't changed at all since the day I left. Same posters on the wall, a cheap disco ball strung up in the corner of the ceiling. The bed was even still made with her *Hunting Falcon* comforter. She was obsessed with Prey Nightingale. We must have watched that movie every day for years.

This was the only room in the house that was still intact. It was like the GPRE strike forces and looters that surely came after couldn't bring themselves to desecrate a little girl's room. The rest of the house was tossed. I did manage to sort through the wreckage and find clothes that weren't covered in blood.

I snapped a half dozen of the glow sticks and shook them to life, surprised they still had juice after all these years. It was just enough light that I could locate the loose floorboard next to the bed. Lhevus was deranged and paranoid. There were hidden cubbies all over the house. It wasn't the secret Havoc had thought it was, however. She'd kept her diary in there. Lhevus read it all the time.

I pried it open and emptied it. She always kept emergency granola bars for me in there. The last thing I pulled out was the pink falcon stuffie. It was a limited edition. I'd told her I saved all summer for it. I'd lied. I'd beat a kid up and stolen it. She had been desperate for it, which made me desperate for her to have it.

I'd take it and the diary with me. Parts of her should not be left in a place like this.

I tore into one of the granola bars, pulling her comforter off the bed and wrapping it around me. I wasn't even going to check the expiration date on them. Dying from food poisoning in this house after everything we've been through would be poetic. Havoc would laugh her ass off.

This house was both salvation and hell. And right now, I really didn't know which side I'd come out on.

A six-year-old rogue alpha should have been impossible. What happened and how I ended up in Lhevus Saint's house was still unclear after all these years. I'd read the official sealed report about the playground incident. People died, I didn't really remember it, and that bothered me.

Depending on your political leanings, Lhevus was a terrorist or a hero. He believed that registering with the Institute, forcing omegas to take the injection that would prevent their eyes from turning gold, and becoming gold pack, was barbaric. He believed that gold pack omegas and rogue alphas were our natural state of being. He wanted to see the end of the Institute and the artificial control they had over society.

Rogues could not be bound by law or pack. They unbalanced society. They were a threat. The only way to control a rogue alpha was to kill them or prevent them from being born.

Rogues could only be born to a gold pack omega parent. Therefore, the Institute made life hell for gold pack omegas. After you perfumed as an omega, you had a year to register with the Institute and get the injection that would keep you from going gold pack. If you didn't, after a year, your eyes turned gold and you were a target.

Gold pack omegas were non-citizens. They couldn't have passports. They didn't qualify for free healthcare or the income assistance offered to all omegas. They were pushed to the fringes of society and hunted. It was completely legal to dark bond a gold pack omega who was compelled by pack bonds to obey or suffer. They were trafficked and abused.

When Havoc perfumed at 12 or 13, I knew exactly what would happen. He would force gold pack status on her, to keep her "pure" and untainted from the poison of the Institute. He said it was her choice, but she didn't understand the consequences of it at all.

He and I fought about it every day. The fights turned physical. He had beat me as a kid, starved me, shoved me in sensory deprivation tanks and more, just to see what it would do to my aura. And I never fought back, not really. But for Havoc, I'd risk it all.

She'd only had days left to get to the Institute before her eyes would turn gold. She got really sick, puking on the floor sick. Lhevus took a baseball bat to me. He told me he'd poisoned her, just to show me that he could. Said he would kill her himself if I didn't leave, vow to never see her again. So, I did. It was the only thing I could do to keep her safe.

I was on the streets doing petty crime to survive. Until these three guys were on a stakeout in the Gritch and got jumped. Two of them were down, I stood over their bodies and defended them until their pack lead could crack some skulls. Talon needed help evac'ing two big dudes. He made me the first solid meal I had in a year, and I just never left.

Talon knew I was a rogue from the moment I met him. He had heard the stories. Lhevus was on every government watch list you could think of. So was the foster son he took in. Talon and Duo worked together to doctor paperwork and erase everything about Lhevus's foster son. Talon thought the perfect place to hide a rogue alpha was in a pack that hunted rogue alphas. He never told my new pack mates.

A couple months ago, Lhevus ran out of luck. Our pack was assigned his execution and the transfer of Havoc into Institute custody. I begged Talon to step in, promised him everything and anything. I knew there were no good options for Havoc once she was in the system. There were no good options for gold pack omega. Period.

The deal he'd struck with me was that I had to promise not to see her, contact her or seek out any information on her. To know the truth about what happened to her would kill me. No, it would kill other people. My aura had flared out of control. We were alone up at the cabin when he told me. Cross and Jackson were far enough away that they knew something was wrong, but not what. They had no idea they had bonded a rogue alpha who just lost control and was capable of killing anyone, including his brothers.

EIGHTEEN

RUBY

I was stuck on O's.

My cheek was pressed against the floor. My right hand had inched toward the bath on the other side of the room. I'd never reach it. I was as close as I dared.

Only. Organ. Official.

My outstretched arm and shoulder were underneath the bed. I bet you could fit a small car under here. I'd never seen a bed so tall before.

Obedient. Oatmeal. Oasis.

. . .

My bed, back when I was allowed to have one, had been on the floor. Not even room to tuck your slippers under.

Object. Owner. Only.

Would this be nesting? Having my arm under the bed like this? Would Cross be mad? Punish me? He said not to do that again.

Only? Already tried that one.

They all had O's in their names. Luther had been easier.

L-oyal
    U-nbroken
    T-ouch
    H-elp
    E-xplosion
    R-eal

When I was younger, right after I perfumed, I would make up elaborate stories. Picture a normal day as a beta. Describe it to myself with all the tiniest details. A scratch on the red tea kettle that was on the stove. The squeak the medicine cabinet made. The little motes of dust that would get set free to dance in sunbeams when the cushions on the sofa got fluffed.

Hours and hours locked in a basement, or in the kennels,

when my smell got too bad. There was nothing for your brain to do but make pictures.

I stopped after a while, knowing I'd never have any of those things.

Just plain words were less... threatening. I tried to match the word, to the letter, to the name, to the person. Billy had been the first. It was simple.

Barf. Ill. Loathsome. Liar. Yuk.

One O word that refused to get out of my head even when I banged it on the floor. It crowded out all the other O's. It screamed for attention, slicing hot knives through me.

Orgasm.

I could taste his anger. It burned my tongue like his cherry scent. He was dangerous and terrifying. He was everything they said alphas were.

And, it had made me horny. I banged my head a few more times.

I rolled over on my back. Inviting gravity to press down on me. I pictured the weight of everything sitting on my stomach. Sometimes that worked. Sometimes it drove the growling hunger pains away.

Fried rice. That was the last thing I ate. But when? Not today. Not yesterday. They forgot food for me all the time.

I twisted my head and looked at the door. It had to be late. Or early. Whatever. This was a home. They had to have food somewhere.

Stay in this room.

I tapped my fingers on my forehead. And swallowed. Again.

I'd risk it.

Cracking the door open just enough to slide my body out. I kept the doorknob twisted as I pulled it shut and then gently let it go. I've been caught out one too many times by noisy doors.

I turned toward the only source of light at the end of the hall to my left.

My breath caught.

I was caught.

Cross sat on the floor. His back was against the island counter of the kitchen. His legs outstretched, and facing down the hallway toward this room. His feet bare, crossed at the ankle. He was smoking. White blue wisps curled above him in the slice of light the kitchen granted him. He tilted his head up, blowing smoke away from him, never taking his eyes off me.

He put the cigarette down to rest in a rusty metal tin. It was palm-sized. Well, the size of his palm, not mine. It was perched on a stack of thin books. A few papers were scattered about him, and at least a dozen markers, too. He stretched to his left, the t-shirt riding up a few inches. Black ink crawled above where his belt bit into his side. I looked down and away, desperate to not let my mind linger on exploring how he turned his body into art.

Cross rolled a bottle of water down the hall toward me. It veered sharply to the right and collided with the wall. I stared at it like it would explode. Cross stared at me.

I sat down next to it. The rip in my skirt making it less awkward. I didn't have to do that side saddle thing. I hunched into the bottle and cracked the top. The breaking plastic was loud in the silence.

When I looked up, he had his head tilted back, like he couldn't bear the sight of me. He stretched his arm, hiking his shirt again to bring the cigarette to his lips. I wiped my mouth with the back of my hand.

With a crinkling sound, he scooted a granola bar or something my way. I didn't even bother to look at what it was. The wrapper fought me. And it was winning. It didn't have a handy "tear here" marker.

Without warning, he shifted his position. Before I could even choose to freeze or flee, he plucked the bar out of my fingers, tore it with his teeth, and handed it back. He settled back to where he was, raking a hand through his hair, pulling it all to the left side. The sides of his head were shaved. Would it be soft or prickly? The cold kitchen light made strands of red and gold dance in the chocolate brown.

I struggled to take normal sized bites. I wanted to shove the whole thing in my mouth so they couldn't take it away. The protein bar was kind of gluey and thick, tasting vaguely of peanuts and cheap chocolate.

"What time is it?" I asked. I don't know why I asked. It didn't matter.

"3:24." He said, shifting his glance away from me for just a second. And then his eyes were back on me.

Not like how Billy or Bennett looked at me, or other members of the Reset. To some of them, I just looked like a take-out meal, something to put their dicks in for quick and cheap satisfaction. Others looked at me like the threat I was. The horrible abomination that would bring everything they loved to a fiery end.

Cross looked at me like... like something he wanted to figure out and understand.

He's quiet, and strong and smart. He'll fix anything that's broken. That's what Jackson had said.

"Aren't you going to bed?" I said, chewing, playing with the edge of the wrapper where his lips had touched.

"Nah, Darlin'," he said, blowing out a breath of smoke.

My breath hitched, the word "Darling" sent shivers down my spine, my legs twitched reflexively. His eyes roamed over me from head to toe, lingering on my lap.

"You don't have to guard me. I won't be bad. You could..." I didn't know if there was a basement to lock me up in here.

He took a long pull on his cigarette. The extended silence

making me feel dumb. No, worse, like I had said something wrong.

"It's a pack thing. It's hard to relax when we're apart like this. Sleep is impossible. Being awake is torture."

"Oh." I frowned and took another dainty bite of the bar. I didn't expect... honesty.

Cross stood in a graceful movement, like he knew exactly what his body was capable of. He stepped out of my sight for just a second before he was standing over me. I looked up and got dizzy, my eyes fluttered. His scent pushed into me, making it hard to breathe, but I was desperate for more of him.

He crouched next to me then. His attention was on my lips as I licked them. He tore a little package open in his hands and held it out to me.

"Thank you." I took it, thanking him even before I knew what it was.

He stood again and was gone from my sight again. I peered down, turning the package in my hand to read the label. Fruit snacks. Cross was back before I finished the second one.

Setting a neatly folded stack of clothes next to me, he took up his spot again. He rolled his head on his shoulders, like he couldn't get comfortable, and sighed heavily.

I pulled the t-shirt closer to me. It had the Jade Falcon on it from "Hunting Falcons".

"They're Jackson's," he answered before I could even raise a questioning eyebrow. "They'll still be too big for you, but it will have to do."

"He won't mind I'm wearing his clothes?" I fingered the edge of the t-shirt.

My head came up at his barking laugh.

"Your scent will be all over them."

"Oh. I'll wash them."

Cross snorted. "He'll sleep with them under his pillow for the rest of his life."

I frowned. I couldn't tell if he was making fun of me.

"I don't think you fully appreciate how good you smell."

I quickly turned my back to Cross, so he didn't see the tears that came from nowhere. How could I possibly smell good? There was nothing good about me.

I pulled the t-shirt over my head but didn't push my arms through the holes. I was an expert at changing without letting anyone see my body. With the shirt tented around me, I unbuttoned the blouse and peeled it off. The skirt was trickier, but I managed. I fumbled for the fabric that was under the t-shirt and shook it out.

Boxers? My eyes went wide and my cheeks flashed hot. They had cartoon depictions of rope and the phrase "Knot like other boys," printed all over them in a repeating pattern. It was one of the Alphabetas' popular songs.

I tucked a lock of hair behind my ear before shimming them up my legs. I wiped my eyes on the t-shirt before turning around again, and getting real interested in the fruit snacks.

Cross moved the rusty tin and picked up one of the thin books. He slid a battered-looking leather journal onto his lap, a fancy one, the kind they sell in the good bookstores, to use as a work surface. He shoved the rest of the stack towards me. I inched closer to him to see what they were. Pulling the top one off the stack, I opened it without looking at the cover.

"Coloring books?" I asked, completely confused and mystified. He expected me to color? With an alpha?

"Yeah, I can't get the satellite up, so there's no TV. It's going to be a long night until the rest of the pack shows up." He shrugged like that was enough of an explanation.

I stared at the first page like there was a secret message hidden there that would help all this make sense.

"Art therapy has been scientifically shown to reduce stress, relieve executive dysfunction and help people process trauma." He picked up a marker, a blue one, and pushed a few towards me. I couldn't reach, so I scooted closer.

"Making art can be daunting and stressful. This," he tapped the stack of coloring books with his foot, "is like a cheat code. Gives you some of the same satisfaction at making creative decisions, but with less pressure because you're following someone else's design."

He worked silently for a few moments while I just gaped at him. I was firebombed, shot at, ran for my life and met my scent matches... and now I was sitting in a kitchen with fruit snacks, coloring books and an alpha.

I flipped it open to a random page and my jaw dropped.

"This is dirty!"

Cross looked over at the page that read "Knot me please, Alpha".

Was he blushing?

"Oh yeah, that was a buy one get one, at Under Covers Bookshop."

I flipped through the pages that had mosaics, and flower patterns with words like "slick" and "heat" and "fuck" embedded in them.

I grabbed a different book, this one with plain, safe, flower designs only. I picked up a green pen and colored in a leaf. And then another. I looked over at what Cross was working on, he seemed to be picking a different color for every square.

I stretched out on my stomach, using my elbow to pin down the book cover and prop up my head. I absently colored another leaf.

My head slipped off my palm, jolting me awake. I looked down at the page and frowned. An ugly green dot from where the marker rested too long ruined the whole thing, made it look wrong.

Cross hadn't moved, but I was now eye-level with his feet. His jeans were worn, frayed in spots at the cuff. And not in that designer way, but from actual use.

He had a collection of dots tattooed on his ankle, behind the knobby bone that sticks out. The Big Dipper, other constellations I didn't know the names of. And a shooting star, with a wispy fiery tail trailing down his foot like that's what Heaven itself used to send him to earth.

I had to. I had to run my finger down it, be connected to something solid and strong. I heard his breath shake and then he stood suddenly. He stepped deeper into the kitchen, around the corner where I couldn't see him.

"You should go to bed." His voice was rough, like he hadn't used it in a while.

He left the kitchen without looking at me, leaving me... spinning. Lost in a space with nothing to hold on to. Biting my lip, my fingers snagged one of the coloring pages he had torn out. It looked like stained glass in greens and blues.

Folding it messily, I tucked it into my bra. Stealing a part of him. I ran back to the room, sliding to the floor with my back against the closed door.

O

Orbit.

Cross' O was *orbit.*

NINETEEN

CROSS

My finger made lazy circles on the trackpad. I had been staring at the computer for hours, not really seeing it. Connectivity was spotty. I needed daylight to see what was up with the satellite. I was hoping for a frayed wire.

I could still feel her fingertips on me. It burned and crackled.

I should be doing work. Putting together a timeline, highlighting where there was missing information that the rest of the pack could fill out. One of them would have gotten a plate number. Make and model of the vans. All I had so far was:

Luther's warning.

Duo's call.

Breach.

Run.

Not fucking helpful at all.

That's what I should be doing. But I was sitting here replaying that conversation over and over.

I won't be bad.

Who the fuck says that? None of this made sense. She didn't

make sense. I kept searching her, consuming her with my eyes, like the answers would be written on her skin.

On a sharp exhale, I clicked through to our open cases files. It was everything off book we were keeping tabs on. We had gigabytes on the Kingsman and Oxford packs. Riot could have his own dedicated server at this point.

I clicked open the "Bad Guys" file but immediately closed it. We had files on dozens of informants and general bad actors in the Gritch District, the poorest and most dangerous area of New Oxford. Talon and I both grew up there. The answers I needed weren't going to be on this stupid computer.

It took more than a dozen clicks to get to the folder I had hidden from myself. I knew it was there, of course, but I didn't want it easy to access. The folder was labeled "then" and it had four sub-folders that were numbered as identifiers.

Folder "1" I would never open again.

I forced my finger to move the cursor away from "2". Her face kept popping up in flashbacks all night. Images from before... the sad disappointment that always lingered in her eyes. And after... her face, too pale to be real, stained with my bloody fingerprints as I tried to bring her back. And failed.

I double tapped on folder "3" and brought up the latest pic. It was a shit quality screen grab of security footage. Focusing on Roy was the safest of the 4 options.

I didn't really know why I bothered. Our pack bonds had shattered when both Stella and David died. Roy was nothing to me anymore. I wasn't going to contact him or see him ever again. But some dirtbag here or there who knew our history would feed me bits of information about him. I had no idea if they thought they were currying favor or pouring salt in a very large wound.

I saved every bit of it. Only pulled them out when I felt good enough to torture myself.

I couldn't even tell if it was actually Roy in this pic. His face was in profile and blurry, like the camera caught him in mid turn. Of course, I had run it through every facial recognition program I had access to, legally and illegally, and there was no match.

Lately, I had been focusing on the location, not on him. Where he was, where this photo was taken, to my knowledge, he wasn't in New Oxford. He could be anywhere, though.

A soft sniff brought my head up and my heart rate.

Ruby stood in the entry into the kitchen. Her fingertips lightly on the wall as she hesitated like she didn't know if she was allowed in the space.

Fuck.

I should not have put her in my pack mate's clothes. It did very primal things to me. I could feel a growl rumbling in my chest. And that made me angry.

When you grew up beta, you knew the world to be one way. There were absolutes, you knew how things worked. It was all simple. Boy meets girl, move on to 2.5 kids. Friends are friends. You chill with them, maybe love them. Back them up in a fight.

Then your alpha aura presents and all of that changes in a heartbeat. It's like the rules of math and physics get rewritten overnight and you have to figure it out all over again.

A pack bond poured s napalm on all of that. You get all these feral and primal feelings that you can't quite express and would not be welcomed in polite society.

As a beta, jealousy and possessiveness had you clawing out your own space with your own stuff.

As pack, "mine" became "ours". Your wants and needs multiply. On a certain level, you feel driven to satisfy other people's needs like they were your own.

Jackson already loved her. I knew that on a cellular level. He wanted her, and that want was going to turn into a need. I closed my eyes and gritted my teeth.

Because now I wanted her, for him.

And she made that happen with her scent and her fingertip on my foot.

"Do you want coffee?" I asked. I needed to put normal, mundane things between us.

She flicked her eyes into the kitchen, like she was unsure how to answer that question. I got up, grabbed a mug, poured some out for her. The crisp smell of coffee pushed her scent away so I could take a clean breath.

I looked up to ask her how she took her coffee. She had moved, now sitting on the bar stool next to my laptop. I dumped in some powdered creamer and a spoon of sugar.

She was looking curiously at the screen. Her eyes darted around, taking in all its features. I put the coffee next to her, taking my seat again. We weren't even touching and I could feel the heat of her body.

"Who's this?" She asked, and immediately ducked her head like asking questions was a bad thing.

"Someone I'm trying to find." I should have just closed the laptop.

"The image quality is terrible," she said, and I smirked.

"Yeah, I've given up on identifying the guy, officially anyway. I'm trying to run down the location. I'm out of ideas on that."

"Have you checked the pics metadata?"

I raised an eyebrow at her. That was astute. It wasn't secret knowledge that modern digital cameras embedded information, like locations, into every photo. It just wasn't something I expected a meek little omega to know.

"It's been stripped." I breathed deep again. Ruby's sweet citrus scent made me believe for a second that everything was going to work out. I could believe that lie for a couple breaths.

"I, uh, could try something if you want." She was biting her lip.

My eyes narrowed. What did this little wisp of an omega think she could accomplish that I couldn't?

I angled the laptop toward her in invitation. No, it was a challenge. A desperate hope that she would do something awful and I could go back to hating her.

Nervously, she brought up the HeatMatch App website, the dating site. I cocked my head and watched as she clicked into a group titled "AYDMP" and typed a message.

"Could you attach the pic? I don't know where the file is."

"Is this all code?" I said as I queued up the file and she clicked send.

"This is the "Are You Dating My Pack" group. I really shouldn't be showing you this. It's a whisper network."

My finger scrolled up and down, looking at some of the posts. They were, well, gibberish. Ruby's read:

AFAF. Location only. No LT. POIDH.

"Is this a foreign language?" I nodded toward the screen.

"It's kind of like a code. I know it's overly complex, but that's on purpose."

"Why?"

"So you don't get caught?" Ruby offered without conviction.

My hand was still hovering over the trackpad. She slid hers under mine to scroll back to her post, and then pointed at the words.

"This means "I'm asking for a friend", it isn't my pack, or my boyfriend."

"Wait. This group is called "Are you dating my pack'? Why?"

She cringed a little bit, not wanting to say.

"Is this to catch cheaters?"

She continued without answering me. "LT means "loyalty test". We don't want people to actually contact the people in the photo, right? So no loyalty test."

"Loyalty test?"

"Yeah, So," she scrunched her face up in this adorable way like she was embarrassed, "if you ask for a loyalty test, someone will slide into your pack mate, boyfriend, whatever, DMs and flirt lightly and then ask if they have a significant other. You know, a girlfriend, wife, if they are a beta, omega, pack mate. You know..."

I looked at her, mystified.

"Well, if someone is chatting with your boyfriend and they say they don't have a girlfriend..."

My eyes went wide at the realization.

"Guys actually lie like that?" She looked at me like I was simple. "And P-O-I-D-H?" I spelled the last acronym out, leaning in toward the screen.

"Pics or it didn't happen. I'm asking for photo proof here. Everyone will get that we're trying to find the location and I want to match photos."

There were three soft dings, one after another. She had pressed send maybe 45 seconds ago and already had response notifications. She double tapped to open up the comments.

B-Heaven

B-Heaven. Gritch. Same decor

The Gritch's B-Heaven. Recent too. Pic 1 from a year ago. Pic 2. A month ago. See new art?

.   .   .

And the pictures kept flooding in. The comment section seemed fixated on the graffiti art canvas in the background. They tracked down the artist, found his posts about when it was commissioned, even a short video of it being made.

I was astounded. I got more information on Roy's whereabouts in ten minutes than I had in the past year.

"Is this what girls do on the internet?"

She winced.

"I get it. Men are dogs." I chuckled.

My head came up at the muffled beeps of the security system at the mudroom door.

My chest got tight in relief.

Talon.

Ruby's anxiety skyrocketed. Her orange scent, going bitter on my lips.

TWENTY

TALON

Luther's bike was parked right where I expected it. There were no other cars. No one else had gotten here yet. If everyone stuck to the protocol, it would be a full 24 hours before they would all arrive. I'd cut Cross some slack for getting here sooner, since he was responsible for getting comms up and the house running.

I pulled the tailgate down on the borrowed farm truck to pull the dirt bike out and wheeled it out behind the garage. It was almost out of gas. I'd have to remind Luther to fill it. He was the one who usually took care of the vehicles.

I stepped into the cabin and smiled at the scent of coffee that hit me in the face. None of us would have slept last night. We'd need a shit ton of coffee to get through the day. I popped open the built-in gun safe with my fingerprint, to stash my gear. The cabin was off grid in all ways that mattered. It didn't even appear on satellite maps of the area. I had no idea how Duo pulled that one off, but we were ghosts here. We worked hard to make this place a fortress.

I stepped out of the mudroom into the kitchen. Vanilla and orange overpowered the coffee scent.

Fuck.

She was sitting at the island counter with Cross, a mug of coffee halfway to her lips. Her hair was damp, and she was wearing one of Jackson's Prey Nightingale t-shirts.

Fuck.

The sight of her in my mate's clothes enraged me. Because it made my dick instantly hard. I wanted to rip every thread from her body, turn her over my knee, punish her, make her count each spank, trail fingers down her inner thighs until she got distracted and we'd have to start all over again, until her ass was rosy and sensitive to a whisper of a touch, her slick everywhere and then I'd have her…

"Talon? You alright?" Cross thankfully interrupted my thoughts. He strode across the room and we hugged. Relief seeped into the pack bonds. They wouldn't settle down completely until Jackson and Luther got here.

No. They wouldn't settle down completely until we took out whoever attacked us. Not until we got rid of the little omega sitting all sweet looking in my mate's clothes.

"Jacks or Luther check in?" I asked, ignoring her for now.

"Satellite is down, so no TV, Wi-Fi or cell. I've had the sat-phone running, but nothing on that either." Not that I expected there would be, as per protocol we should be radio silent.

"So, what, you thought comms being down was the perfect time to sit back and have a leisurely brunch? Bust out the mimosas? Play house?"

Cross opened his mouth to reply, then thought better of it. He knew I was right. Regardless of the vulnerable civilian sitting in my kitchen, there was work to do.

"You think we're just going to magically figure out who planned this attack and if it's connected to Ruin Winters? We need intel from Duo. We left bodies on our front lawn. We're not on a honeymoon here." I snarled, but reined it in at the sense of terror dripping from the omega in my kitchen.

Cross snatched a jacket that was hanging off the back of a chair and stormed out.

I turned my back on her and took a deep breath. Her scent was so fucking good. Good to the level of distraction. I stalked out the way I came. I'd put gas in the vehicles myself. Anything to get away from her scent.

JACKSON

Luther cut me off in a busted up Honda. Lord knows where he got it from.

I couldn't even rev the engine in Jonnie's little electric car to make a show of catching up with him.

I parked next to some ratty pickup, got out and popped the trunk. My job was provisions. Cross was comms. And Luther was muscle.

The trunk was packed with basic groceries. We hadn't been to the cabin in a while. There'd be pasta and stuff in the freezer, but I knew Luther would want to make pancakes and work out some frustration cooking. And Cross would be grouchy without cream for his coffee.

"You look rough, man." I clasped Luther's shoulder as he joined me at the trunk. Immediately, the bonds eased up, and we both exhaled.

"Yeah, I think I got another concussion. Hit the ground after the fireball. I think I'm seeing things now."

I did a double take. Shit. It must be bad if he was confiding in me. We were pack, we were close, but he went to Talon with the things that really got to him. Luther was just 18 when Talon bonded him in. Being almost 10 years older, Luther had always seen him as a big brother and mentor.

"What do you mean, seeing things?" I asked.

"I don't know, man, I keep seeing this woman..."

I cut him off, "Boy, do I have news for you." A giant smile wiped across my face.

"What?" Luther was a bit taken aback by my obvious glee.

"You'll see. Let's get this inside. Can't have the ice cream melting."

"Ice cream?"

I slung the duffel over my shoulder before hooking fingers through the cotton grocery bags. We'd be at the cabin for a few days at least. I'd have to find time to do some quick shopping for her. It would take all my strength not to pop into Black Lace, the most expensive lingerie shop on the West Side. Jeans, T-shirts and some comfy clothes would have to do.

I shifted all the bags to one hand to punch the keypad next to the door. It beeped, and I stepped into the mudroom, holding it open with my foot for Luther and his load. My breath caught as Talon stepped around the corner. It was like sinking into a warm bath and getting a jolt to my libido at the same time.

I drank him in, flashing back to the last image of him in the backyard, fierce and desperate, pure alpha, walking into bullets like it was nothing. We crashed into each other, relief pouring into the pack bond like all the tension was finally resolved. He crushed my lips to his briefly and eased me back to double check all my pieces were where they were supposed to be.

I saw her over his shoulder. She was sitting on a bar stool at the island wearing a Prey t-shirt. My knees went weak. I slid from Talon's hands. I wanted to tackle her, scoop her up, bite her, touch her everywhere, but I held back, and instead tucked a lock of hair behind her ear.

"Hi." I said softly. Her eyes fluttered when I drew a finger down her cheek. "I'm so relieved you're OK. Cross took good care of you." That was a statement, not a question. I had no doubts about his abilities.

"There's someone I want you to meet. Luther."

She stood so quickly she knocked over the bar stool.

TWENTY-ONE

LUTHER

She was real, and she was standing in my kitchen.

My head swam, and my vision got fuzzy when her scent hit me. She smelled like summer and sunshine. Just like in my dreams. I shook my head to clear my vision. I looked at each of my pack brothers and then touched the counter to test reality.

She was a hallucination. A mirage my scrambled brain spit out. I blinked, my chest tight.

"She's…" I started.

"She's our scent match." Jackson beamed at me, giddy like it was Christmas Day and he'd won the lottery.

I was cracking up. I was actually losing it. Now that she was standing here, I couldn't remember what she looked like in my dreams. She was slight, almost insubstantial in the oversized t-shirt she was wearing. She looked at me like she couldn't quite decide if I was a dream come true or a nightmare.

"Man, you alright?" Cross pushed off the wall, concern wrinkling his forehead.

"I know it is a bit out of the blue. But it happens like that, doesn't it? This is Ruby Frost." Jackson angled the girl forward with a hand on her back. She was reluctant, darting glances between Cross and Jackson. "Luther has terrible manners, but I swear he's a giant teddy bear once you get to know him."

I closed my eyes and breathed deep. Her scent filled me, got into every corner of my brain. I felt my aura light up like a pinball machine. She reached out a hand. I jerked back like it was a bomb about to go off. She was dangerous.

"Who the fuck is she?" I spat.

"Luther?" Talon edged forward. Didn't he see? Couldn't he tell? She was a threat.

I stepped back, rubbing my face. Jackson put a comforting arm around her shoulder.

I growled.

Mine.

The single word chimed through me, making my aura sizzle, and my vision lost its color again.

This wasn't right. None of this was right.

"Someone needs to explain what the fuck is happing right now."

"Luther…" Talon started, but I cut him off.

"No. Jackson, tell me." I nodded in his direction.

"I told you. I met Ruby, we discovered the scent match, and I brought her home to meet the pack." Jackson was staring at me like I was a puzzle, a dangerous one that could bite.

"Why don't we take a walk?" Talon angled his body between me and Jackson and the girl, pushing me with the force of his aura back down the hall.

RUBY

It was *him*.

The angel. The killer.

And he knew.

He knew I was Ruin Winters.

I wobbled on my feet. Jackson had me by the elbow and Cross righted the stool for me to sit again.

"Cross, get us a glass of water, will you?" Jackson effortlessly picked me up and eased me back to sitting.

I was going to die. Or worse.

Ruin Winters was branded a terrorist. Enemy number one. And these men, this pack... *my* pack... were the ones who would bring her... me... to justice.

And when they came for me... Bennett, Billy and the rest... they would try to kill them again.

"I'm so sorry. I don't know what's up with Luther. He's had a concussion, so he's a bit off."

Jackson continued to talk at me, soothing words that did nothing to soothe. But I smiled. I leaned into Ruin's confidence.

"It's been a difficult day." I murmured.

Jackson traded glances with Cross like they had a wounded animal on their hands and they didn't know what to do with it.

"I brought some things for you, some clothes. We'll probably be here a few days, so why don't we get you set up and Cross can get to work putting groceries away?"

He led me by the hand down the hall to the bedroom I had stayed in. His aura was bright and shiny. It wrapped around me, and that did more than all his words to bring me back to myself.

He dropped the duffle on the bed. Some thought crossed his mind that wrinkled his brow. He shook his head like he dismissed the thought.

Jackson brushed his knuckles down my cheek again. I shivered and leaned into him.

"Everything is going to be alright. I promise." His voice husky, making me vibrate.

I wanted to believe him. If I searched for the lie behind his words, I knew I would find it. But for just this moment, I'd lie to myself.

TALON

I herded Luther away from the house. We needed some distance for a private conversation.

"She's..." he rounded on me and spat out the word.

"No. First," I held a finger up to cut him off, "how are you?"

"What?" Luther reared back like I had slapped him.

"The last time I saw you, you were jumping into a van with people who just tried to kill us all and your aura was white hot."

"I'm fine."

"You're lying."

"Another concussion I think. It's fine."

"It absolutely is not." I grabbed him by the neck and tried to get a read on his pupils. He twisted out of my grip and burned off some energy, pacing in a tight circle. "Tell me what happened."

"They were chasing Cross..."

"No. Before that."

"What?" Luther was already losing the thread of the conversation.

"Back all the way up to before the attack. We got fucked up shit through the bonds. You were running?"

Luther nodded and took some deep breaths. The trick with Luther was to force him into a logical order. Didn't matter what the topic was, if you could get him to focus on a pattern, he'd fall in line.

"I went for a run through the preserve and stopped for a drink."

"How's Moxie?"

"A pain in the ass."

"And then?"

We fell into a call and response pattern until he got the whole story out, right down to dumping the bodies and walking out of the Gritch. There was something he was avoiding telling me. But we could get to that later. Getting his side of the story, his interaction with the betas was more important.

This was a well-planned attack. That took coordination and money. Luther was still pacing circles in the clearing behind the house, before the woods got really thick.

"What the fuck is the deal with the girl?" Luther finally asked.

"I don't know what you want me to say, Luther. Jackson found her and brought her home."

"So. Just like that, we're making her pack?"

"No."

That stopped him in his tracks. Obviously, it was not the response he thought he'd get.

"But Jackson..."

"Didn't yesterday just prove we can't have nice things?"

He turned and walked a dozen feet away from me. Taking some calming breaths again.

"Just come out and say it."

There were a lot of directions this conversation could go. Luther was always on the "no" side of the omega question. He'd never say it outright, but he didn't want to love something and have it taken away from him again. Not to mention kicking all his rogue instincts into high gear with a mate to protect. I waited him out.

"You don't think it's strange?" He finally said, his back was to me, which made me suspicious.

"Strange that Jackson just shows up with a scent match out of the blue? Absolutely."

"No. Jackson shows up with a scent match and minutes later our home gets firebombed, raided and we're running for our lives."

I felt like I was hit with a bucket of ice water. I turned and looked back at the cabin, our real home, the place we could all let our guard down and relax. The place we felt safe.

Did we just walk a ticking time bomb right into our lives?

TWENTY-TWO

JACKSON

I twirled pasta on my fork, desperately thinking about how I could break the tension. Cross said Ruby spent most of the afternoon in her bedroom. *Her* bedroom. I just loved how that sounded. We were all caught up in getting the property in order. Talon and Cross spent most of the afternoon fiddling with the satellite. Luther and I checked the trail cams on the perimeter fence.

We now had Wi-Fi, cell access was spotty, and the TV was still out. I grinned to myself. I could think of a billion ways to entertain ourselves tonight, and all of it involved Ruby giggling and gasping.

Talon sent me a dark look. He knew exactly what I was thinking about. Good.

Ruby fidgeted with her fork, not eating much. And Luther seemed to take that as a personal insult. Cross kept giving her sidelong glances like he couldn't keep his eyes off her, but didn't want to stare.

And the sexual tension was exquisite.

We were all civilized and too polite to make outward signs about what an omega, *our* omega, was doing to us. I was the only one willing to make a slutty show in public. Ruby seemed reserved for an omega. Made sense. She barely knew us and a lot had happened.

Ruby shifted her posture and her aura danced. We all picked our heads up, noticing the change. Cross did that puppy head tilt thing like he was trying to figure something out.

"So," she put down her fork with a dull click, "no one is going to explain what is happening and we are just going to pretend that you didn't kidnap me?"

My eyes shot wide, and I had to stuff a fork full of spaghetti in my mouth to cover up a smirk. My girl's got some sass in her.

Everyone shot a glance at Talon. He wiped the corners of his mouth with a napkin and scratched his eyebrow. His dark hair was short right now and always looked like he just got done with strenuous bedroom activities. He hadn't shaved. The dark fuzz on his jaw made his skin look paler than usual. He was silent for a long time.

Ruby picked up her fork and delicately placed a bite of pasta in her mouth.

"We have very dangerous jobs. This is a consequence." He finally said.

"And the kidnapping part? Or is this normal for your pack?"

Talon flooded the room with irritation. Not good.

"We couldn't very well leave you behind. We have to make sure you're safe," I added before Talon got snippy.

"There's nothing safe about our pack." Talon's voice was cold and flat.

"Obviously." Ruby said with an eye roll. Cross snorted at Ruby's comeback.

"Jackson is a top academy grad and expert marksman. Luther gets contracted out to break up prison riots. Cross is a convicted murderer." He pointed at each of us in turn. I cringed at the Cross comment. It was technically true. I bribed that conviction off his record a few years ago. Talon leaving out the part where his pack lead went rogue and killed their omega and he was defending himself was a dick move, however.

"And you?" She asked.

He pushed his aura out with just enough "I'm pack lead" to be uncomfortable. He stared her down until she caved and looked away. Also, a dick move. He was trying to scare her, and it was working.

"We'll get you back to your life so we can get on with ours as soon as we can."

The fuck we will. I drummed my fingers on the table. Talon and Cross had always been opposed to the idea of having an omega. For obvious reasons. I bet they all thought that since Cross had scent matched already with his previous pack, a scent match wouldn't be in our pack's future.

But now that we had, now that Ruby was ours, they'd have to change their minds.

"I think we need to establish some rules here." Talon put down his fork and leaned back in his chair.

Ruby instantly got nervous. It was the oddest thing about her. One second she'd be flirty and out going, pulling me, everyone, towards her just to be in her citrus scented sunshine, then she'd flinch. Actually flinch and curl into herself, retracting all that light. It almost seemed like she was faking a certain level of confidence.

"We're going to put Ruby in the spare bedroom. The one across from Luther, not Cross."

I smirked. He didn't want her in the pack bedroom. That would be too promising.

"What? Why?" Luther asked like he was offended.

"To give Ruby some space. There's already too much testosterone around."

Ruby cocked her head and looked at Talon.

"We're in a bit of a crisis mode, but we still have jobs to do. We're going to have to drive into the city every day to track down the people who did this, but I want someone here at all times."

"This place is secure." I said.

"That's what we thought about the West Side house, too." Luther was a little ray of sunshine tonight.

"Luther is going to be in charge of cooking and the vehicles. Jackson on clean-up. Cross, I need comms back up, and we've got to get patched back into our sources. We've got a partial plate on both vans. You're going to have to see what the security feeds at the house turns up."

I frowned and twirled my fork.

"She's not pack. She's a guest. She's not doing your laundry or fixing you a sandwich. You're big boys. You can take care of yourselves."

Ruby did a double take. It was subtle, but I caught it.

"Unless, of course, that's something you need." I took Ruby's hand in a comforting grip.

"Jackson." Tal admonished.

"You have not spent a lot of time around omegas." I dropped her hand and wagged a finger at Talon. "My mother would have a complete nervous breakdown if you told her she wasn't allowed to cook. We all know how I positively love when you get bossy, but we usually keep that to the bedroom. We don't know if that," I wrinkled my nose at Talon, "turns Ruby on yet. You should let her decide how she wants to spend her time."

Luther's aura flared. He could get a little possessive about the kitchen. He grew up having to cook for his sister. It was one of the few things he had any level of control over. He really didn't like other people in the kitchen with him. Now, I was second guessing myself. Putting him in a kitchen with an omega he didn't like might not be great. He'd need more neutral ground to fall for her.

"Speaking of," Talon's eyes narrowed while he made a sweeping gesture around the table. "And this goes double for you, Jackson. Everybody keep your dicks to yourself."

"Excuse me?" Ruby blinked in shock, her cheeks flushed bright red. I suppressed a smile. It wasn't often you could get an omega all flustered at the mere mention of sex.

"You heard me. You're not fucking my pack."

"Hold up a second." I broke in. "You're pack lead. That gives you some say over our behavior. But like you said, she's not pack. Don't tell her what to do... unless..."

"Fine. You," he pointed at Ruby, "you'll be leaving soon. Keep that in mind and don't fuck with my pack."

"Woah, wait. You're telling us what to do with our dicks," Luther gestured at his lap and then at me, "and you're gonna run upstairs and fuck the little slut into next Tuesday? You really think that's fair?"

"Well, you know, the pack bed is huge, if you and Cross..."

"Great. Perfect. No one is having sex under this roof until we deliver Ruby back to her life. Happy now, Luther?" Talon threw his napkin on the table.

"Tal, you can't be serious?" He had to be joking. "Fuck me." I muttered under my breath. The tone of his aura was deadly serious.

"Apparently not." Luther was smug.

"You overgrown piece of..." my filthy jab at Luther was cut off by Ruby clearing her throat.

"How do I know I can trust your little rule and I won't be fighting you off in the middle of the night?"

We all turned to stare at her. What an odd question. It wasn't like alphas were uncontrollable beasts. Sure, some alphas could be aggressive and demanding, but it's not like we went around raping omegas. Incidents of sexual assault weren't much different in the general beta population.

Talon held us in silence for a long time. He had the pack bonds locked down tight, so it was hard to know what he was thinking. His eyes drove right into her until she looked down and toyed with her fork.

He leaned forward, reached behind his back and pulled his handgun out and put it on the table in front of her with a dull thud.

"You know how to use that?" Talon nodded at the weapon.

Ruby stared at it. Her sunset hair hiding her features. She robotically picked up the gun, expertly chambered a round, flicked the safety on and off, and put it back on the table. She nudged it with a fingertip until it lined up perfectly with her place setting.

"If you doubt the integrity of my pack, you can now defend yourself." He pushed back from the table and took his plate to the kitchen.

Awkward silence seeped in around us. Luther couldn't take the tension and headed for the kitchen, too.

"Well, this is a hell of a second date, isn't it?" I said.

Cross chuckled and shook his head, getting up from the table, leaving me and Ruby alone. I ate a few more bites, hoping to encourage her to finish. She had barely eaten anything. There was something off about that. A lot of women, especially omegas, got caught up in diet culture, but Ruby had an unnaturally thin look about her, like she wasn't trying to be thin, but just didn't have enough food. Maybe it was just alpha instincts on hyper drive, wanting my omega happy and fed and content.

"You want some dessert?" I asked. No omega passed up ice cream and cake. She shook her head, and I frowned.

"Tell you what, come sit, keep me company in the kitchen while I clean up, and I'll tell you how I met Talon."

"You're doing dishes?"

"Yup." I picked up my plate and held my hand out for hers, "since the cake incident, they don't let me cook. So, I'm on dish duty."

She looked at me like I had two heads while handing me her plate.

RUBY

Jackson could almost make me forget everything. With his sleeves rolled up and his hands all soapy, I had to grip the edge of the counter to keep myself at a safe distance. Talon wanted to drive home how scary and dangerous they all were. But Jackson was the most dangerous one of them all. He could make me hope for a different life.

He stood in the middle of the now clean kitchen, drying his hands on a dishcloth and looking at me like I was dessert. A little bubble of panic rose. I was alone in a house full of alphas. Killer alphas at that. They could take what they wanted at any moment. Talon's little gun was meaningless.

But, I felt safe. And that made me uncomfortable. They were nothing like the alphas I had learned about. But I could see touches of that aggression and violence. I excused myself and tried really hard not to run to the bedroom.

I closed the door and put my ear to it. Jackson made some comment about tucking me in. I didn't think that was a good idea. It was early, like 8pm. I wasn't going to sleep, but I needed some space.

By now, I had been pacing around the bed for what seemed like hours, trying to figure out who knew what and how I was going to get out of here.

Luther knew. He had to. I saw it in his face. But he hadn't said anything.

Sent to break up prison riots. He could probably kill me with his bare hands. I pictured them around my neck, in my hair, sliding down my arms. I dug my fingernails into my palms, hoping the flash of pain would snap me out of this. I had to stop thinking about sex. Thinking about their hands on me, lips... other things.

I looked at the bed like it was an obstacle course. It was just a stupid bed. I shouldn't feel weird about sleeping in it. It felt huge and empty and forbidden. I peeled a corner of the comforter back and slid in. It was soft and plush, the blanket instantly warmed me and tucked itself around my curves. I closed my eyes, but my breath became ragged. I jumped off the bed like it bit me. I pulled the comforter straight again and smoothed it out, erasing all evidence of my transgression.

I heard a door open and close. My heart jumped into my throat and choked me. I fumbled for the gun I had tucked away, and scooted back into a corner, aiming it right at the door. I held the gun out until my arms shook. But no one came.

TWENTY-THREE

RUBY

I waited until I couldn't resist the smell of coffee anymore before stepping out of the bedroom as quietly as I could. I hadn't slept. Every sound of the foreign house, and the men in it, had jolted me awake. I showered and put on the jeans and t-shirt that Jackson had brought me. They were loose, but I didn't have any other options.

Smoothing down the shirt, warmth spread through my whole body at the thought of Jackson choosing my clothes. The idea of him dressing me was almost as sexy as the idea of him undressing me. The throbbing between my legs was a constant annoyance. Their scents all combined and made me light-headed. I felt like I had to run to the bathroom every five minutes to wipe away excess slick that dampened my panties.

They were all in the kitchen, their voices became more distinct as I crept closer.

"As far as I can tell, it was the Reset. They are talking like it was a great victory. Not a single mention of the deaths or injury." Cross' voice was matter of fact.

"What's the GPRE saying?" Luther asked.

I pictured Talon shrugging.

"Duo somehow got the Greyson pack there before the local PD. There's some water and smoke damage in the house, but it should be structurally sound. They transported two to the hospital."

"Transported or dumped?" Jackson asked.

Again, I pictured Talon shrugging.

"And Luther took out two, right?"

I covered my mouth to hold in a gasp. When Cross ran with me across the lawn, I saw Billy, so I knew Bennett was there. And the rest of his boys, Lance, Greg, Steven, they all would have been there. I closed my eyes, praying it was Bennett that was dead. It didn't matter, though. Bennett had drawn the short straw and was on keeper duty. Billy got pulled when he gave me a black eye and it messed with the videos. Greg had been last year. They all got a turn.

"And Winters?" Talon asked. The question stole my breath. This was it. This was when Luther would tell them.

"Not a peep in two days. It's really fucking weird." Cross said. I bit my lip. "She has recycled content in the past but there is something new every day. All of her accounts are silent."

"So can we talk about..."

"No." Talon cut Jackson off.

"Talon..."

"We're not doing this right now."

"We need to talk about this as a pack." I pictured Talon and Jackson staring each other down and the other two sitting back to watch the show.

"I think..." Luther started. My mouth went dry at the sound of his voice. It was rough and grumbly, like he just woke up.

"I think Ruby's in the hall eavesdropping." Talon said.

Panic flared. I started taking slow backward steps. If they caught me...

Jackson popped out from around the corner. His smile was huge and bright and went right to my core.

"Hey, good morning. I hope we didn't wake you." He walked toward me and I tried not to flinch back. His eyebrows pulled together in confusion. He put a tentative hand to my back to guide me into the kitchen.

Cross closed his computer and got up from the stool he was sitting on to make space for me, as Jackson went to the coffee pot. Talon and Luther avoided looking at me.

"Cross said milk and sugar, right?" Jackson put a mug in front of me. It smelled heavenly. "Did you sleep alright?"

"Hmmm," I lied and took a sip. I hadn't slept at all.

Talon stood at the sink to refill his mug. He took a breath like he was settling himself.

"Luther, I want you to go lean on Elmont. We haven't poked him yet for what he knows about Winters. Jackson, go to the house, make sure it's secure. Empty the safes and transport it all up here. Cross, get what you need to fix the satellite," Talon said, like he was commanding an army. I thought about that for a second. They were an army of sorts.

Jackson grazed my cheek, and I leaned into his touch. They all gathered up their things and got ready to leave. They were discussing driving arrangements. There was a stolen car, a borrowed car. I didn't really track the conversation. I kept stealing glances at Luther, wondering when he was going to tell everyone.

Talon leaned against the fridge and stared at me. I pulled Ruin around me to act like I didn't care. I felt like Talon could see right through it but was humoring me, anyway.

Jackson popped back into the kitchen to give my arm a squeeze before leaving. He walked up to Talon and took the mug out of his hands, setting it carefully and deliberately on the counter. Then he stepped into Talon, slid his hands up his chest and pulled Talon down for a kiss that scorched the earth. I gaped, my breathing got tight and short. I pressed my legs together, fearing I'd get wet with slick. The kiss lingered until Talon finally met Jackson with the same ferocity.

I stared down into my coffee like it held the answers to all the conflicting ideas spinning in my head.

I was raised in beta foster families after my mom died when I was little. There was an accident in a park. I don't even remember her anymore. In all the homes I had lived in, no one kissed in the kitchen like this.

Pack behavior was disgusting and immoral. You weren't supposed... I licked my lips, trying to get the word to form in my brain... you weren't supposed to love more than one person. I should be feeling jealous. I... I felt something for Jackson and... I squeezed my eyes shut. My thoughts and my feelings weren't matching, and it made me feel woozy.

When I opened my eyes, Jackson was gone and Talon's presence grew to swallow the whole room. He was looking at me like some men look at car engines to figure out what's wrong so they can make it purr properly. And I didn't want him to stop. I wanted him to crack me open like a book and lick his finger and turn every page.

I set the coffee down on the stone countertop and pushed the stool in.

"I'm... I'm going to go for a walk." I lifted my chin and waited for his response. He held me there wordless for the longest time, until the jittery nerves melted, leaving me feeling like I could wait forever.

Finally, he nodded. I swallowed hard. I had to walk right past him to get to the door. I tried to be casual, but my heart beat harder and faster as I got closer to him. I tried to keep as much space as possible between us.

"Stay close to the cabin. Keep it in sight. We don't want to lose you in the woods." He said as I carefully edged past him.

"Yes, sir," came out on a soft breath. Why the fuck had I said that? I picked up my pace until I was running out the back door.

TALON

I gripped the edge of the counter to take some slow, even breaths. I had to get this girl gone as soon as possible.

That "yes, sir" ripped through my soul.

I'd made her stand there, just to see what she would do.

Would she flip me off? Would she cower under assumed disapproval? I had tried to get a read on her aura, gain some insight into what she was thinking, feeling, and it was a confused mess. It felt like her head and her instincts were running two different programs. I made her wait to see which one would win.

She didn't act this way with the rest of my pack. Jackson brought out a comfortable, playful side of her. She was quick to laugh with him, and I could get drunk on that sound. Cross' quiet presence seemed to make her think, bolster her courage maybe. She and Luther? I didn't know what the fuck was happening there, and I hoped she'd be gone before that developed.

I had given Ruby enough time that she probably wouldn't think I was following her. I went out the front door that we rarely used and circled around the house. I could pull up the cameras and see exactly where she was, but I tracked her by scent. That maddening infectious orange and cream scent that made me hungry for things other than ice cream.

I dipped into the edge of the woods to keep out of sight. There was a clearing, where Cross had a fire pit. He was out here most nights, reading by firelight. She was crouching next to the circle of stones.

The jeans were a little too big for her. It was too cold for her to be out here in just a t-shirt. It was March, but still chilly. A snarl rose as I pictured her in Jackson's clothes, still unsure if it was contempt or lust.

She touched one of the charred logs, rubbed her fingertips together and brought it to her nose. Whatever she was smelling, she savored, like hot cocoa and marshmallows. She stood and hugged herself, walking a lap around the fire pit. I could see her lips moving, talking to herself. I would have paid in blood to know what she was thinking.

She looked back towards the cabin, nervously, like she didn't want to get caught doing something naughty. I rubbed at my temples to push away any thought of catching her and what I could do to her after. She sat down tentatively on a patch of newly green grass, leaned back and fanned her arms out like she was making snow angels. She was reveling in the feeling of it on her skin, like she hadn't seen grass in a long time.

I took myself silently back to the cabin, wanting to give her this private moment.

The math was not adding up on Ruby Frost. I clocked people really well. It was a combination of being able to read auras, as well as an alpha who was not a seer could, and she had terrible control over her aura, so that helped. Another part was experience, from seeing the worst in society, and what people could do to each other, and the cleaning up the aftermath of that.

The pack was an elite strike force for the Gold Pack and Rogue Enforcement Agency. We ran off book missions all the time. Justice was merciless in the system. Flying under the radar, we did what we could when we could.

The day I'd met Luther, we were tasked with eliminating a rogue alpha and an omega he was trafficking. We got caught out and jumped. Cross and Jackson were both down with bullet wounds, and we were being circled by a pack. This huge kid came out of nowhere, stood over my pack mates, and let nothing touch them just by the force of his aura alone. Our plan was to kill the alpha and spirit the omega to a safe house. But the alpha had broken the omega's neck before I'd killed him.

We lost that day but gained Luther.

I knew he was a rogue instantly. When I figured out that Lhevus Saint was his foster father, the only solution I could come up with was to bond him into the pack and train him to hunt rogues. I'd hide Luther in plain sight. It was a constant battle, helping Luther keep his aura under control, and keeping his paperwork clean. It helped that Jackson fell in love with him instantly.

Just like he had with Cross a few years earlier.

And now Ruby.

Fuck.

TWENTY-FOUR

CROSS

The only sound was water squelching up from the carpet.

We entered the house in a well-practiced formation. Luther, big and fast, on point. Jackson last, his deadly accuracy providing cover.

I opened up the pack bonds to pull in additional perception. Not helpful. We were all too amped up. All the wrong kinds of emotion were sizzling between us.

This wasn't a job. This was our home.

Alphas were naturally protective and territorial. Luther could barely stand letting anyone in his room, even pack. No one drove Jackson's car. Talon's office was off limits. In the early days, I'd broken Luther's finger when he snatched one of my pens. To have someone threaten the pack house? We'd do more than break fingers.

And our mate was in the house.

Mate.

Just thinking the word brought calm agitation.

Fuck. We had to figure this out and get her out of here.

You didn't know the hold a scent match had until it walked into your living room. We were all avoiding the subject. There was an unusual tension between us, things left unsaid, heavy in the bonds.

I heard Jackson announce "clear" from the basement, where the unused pack bed was. Luther was in the back bedrooms. I was crouched low, opening closet doors in the front of the house, until we were sure no one was here, nothing was out of place.

The whole house smelled damp and smoky. It bit at my nose. Not at all soothing, like Luther's applewood scent.

Satisfaction purred through me. I had installed fire suppression during the last renovation. The carpets were ruined, but no one would have died if we had been trapped inside.

"The fuckers didn't break in." Jackson finally said when we all circled back to the living room. He tucked his weapon in the small of his back.

"They probably ran when we did. We'll need to check the back, where they rammed the house." I was already compiling a mental list of what needed to get done before we could move back in. I'd get a crew out here to rip out the carpets. That would have to come first.

Luther picked up his feet, grimacing at his waterlogged sneakers.

"Grab anything you want me to take up to the cabin," Jackson said as he toppled the little stack of ballistic vests with the toe of his boot.

I slung the MP5 over my back.

"So..." Jackson started, hands on his hips, rocking slightly on his feet, like he had too much energy and didn't know what to do with it.

"No." Luther answered the question before it was born. He didn't need to state it. We all knew what the question was.

Jackson's face morphed from his easy-going fuckboy look to

determined alpha in a heartbeat. It was impressive. Normally, that would have been the end of the discussion.

Talon was already a clear no on the Ruby Frost question. Three "no's" to Jackson's obvious yes.

Fucking Jackson.

I slung the MP5 onto my back and scrubbed my face. He wanted her, and this piercing voice in my head wanted me to want her, for him.

Jackson needed someone to care for. Talon and Jackson had a desperate love for each other. Had since the day I met them. But their relationship didn't satisfy alpha instincts, and Jackson was slowly discovering he couldn't fuck that away.

"She's a scent match, Luther." Jackson's voice was matter of fact. Like that was the only detail that mattered. Both of their auras flared and scrapped against each other. Maybe we shouldn't be having this conversation armed.

"She's..." Luther scrubbed his face with his hands and shook his head, like he was shaking off a thought. He let out a breath and changed tactics. "We agreed years ago. No omega."

"That was before Ruby."

"You don't even know her. What if she's..."

"What? A bad person? She works in a salon, for god's sake." Jackson said, as if that was a marker of moral upstanding.

"I'm telling you, there's something. She's..."

"I don't care." Jackson's voice was cold and resolute. "I don't care if she kills puppies and eats them for breakfast. She could be gold pack in hiding. Or Ruin Winters herself. I don't care, she's mine. Ours."

I looked at Luther. Something bubbled up in his aura like outrage but was then swamped by conflicting emotions. Jackson caught it too. His eyes narrowed. He was prepared to fight about this. Physically, maybe. He'd lose against Luther, but that didn't matter.

Jackson was spoiled. Not his fault, really. He came from one of those sprawling rich packs. He got his way with obscene confidence, sex, or wearing you down with his cheerful optimism. He squared up with Luther and took a deep breath to get started.

"You're being selfish." That was the biggest insult to Jackson, second only to being bad in the sack. Jackson always put pack first.

"This *is* about the pack."

"The pack needs an omega."

"*You* need an omega."

"I do. So do you." Jackson gave Luther a head-to-toe scan like he could physically see Luther's aura.

"Think with your brain and not your dick for once in your goddamn life, Jackson. She walks into our house and minutes later, this?" Luther showcased our soggy living room with a sweeping gesture.

"Right. Like this was Ruby's fault? That wonky aura affecting your brain now?"

Luther was biting back a growl. Bringing up his aura was a low blow.

"I want her. I'll challenge for pack lead if I have to. She's mine."

Luther's aura crackled and rocked me back. We gaped at Jackson. He wasn't joking. He'd challenge Talon. His aura was totally backing up his words.

"Then you'll be my little bitch instead of Talon's." Jackson's smirk was created by God herself to piss you off.

"Listen, you spoiled brat of a fucktart..."

Once the insults started flying, it was going to get messy.

"Himbo." Jackson pivoted his body to a fighting stance.

"Whoa, whoa. Let's not do this." I stepped forwards, palms up to try to bring this down a notch.

"You want to go? Alright shorty," Luther said, completely ignoring me.

"No gun play in the house." I pushed my aura out to get their attention.

Jackson smiled. It was all eager and confident. He slid the gun out from his waistband and tossed it at me without taking his eyes from Luther. Reluctantly, Luther followed suit.

Jackson struck fast and popped him right in the mouth, splitting his lip. Luther had at least 60 pounds on Jackson. I had no doubt that he'd wiped the floor with Jackson. But Jackson fought dirty.

"Asshole." Luther said, wiping blood off his lip with the edge of his fist.

"I have no problem knocking some sense into you. I would burn the world down for my mate."

And it was on with a full growl from Luther.

"Oh, don't like the word mate?" Jackson pushed.

Luther was fast, but Jackson was faster. He easily ducked a wild punch from Luther, who put too much body weight behind the swing and had to correct mid punch. Jackson caught him right in the ribs. Looked like he pulled that punch, just tapping Luther, but showing him he could do some real damage if he wanted to. Luther grunted and caved to one knee.

"Or maybe you like the word mate a little too much." Jackson danced back when Luther made a grab for his legs. "Is that it? You want to want her, but you just can't let yourself have her?" Jackson taunted.

"She's a threat." Luther bit out, his fist glanced off Jackson's shoulder, doing nothing but forcing a snarl from Luther.

Luther had had enough. He went to sweep Jackson's leg to grab him around the middle and take him down to the ground. Jackson went with the movement, but twisted his body around Luther, entwining his legs. Catching Luther off guard, Jackson had him immobilized in a heel lock. All Jackson had to do was apply pressure, and he'd dislocate Luther's knee, popping it right out. Luther's lack of flexibility had him flailing his arms as his only counter move.

"You know you need an omega." Jackson said around grunts made by the effort to keep Luther in place.

"Get the fuck off, man." Luther snarled.

"Say it. You want her."

With a massive heave, Luther rolled them over, the wet carpet soaking both of them. I crouched and rubbed my temples. Under different circumstances, seeing Luther and Jackson grappling on the ground would be super fucking hot, not to mention funny. But reading their auras, neither one of them was going to cave.

"Tap out Luther." I shot Jackson a glance. He'd do it, he'd break Luther's leg.

Luther arched his back sharply in another attempt to free his legs from Jackson's hold.

"She will ruin us," Luther said between gritted teeth.

Jackson rolled him face down into the soggy carpet, and got an even better hold on Luther's heel, wrenching his ankle to the side. This had gone too far. Luther didn't need a cast on top of his concussions.

"You really think Ruby wants to be in a pack that has to be beaten into wanting her?" I leaned into the wall, just in case either one of them came up swinging at me.

Jackson immediately relented. Disgusted, Luther kicked Jackson off, now that he had control of his legs back. Soaked, Jackson got to his knees, shit-eating grin plastered on his face, like he'd won the biggest victory. Luther panted on his back.

"Doesn't matter. Talon says no. He is pack lead. You will never be." Groaning, Luther got to his feet, breath coming hard and fast.

Jackson didn't need to respond. He was confident he'd get his way, eventually. Jackson and Talon weren't often at odds, not on anything that mattered, at least.

Luther held out his hand for his weapon, silent, not looking me in the eye. Then he stalked out without another word, his applewood smoke and cut grass scent heavy and bitter.

Jackson clasped me on the shoulder, bouncing on his feet.

"We're going to have to add on to the house," Jackson said over his shoulder, then he headed for his bedroom. "The spare room isn't big enough for a nest. What do you think she'd want? Something cozy, for sure. So long as it's not all pink. I don't think Talon could stand an all pink nest."

I hung my head. The exhaustion of lying in bed and thinking about her all night was getting to me.

Fucking Jackson.

TWENTY-FIVE

LUTHER

"Wait, wait. I'm not ready."

"You gotta relax, my man, or it's going to hurt more."

"OK, I'll close my eyes and count to three... Ready... One..."

I popped him in the nose before he got to "two". I shook out my hand from the sting. Elmont Evans writhed on his back, cursing. I sorted through the debris of take-out containers on the coffee table for the cleanest looking napkins and handed them to the snitch. I was a gentleman, after all.

"Was this really necessary?" I grumbled.

"Look, I got a reputation to uphold," he said, dabbing at his nose and wincing. "You think it's broken?"

I leaned over him and squinted, like I knew what I was looking for. I reached out, grabbed his nose, and pulled. If it was broken, that would line it up. If it wasn't, well, maybe he'd think twice next time he asked to get punched in the face.

"Now that you have black eyes to show off around the Gritch, can we get on with it?" I wasn't in the mood to deal with Elmont's bullshit, anyone's bullshit, including my own. I picked at the collar of my shirt. It was still damp from the tussle with Jackson.

Elmont was your average everyday low life scraping together a living in the Gritch District. I had acted as lookout for him when I was on the streets, before Talon took me in. He knew everyone and everything. I don't know why, but people were just compelled to tell this dirt bag their deepest, darkest secrets. I had asked him once. He said it was because he was a "Pisces sun, Pisces moon, Pisces rising". Whatever the fuck that meant.

Talon didn't like using him as a snitch, because he always pulled some nonsense like this.

"I can't have you walk in here and walk out with valuable information. If you're not going to pay me, then it's gotta look like you got the information out of me the old-fashioned way."

I offered a hand to pull him up. He stumbled to the couch, sat and put his head back to staunch the flow of blood.

"So…" I made a get on with it gesture. "The pack house that was raided? You have names?"

"No, but sounds like it was an inside job."

"Inside job?"

"These three kids I'd never seen before flush with cash, saying how they torched this pack house."

"Can you get names?"

"Tried." Elmont dabbed at his nose. "Said their names were Cash, Zeke, and…"

"Dashing." I listed off the last name of the villains from the latest Prey Nightingale flick.

"Unoriginal." Elmont said as if that was the worst insult he could think of.

"What do you mean by inside job?"

"The way they were talking about their payday, the only people who have cash like that is the Institute themselves."

I frowned. The Institute wouldn't put a hit on their own,

would they? That didn't make sense. We were the most effective team at the GPRE. If they found out... Nah, if they found out I was a rogue, they'd send another GPRE team for us, not a gaggle of betas.

Who else had big money? Lots of people, but who had big money that would come for us?

"Can you dig around on that?"

Elmont shrugged. His information wasn't totally reliable. People bragged, made up stories. You could count on Elmont to tell the tales, but who knew how accurate they were?

"What do you got on Ruin Winters?" I asked.

He perked right up.

"You know, I've said this from the start. I don't think she's an omega."

"She looks like an omega."

"Any chick with some makeup skills can look like an omega. That's not the point," he said, shoving a napkin up his nose to stop the flow of blood. I didn't know if I could take him seriously anymore looking like that.

"When the whole Crimson Bullet thing happened," Elmont continued, "you remember when they strung up that omega in a cage in the middle of the dance floor and forced heat on her?"

I nodded. Two people died in the riot that followed. That's when the all point bulletins on Winters began. She never officially claimed responsibility, but notecards with black lip prints were found at the scene.

"Anyway, I was out at that gentleman's club on the way to Berry Creek," Elmont sniffed and wiped his bloody fingers on his jeans, "I don't remember exactly what they said, but I left with the impression that Ruin Winters had been with the Reset from the start."

"You're going to have to do the math on this one for me, man. I'm not following you."

"There's no such thing as an omega from Berry Creek."

"And?" My stomach suddenly turned sour, the hairs on my neck standing up. Something was digging at my brain, trying to get out.

He looked at me like I was slow.

"The way they were talking made me think that Ruin Winters was like some big psy-ops campaign run by the Reset." I narrowed my eyes at him. Elmont was *this* far from tinfoil hat conspiracy theorist. "And as we all know, you don't perfume or present an aura in Berry Creek. On a good day, you pray they'd kick you out on the street. On a bad day..." He let that hang in the air.

We'd ridden back-up on a raid on the outskirts of Berry Creek a few months back. Two twins, little girls, fourteen, had turned up dead in Lake Iota. They had perfumed and their father had beaten them to death. Betas made up the majority of the population and Berry Creek was home to every fringe group, like the Reset, that wanted to see alphas and omegas stamped out. Or at least not glorified in the media.

"So you think Ruin Winters is from Berry Creek and therefore, not an omega?"

"I'm just telling you the chatter." He made jazz hands for emphasis.

"That's not helpful. I need more."

"What are you going to do, beat it out of me? If I had it, I would give it to you."

"Are you serious? You asked me to hit you, and now you're offended?"

"Well, you did break my nose."

Disgusted, I walked out of the house and slid behind the wheel of Cross' truck and banged my head against the headrest. I still had a dull ache pulsing behind my eyes. That jab to the ribs from Jackson wasn't helping.

The little shit.

Ruin Winters was from Berry Creek. Berry Creek was home to extremists. I tapped my fingers on the steering wheel of Cross' truck. There was a connection there. I knew it.

There's no such thing as an omega from Berry Creek.

Mason Forthright saw to that.

I couldn't shake the memory of Havoc decapitating that doll right in front of him. He had been simmering with that special kind of anger that only men who fundamentally hated women had.

If Ruin Winters really was an omega from Berry Creek... I rubbed at the bruise on my side. We'd seen plenty of omegas, gold pack or not, beaten into compliance. If you grew up in that, what might you do to make it stop?

I was missing something, some connection I wasn't getting. I was the Leroy Jenkins of the pack, not the Sherlock Holmes of the pack. I turned the key in the ignition. I texted the group chat that I'd get take-out. I didn't want to be in the kitchen with a helpful omega throwing off nesting vibes.

I looked down at my phone and rolled my eyes at the half dozen messages from Jackson, wondering what Ruby's favorite food was. Disgusted, I tossed the phone on the passenger seat and put the truck in gear.

TWENTY-SIX

RUBY

I rested my head on the cool tile of the shower. I had to wash the scent of grass off me. *His* scent. It clung to me like hope. It had been the thing that sustained me since the warehouse.

His scent and the look of recognition on his face. I didn't know what it meant then, but I do now. Mates. I had scent matched to Luther in the warehouse. And I didn't know it.

I didn't know anything about being an omega.

They were all so very different. Jackson was charming and funny, with this river of sex that ran under everything. Cross made me think of that meme "looks like he could kill you, is a cinnamon roll." Talon was the most unsettling right now. Which surprised me. Luther should have been the one I was concerned about. He knew I was Ruin Winters. He had to know. And with one word, he could bring about my death.

But Talon... Talon was just everywhere. His sea salt and pine scent chased me. It wrapped around me, it made me feel safe and scared at the same time, like disappointing him would be worse than what was waiting for Ruin Winters.

There were three different body washes on the edge of the shower. I picked the unscented one, wondering why they didn't have that de-scenting soap handy. My foster parents could barely tolerate having me in the house because of the smell. I squeezed more soap than was necessary in my hands, hoping it would wash away this disgusting citrus. My hands glided over my body, making everything, even the still-healing bruises on my stomach, tingle.

I glanced at the door. There was no keeper to watch me. I even had a shower curtain to hide behind. The apartment didn't have a shower curtain. No one would know.

I bit my lip as my heart pounded. I slid my hand between my legs and gasped. Jackson had soft hands, long fingers that would glide effortlessly with my slick. Cross' beard would be soft against my breast. I stroked my neck, where Talon's fingers and teeth would be. And Luther... he would press himself against me. He was huge, bigger than all of them. He'd fill me and his knot...

My eyes shot wide. Knots. And ruts.

My heart began to pound. All those lessons, the police reports, dead omegas everywhere, torn open during ruts by knots and maniac alphas lost to their animal instincts.

More soap. I wished I had a scrub brush. I was unnatural, immoral, debauched. The only way to be safe was not to smell so slutty.

I stepped out of the shower and covered up immediately, pulling on the jeans and the t-shirt even though my skin was still damp. I leaned on the counter, digging my fingers into the stone. The ache between my legs spread and consumed half my body.

I towel dried my hair. This is the longest I've gone without styling it, not because I wanted to look pretty, *they* insisted I looked the part. I looked plain and drab in the mirror, the clothes too big, my hair limp.

I wasn't used to being alone. It was... creepy. Every little noise made me jump, and I didn't really know what to do with myself except to walk back and forth around the bed. I didn't want to go out there and get caught in Talon's magnetic pull. I wasn't actually a prisoner here, at least I didn't think I was. Jackson hadn't said I had to stay in my room.

"Fuck. It's not *my* room." I said aloud. This wasn't my house. This wasn't my pack. I couldn't stay here. I had to get back and figure out some story to tell to keep the Reset away from them.

I slipped out of the bedroom, my stomach growling in the quiet. My bare feet carried me soundlessly past the kitchen without a glance, the soft sound of keys tapping pulled me to the dining room. The room was homey. The whole house was actually. It was done up in greens and blues with brown accents. It had a much more lived-in feel than the other house in the city. That felt like a hotel, almost. Here, I could see touches of their personalities.

Cross sat at the big table, a computer, tablet, and a folder of papers all spread around him. The table was a giant slab of wood; the edges were rough and looked like they still had bark on them. There was a crisp cut down the center, splitting the table into two wood sections with a transparent sapphire blue section, made of glass or plastic, running down the middle, like a river perfectly splitting the wood. The eight chairs around the table were mismatched, but in that glossy fashion magazine way, where they all still seemed to go together. The table was polished to a high shine.

I lingered at the entry into the dining room. He was working, I didn't want to interrupt. He was scribbling something in a leather-bound journal when he froze, closed his eyes and took a deep breath. Damn it. Maybe I should have gone with one of the scented soaps.

"Hey," The softness of his voice didn't match his gruff exterior.

"I don't want to interrupt." I said, my voice more desperate than I wanted.

"You're not." His voice and cherry whiskey scent just drew me in.

"I'm just trying to cross-reference all the Ruin Winters' incidents. It's kind of boring and tedious, actually."

I swallowed hard, anxiety fluttering in my chest. Luther knew. I knew he knew. I didn't want Cross to figure it out. I leaned on the back of one of the chairs looking at the papers he had spread out. There were documents that had "New Oxford Police Department" letterhead and a map with sticky notes attached.

Glancing at his laptop, I shivered. He had a Ruin Winters video playing on a loop. It was an old one from just after the Crimson Bullet incident. My stomach soured, bile crept up my throat. I had been live streaming from the ladies room. One of the omegas from the Evendale pack was planning a date with a beta and I was capturing all the drama. I had no idea Billy and Bennett had taken one of the omegas from the Berry Creek house and drugged her.

He closed the laptop and relief flooded me.

"When can I leave?" I had to get out of here before Luther told them.

Cross pushed back in his chair. His eyes fluttered all over me. I felt like a puzzle and he was trying to figure out where the missing piece went.

"You really want to go?" he asked. I nodded and cringed.

Ruin not Ruby. Ruin not Ruby.

I flashed a smile and rolled my shoulder toward him. His brow wrinkled like a confusing thought floated through his mind and he glanced down at his computer.

"Well, you did kidnap me. I do have a job, friends, a life. People will miss me."

"You're unbothered by the scent match?" He asked. Cross was direct, there was something comforting and terrifying about that.

"Why should I want you, when you clearly don't want me?" I pitched my voice low, using that tone Bennett insisted on in his special videos.

"Luther will be back with dinner shortly." Cross said, piling some papers and his leather journal on top of his computer, before walking out of the room.

A bubble of excited anticipation fluttered my stomach and sent a pulse to my pussy. I squeezed my eyes shut. The thought of Luther should be filling me with dread. I should not be longing for him.

I should not want Luther.

It wasn't safe.

TWENTY-SEVEN

RUBY

My knife and fork hovered over the plate, unsure of what to do. The rich spices momentarily overpowering the whiskey, grass, sandalwood, and sea salt of the alphas at the table. I didn't know what we were eating. It was take-out from some place in the city. Rice, saucy dishes and little misshapen flatbreads. Cross picked up one of the flatbreads and tore a piece off, and ate it with his hands. I put my knife and fork down when Luther did the same.

Looking down at my plate, I ripped a bite of bread off. I ate a lot of food with my hands. I wasn't allowed to have a knife, and sometimes they forgot to give me utensils, saying I was an animal, I didn't need utensils. I didn't know how to act, what was expected, and it put me on a razor's edge.

"What did Elmont have to say?" Talon asked. He was across from me. Luther was on my right and that seemed like it was the wrong move for me. Maybe I was sitting in his seat?

Luther shot a significant look my way. Obviously, he didn't want to discuss business in front of me.

"She's part of it. She was there. So, she should know." Jackson said with a grin, popping bread into his mouth.

"Fine." Luther said in a way that was absolutely not fine. "After I broke his nose, Elmont said…"

"You broke his nose?" I asked. I don't know why the question came out of my mouth and I deeply wished I could take it back. His aura went all prickly and grated against me like sandpaper.

"He asked me to," Luther spat out, like that was all the explanation that was necessary.

"That sounds like Elmont. Did he manage to tell you anything useful or did he just whine like a bitch?" Talon asked, wiping his mouth with a napkin.

"He told me there were three betas talking about a hit on a pack house, said they were throwing around so much cash it could only come from one place."

He left that statement hanging in the air like everyone but me knew the answer. Talon sat back in his chair, chewing thoughtfully.

"The only person who would have access to cash and would want us dead would be Riot," Jackson said.

"Riot wouldn't pay people off. Not his style," said Luther. "After Elmont, I got Brian to meet me for a coffee before I picked up dinner. There's nothing from local PD."

"What do you mean, nothing?" Talon asked.

"No police report. No 911 calls from neighbors. Nothing."

They all pondered that for a bit while I resisted the urge to squirm. When they all found out, I would be the first one in handcuffs. I pushed some rice on my fork and took a bite. The butter hit my tongue and made my stomach growl, catching looks from everyone at the table.

"Anything else from Elmont?"

"Just that he doesn't think Ruin Winters is an omega because the Reset wouldn't work with an omega."

Jackson snorted. "That's ridiculous." Luther shrugged.

Heat crept into my cheeks. Their enemy was sitting at the table with them and I was garbage for just sitting here, playing along. I was garbage for sitting here, pretending, eating their food, feeling welcomed in their home.

My gut twisted. I could solve this for them. I could solve it in an instant. Give them all the answers they wanted. Names, locations, where they kept their weapons. Everything. And it wouldn't matter.

Bennett and Billy were just two worker bees in a vast organization. They could never take down the Reset. If they tried, they'd be dead. My heart ratcheted up. Panic swirled around me. If I told them, they'd respond, and they'd all die. But if I... did what? I had to figure out something I could give the Reset that could buy the pack's safety. First, I had to get out of here. I didn't deserve to be here.

"Ruby?" I heard my name. "You don't like Indian?" Jackson said softly.

I knew he meant it to be kind, but all the focus and attention was now on me and that felt awful. And it got worse when I met his eyes, and this wave of care and concern swamped me. My chest tightened. He cared if I ate. And I was going to destroy all of this. I looked down at my plate to avoid his eyes because I couldn't help conjuring how he'd look at me when he learned I was Ruin Winters.

Luther next to me made a disgusted sound. He already hated me. He wanted nothing to do with me. I needed to convince the rest of them. Maybe I could get them all to dislike me?

I pulled Ruin Winters around me like a winter jacket. I rolled my shoulder forward and got that snotty stuck up omega look on my face and turned to Luther.

"Who pissed in your soda?" I said to the stunned alphas. Even

Luther could only blink at me in response, until his lip curled and his eyes narrowed.

"Our food not good enough for you? Turning your nose up like a duchess walking away from a princess bond."

"Well, you know," I gave him my best "hun" look, that look women used to put other women down, "it's hard to find food appealing when you're being held captive, your food chosen for you, your clothes." A snotty duchess would say that, wouldn't they? I hadn't chosen my own food in years.

"We make decisions as a pack. You're not pack. And you're not going to be."

"Who said I wanted to join your stupid pack, anyway? You're holding me captive. I just want to go home." I had the over-whelming urge to call him a doodie head like I was twelve again.

"Say you're not hungry and get up from the table, and don't play with your food like a child," Luther said, looking down his nose at me. I caught Jackson and Talon exchanging a look of concern. "You're acting like you've never seen food before." He grumbled.

"Oh, I'm sorry." I leaned forward, putting delicate fingers to my chest and tossed my head back. "I'm sorry I grew up poor with a foster family, and not fancy rich packs who went out to eat all the time like the rest of you. Maypole is not exactly known for their international cuisine. I don't know what any of this is, and I didn't want to be rude and ask."

Panic fluttered in my chest. I had said something wrong, gone too far. They were all staring at me like I had a live grenade in my hand. Luther turned toward me with narrowed eyes, flicking his gaze all over me.

"A foster family? In Maypole?" Talon asked, his tone carefully neutral, but he gave Cross a significant look. And that spiked my anxiety through the roof. Whenever someone was careful like that, bad things happened.

I nodded. I had a carefully constructed story about my upbringing. It was mostly true. "My mom died when I was six, some sort of accident on a playground. I don't remember it. So foster families took me in. I moved to the city when I perfumed at 18." That last bit was the lie, but I had said it so often I almost believed it myself. I was 17. If my stupid fucking hormones had held off for just a few months, I would have been free.

I looked around at the alphas at the table. My back story was tragic, sure, but their reaction, as a pack, wasn't something I had encountered before. Most people would hit me with a "oh your poor dear" and move on to better topics.

Something passed between Jackson and Luther, a silent communication I wasn't a part of. Pack bonds.

"I just want to go home." I said to my plate.

"To Maypole?" Talon asked softly. I just nodded.

They went back to their conversation about criminals. Luther stewed next to me. His scent became thick, smoke and grass flooded the air around me. I hated myself for wanting more than just his scent in me. I crossed my legs under the table, pressing my thighs together and pretended to eat more rice.

TWENTY-EIGHT

JACKSON

I bit my lip, taking in the scene, practically purring. We were all in the kitchen, having survived the fireworks at dinner. Talon and Cross were packing away the leftovers. Luther was washing up a little more vigorously than the chore required. This was what pack life should be, what we'd been missing.

I was determined to ride the school yard fight Luther and Ruby just had, and get them to the kiss and make up part.

And Ruby was adorably flustered. She was still holding her dinner plate, unsure of what to do, bobbing on her bare feet. I wondered if we were stepping on her omega instincts. We were self-sufficient. When we made her pack, I didn't think anyone would expect to dump all the household duties on her. We were progressive like that. Not like my birth pack. Alphas didn't lift a finger in that house.

I took the plate from her hands. Slut that I was , I took the opportunity to trail my fingers down her arms. It made us both shiver. It was getting increasingly hard not to touch her all the time. I had to keep reminding myself she had only known me for

213

days. I'd been stalking her for a while. I had weeks of unfocused desire under my belt. The second your scent match locked in, all your instincts fired off. I was surprised I'd kept it together this long.

Cross would come around. So would Talon. It had only been a day. A traumatic day at that. If I could just show them how good this could be, they'd get it. They'd want it. They'd curse themselves for ever putting up resistance.

"I know," I said, placing her dishes by the sink, leaning on the edge of the counter. "We should have a pack battle."

"A battle?" Ruby said hesitantly, brushing hair out of her face.

"Video game battle. They," I gestured to Talon mostly, "won't let me play my favorite anymore, though."

"That's because you cheat," Talon grumbled.

"You just don't like losing."

"I wasn't allowed to play video games." Ruby's lip trembled, like she wanted to take that statement back. I was getting the sense she came from a strict family. A video game ban would fit with that.

"We have a go-cart driving game. It's super easy to learn."

"You cheat at that, too."

"It's not my problem you can't concentrate when someone is biting your neck." I leaned into Ruby and whispered loudly, "I distract him with sex when I think he's going to win."

Ruby flushed and giggled. God, I could eat her up. I *would* eat her up. My breath caught at the idea of going down on her while she was trying to concentrate on driving a little go-kart. Slick coating my lips, then pulling Talon in for a kiss so we could taste her together.

"OK." Ruby said, crossing the room to put her glass in the sink. "I guess since you gentlemen are in charge of my incarceration this evening…"

Luther froze and then exploded.

Everything happened in a flash. Luther growled. His aura burst, rattling the cabinets. Talon, Cross and I were jolted back a step. Ruby yelped and dropped the glass. It shattered everywhere. She teetered back, screamed in pain. The scent of blood rose sharply.

Luther moved faster than I could track. He had her by the neck and shoulder, up against the far wall. Her toes barely touching the floor, scrabbling for a hold. His rolling growl vibrated the air.

"Luther." Talon said, slowly uncoiling his aura with the command pack lead afforded him. "Put her down."

I shifted my weight to lunge for Ruby, but Talon's unspoken order kept me in place.

"Put Ruby down, Luther."

"Can't."

LUTHER

I'll be in charge of your incarceration this evening.

The words registered immediately. I had said them in the warehouse. Showboating. Making an ass out of myself.

Ruin Winters.

She was Ruin Winters.

She was in the warehouse... With those betas... Gun in my face.

Her scent was all over me. Orange. Vanilla. Ice cream on playgrounds.

She had been... terrified... Not of me. Of the betas.

Please, do it.

Begging. She had begged. Begged with her sweet black lips. Begged me to kill her.

My chest shrank, all the air squeezed out. She had been at the house. With the betas. The same betas. Ruin Winters. Attacking my pack.

Orange. Vanilla. Grass. Smoke. Blood. Her blood on the floor. On the grass.

Because of me.

"Put Ruby down, Luther."

Talon's aura tried to swallow mine. It wouldn't be enough. Never enough.

The alpha urge to protect... Protect the pack... From her... From our *mate*... Protect her... From me... From everything.

"Can't."

She was a threat... She was threatened.

Ruin... Ruby... She put her hands on my face. Her aura drank mine in, containing it, shrinking it to child sized. Her thumb stroked my lips. I put my forehead to hers. She breathed into me until there was only orange and vanilla, and her.

I stroked her pulse at her throat with my thumb until mine matched hers. My heart, hers.

RUBY

Can't.

I can't either.

I felt my aura for the first time.

Really felt it, a force unto itself. Made of nothing but energy, it was real and solid. It knew who I was, not Ruby, not Ruin. Just omega, his mate. My aura mingled with Luther, like teeth in a zipper, locking into each other, impossible to part.

I breathed him in. Smoke and grass all around me. And he could destroy it, destroy me. I'd let him, so long as he held me like this.

I felt them press around us, the rest of the pack. A hand grasped my arm, another slipped behind my back. Cross appeared over Luther's shoulder, his arms circling Luther's chest. I felt Talon's attempt to pry Luther's fingers from my neck.

I growled. Low and soft. I would not be forced from my mate.

"We're all going to let go and take a step back," Talon's voice whispered across my awareness. My fingers dug into my mate.

"Luther, she's bleeding. We need to look at her foot." Luther squeezed my neck in response, ignoring Talon's words.

I grunted. Not from fear or pain, but from need.

"Omega." I felt the word spoken into my ear like a whip crack. Confusion forced panting breaths from me. The need for my mate wrestled with the need to comply. I darted a glance away from Luther. Talon's eyes were dusky, his pupils huge, and utterly captivating.

"Let go of Luther." Talon said gently. I instantly obeyed, but my fingers were cramped and had a hard time letting go. The sounds of Luther's breathing got harsh and ragged.

"Good girl." Talon purred. My eyes fluttered at the sudden shock of pleasure that rippled through me. I felt Luther's shudder against me, feeling what I was feeling, maybe.

Talon had me by the waist and arm. He slid me along the wall, out from the cage of Luther's body. Luther didn't let go, but he didn't grasp for me. His fingers only fully releasing when Talon had me just beyond his reach.

It hurt. It hurt to lose touch, lose connection with him. I took a step back. A sudden spike of pain in my foot caused a hissing breath.

A snarl rose from Luther, Cross and now Jackson tightened their hold on him. Talon scooped me into his arms and strode down the hall. Each step away from Luther ripped open a fresh ache.

Talon set me in the middle of the bed. A huge expanse of white stretched under me. My eyes popped wide. I scrambled off the bed and cursed as my foot connected with the floor. I tried to hobble away from the pristine bed. I was all emotion, no thoughts.

"Sit on the bed, Ruby." It was a command, an order.

A new sensation of pain coursed through me and then as a realization rocked me.

It was true.

They had said omegas can't say no. They can't disobey. It physically hurts when you disobey. Anxiety spiked, I took a few pained and panicked steps from the bed.

"Ruby..." Talon looked from me to the bed.

"No. I'll ruin it. It'll be garbage." I bit my lip at the shocks of pain in my foot. I reached forward and gave the comforter a tug so no one would know I sat on the bed.

"It's just blood. We can wash it out."

I shook my head furiously, eyes fixated on the bed, like it was a viper about to strike. Talon picked me up again. I stiffened to struggle when he forced me back on the bed. But he sat smoothly on the floor, with me cradled in his lap. His scent was sharp in my nose.

He grasped my ankle and bent my knee so he could examine my foot. I nervously watched him. I eyed the bed over his shoulder like it knew my secrets and now that I violated it, it would tell on me. The bed and Luther could destroy me. And I'd deserve it.

Talon glanced at me and did a double take. He didn't like whatever I was showing on my face. I tried to give him Ruin's winning smile, but it wouldn't come to me.

"Hey," he said gently, holding my face and stroking my cheek. "You're OK. It's just a little piece of glass in your foot." I leaned into his touch, dropping my eyes when he frowned.

Jackson slid to his knees next to us with a plastic box in his hands.

"Well, that was eventful. Scent matches can be unsettling at first." His words were light and airy, but there was darkness in his eyes.

They set to work silently, each one predicting what the other would need next as they took care of my foot. Mates. They could act seamlessly because they were mates. Jackson threw his leg over Talon's so he could scoot closer and see what he was doing. Talon held his phone's flashlight for Jackson.

I hissed and curled into Talon's shoulder when the sting of disinfectant hit me. He rubbed his thumb in little circles on my hip.

"You don't need a bandage, but I'll put one on, anyway. It was a tiny piece of glass." Jackson stroked my foot. Talon rocked slightly. "You want me to kiss it better?" he said, a sparkle coming back to his eyes.

I nodded tentatively. He made an exaggerated smacking kiss sound as he held my foot like a prize and kissed the sole. Fiery tingles dance up my leg, burning need through me.

"I think we deserve some ice cream and video games after all that excitement." Jackson stood. I reluctantly put space between me and Talon. My hand touched my neck where Luther's fingers were. I wanted them there again. Needed them. Jackson reached down and lifted me off the floor and into his arms.

"I can... I can walk."

"It's my turn to hold you. Luther and Talon had their chance." He winked at me, as he side-stepped to maneuver us out the door.

TWENTY-NINE

TALON

I shook out the ache in my arms that didn't like her absence, listening to Jackson's lighthearted banter as he carried Ruby to the living room. Jackson could always be counted on to diffuse tense situations. While Luther couldn't help but ratchet things up.

His aura was to blame, mostly. The concussion and an unconsummated scent match was a volatile combination. I couldn't help but think there was something else going on. Luther was quick to fly off the handle, but something about this was different.

I turned to get up off the floor. There was something about the bed, too.

Ruby's reaction to the bed was very... odd. It was perfectly made, like she hadn't slept in it, the pristine white was unwrinkled. Maybe it was the duvet and not the bed itself?

I couldn't quite put my finger on what was happening with her. Snow angels in the grass. The fake smile and bravado. It all added up to a meaning that wouldn't come to the forefront of my brain.

Thoughts swirled as I followed Jackson's path to the living

room, passing the kitchen. Cross was alone, elbows on the counter, cradling his head. I stepped in and gave his shoulder a squeeze. Physical touch helped ground you after a mishap with your aura.

Touch. She was touch starved.

She'd practically melted into me once my arms were around her. And that shock of pleasure when I called her "good girl"? It could be run-of-the-mill omega praise kink, but it didn't feel like that. A touch starved omega wasn't natural.

"How's Luther?" I asked Cross, we kept our voices low, knowing they wouldn't travel far.

"Freaked out. Went for a run."

I nodded. Probably the best thing for him. "He tell you what that was all about?"

Cross shrugged and leaned against the fridge. "He said alpha protectiveness. You know how he can get around omegas. He almost stomped a guy the other day for making a crack about gold pack."

I ran a hand through my hair. It was time to tell Cross and Jackson. At first, I wanted as few people to know Luther was a rogue as possible. His aura had been relatively stable the past few years. On bad days, I could anchor it. They chalked it up to child-hood trauma. It fit, it worked. Trauma could make your aura sensitive. I'd left it to Luther to tell them, and he never did. He feared ruining his chances at pack and family. I cringed every time Jackson would spout off slurs about rogues. He didn't mean it, not really, it was just habit, and training from his birth pack.

"Jackson and Luther went at it," Cross said softly.

"The split lip?"

Cross nodded.

I didn't have to ask what the fight was over. Ruby was turning over all our apple carts.

The opening music of the racing game blared from the living

room, pulling our attention that way. A giggle from Ruby made it all the more alluring. Jackson, as always, had the pack bond wide open. He was gleeful, and that was infectious.

"There's another thing you should know."

I braced myself. We didn't need more bullshit on our plate.

"I know you told me not to, but I put a bug on one of Luther's records. His birth certificate."

The fake birth certificate. The one Duo and I had doctored. I sighed and scratched my eyebrow. The less we fucked around and left a trail for people to follow, the better.

"If anybody pulled it, it would send me an alert."

"Who?"

"Kai Ekon."

"Fuck."

"Yeah, Luther's sister's pack is looking for him."

"How the fuck did he make that connection?" I ran my fingers through my dark hair for comfort, not to make it look nice.

"I don't know, man. He must have pulled every birth certificate for every male born that year, throughout the whole country. Done a manual search or something. Kai is good. And he's fucking crazy. I don't trust him to not take risks."

I gripped the counter and hung my head, trying to force out some of the tension.

"You know we can't let there be any connection between them."

"I know. I reached out to Kai."

"And?"

"Told him that if he kept looking, what he was looking for would be dead."

"You think he's going to stop?"

"No. Kai will just be cleaner now. Leave no trace. The fact that I called him on his unlisted cell about 8 minutes after he pulled the record would be enough to tell him he was being sloppy."

"OK." I rolled my head around on my neck. Luther was currently physically and emotionally beating himself up. He was losing the ability to control what he sent through the pack bonds. His aura was out almost all the time now. We were not going to be able to hide him as a rogue for much longer.

"I want you to do something for me." I said. Cross eyed me suspiciously. "And I don't want you to tell the other two."

That was a big ask, and Cross knew it. Secrets in a pack were problematic, and we were living out that reality right now. I squeezed my eyes shut and rubbed a thumb nail along my eyebrow.

"What?" he said, stroking his beard.

"Pull Ruby's file from the Institute."

"That's... invasive."

"There's security concerns."

"You're not worried about that." It was a statement, not a question. "Maypole." Cross didn't need to elaborate. We all knew what that meant.

Maypole was where you said you were from when you didn't want to say you were raised in Berry Creek. It could be nothing. Normal, average, everyday people lived in Maypole, but its proximity to Berry Creek, being the last town before the farms and compounds of the insular, paranoid, anti-traditionalist beta organizations, always made it suspicious. We had run backup on a few raids in Berry Creek. Murdered twins, lots of credible allegations of abuse. Everyone knew Berry Creek was the HQ for the Reset. Omegas and alphas almost never claimed to be from that area.

So yeah, the Maypole angle was something to look at, but we had other concerns. Protocol, evidence handling, the law, all that would be applied differently if she was pack, but she wasn't.

And she wasn't going to be. It didn't matter how I was feeling right now. She was a destabilizing force that we couldn't sustain.

A giddy squeal erupted from the living room. The sound went

right to my groin. Cross dipped his head. He'd been thinking along the same lines. I had to get this girl out of my house.

I held Cross rooted in place until he nodded and agreed to get her file. It didn't matter what we found, but it would be justification for sending her back to her life. Tonight proved adding her to the pack was the wrong decision. There was too much at stake for that.

"I don't want her in the pack." Cross said to my back as I walked out of the kitchen.

THIRTY

TALON

Fucking omega auras.

Cross was eventually pulled to video game hour by the hum of delight coursing through the cabin. Ruby was sitting on her knees right in front of the couch, turning the controller with her whole body to move around the figure eights of the go-kart track. Jackson was offering helpful pointers, and Cross and I were trying to lose as best we could.

"Can you show me how to do that slidey thing again?" Ruby took her eyes off the TV and immediately crashed her cart.

I was stretched out on the length of the couch, cursing myself when I realized I wanted to be closer to her scent. It was maddening, to the point of distraction. And that was the point. We weren't keeping her. She wasn't a stray puppy Jackson brought home. It didn't matter how she made us feel. She was a security risk. She unbalanced Luther. We were a risk to her. I was a risk to her. I'd already proven I couldn't take care of an omega. They were too needy, too easily influenced.

"Tap. Tap. Press. Hold. Release." Jackson leaned over to show her again.

I squeezed my eyes shut. And gave in. For one night, for the next hour, I'd let this little fantasy of a pack we'd never be able to sustain play out.

I shifted and kicked my leg out over her head and scooted to sit on the edge of the couch. Ruby was between my knees now. I put down my controller and slid my hands down her arms. She jumped and stiffened, her citrus scent going bitter with anxiety. I paused. Maybe this wasn't a good idea. She was like a baby bunny that startled and froze at the slightest movement from something bigger.

"Let me show you." I whispered in her ear.

She nodded, hesitantly, almost like she didn't believe what I was saying and was waiting for me to bite. I moved her fingers to the right buttons, putting mine over hers. I guided her fingers to make the right patterns.

Her scent sweetened as she relaxed. Her skin heated up under my light touch. After a few laps around the track, I let go of her hands on the controller, the heat of her skin still lingering on my fingers. She shifted her weight slightly, leaning her shoulder into my leg. I burned under her touch, and shut down the pack bonds. I didn't want them knowing, didn't want to share the swirl of thoughts and emotions and the sharp disappointment that was already building at knowing I couldn't have her, shouldn't have her.

I shifted and swung my leg over her again to stand. The sudden scent of fear flooding the cabin burned my nose. She skittered back, dropping the controller, panting at the jump scare.

We both blurted out, "I'm sorry" at the same time.

"I'm sorry I startled you." I said, my eyes narrowing. She was touch starved, that much was obvious and in a house with four strangers. Some apprehension was to be expected. And we did have to pry her out of Luther's grip an hour ago. I could have heard her heart pounding if mine wasn't so loud.

And then she shifted, going from soft, scared little bunny, to coiled pit viper.

"Captivity has made me jumpy." Her voice became rich and sultry.

She was manipulating us. Anger settled onto my shoulders. Our unusual circumstances, the attack, holding up here, could account for some of this personality shifting. She didn't know us, she had every right to be on guard and defensive. But there was more here.

She skirted the room, keeping as much distance between us as possible.

"I think I'll go to bed." Ruby's voice was solid but laced with anxiety. She turned and walked down the hall. I jolted forward. Cross put his body between me and Ruby, a growl caught in my throat.

"We're not hunting her. She's not prey." He said, putting a hand on my hip to stop me from going after her. I pushed back from Cross, not realizing I was going after her to... To do what, exactly?

"You want her." Jackson purred with satisfaction.

I cracked my neck and tightened my hold on my emotions. Jackson was flooding them with all his lusty thoughts.

"It doesn't matter what I want," I said, stepping away from Cross and Jackson both, now that she was safely down the hall and out of sight. "She's manipulating us. It's not good for the pack."

"I think you're scared, Tal, and making up bullshit."

"I think you're obsessed and blinded by the lure of a scent match."

"You're projecting. I can feel you, Tal," Jackson said, stepping into my body, hooking fingers into my belt. "I can feel all of you. Even Luther, he wants her. And Cross. He'll never admit it."

I wanted to deny it, deny it all. Jackson knew, though, he knew I could never refuse him anything.

"She isn't a toy or a puppy you brought home," I said, my voice low, covering up my conflict.

"Oh, I know. She's our omega. Our scent match. And that is what makes all the difference. This isn't like before. She isn't Melodie..."

"Shut up," I cut him off. His eyes narrowed on me.

"You can try and push that away all you want, deny it, deny your desire, your own needs." The fucker was reading my mind now. "But it's only going to work for so long."

The pack bonds lit up with a giant fuck you as Cross stormed out.

"Stop fucking with Cross." I growled. Jackson wasn't so cruel that he'd torture Cross with his dead omega, but he would capitalize on it.

Jackson slid his hand down the front of my pants and squeezed my cock.

"This right here, tells me all I need to know, my love."

I closed my eyes as he stroked me through my pants, my fingers biting into his shoulder.

"Don't do this, Jackson." Lust and frustration cracked my voice.

"Oh, I'm not doing anything. You said no sex, remember?"

I groaned weakly. Jackson always made me weak.

"Save it for her," he said into my neck, nipping at me, right where her claiming bite would be, before letting me go and turning toward the kitchen.

I staggered at the loss of contact, my breath coming hard. I looked down the hall toward her bedroom. It was only years of discipline that kept me from throwing her door open. No, not years of discipline. Fear. It was fear that kept me from putting teeth in her. I couldn't be trusted with an omega.

THIRTY-ONE

LUTHER

I let the gravel of the driveway bite into my back. It was getting close to dawn. The run didn't ease the panic. I couldn't go back in yet.

Ruin Winters was in my house. With my pack mates. My brothers.

I had convinced myself it was a dream, something my concussed brain kicked out. The memories lined up like grainy security footage snapshots.

Three betas in the warehouse.

I hit the ground.

One perp broke free and ran.

I chased. Caught him.

It was a woman.

An omega.

Black hair and lips.

Her scent.

Mate.

Explosion.

Her lips, black and full, consumed my vision. "Go. Please. They'll kill you." I couldn't hear, but that's what her lips had said.

The omega terrorist ran, not to get away from me, but to get *them* away from me.

I shook my head, dull rocks from the drive poking the back of my head. I had to get this straight in my own head before I could go to Talon with it.

There was something else.

Something else happened before all this, maybe? Something about... Maypole?

I looked at the house and reached for the people inside. They were all asleep. Dreams didn't really come through in the pack bonds.

Fuck.

That's what was new in the pack bonds. He was in love with her.

I stood and paced around the drive, touching the split lip Jackson gave me... yesterday? The day before? It seemed like a decade since the warehouse explosion.

What the fuck was I going to tell Jackson? I couldn't walk in there and say "yo, check this, your omega hottie has a body count and not in that way." Talon himself would turn me into the Institute for scrambled brains.

Jackson loved her and I couldn't break his heart.

I needed some kind of proof. Get her to admit it, find evidence on her phone. And then what? Tell Talon so that he would have to be the one to tell Jackson? I was a fucking coward.

She was just sitting in our house all coy and sexy, worming her way into Jackson's heart.

A realization kicked me in the balls. Elmont said big money was behind the attack on the house. The Reset had big money.

This was all a setup. Jackson just happened to meet the girl of his dreams. We just happened to get attacked?

Rage simmered in my gut. Every second she was here, she was a threat. A threat to Jackson.

RUBY

I paced another circle around the bed. Sleep was impossible.

I wanted them. All of them. I wanted their hands on me, their scents coating me. I knew I couldn't have them. When Luther told them, they would never want me.

My mouth was dry, my skin felt hot. I dragged myself to the bathroom, flicking off all the lights along the way. The brightness made everything too real. I cupped cool water in my palm at the sink. I drank some and splashed my face. I stood and avoided the mirror as usual and reached for my... vitamins? My empty hand hovered over the spot on the counter where they should be.

Oh god... heat.

It was in the rule book. Vitamins every day because a healthy body prevented heat. And sex. Vitamins and sex. That was the only thing that prevented heat. How many days had it been? Two? Three?

I was going to go into heat in a house full of alphas.

I closed my eyes and was met with all the pictures they had shown me. Girls and women mutilated, turned inside out by alphas who lost control when an omega went into heat.

Next time it will be you.

The night of the Crimson Bullet, I had tried to run. It was chaos, people were screaming. Billy caught me, dragged me to the van.

. . .

Next time it will be you. No cage. Naked. You in heat with all those knotters.

Screams from the club ringing in my ears.

I looked around the room, panicked. The enormous bed. Would that be where it would happen? Would they hold me down? Talon's teeth in my neck. Jackson's hands on my thighs. Cross' lips on mine. Luther pushing...

His hands on my neck. His body pressing into me. His cock pressing into me. I could feel the wetness between my legs. Heat.

I ripped the sweater over my head. I was too hot.

Oh god, was this heat? Was it starting already? I had to have sex to stop heat.

My head came up at the sound of the doorknob turning. It pushed open far enough for Luther to slip into the room. His chest was bare, glistening in the low light. He came at me. *Run.* I should run. But all I wanted was for him to catch me, take me.

His scent flooded the room with all the good things in life. Summer days, cookouts, sunshine, love. I clutched the t-shirt to my chest. Chilled to the bone, and on fire at the same time.

He had a furious beauty, like an explosion in slow motion. His presence was like a living thing coiled around him and striking out into the room all around me. It was thick in the air. I could taste it, taste the rage and anger, all the acrid smoke and wildfires filling my mouth. I shivered. I needed him in my mouth.

The emotion pouring out of him pushed me back, and he kept coming until I had nowhere left to go, the back of my thighs bumping into the edge of the bed.

His fingers curled around my neck. My pulse protested and beat against his thumb.

"This is familiar, isn't it?" His voice was a dangerous hush.

"Wha... what are you talking about?"

"The warehouse."

I shook my head.

"Ruin Winters," he said her name like it was a curse, a magic spell that would end us all. "Was Jackson the target all along?"

"No." Jackson was a secret pleasure. A taste of hope I wanted to keep all to myself. But I wasn't allowed to... to love anything.

"Ruin," he growled in my ear and squeezed my neck harder. I moaned.

I was lost. I had lost. It was over. Luther would tell the pack and they would kill me. The Reset would find me and they would kill me. I would go into heat and die. And I would lose him, lose Luther forever when I had just found him.

He stroked his thumb along my neck and I quivered. His hazel eyes shifted, fury burning up, leaving behind a rich darkness. A growl vibrated the space between us. I stretched my neck wanting his fingers to dig in deeper.

He put his hand to the small of my back and crushed me to him. I felt his length press into me, hard and growing harder.

I reached a hand between us to feel his cock, whimpering at the contact, thin fabric still separating us.

"Please."

LUTHER

Please.

I came undone. I was here to force a confession, to protect my pack, to protect Jackson.

I put my hands on her and the only truth that mattered was that she was mine. Her scent filled in all the gaps in me, pulling my pieces together. My aura condensed around her, to take her, make her mine.

With her hand on my cock and 'please' on her lips, I knew the truth of that, too. I was hers. She was answers to questions I didn't know I had.

"Ruin," I breathed as she stroked me, "we can't." Some sense came back to me. She was the target we were hunting. She was a terrorist. Jackson was in love with her. We couldn't have an omega. She could destroy the pack. All the reasons scrolled out in my mind, and evaporated into a need that was greater than the danger we all faced.

Need, lust, and fear pooled in her eyes. She knew it. She knew the stakes, what was at risk, better than I did. And she knew the truth of it, too, that she was turning me to marshmallow in her hands. She swallowed and begged, "please" again. Our scents mingled, creating the perfect summer day, the kind of day that I had never had, carefree, easy, full of laughter and love. That's what she was, a promise of love.

She held me with her eyes and fell back, knowing I'd catch her, I'd always catch her. Gravity took us to the bed. This could all be a manipulation. A way to get to Jackson, the GPRE, the Institute. I squeezed my eyes shut to gather my resolve and pull away from the promise of her. I dug for the anger that had been boiling in me and grabbed her throat. She responded by parting her legs, making a home for me.

"You want me to fuck you?" My voice was barely a whisper, thick in my throat.

She nodded slowly, dipping her hand into my running shorts. I bit back a growl when her flesh touched mine. We shouldn't be doing this. I needed to be sure.

"Say it." I squeezed her neck again.

"Fuck me." Her voice, full of omega need, penetrated me, my aura, my brain, claiming space there. With her free hand, she pulled down the boxers she was wearing and kicked them off. Jackson's boxers. I grunted and forced the thought away.

I slid my hand between us, joining hers on my cock. I rubbed the head along her entrance. She was already drenched with slick.

I pushed into her slowly, wanting to feel every inch of her take me in. I was fixated on her eyes. They danced and sparkled. She breathed in a long gasping inhale, and shattered around me. Her eyes fluttered and her head lolled back as she came, her body tightening and pulsing.

"I didn't know," she panted, "it could be like this."

I began to withdraw, so I could do it again, feel her pussy clench, feel her body tremble and her scent rise off her. Again.

She sat up with a gasp. Eyes wide with almost panic. Her free hand dug into the back of my neck. Her legs squeezed around me, not wanting me to leave her.

I rested my forehead against hers and pulled back more. A high-pitched squeal of protest sent me over the edge.

"You want me deep in you," I growled softly. It wasn't a question, but she nodded, anyway. "Say it."

She hesitated like she was fighting with herself, not wanting to admit that this was what she wanted. Needed. I pulled all the way out of her.

I buried my nose in her neck, and they were there. My pack brothers' scents clung to her, like she was always meant to be here, be a part of us.

She cupped the back of my head, her nails biting into my shoulder. I smiled. I'd have to grow my hair out for her, just to feel her fingers get lost and tug at it, putting my head exactly where she wanted it.

"Yes," she said with a breathy moan. "I need you in me." It was barely loud enough to hear.

I smoothed my hand down her perfect leg to grasp her foot, hiking it up, settling her heel in my lower back. I wanted her leg high so I could go as deep as possible. I ran the head of my cock up and down her slit, drowning it in her slick, teasing her clit until she was right on the edge of coming.

In a quick fluid movement, I pushed deep inside her until my knot prevented more. She stopped breathing for a moment as the waves of the orgasm crashed into her. She stiffened, her breath returned sharp and shuddered. I didn't move, biting my lip to fight every urge to push my knot into her.

I didn't deserve that. Not yet.

I waited until she came back to me. Her eyes fluttered open, a tear in the corner quickly blinked away.

She cupped my face with her palm, her thumb brushing along my lips. I parted them and took her finger into my mouth, and started to move. Short, deep thrusts, while I teased her fingertip with my tongue.

I could watch her face all day for the rest of my life. Each new sensation was like a discovery of something she didn't know existed. She came again when I bit the pad of her thumb.

She planted a foot on the bed to grind herself against me harder. Faster, I was getting close to my release. I buried my face in her neck.

"Ruin," I growled softly into her ear.

"Don't call me that."

"Ruby," I whispered before grazing my teeth on her neck.

"Don't call me that either." Her voice was rough.

"What do you want me to call you?" I breathed deep to take in her scent, oranges and vanilla, and pack.

"Yours," she moaned as she tumbled into another orgasm. "Call me yours."

"Mine." I slipped my hands under her ass, to hold her as close as possible. My cock kicking in her as I came.

RUBY

I squeezed my eyes shut to keep tears from escaping. I felt like a real person for the first time, like my body and soul occupied the same place. So much had been done to my body, what it should wear, what it should eat. Things I didn't ask for or want.

This? I wanted this. This was all mine. He was mine.

He thrust hard. I felt him release in me. I bit my lip and arched against him, wanting him to fill me in all the ways he could. Coming with him, our bodies trembled together like we were one being. He rested heavy on me, nuzzling into my neck. I took a deep breath, as the shuddering quieted in both of us. I allowed my fingers to dance in his hair. It was like peach fuzz but better.

Luther sighed and pushed off me, pulling out of me, and stood. I clamped my legs shut, wanting to weep at the sudden emptiness and disconnection. With gentle hands he pulled me up and maneuvered me to the bathroom, holding me by the wrist. I managed to tug the edge of the duvet, straightening out most of the wrinkles. I squinted in the harsh light.

"Well, at least I won't go into heat now." I muttered to myself.

"What?" Luther said, pulling up his shorts, tossing my shirt and boxers to the bathroom floor.

"You have to have sex to stop heat."

"I'm not sure that's how it works..." he said turning to me.

I gasped at his smile. He looked so peaceful, blissful. His eyes danced down me, taking me in like he was seeing me for the first time. His grip on my wrist tightened almost to the point of pain. Storm clouds raced across his beautiful face.

A new kind of rage, hot and stinging, burned through his aura like a back draft and filled the bathroom. This was danger. This was the alpha rage I was taught to fear. He flicked on another light and turned my body.

"Who did this..." His voice was sharp like shattered mirrors, "what happened here?"

LUTHER

Real fear and panic doused her. She broke from my grip and fumbled for the shirt on the ground, frantic motions to get it back on. She stepped into the boxers and retreated into the bedroom, not turning her back on me. She didn't break my grip to save herself. But to cover herself, to hide what had been done to her.

I grabbed her upper arm and turned her toward me.

"Tell me."

One single head shake.

A tap tap at the door, it eased open with a questioning, "Ruby? Are you up?"

She spun and put her body between me and the door, like a kid caught with a forbidden snack. Jackson poked his head in. His devastatingly beautiful smile fading instantly when he saw me in her room.

He stepped all the way in, his posture aggressive.

"Everything OK here?" he asked, looking at me, not at her. I clamped down the bonds as best I could.

Ruby morphed into the pleasant and pleasing little salon girl Jackson had brought home. Ruin Winters. She became Ruin Winters right before our eyes.

"Oh, yes, everything's fine." Ruby's voice was full of sweet nothings.

"Luther?" He eyed me, not believing this for a second. Jackson was not dumb.

I took a breath to reply, my brain frying itself to come up with something, anything that would seem plausible. I had just attacked her hours ago, for god sakes. Jackson had to peel me off her.

"Luther was just apologizing. For earlier. The kitchen." Ruin… no, Ruby offered as sweet as can be.

Jackson eyed us both as he stepped fully into the room, a pink handbag hanging off his fingers. She had lied. To protect me?

"I, uh," Jackson, still eyes on me, stammered, "Talon and I have to head into the city early. But I forgot this last night. We stopped by the house. There may be some water damage. I'm sorry about that." He held out her bag and pulled a phone from his pocket.

"Oh." Ruby took a step forward with a glance over her shoulder at me.

She took the phone and the bag and peeled it open, inspecting the contents. Nervously, she tucked a lock of hair behind her ear, and tried to look interested in her bag.

"Do you want to come have coffee before we go?" Jackson said, his eyes still on me.

"I, uh, think I'll take a shower first."

"Luther?"

"I need a shower too. I went for a run."

I stepped by them and out into the hall.

"Luther?" My name on her lips stopped me at the door. I couldn't turn back to look at her. "Thank you."

I squeezed my eyes shut and stepped into my room across the hall. All the lights were blazing and it still felt too dark.

Fuck.

What had I just done?

Jackson could never know.

He couldn't know that she was Ruin Winters. Jackson's worldview was very black and white. Once you went bad, that was it. You deserved what you got. Since joining the pack, I'd cringed at every cut he made about rogues. He'd toe the line about eliminating the threat they posed to society. I had become immune to it.

When Jackson found out she was Ruin…

I stalled out at the foot of my bed. I rubbed my side. I still had bruises. They were yellow now. A dull ache was still there.

Her bruises? Violent and purple. Recent. Some older ones had faded to that yellow green. She was covered in them. Her torso, stomach, upper arms. Old and new layered on top of each other. And a cut on her chest. Right above her heart. Still angry and red.

Someone put marks on her body. My mate's body.

THIRTY-TWO

RUBY

"Come have coffee." Jackson beamed and tugged at the sleeve of my shirt.

I moved my bag to my elbow, like it could shield me from what I'd just done. "Let me shower first." I pulled out of his grasp.

"OK, be quick," he said with a wink. I caught the glare he shot at Luther's door before he closed mine.

I ran for the shower, stripping my clothes off on the way. I didn't even bother to wait for it to get hot. I sobbed as I scrubbed between my legs with the medicinal smelling soap. I cupped my pussy wanting to keep Luther inside me. But I couldn't. I couldn't have breakfast with Jackson and Talon knowing I was filled with Luther's cum.

I pushed my palm against my mound and another orgasm bubbled up. I tilted my head back in the spray. Sex was supposed to stop heat. That's what they'd told me.

My hands shook as I covered my mouth and scrambled out of the shower, soap bubbles still clinging to me.

Had it... had it all been a lie?

Sex wasn't supposed to be... that.

Sex with an alpha was dangerous. It could kill. It *did* kill omegas every day. That's what they'd said. That's what they'd told me, showed me.

That was...

Luther knew I was a terrorist. He had to know that the attack on the pack was my fault. He hated me, what I represented. What Ruin Winters represented. It was his job to hunt me, stop me, put an end to me.

But he... He said her name like he... I could even make myself *think* the word. But I felt it. I felt it in his... aura... that energy so sharp and clear around him... when he...

I felt... When he was inside me... I felt... I felt right, whole... I felt like me. Not Ruin, not Ruby. Me. It felt like he was giving a piece of me back. Like he'd been holding it for years and years.

Was everything a lie?

If sex, sex with an uncontrollable alpha, was that... amazing... what else was a lie?

I scrubbed my hair with a towel and threw on a clean t-shirt. I stepped into fresh underwear, cupping myself again, desperate to hold on to a piece of Luther.

I took some settling breaths and stepped out into the hall. I refused to even look at his door or I'd want to bust it down so he could have me again.

They were all in the kitchen. Cross, Talon and Jackson. Jackson's smile was radiant as he put a mug of coffee in front of an empty stool for me. I sat and crossed my legs, squeezing them tight.

Ruin not Ruby.

Ruin could drink coffee with a pack after fucking one of their brothers. Ruby would never do such a thing. I looked at Talon and froze.

Don't fuck with my pack.

Ruin not Ruby.

I kept saying it over and over in my head to push away the panic.

CROSS

Jackson placed a waffle on her plate with a smear of butter and a puddle of syrup. They were the good ones. The fluffy, crispy ones made for dessert, not breakfast.

Luther ambled into the kitchen. He must have just showered, his t-shirt was sticking to him. I eyed Ruby as she stiffened. Luther did basically attack her last night. But that was not the vibe I was getting off her. She crossed her legs again, and twirled her fingertip along the rim of her coffee cup. I frowned. Her body language was not matching up. I breathed her in. Her scent was rich and deep behind the artificial soap scents.

We'd have to get her to use unscented soap when she joined…

Fuck.

She was not joining the pack. She was not ours. We were not having an omega.

Luther picked up the box of waffles and grimaced, looking over at Ruby's plate. It was the last waffle. He tossed it in the trash and got out flour, powdered buttermilk, eggs and the big ceramic bowl.

"Good pancakes or bad pancakes?" Jackson whispered to me in a loud stage whisper.

"Undetermined." I said.

"Luther only makes pancakes," Jackson explained to Ruby, "when he's super pissed off, or when he's really happy, like after sex."

Ruby choked on her coffee, splashing some on the counter. Luther squeezed the egg he was holding, it shattered, raw egg goo oozing everywhere. Jackson couldn't stop laughing as he mopped up the coffee spill with a napkin.

"You know what, fine, you motherfuckers can make your own god damn breakfast." He swiped at the egg mess with a dish towel and put the ingredients he just took out away.

"Luther! Language!" Jackson clutched his pearls at me.

"That," he flung a finger at Ruby, "is not a delicate flower that has never heard the word motherfucker before."

"Fuck you, I'm a fucking lady." Ruby spat with honey and sweetness in her tone.

I snorted, couldn't help it. Jackson cracked up. The only one not finding the humor was Talon. I bet he giggled on the inside, though.

"Aww see, she's going to fit right in. "Fuck you" is our love language."

"Fuck you, Jackson," Luther said, pissed off, turning to pull leftovers out of the fridge.

"Fuck you, too, baby." He said like he was talking to a lover.

"Cross, what are you doing about the satellite?" Talon said, being the adult in the room.

"I need some parts. I'm hoping it's just a frayed wire."

"I'm going to see if I can catch up with Leighton," Jackson interjected, drawing a finger through the syrup on Ruby's plate and sucked his finger with a sexy grin. I rolled my eyes.

"Leighton Winston? This isn't a public relations problem she can solve." I muttered.

"True, but all of our contacts in the Gritch have failed. Maybe we're going about this wrong. Maybe high society has the answers we need. She and her contacts have their fingers in all the behind the scenes dirt."

Luther and I both gave Jackson a heavy dose of side eye.

"You're... You're going to go see her alone?" I asked delicately.

"Of course. Talon is going to go meet with the Greyson pack.

Duo sent them to the house right after we bugged out. They might have seen something we missed."

"Do you think that's wise?"

"What do you mean?"

"Leighton is the only woman in this city who is not, uh... susceptible to your charms. It makes you, uh, try harder." Luther said.

That was a fucking understatement. A year or two ago, Jackson had spent months throwing himself at Leighton. There was an embarrassing incident at a picnic hosted by his birth pack where Jackson practically groveled on his knees.

"Leighton is a female alpha. It's not my fault that makes her the second most desirable thing in this city." Jackson flashed us two fingers for emphasis.

"What's the first?" Ruby asked in a small voice, like she didn't really mean to say it out loud.

"You." Jackson ripped off a corner of a waffle and popped it in his mouth, managing to make the act of chewing downright seductive. Ruby blushed and ducked her head, crossing her legs again.

Talon leveled concerned looks at both Luther and Jackson, like he didn't know which one was going to fuck up worse today.

"Can Luther go get parts for the satellite?" Talon asked.

"Not really. I'm not 100% sure what I need. It was a custom install, so I'm going to have to find a solution on the fly. Also, that report you asked for? It was sealed so I'm waiting on a call from Duo to see if he can get it for you."

Luther quietly fumed, red in the face. His scent was vivid this morning, despite the shower. He was getting the subtext of Talon's question, or at least part of it. After the blowup in the kitchen last night, no one was keen on leaving Ruby alone with him. Not that we thought he'd hurt her, but well, his aura was unpredictable.

"I've got vehicle maintenance to do. I'm sure your princess

can entertain herself for the day." He said around a bite of leftover pasta, answering the unasked question.

Jackson made a show of snapping out his wrist to look at his watch. "It's not even 8am and someone needs a nap already."

"C'mere," he said, putting down the bowl, "say that again, you little slut. Let *me* pop *you* in the mouth this time."

Jackson leaned over the counter and bit his lip. "You know how I like it rough."

"Are you two going to do the fight or fuck thing now, too? I thought you settled that years ago." I moved Jackson's coffee out of the way, unsure if he would launch himself across the kitchen.

"If at first you don't succeed..." Jackson winked.

"Jesus Christ," Talon groaned with an eye roll and stalked out of the room.

"Is this normal breakfast conversation?" Ruby said, dragging her fork through a puddle of syrup. Waffles still uneaten.

"Ha!" Talon barked from down the hall.

"So, uh," Ruby's hesitant voice sucked all the playfulness out of the room, "this has been an interesting vacation, but I do need to go home."

"Back to Maypole?" Luther asked with an odd tone in his voice, making the word circle around my head.

"No, I have a place in the city. But, I... have a life to get back to."

Dismay and shock fluttered through the pack bonds originating from Jackson. The sassy smirk remained on his face, but his emotions told another story. I didn't think it had occurred to him that she might want to leave.

"Ruby, we need to get a better handle on the situation to know where the danger lies. It's doubtful whoever attacked us knows who you are, but we need to make sure you're safe."

Talon was back with their jackets and a go bag. He slid his arms into the leather coat, a critical eye roaming over Ruby.

"You should eat," he said softly. She immediately cut a perfect waffle square and put it in her mouth. "You good?" He jutted his chin in Luther's direction.

"Peachy," he said, pulling pasta out of the microwave with a dishtowel. He sauntered down the hall to his room. We all stared at him. Luther hated eating anywhere except at a dining table.

RUBY

They all filed out of the kitchen, leaving me with waffles I couldn't eat. I blew out a strained breath.

I stared at my waffle. It had gone soggy in all the syrup. The sweetness clung to my tongue, making it hard to swallow. *Right, that's a good lie, Ruby. "It's too sweet" rather than you're going to die any second.*

I heard the door open again, panicking, I stuffed the whole plate in the trash, and spun around with my sticky fingers behind my back.

Jackson prowled back in, looking at me like I was the sweet thing he wanted to dip his fingers in. He slid a hand around to the small of my back and cupped my face with the other. Desire flashed through me, stealing all the air in the room.

"I wanted to take your scent with me." He closed his eyes in bliss. He pressed his lips lightly to my forehead and then pulled away. I grasped the edge of the sink as he dragged his hands from me, lightning sparking beneath his fingers. I bit my lip to keep a moan in.

He held a sticky note and swiped it to the fridge with a careful finger.

"Our cell numbers, if you need us."

He turned and groaned on his way out. "I have to go before I'm never able to leave again."

I ran the water, rinsing my sticky fingers and splashing water to cool my face.

I had to leave before *I* was never able to.

THIRTY-THREE

JACKSON

"Jackson." Talon's voice was soft. It was his 'I have bad news' voice. "We have to take her home."

I rounded on Talon like frogs jumped out of his mouth. The sound of the wipers, squeaking at top speed, the only sound in the car.

"No, we don't."

"She's asked to go home more than once. We are getting really close to the kidnapping line."

"It's been a traumatic few days. She doesn't know what she wants."

"That's the point, isn't it?"

I unclicked my seat belt and turned toward him. "She's our mate. You can't just send her away and pretend like that's not a fact." Ruby was ours.

"Scent match or not, she still gets a choice in all this."

"You just don't like change." I traced a raindrop as it raced down the window. I didn't need to look at Tal to know what he was feeling.

"This isn't the same as you hunting me when you were sixteen."

The tires screamed as he pulled us over, just before the turnoff to the cabin. He curled his fingers around my neck to make sure he had my attention.

He didn't understand. He had never understood. The second I'd met Talon, I'd known I was his.

My aura had presented when I was fourteen. By sixteen, I was one of the most eligible alphas in the city. The pack dads entertained inquiries every day from packs looking to court me. My mom, Mary Ellen, and the other omega moms in my birth pack spent hours with pack registries shopping for the most perfect potential mate. I wasn't interested in all their plans. I was too busy sticking my dick in anything that moved.

Most people looked past the fact that I was technically, legally, a minor, including my own parents. The fact that I was an Albright alpha was what mattered. The dads set me up on my first date with a duchess that year. Duchesses were omegas who walked away from Princess bond, elevating them in society. This made them desirable and worth every penny for the privilege of spending time with them. They even negotiated a consensual sex clause in that contract. And thank god for that. The duchess Sparkle took extreme delight in teaching me exactly what an omega wanted.

The only person who had a problem with my age was Talon.

We were at a ball. My mother was parading me about, showing me off and salivating over my potential. Talon had just joined the GPRE and was working security. He was dressed all in black, looking mean and deadly. I was already bored. Not just of the ball and the line that had formed at our table of interested parties desperate for my attention. I was bored with high society, the rules, the etiquette.

Talon stood behind our table and watched me, rather than his job for the night. I felt his eyes all over me, scorching touches that no one else knew about. Every sweeping glance he stole made me hard. I broke away from the social scheming at the table and darted down an employee-only hallway. He followed. To make sure I was safe, he said. I grabbed his hand and put it on my cock saying 'this is what you do to me.' He grabbed me by the throat, 'You're far too young, Mr. Albright,' he said, stroking my cock through my pants, 'find me in four years when I can properly make a mess of you'. He left me on the edge of coming. No one had ever denied me anything before.

I rearranged my entire life to have him, worked hard and waited four painful years. I became the best. Bent all the rules. I bribed a professor, poisoned people, I even used the pack dads and all their influence to get me to the top of the class. All just so I could have Talon.

That was nothing compared to what I'd do for my omega.

"Did you forget someone tried to kill us? She's part of that now. We can't send her home with no protection." This was the only line of attack that might get through his head right now.

"Exactly. She's safer without us. She will always be in danger with us."

"Are you saying we're not enough to protect her? Our mate?"

"I'm saying we shouldn't have to."

"Whatever. We can't send her back to her apartment alone."

"We'll put her up in a safe house until the threat is neutralized."

"No." I leaned into his hand around my throat until he broke contact and sat back.

"What she wants doesn't matter?"

"Talon. She's our mate. What part of that don't you understand?"

"The part where consent comes into play. She gets a choice in this. We all get a choice. And my choice is no right now."

"Ah, *right now,*" heat flared in my gut.

I had him. He didn't want a mate, but he did. He wanted this as much as I did. I could feel it. I grinned and bit my lip. It was a challenge now, and I'd win, just like I won him all those years ago.

Sometimes I thought Talon was fundamentally impatient. If he couldn't see a successful outcome in a reasonable timeframe, it wasn't a game he would want to play.

"I am not asking her to join this pack."

"You're afraid she's going to say no." Was he getting closer to rut? He always got super fucking cranky. "No. You're afraid she's going to say yes. Aren't you?"

"We can't have something that delicate in our lives." He said through gritted teeth.

He said 'we', but he meant 'I'.

I knew Talon was haunted by the omegas in his past. He blamed himself for Melodie's breakdown. Guilt ate at him every day about Havoc. There were countless omegas that we had pulled out of terrible situations, and Talon blamed himself for every single happily ever after that would never happen.

But this was different. Ruby was ours. We'd make it different.

Talon rubbed the heels of his palms into his eyes. He couldn't rub out the truth, though. She was ours. He wanted her. He just didn't think he could have good things.

High beams flashed behind us. Cross had caught up, his truck making a comforting rumble behind us.

"We have to let her go, Jacks."

The fuck we did.

I popped the door open. "I'm riding back with Cross. You can enjoy your denial all by yourself."

I was drenched to the bone in the short distance between the cars.

I slammed the passenger door shut, shaking out excess water from my hair and jacket. Sniffing to bring in Cross' biting booze scent, I cracked my neck. I needed a moment to let go of the angry frustration. We would be back at the cabin in a couple of minutes, and I didn't want to drag this with me.

"I see we chose fighting over fucking today," Cross said, his tone unreadable. And of course, the selfish bastard had the bonds on lockdown, so I got nothing from him.

"Fine, asshole. You pick one. Fight, fuck or drive."

Cross chuckled. Talon pulled back onto the road and Cross followed.

RUBY

57 messages.

My cell phone lay face down next to me. I had found a charger for it. I powered it on, saw the message count from Bennett and was too afraid to touch it again.

I lay on the bathroom floor, my feet in the linen closet. Luther was working outside all day. I could see him out the kitchen window, working on cars and dirt bikes. He'd popped his head in a while ago to tell me he was going for a run, and I should stay in the house. Like, where was I going to go?

I was hiding inside a blue hoodie I found in the laundry room. It smelled like Cross. He was the safe one right now. Anything to push away Jackson's scent. Luther's scent. They both were things I could never have. Things that would be destroyed when the monsters crawled out of those 57 messages and killed us all.

I pressed my cheek into the tile, the phone inches from my face. My hand crept towards it. I snatched it back and tucked both between my thighs like a kid told to keep their hands to themselves. I ached to be filled again.

I want your scent all over me.

Good girl.

Darlin'.

Ruin.

Their scents lingered on my skin like touches. I eased my finger behind the fabric of my panties. I was drenched in slick. I had been all day. I nuzzled into Cross' hoodie. I needed their scents in me. I needed them in me. I slid in two fingers and groaned in frustration. It wasn't enough. It was never enough. Fire flashed through my body. I swiped my tongue across my lips and shivered. Sweat broke out on my forehead. It jolted me upright. Disoriented, I tried to stand too fast, one hand slippery on the tile.

My heart pounded. Was this heat?

I jerked my foot back when I stepped on my phone. If I broke it, they would...

I had to get a grip. I had to get myself under control and think logically. I had to think like Ruin.

The Reset would come for me and they would hurt the pack. I had to figure out how to get back to them. Pretend I escaped. Do whatever I had to so they would be safe. I paced the small bathroom, ticking off options on my fingers.

I could walk out of here. I had my phone now, I had GPS so I wouldn't get lost.

I stopped short.

I would need shoes.

Nodding to myself, I crept out into the living room. The mudroom had all sorts of things. Sleeping bags, extra phone chargers. It was like a mini garage. Maybe there were shoes in there?

A knock at the door made my heart leap. A huge smile spread across my face as I bolted across the room. He was back.

My hand froze, reaching for the knob.

Luther would not be knocking on his own front door.

The pack didn't use this door. They used the back one. The one that led right into the laundry room.

They kept a shotgun by the front door. Cross said it was for bears. I raced back to my room for the handgun, stuffing that in the waistband of my jeans.

Another pounding knock came. More urgent.

I held the shotgun at chest height and let it lead the way.

A tall, thin man whirled on me. He had on a light jacket and jeans. His hair was cropped close to his head. He looked tired, like too many late nights had caught up with him. He held a yellow envelope, tapping his fingers on it. He stopped dead with the muzzle inches from his chest.

"Who the fuck are you?" we both said at the same time.

"You first." I said.

"Fuck you."

I took a step forward with the gun, eating up the space between us, forcing him back. He looked behind him. He was rapidly losing space on the porch. He had a foot until the steps.

"Who are you?" I asked again, hiking the gun up so he'd get the point.

"Where's Talon?"

I took another step forward, forcing him down the stairs. He made the smart move and backed all the way down the steps. I followed until we were both standing on the field that spread out in front of the cabin.

He did a double take like he just realized something.

"You're an omega." There was a touch of wonder in his voice.

A raindrop splashed on my cheek, droplets of water clinging to my lashes. He looked up at the sky, like that would be the determining factor in this standoff.

"I work with Talon. He asked me to come up."

I didn't believe him. I didn't know everyone in the Reset. Berry Creek was small, but new people were always being brought by, especially to gawk at the omega in the kennel.

The tracker. It must still be working. They'll all come.

"This is bullshit." He took a few overconfident steps forward. I cocked the shotgun and fired off into the field, the recoil rocking my body back until I took up a better stance. He backed up again.

He attempted to dodge left. I fired again.

I pulled the handgun from my waistband and trained that on him, I wedged the shotgun under my arm and pulled cartridges from my pocket to reload.

The man was fascinated with every movement, like he'd never seen a gun before.

The rain started coming down in earnest now.

"Can we just…"

A growl burst from my chest that silenced him.

He looked up at the sky, like that alone would stop the rain. Wiping water from his face, he looked around for something to solve the problem of an armed omega between him and my pack.

"Can we at least get out of the rain and move to the porch?"

He was not touching this house. He looked down at the rain-stained envelope in his hand before zipping it up inside his jacket.

As the minutes bled together, he got increasingly uncomfortable. Rain was too much for his delicate soul. I'd stand here until I died to protect my pack.

TALON

The dirt road to the cabin was a mess. We should just pave it this year. I didn't want to hear Jackson complain about how dirty his sports car got driving up here. It was a safety issue, too. If it iced over next winter, four-wheel drive might not be enough. And I didn't know how well Ruby could handle a car in icy conditions.

"Fuck." I hit my fist on the steering wheel. God damn you, Jackson. I was already making future plans for a woman I didn't want in my house.

Rounding the last bend, I saw Duo's car parked in his spot by the front door. He didn't come up to the cabin often. That was a bad sign. We didn't fully trust the GPRE to not put illegal wiretaps on their employees' phones. So, if Duo was here, there was bad shit happening.

I squinted through the rain. The wipers were not quite keeping up. That, or I was hallucinating. I wasn't understanding what I was seeing. A cactus with bunny ears would make more sense than this.

I parked next to Duo, not behind the house as usual. Jackson met me at the bumper. He was jiggling his keys in his hand. It was an unusual show of nerves for him. Cross joined us.

Obviously, none of us grasped what was happening right in front of us.

There were two omegas having an armed standoff in the pouring rain on our front lawn.

"Ruby?" I said, stepping closer to them.

"Is she growling?" Cross said, a hint of pride in his voice. Sure enough, there was a sub-audible vibration in the air.

She was soaked to the bone. The blue hoodie acted like a sponge, water dripping off at the elbows and cuffs.

Duo was shaking. Not from fear, but from cold. It was still chilly for spring.

"How long have they been out here?" I asked no one in particular.

"OK. Let's take this inside." Jackson said, taking command. The snarl from Ruby buzzed in my ears.

Duo took a step toward Jackson.

A shotgun blast burst through the air. We all froze.

Cross made a movement but thought better of it.

"So, what do we do now?" asked Jackson. Ruby obviously knew her way around a shotgun.

"Well, she's only got one shot left." I looked at Cross. True, but what were we going to do? Tackle our omega to the ground to disarm her? And where the fuck was Luther?

"Oh, don't worry, that bitch can reload one handed." Duo added unhelpfully.

An ungodly sound rippled out of Cross that had the hairs on the back of my neck at attention. We needed to bring this all down a notch.

I pushed at Ruby with my aura. Not quite an alpha bark which would compel her, like any omega, to obey. But instead, I wrapped her in the certainty that what I wanted was what she wanted. I watched her eyes flutter, like when I called her a good girl.

I approached her slowly, not like the danger she was, but like a feast, deciding where to sink my teeth in first. When I was at her side, I covered her hands on the weapon with my own, and put my other hand to the back of her neck.

She tilted her face toward me but did not break eye contact with Duo.

I dug my hands into her drenched hair, pulling with just enough pressure to get her attention. She blinked rapidly, taking little gasping breaths, like I had pressed her reset button and she was rebooting. She finally broke eye contact with Duo.

"Help," she said so softly I wouldn't have heard it if I wasn't drinking her in.

I tightened my grip on her hair. She leaned into my hand. Her growl became the slightest of moans.

Touch starved, needy, pushed to a physical extreme from the cold. Her natural submissiveness had her melting in my hands. I tugged on the gun until she obeyed and released her grip.

Jackson ushered Duo into the cabin and out of the rain.

I knew I should do the same with Ruby. Get her warm, cozy, feed her hot chocolate and whipped cream. But having her here, practically inside my aura, so responsive, receptive, waiting, needing dominant control, needing... me. We hung in this silent moment for an eternity.

She was truly beautiful.

There was a soft touch on my elbow. Cross' voice low in my ear.

"She's cold."

I nodded slowly, trying to come back to earth. I slid my fingers out of her hair to the back of her neck. I moved my hand to her back, shocked to find a handgun in her waistband. I pulled up the soggy hoodie to take it from her. With gentle pressure, I got her moving toward the stairs. I couldn't break contact with her. Not yet.

Cross closed the door behind us. In the living room, she turned into me, pressing her whole body against me. She was cold, soaked. Her lips had a faint blue tinge.

"Who the fuck is the omega?" Duo said, clattering down the stairs with Jackson. Duo was wearing a pair of Jackson's sweats. He was just a bit shorter than Jackson and thinner. Drips of water fell from the laundry basket Jackson hauled down with them.

Ruby turned at the sound of his voice, giving Duo a critical up and down look. And then she launched herself at him with a sharp growl.

Cross caught her by the waist. Duo back peddled. Jackson's head ping ponged between the two omegas.

"OK. I think we need some space here. I'm going to put Ruby in the bath."

Ruby caught herself like she'd snapped out of a trance and didn't know where she was. She looked down at her dirty bare feet and danced back a step, like muddy toes and puddles on the hardwood were a capital crime.

"I'm sorry," came out in a rush.

CROSS

Gentle. Gentle. She's fragile like eggshells.

I didn't even touch her. My hand just hovered over her back as I ushered her down the hall. I twisted the doorknob to her room open with the lightest touch possible. I couldn't touch her, I'd be too rough. I was too close to some feral part of myself.

Don't even look at the pristine bed.

My instincts and aura were surging. Too much conflicting energy was flowing through me right now. I wasn't sure I knew what my strength was. Just like when your aura presents for the first time. You have access to all this power, and you have to relearn how to move through the world.

I stepped past Ruby into the bath, flicking off one of the overhead lights. With all the white glossy tile, it was way too bright. I cranked the hot water knob, leaving the cold untouched. The only downside to the cabin was it took forever for hot water to reach the tap.

Bubbles? Would bubbles be soothing right now?

We needed to pull Ruby back from whatever edge she was on.

I turned, my fingers reaching for the linen closet door. The door that wasn't there anymore. I pounded a fist into my forehead. I couldn't really pencil in a mental breakdown today. I turned my back on the closet, taking some shallow breaths to push away flashbacks to dead omegas.

Fuck the bubbles.

"Ruby, do you..." ducking out of the bath, I pulled up short. She was standing in the bedroom, a puddle forming at her feet, staring at the bed. I followed her gaze. It looked exactly the same as when I pulled the dust cover off it. That was wrong somehow, but I didn't have the extra mental energy to parse that.

"Hey," I said to get her attention, and continued when she

didn't acknowledge me, "You need to get out of wet clothes and warm up."

"What happened?" She looked confused, but more than that, she looked afraid.

I grasped the edge of her sleeve and gently pulled her into the bath. I balled my fists and stuck them in my pockets to resist the urge to help her out of the soaking sweatshirt.

"Cross?" she asked when I didn't respond.

She really had no clue. An omega who didn't know what it was like to be an omega?

Her face was chilling. Her brows were drawn together, a faint blue tint colored her lips. I wanted to take a step back. Fuck that, I wanted to run. I blew out a slow breath to give myself a moment to figure out how to say this.

"Omegas can be territorial just like alphas. You felt threatened. You acted accordingly."

She lifted a hand to wipe her face. It was covered by the wet sleeves of the sweatshirt. She seemed completely mystified by that.

"Do you…" No, you are not asking if she needs help. "Go ahead and adjust the water temperature and warm up in the bath for a while." I jutted my chin toward the bath to show her a direction to go.

She nodded. I stepped back and closed the door. I had to get the fuck out of this room that smelled like the ice cream man.

In the hall, I jammed my fingers in my hair and pulled hard. I had to sort through my emotions damn fast or I was going to break things. I paced the hall, forcing my breathing to be slow and even.

Fear.

She was the one with the gun, but she was so damn breakable. Duo had training. Not as strong as Luther. Not as good with a gun as Jackson. But he could hurt her. Everything could hurt her. I could hurt her. I would hurt her.

Failure.

What kind of fucking alpha puts their omega in a position where they had to defend themselves in the rain like that? I'd already failed as an alpha. Stella had died with her blood and pain everywhere. I'd failed her. And Roy, I'd failed him too, when I killed our pack lead and let Stella die.

I rested my forehead against the wall, my breath turned to pants.

I didn't even know what to call this emotion.

To see her... putting her body between the world and us... me. Unmoving, unbending, fierce and determined. "Proud" "hot", "sexy," "turn on," those words weren't primal enough. Her standing there with a gun on my front lawn... she reached right into my lizard brain, and put me in a choke hold, claiming me as her own. No woman had ever... loved... me enough to do that, take that kind of risk. No one had ever loved me enough... except... for Luther.

Luther didn't even know me the day he saved my life. The first time he saved my life.

We were deep in the Gritch, masquerading as NOPD on a raid for a rogue who blew his aura and was on a killing spree. Jackson had taken a bullet to the thigh, his expert aim hampered by blood loss, pain, running low on ammo. I had a punctured lung, lying useless on my back, just concentrating on gurgling sips of air, choking on blood. Luther had stood over us and, with the force of his aura alone, kept us safe until Talon could pull us out.

The water cut off, the sudden silence bringing the murmurs from the kitchen to me. I refused to look back at Ruby's door.

I scraped my damp hair back and put it back up with the elastic. Certainty settled about me as I rejoined my brothers in the kitchen.

Fear had won.

I couldn't lose someone else. I couldn't have Ruby in my life. I would fail her. Like I failed my first pack, Stella, my first scent matched omega. She would die because of me, and that would take everyone else I loved. Again.

I shut down the pack bonds and stepped back into the kitchen.

THIRTY-FOUR

RUBY

My pack.

They weren't my pack.

The lesson, carefully copied, over and over, a million and one times, spooled out in my head.

Auras are an unnatural construct, an abomination, reinforced by illicit drugs, corrupt spiritual practices, propaganda, by a ruling elite seeking to solidify power and control in an unending class struggle. The notion of inherent instincts masks aggression on the part of "alphas," and weak-mindedness on the part of "omegas." These fabricated instances are indoctrinated by means of tradition, culture, and practices such as the indulgent and narcissistic impulse of "nesting" and pack formation. These instincts do not exist and must be stamped out and eradicated for society, the wholesome and pure aspects of society, to prosper and survive.

. . .

I could see the words just appear on a page in my mind.

I stared at the water filling the tub. I shut the tap off, unsure about what to do.

I wasn't allowed a bath. Not since I perfumed.

I wedged the little wooden chair under the door handle. I was old enough to bathe unsupervised, but none of the doors had locks on them. It wouldn't keep people out, not really, but would stop someone coming in by mistake.

I was too hot, too clammy. The Morganstern's, two properties over, paid me $50 to muck out their kennels. It was hot, and I was filthy.

I had to scrub out the tub before I could get in. I had already peeled my t-shirt and jeans off while I waited for the tub to fill and then kneeled next to the tub, trailing my fingers in the water.

My skin was too sensitive. Anything that brushed against it burned or tingled.

I splashed cool water on my face. I rested my cheek on the tile and squeezed my eyes shut. I knew it was wrong. But I couldn't help it, I couldn't keep my mind from wandering.

I climbed into the tub before it was full and let the water rush around my skin, hoping that would bring relief. It didn't. It just felt like a million fingertips on me.

I had asked him to go slower, to be softer. He'd said he was too excited, nervous. His hands were rough on my breasts. It felt good, but I knew it would feel better if he slowed down.

Bennett had said he wanted to wait, wait until we were married, but we could still do stuff.

I shot a glance at the door. The chair was still in place.

I'd sat on his lap in the car, my knees straddling him. He'd had his pants open. I'd stroked him with one hand for a while. I'd pulled his hand between my legs while his other hand dug around in my shirt.

I closed my eyes and slid my hand between my legs, to that place you weren't supposed to touch or even speak about.

I lazily stroked the hard bit of flesh until lazy wasn't good enough anymore. I bit my bottom lip to keep in the sounds that were desperate to be free.

I adjusted the tap with my toe, turning off the hot water completely. I felt like I was boiling.

Bennett had said just the tip, that's all good girls were supposed to do. But I wanted more, needed more.

I slid two fingers inside myself and I couldn't hold back the groan. Not even this was enough.

I knew what an orgasm was. We all giggled and were scandalized over videos downloaded onto phones we weren't supposed to have.

Bennett had never given me an orgasm. I was on my third when the door burst open.

Mama Pauline stood over me. She was more prison guard than foster mother. Her eyes were wild, panicked. Terrified.

"What have you done, you stupid fucking whore?"

I shrank back. Touching yourself was #27 on the rules list.

"Don't you smell it?"

I covered my breasts and sank down into the water, turning to my side.

She grabbed me by the hair and pushed my head under the water. I was stronger. Bigger. I fought back.

It would be the last time I fought for a long while.

Exhausted and soaked, she fell back on her ass and shook her head at me.

"Oh girl, you're gonna wish you let me kill you."

She was right.

.   .   .

I climbed into the tub with all my clothes on. I should have let just the cold water run this time, too. I was hot all over, even after standing out in the rain.

I'd just had sex with Luther. That was supposed to stop heat. It always had in the past. I rubbed my eyes. I forced myself not to think about Luther sliding more than just the tip in me and how it made me feel right.

I flopped my arms back into the water, some splashing out of the tub. I didn't understand what was happening. All these new feelings were flooding me.

It used to be simple. My life used to be simple. I knew what to expect. I knew what was going to happen every day. I knew what Bennett and Billy and all the rest wanted.

I stood up in the tub to struggle out of the wet sweatshirt. It was heavy, and it stuck to me. It made a wet thud when I finally managed to tug it and the t-shirt off in one go. The water fought me as I struggled to get my legs out of the jeans. Hobbled with the fabric caught around my knees, I swung my legs out of the tub to kick and wrestle them down.

Averting my eyes from that cozy space Cross told me I couldn't be in, I grabbed a towel, dark blue and thick, to wrap around myself.

I collapsed on the edge of the tub. I didn't know what was real anymore. I shot my eyes back at the linen closet. Nests, packs, all of this. It wasn't supposed to be real.

It felt real.

When that man tried to step into this house, that felt real. The anger felt real. Why? My head sunk into my hands, the confusion making it too heavy, like the wet hoodie.

If all these instincts were just propaganda, how could it feel so real?

Walking limply into the bedroom, I pulled on a t-shirt and the boxers from the other night. I wanted to pace around, pound my fists into my brain until this all made sense.

I looked at the door and all that lurked on the other side. I was probably in trouble. Whoever that was, Jackson had given him clothes, so he was probably important to them. And I had shot at him. Not once. Three times.

Fuck. I was screwed. What would be the corrective action for this misstep?

I pulled the door closed softly behind me, the deep rumbling voice drawing me down the hall.

THIRTY-FIVE

TALON

I gripped the edge of the counter, trying to bring myself down. My head snapped up when Cross disappeared from my awareness entirely. Out of the corner of my eye, Luther's knee gave out like someone ripped the rug out from under us. He had been out for a run. Jackson quickly filled him in and surprisingly did not rip into him for leaving Ruby alone. Probably because when Cross closed up like that, it threw us all off.

It was like that with Cross. He gave us crumbs of himself, always holding back. I had asked him once, about a year after we formed the pack, before Luther. He laughed it off, saying Jackson felt enough for all of us.

Luther was the most unsettling of all. His aura was always like tinfoil on teeth. After he was pack for a few years, it stabilized, as best it could. Pack bonds could anchor you like that. Jackson and Cross totally believe the abused childhood story. Because it wasn't untrue.

They could even believe that Luther's increased instability over the past few months was due to Havoc.

Duo and I had been a little too successful in hiding Luther's identity. We faked paperwork, bribed people, anything we had to in order to create the paper trail, confirming he was registered as an alpha, got his ID and then was orphaned and was on the streets. The pack thought we were hiding his connection to Lhevus Saint, a known extremist. That was true, and it was great cover for the rogue thing.

The day I got the mission brief, I almost lost consciousness.

Nothing in life prepares you to go tell your brother, a person who is part of you, who lives in your brain, in your soul, that you have to go kill his father and sell his sister into slavery.

The Gold Pack and Rogue Enforcement Agency's official mission statement was to police, regulate and control registered rogues and gold pack omegas. Its unofficial mission was to eliminate threats to the Institute and society at large.

Lhevus Saint had been straining the patience of the Institute for decades. He had his fingers in every illicit trade imaginable. Illegal research in aura development. Medical experimentation on omegas. He didn't actively participate, but collected information and connected people. Depending on where you stood politically, he was either a hero or a terrorist. He believed that our natural state was rogue and gold pack and all the fuckery the Institute got up to, the omega injection, the training, the pack bonding ceremonies and registries were an affront to nature itself. There were far too many people who agreed with that. And that kind of rebellious thinking could be allowed only so far.

When closer ties between Saint and the Reset began to surface, the decision was made not to let that progress.

My pack, one of the ranking strike forces, with countless missions to capture or kill rogues, was assigned the task of the extrajudicial execution of Lhevus Saint. We were then to take his daughter, Havoc, into custody and deliver her to a prison. She hadn't done anything wrong, so there would be no trial. They weren't incarcerating her. They were *volunteering* her to serve as a rut helper for the dangerous alphas they couldn't be bothered to kill. That was, if someone didn't outright buy her so they could dark bond her.

Duo and I knew we had one shot at altering that course and saving Havoc's life, saving Luther's life in the process. He would not have survived Havoc's sentence. In the chaos and confusion of the order being issued, we put out back-channel chatter that made it known an investor in Gavin's Treasures, which was basically a fucking brothel, was owed a debt and that debt would be settled with Havoc.

No one would question it at face value. "Investor in Gavin's" was universally known to be Kingsman pack. Kingsman was one of the families that ran the Institute, the GPRE, all of the city of New Oxford. If anyone looked closely, asked the right questions... that trail would lead right to Luther, an unregistered rogue, foster son of an executed terrorist. We'd find a GPRE strike force at our door. And Havoc? There were worse things than being dark bonded if the Institute wanted to make an example of you.

And Luther had to pay the price of never seeing his sister again. The shock and the emotional damage made him and his aura too unstable. He couldn't risk having it known that GPRE agents were losing their shit to get to Havoc. All the wrong people would start asking all the right questions. If he saw her even once, it would cause her death, or worse. If a connection was made between them, you wouldn't have to be a rocket scientist to connect the dots.

We'd made Havoc's older brother disappear. But we could not erase the knowledge that Havoc had an older brother.

And I fucking did that.

I broke Luther.

I caused the tear in his aura.

I killed his father. The double tap came from my gun. Some members of the GPRE like to play with their food first. Not me.

I'd put Havoc in the back of a van. I had expected her to scream and struggle. She didn't. She wasn't calm, not exactly, but fury and resignation had turned her to stone.

I broke Luther, and I destroyed his sister.

Then I demanded that he never see her again. I fucked around with so much, put so much on the line to make sure she didn't get auctioned off or put in a prison as a rut helper for serial killers.

It wasn't just about my pack and hers. They'd find everything we'd been doing. All the omegas we'd hidden, rogues we'd relocated. People we'd killed because that was the lesser evil. Luther and Havoc were the weakest links to having it all crash down.

And then the GPRE would make an example of us.

I'd made a choice, knowing all the risks. I'd walked Havoc into a brothel that day.

It was the best option she had. It was the only option she had.

I knew the guilt of that would put me into the grave early.

After all that, Luther still loved me. He cried and fucking thanked me for it.

And right now, his aura was intense, but cool, calm, determined. Like it knew itself and had purpose.

"OK. I don't have a lot of time now after that fucking stunt." Duo broke into my wallowing guilt, his omega aura sharp with anger. "First , Treyfor is hot for you."

"Who the fuck is Treyfor?" Luther asked.

"NOPD commander. Lead on the warehouse incident."

"Treyfor? What's his first name?" Jackson asked.

"No clue."

"Huh, I saw Vex the other day. She fed me some nonsense about NOPD, shaking her down for GPRE dirt. Said the name was Ray or something."

I snorted. "Watch this be the one time we pay her for information and the information actually turns out to be good."

"But what the fuck did we do to get NOPD's panties in a bunch?" Luther asked.

"You let the warehouse blow up."

"Are you shitting me?" I narrowed my eyes at Duo.

"Jurisdiction."

"We didn't have jurisdiction." Jackson jumped up to sit on one of the counters. An odd move for him. He was always in motion, all kinetic energy all the time. He was in overload too, if he had to nail himself to one spot to process all the bullshit.

"GPRE out ranks NOPD, so he's trying to run that failure as your fault."

"A warehouse blew up. That's no big loss." Luther shrugged.

"Are you kidding? The pack lead of every elite pack in the city now has hysterical omegas losing their haute couture clad minds. I can guarantee you no one is getting any sleep, no one is getting laid in their pack beds right now."

We all went silent, taking that in for a minute.

It was times like this that I solidified my opinion that Jackson is an alien from another universe. He grew up in an influential pack, rich, loved.

I grew up with a junkie for a mom and an alcoholic for a dad.

"What?" Cross asked, as mystified as I was.

"There's what, a dozen packs that run the city, right? Unofficially. Every one of their omegas has personally hot glued a fake flower onto one of those floats that Ruin Winters destroyed. You don't think they are going to be pissed off and spewing balls of omega rage everywhere? Their pack leads are going to be out there slaying dragons to make the pain stop."

"Fuck." Cross murmured.

"Yup." Jackson nodded, kicking his feet with soft bangs into the dishwasher door. "It was a fucking genius move by Ruin, if

279

you ask me. The fastest way to bring this all down is to fuck with the omegas."

I crossed my arms, pinching my bottom lip in thought.

"That brings me to the next point. We're going to have to cut Ruin Winters loose." Duo said.

"How do you mean?"

"I know we had hoped to get to her first. Convince her what the future will hold if she didn't shut the fuck up. Save her life. But that's off the table now."

Jackson hopped off the counter, running his hands through his hair, the tension finally getting to him.

"One more event," Duo continued, "and they are going to put a bounty on her head. She will be lucky if she's hunted by every psychopath in the city rather than being auctioned off."

The urge to duck hit me a millisecond before Luther's aura boiled over, the force of it making him stagger.

"I'm fine. Back the fuck up." Luther said to his knees when Cross got too close.

"So, it's now or never boys. You're going to have to make the decision if you want it to be your bullet or someone else's."

Luther slid down the fridge to put his head between his knees and breathed for a bit.

Duo looked at his watch. He still had an hour drive back into the city and it was a risk coming here. He knew that.

"So," he said, dusting off his hands, "go bite your omega, stick her in the Valkyrie for a few days. A heat hotel is the only place with good enough security. And go do your fucking job."

"She's not a prisoner or a thing" Luther said it so softly I might have imagined it.

Eerie quiet spread through the kitchen. Duo raked each of us with a searching look. Duo was an omega in an alpha world. He'd had to develop a good read on alphas auras just to survive.

"You dumb motherfuckers. You can't seriously be thinking of rejecting her? A scent match?"

Of course, Duo would have clocked her as a scent match. The way she'd defended the house, it would be the only thing that made sense.

It was now Duo's turn to stalk off some anger with a few laps around the kitchen. He stopped in the middle of the room and put his hands on his hips.

"OK, this is your come to Jesus moment. And I am not saying this as your best friend, but as your boss." He nailed me with a pointed finger. "And you," he rounded on Luther, "you keep your ass on the floor and your shit together."

"You are slowly disintegrating as a pack. It is going to get one of you killed. And no, this is not all about Luther, *Talon*." He said my name with emphasis so I would know what he was talking about. He didn't agree with me about keeping the rogue thing from Jackson and Cross, but it was my decision as pack lead.

"You," Duo tapped on Luther's foot, he didn't look up, sulking like a kid called to the principal's office, "none of this is your fault."

"Cross, you can't survive in a pack half in and half out. They don't deserve that."

Duo crossed his arms and stared me down. Now, I felt like I was waiting for the switch.

"Just say it, Duo."

"Rut." Duo spat out the word.

"The rut thing is fine…" The look on Duo's face said "bullshit".

"Dude, you put Jackson in the hospital last time."

"Minor dehydration. Two IVs and he was fine."

"You broke his pelvis."

"Hairline fracture." I pinched his fingers together to show him how itty bitty it was. "Besides, the little slut loves bragging about how he got fucked unconscious and couldn't walk for a week. Literally. "

"You took on pack lead. Lead or get the fuck out of the way."

I raised my head in defiance. Everything he said was true, and it didn't fucking matter.

"We are not taking on an omega."

"You sure about that? All of this," he nodded toward Luther specifically, "all goes away with an omega, a scent matched omega."

"No." Cross' voice was low but certain.

"Alright geniuses, what are you going to do if you force Jackson to choose between pack and an omega and he doesn't choose you?"

I snorted, Jackson would never... I flicked my eyes to him and my world fell apart.

He was leaning against the pantry door, hands in his pockets. He would not meet my eyes. For the first time since I made him mine... the first time in 10 years, ... Jackson shut down the pack bonds. He closed me out. Cut me off.

I blinked. There was no oxygen in this room. I couldn't get enough air.

"Sort your shit out or people are going to die."

I didn't even notice Duo leaving. None of us did. We were all trapped in our own personal hells.

I closed my eyes, feeling a fraction of myself. I was pack lead, but Jackson was the leader of this pack. It was his energy that made us whole. And now that it was gone, now that he took that away from me.

No. *She* took that away from me. She took Jackson away from me.

THIRTY-SIX

RUBY

"We're going to have to cut Ruin Winters loose."

I stopped mid step when I heard my name. Her name.

I was still in the hall. I could creep closer and no one would know. Eavesdropping was on the rules list, too. But that was a rule everyone broke.

"I know we had hoped to get to her first..." it was the stranger talking. I covered my mouth with both hands to keep a growl in.

I was growling? What the fuck was up with that?

"... they are going to put a bounty on her head..." A bounty? What did that mean?

"... hunted by every psychopath in the city..." my heart pounded so loud it was getting hard to hear.

"... you want it to be your bullet or someone else's."

They... they would kill Ruin. They would kill Ruin when they found out.

Silent feet took me back down the hall and behind the door.

I stood in front of the linen closet. An ache in my stomach doubled me over. I got on my knees, tucking my damp hair back.

My breathing got faster, harder. I winced when the ache sharpened. I pushed through and tucked myself in the closet.

Don't fucking do that again.

I swallowed down acid that was creeping up my throat. As soon as I was out of the closet, the pain lessened. It was true, you had to obey or it hurt. I looked at the closet, my hand covering my mouth to hold in a sob. I'd disobeyed Cross.

I didn't trust my legs. Crawling, being close to the ground, was safer. I looked up at the huge bed and squeezed my eyes shut. I curled into a ball and pushed myself half under the bed. Immediately, some of the jagged edges of my nerves softened.

I didn't understand this either. Why it made me feel... safe...

I reached up and slid the piece of paper out from between the slats of the bed. I unfolded it and smoothed out the creases.

I ran my fingers over the blues and greens, like I could touch Cross, touch them, through the marker and coloring page I stole on my first night here.

JACKSON

Cross and I stood opposite each other, holding up matching pantry doors. Cross had installed them himself when we remodeled a few years ago. I tilted my head up like I could see into the bedroom I shared with Talon.

I fucking loved that room. The slate gray walls, the huge walkin. And no furniture, like dressers, to clutter the space. Just a huge bed that cost more than Luther's bike. I huffed out a laugh, shaking my head at the realization.

This whole house was a nest. Built to be exactly what we wanted. A wincing frown squeezed my eyes shut. This house was what *I* wanted. I'd bullied them all into it. And I have zero regrets about that.

As the minutes ticked by, I wondered who would break first. I was struggling to keep the pack bonds on lock down. I had never bothered to get good at that skill. Not like Cross.

I looked over at the stoic asshole. Cross had a lot of muscle memory with biting back the things he wished he had said. The past nine years aged him well. He wasn't a scrawny street rat anymore.

I was surprised Luther hadn't bolted yet. He was on the floor, knees bent, leaning against the fridge. His head was hanging like the weight of it was just too much for a mere mortal to hold. Even though I had the bonds shut down, I still could feel him crackling in the air.

I couldn't bring myself to look at Talon. This was probably painful for him. Like physically painful. I couldn't think of another way to make him understand, get him to see what was crystal fucking clear to me.

We weren't a pack right now. We were just four people cocooned in different flavors of misery.

Cross leaned forward and straightened out of his slump. His bare feet made soft sounds in the dead silence, as he headed left to his room.

With a grunt to get himself off the ground, Luther followed a while later.

Just me and Talon. We couldn't come together and we couldn't break apart, just suspended in this vast space of things we couldn't say to each other.

"I can't, Jackson," he finally said around a regretful sigh.

"I can't not."

I tilted my head back and closed my eyes. I'd pictured us having this fight a million times. I was always screaming and hysterical in it, however. Ranting, pulling at his clothes, crying even.

It was my turn to sigh.

"Sometimes, I feel like I'm the omega of this pack."

Talon took a breath to refute that.

"No, shut the fuck up for once. You know everything I'm about to say, but you need to hear it said." I slipped my hands behind my back and crossed my legs at the ankle.

"There's no space for me to be an alpha in this pack, not a real alpha."

"You sound like your mother."

I smiled and snorted. I knew the fucker couldn't stay quiet.

"Regardless. It's true. You say "do this" and I jump with a "yes, daddy" and I fucking love it. It makes for hot sex. But there's a part of me it can't fill." I looked down at my feet, my voice going very soft. "There's a part of me *you* can't fill."

I could feel his hackles going up even without the bond. "There's a part of you *I* can't fill." And that was a fact that Talon never wanted to look at.

"That's the thing the beta world doesn't get about packs." Talon wasn't raised in a pack. Neither were Cross nor Luther. Wait. I didn't actually know if Lhevus was a beta or not. Didn't matter, he was a shit father to Luther, regardless.

"You let the pack in and it fills all your cracks. It makes you more of who you are."

I picked at a split in my thumbnail, the sharp edge digging into my finger.

"I need someone to need me, Talon."

"I need you." His voice was strained. He sounded like he wanted to grab me by the shoulders and shake some sense into me. He was the one who had no sense right now.

"Oh, you want me. I have no doubt about that, but you don't need me."

"Jacks..."

I shook my head, cutting him off. "We can't fuck our way out of this right now. Which is a fucking pity."

His turn to snort.

I pushed off the pantry door, my fingers skating along the edge of the counter as I rounded it. His face was devastated, crumpled into faint lines around his eyes. Even suffering, he was stunning. His brown eyes were warm but wary.

I took his face in my hands, running my thumb across his bottom lip. I brushed my lips against his before tasting him with my tongue. Our kiss was full of his desperation and my determination. I pulled back and let our breath whisper all the things we didn't say on our lips.

"I love her."

I trailed fingers down his arms as I stepped away, knowing he wouldn't let go until the distance forced us to part. I also knew he wouldn't follow.

I stepped out the front door. It was already dark, the ground wet and muddy. The rain had stopped. I looked up at the sky. No stars to light our way. We'd have to figure this out on our own.

No. *They* had to figure it out.

I already knew what would happen.

THIRTY-SEVEN

RUBY

My lips were numb. The deathly quiet made my bones hurt. I had been blowing air past my lips to make motorboat sounds just to not hear my own thoughts screaming at me.

I didn't dare turn my phone on to see the time. There was no clock in this room. I never cared about time. Things happened if I wanted them to or not. Wishing them faster or slower didn't matter, they still happened.

I had been trying to find the courage to open the door again. After my last failed attempt, I sat with my back against it, braiding and unbraiding a strand of hair.

Ruin.

Ruin wouldn't let a door defeat her. She would throw it wide and march right into the kitchen and help herself to champagne and chocolates.

I stood, hands on my hips, staring down the doorknob. I closed my eyes, fumbled blindly for it and twisted it open, stepping into the hall before Ruby had a chance to object.

Luther's room was in this hall, too. I turned my head to keep my eyes from his doorknob before Ruin stormed in there again.

They were going to kill Ruin.

I knew Ruby should be upset about that, but she was too busy being confused.

I followed the soft light that leaked into the hallway. The rest of the house was dark. I didn't think it was late, not that late, not late enough for everyone to have gone to bed.

I stood in front of the fridge. No padlock on this one. I chewed on my lip as Ruby and Ruin battled it out. One wanted ice cream. The other knew what would happen if she got caught eating ice cream.

Ruin won.

"What are you doing?"

Jackson was suddenly here, next to me, on one knee. I had a mound of ice cream on my fingers. Fear bubbled through me. This was going to be bad.

"Why aren't you using a spoon?"

"There are spoons?"

He tilted his head, like he was trying to figure it out. His smile went all funny around the edges. I had said something very, very wrong.

"I.. I meant... Wh... where are the spoons?" I mashed the ice cream back into the container and tried to wipe the evidence off my fingers. I couldn't look at him. I couldn't watch his beautiful face morph into rage.

I yelped when he scooped me up and deposited me on the counter. I clutched the ice cream closer, like it could protect me. He nudged my knees apart. I opened them, hoping they didn't shake. Sometimes it was worse when they knew you were scared. Metal clinked softly as I tried not to move.

He twirled a spoon in front of my eyes, his smile warm and...

sexy. He dug into the ice cream and held it to my lips. Trying not to breathe heavily, I opened my mouth for him.

The ice cream hit my tongue, cold and rich. I closed my eyes. The last time I'd had ice cream... I couldn't remember, but I knew I'd tried it before. When I opened my eyes, he had another spoonful ready for me. I took that one, too.

The look of pure pleasure on his face confused me. It was just ice cream, and he wasn't even eating it.

The next scoop was melty and heavenly. It coated my mouth and made me moan.

Jackson drew in a quick breath.

"Do that again," he said in a deep whisper, fascinated. His scent creeped up around me. I wanted it all over me.

"Do what?" I breathed.

"Moan for me."

It was my turn to gasp. I froze, my eyes went wide.

He delicately separated my hand from the container, the messy one, dripping with ice cream. He took two of my fingertips into his mouth. His eyes fluttered, like it was the best thing he had ever tasted. His tongue swirled softly around my fingers. The sound that came out of my mouth matched the shivers running through my body.

And then he moaned as my fingers slipped from his mouth. The sound went straight to my core and throbbed between my legs.

He put his arms to either side of me on the counter and leaned in. Our breaths, quick shaky pants, chased each other, mingling. I could feel the heat from his lips on mine.

"Can I kiss you?"

"No," shot out of my mouth without a thought, on reflex. I held my breath. No, wasn't a word omegas were supposed to use.

He grinned wide and his eyes sparkled. He leaned back and pulled open the drawer again. He got out another spoon, sticking one straight up in the ice cream, used the other to take a scoop for himself. Pure satisfaction washed over his face. I was confused.

"That's... that's OK?" I asked hesitantly, "Omegas don't say no?" I whispered softly to the ice cream. I had never said no before without being hit.

"Of course," he said around a mouthful of ice cream. "I'm going to have to work much harder to make you want to kiss me."

He loaded up his spoon again and encouraged me to do the same with a glance at the container.

I took some time digging out a chunk of chocolate and tried to get my brain to figure this out. He liked it when I moaned. It gave him... pleasure? And he was delighted when I said no.

I dug in the ice cream, looking for another chunk of chocolate, lost in my thoughts. Jackson took small scoops around my work in the container. He was content, happy even.

And it was real. It felt real at least. There was no fake smile hiding bad intent. This was honest, and I didn't know how to handle that.

Jackson had unearthed a giant bit of chocolate. He held it out on the edge of his spoon for me. I flashed him a shy look and opened my mouth for him. I made a little happy mmmm sound crunching through the chocolate.

He growled, low and smooth, like it rumbled up from the center of his being. He caught a drip of cream from my lips on his fingertip and held it out to me. I searched his expression. He was just waiting there for me to come to him.

I parted my lips, and he gently placed his fingertip in my mouth. Feeling bold, I reached for the taste of cream with my tongue, his finger warm and hard against my soft flesh. A new sense of hunger rolled through me, making me feel empty.

I pushed my head forward, wanting more of him in my mouth. He slowly pulled his finger back, disappointment shook me, until he pushed his finger back in. My sex pulsed like it was jealous of my mouth. I squeezed my legs shut, but he was standing between them. I wanted to wrap my legs around him as he dragged his finger out of my mouth. I licked my lips and swallowed. I took another small bite of ice cream to cover my confusion.

"OK," I said in a small voice.

"OK what?" he asked, the spoon clicking on his teeth.

"You can... kiss me." I held my breath. He grabbed my spoon and tossed it in the sink with his, where they clattered. He put the ice cream carton on the counter and grasped my hips, lifting me off the counter like I weighed nothing.

I found my feet in the middle of the kitchen, with him towering over me. Jackson was big, but not huge, like Luther. Still, he made me feel small.

He held my face, his fingertips behind my ear, his thumb caressing my jaw. His other hand traced a line from my shoulder to the small of my back.

His hands on me, everywhere he touched, set off sparkles that wiped everything away. All the thoughts, all the bad feelings that endlessly circled my head, were pushed out, put to the side, leaving only Jackson and how he made me feel.

I sighed and closed my eyes, and gave in completely to him.

"You're so perfect, little omega," his voice whispered into my ear and circled my soul.

His lips brushed mine, setting them on fire. I froze, afraid to move, to breathe, afraid I'd break into a million pieces. Until his tongue parted my lips and pushed inside me.

And then I was falling. A ripple of pleasure took my ability to stand. I was weightless, floating in his arms, balanced on his fingertips and his tongue in me. Him in me.

When time moved forward again, he was holding my face in both his hands like I was a flower that would bruise easily. His lips, soft against mine.

Jackson walked me back until I hit the counter. He reached behind me. I heard the water rush and echo in the metal sink. He spun me around with gentle fingers, my back to his front. Fingers blazed a path down my arms to my wrists.

He held both in one of his big hands. I was caught, bound, my cheeks flashed hot.

He stretched forward, leaning into me, his free hand getting a pump full of dish soap. He had my captured hands under the rushing water. Then his fingers went to work, lathering the soap, giving each finger attention.

As he washed my hands and then rinsed them, my lips parted to bring in more air. It was no help. I closed my eyes and leaned into him, his lips were right at my ear. He didn't know I'd never be clean.

Silently, he guided me to the living room. He threw wood into the orange glow of the embers, and the flames immediately jumped up in thanks. Wood smoke curled around me, reminding me of Luther.

Jackson pulled a blanket off the edge of the couch and settled it on my shoulders. I stopped breathing when he knelt at my feet, his face bathed in the soft flickering light. He wrapped the blanket around me, snug and tight.

I wasn't quite sure I could even find the words to describe how beautiful he was. "Impossible" was as close as I could get. It was impossible that he was real. He was here, kneeling at my feet.

He held a hand out in invitation and I put mine in his. He kissed my palm over and over as he guided me to the floor and stretched me out before the crackling fire. A slight frown of disapproval played about his lips.

He stretched over me, his long, lean frame begging my fingers to take action. But I couldn't. What if I touched him and he disappeared?

He dragged pillows and cushions from the couch, tucking one

gently under my head. I snuggled into the blanket as he created a wall of pillows around me. The pack's scents rose from the blanket, each distinct but blending into the best thing I had ever smelled. Tension dropped off me, I swore I could practically hear it hit the ground.

Finally satisfied with his efforts, Jackson settled next to me, his head curled on his bicep. "I want to watch you fall asleep," he said softly. We were so close; his words caressed my lips.

I was afraid to move, even to close my eyes, just in case none of this was real. He ran his fingertips down my nose, over my chin, my lips, finally brushing my eyes shut. The gentle touches slowed my breath and made way for sleep. I sighed and hoped for no dreams. How could dreams be better than this?

When I heard the words, "I love you, Ruby Frost," I knew that must be a dream, too.

TALON

I waited. I waited for the anger and the jealousy to swamp me, capsize my rickety boat and drown me.

It didn't come.

I stood over Jackson, my heart pounding. Contentment so fierce it oozed out of him in his sleep. Jackson was radiant. He literally glowed. A smile painted his lips. He was using his own arm as a pillow, curled in front of the fire with Ruby. He had tucked her up in blankets and pillows, saving none for himself. He had given everything to her.

That summed up Jackson. He had everything. He was beautiful, breathtaking, he had wealth, political power, and connections. He could be sitting in a cushy office, dating a duchess, have a pack of the most powerful and wealthy. He gave that all up for me. For pack.

Her hair, messy on the pillow, reflected the warm firelight. She looked so soft. There was no tension pulling her tight, making her second guess her every move.

They were heartbreakingly beautiful together.

He loved her. I wanted to hate that. I wanted to smash it to bits with all the alpha rage I could find in me. But I couldn't. Because there was none.

My eyes consumed Jackson like a starving man.

He was wrong. I did need him. "Need" didn't even touch what I felt for him.

I needed him, but I couldn't give him this.

I noticed Ruby watching me then. She sat up, looking like she got caught with her hand in the cookie jar.

Anger finally bled into my awareness. Not at her. I was angry at the floor. She should not be on the floor.

I bent and picked her up, the blankets trapped her legs. Her eyes were wide and wary, but she didn't struggle or protest. She glanced once back at Jackson as I carried her down the hall, past Luther's room. Her scent mixed with the packs, making it sharper, more sweet.

I pushed her door open with a foot, settling her in the bed.

A flash of movement, she skittered off it to the other side.

Moving slow and deliberately, I rounded the bed, crouching on the ball of my feet in front of her.

"What's the deal with the bed?" I tried to keep a tone of accusation out of my voice.

She glanced at the bed like that was the real threat in the room.

"Have you been sleeping on the floor?" The bed still looked untouched and cold.

She began to shake her head "no," pausing to look at the bed again before giving me a single nod.

I put an index finger to her chin, turning her to look at me.

"What's wrong with the bed?"

She licked her lips. I could practically see her sort through possible answers to find one I would believe.

"It's..." she swallowed, and continued, "too big."

I searched her face. It wasn't a lie. But it wasn't the truth either. She'd picked that answer, thinking it was the one I wouldn't get angry at.

"Don't move," I said softly.

I flew through the cabin quickly and quietly, not wanting to wake Jackson. In moments, I was in her doorway again.

The sight of her on her knees, waiting for me, stole my breath. She had her head down. I stepped close so she could catch me in her field of vision. She looked up as I shook out and unzipped the bright blue sleeping bag I had fetched from the mudroom.

I held my hand out to her, to get her on her feet. She looked at my hand with crinkles of confusion breaking out between her brows. Unsure, she put her hand in mine, anyway. I held the sleeping bag open, the long side unzipped fully.

"Step in it." She didn't hesitate, even though she must think it was a totally weird request.

I zipped it up around her and scooped her in my arms before she could think too hard about it. Placed her back on the bed, knowing for sure I was right. Yet panic and dread danced in her eyes. The bed might be too big to be comfortable, but that wasn't what was causing the distress.

I stretched out alongside her, swiping hair from her forehead. She turned her face, seeking out more touch.

"I didn't like seeing you on the floor." It bothered me, just the idea of it. I couldn't pinpoint why.

I watched her struggle with unknown enemies. This wasn't working. Whatever was wrong needed a different solution.

She fumbled inside the sleeping bag, finally managing to free one hand. Blindly reaching out, she grabbed a fist full of my t-shirt like it was a lifeline. She caught my eyes for a heartbeat before looking down again.

"Tell me," she said, soft and desperate.

"Tell you what?"

She dragged her eyes back to me. Fear and confusion swirled the blues and greens like the sea before a storm.

"Not to sleep on the floor."

The words gutted me and breathed life into me. Her lower lip trembled. She shied away slightly, as if she had made a mistake and a blow would come.

I traced the edges of her face, knowing that even this small amount of contact would keep her in place. I marveled at the particular kind of courage this request required of her. Just like when she asked for help on the lawn. To have a sense of what you need, maybe not fully understand it and reach for it, anyway. I didn't have that kind of courage.

I ran my thumb along her bottom lip to ease its trembling.

We weren't pack. She didn't wear my bite. She could, perhaps, get a sense of my aura, but we didn't have a bond where she could trust my intentions or emotions. As an alpha, I could compel her to a certain degree, regardless that her skin was unmarred by my teeth. I pulled my aura back as close to my soul as I could, knowing she'd feel none of it, none of the compulsion that I could wield.

"You're not to sleep on the floor anymore, Ruby."

It wasn't a request or an invitation. It was a command. One that came from me, not from my alpha aura.

Relief flooded her like having an order to obey was the only thing that made sense to her.

She closed her eyes and nodded. "OK".

I lifted her chin up with my fingertips, wanting her to see me, just me, what I wanted and expected.

"Yes, sir," she corrected herself without prompting.

"Good girl."

She shivered, a sound that was not quite a moan, left her lips. I held her eyes until she couldn't take the naked honesty of this moment anymore and tilted her head back down.

I felt her breathing slow, but her hand stayed twisted into my shirt. The immediate crisis of being in a bed had passed. I didn't need the reason behind it, not right now, anyway.

I watched her fall asleep by counting the confused wrinkles that smoothed out and disappeared on her brow. When the skin was soft and flawless again, I began untangling her fingers from my shirt.

The jealousy hit when I brought her fingertips to my lips. Kissing them softly so to not disturb her sleep. I was jealous of the courage she had to fill an aching need for both of us.

THIRTY-EIGHT

JACKSON

Talon was all around me when I woke, his scent, his aura, his soul. I stretched my arm wide across the living room floor, totally refreshed despite the sleeping arrangements. I rolled back to my side, touching the cold spot where Ruby had been.

I had wanted to be near enough so she could slip into my dreams, but the "no" she gave when I asked to kiss her meant I was not going to creep into her bed. I had the patience of a saint, after all.

Tossing the pillows back on the couch, I let the promise of the gurgling coffee maker tempt me into the kitchen.

Talon had been watching me the whole time. He probably had been for hours. He sat with his back to the island counter that marked the transition from kitchen to great room. His elbows were on the counter and his long legs extended, crossed causally at the ankles. Blue stained his under eyes. He hadn't slept at all.

Holding his gaze I kicked his top foot off the other. He hitched forward slightly at the sudden unbalancing. I forced his legs wider until I could fit between them. Placing my hands to either side of

301

his body, I contemplated his lips, deciding how I wanted to kiss them.

"With all we've seen," he picked up our argument right where we left it, "all the omegas half dead, and dead," he corrected himself, "and broken, ground to nothing under an alphas power, how could you want that much control over another person?"

Stunned and shocked, I pushed back to see his whole face. The realization hit me like a truck. This was about fear. Guilt.

"This is about Melodie." A perverse kind of wonder dawned on me. Followed quickly by anger. Talon was mine and I would not let anyone torture him, especially Talon himself. "I'm a fucking idiot."

I turned away from him to make my way up the stairs. Talon's hand shot out, and he grabbed my arm.

"Don't run away from this. We need to talk."

"Oh, I am not running, you dumb motherfucker. Sit your ass down. No, make me coffee. I'll be right back." I pulled away from Talon when his only response was to blink at me.

I took the stairs to our bedroom two at a time. Tossing shoes out of our closet until I unearthed the fireproof lock box I kept there. It had a key, but I didn't bother to lock it. They were in a box for protection, not for secrecy. I dumped the collection of thumb drives on the floor so I could find the pink one faster. I replaced the box and made it back to the kitchen before Talon put cream in my coffee.

"Jackson…"

"Nope. Sit down. I get to be the Dom now."

Talon raised an eyebrow and took a sip of the coffee he made for me to hide a smirk.

I slid Cross' laptop to me and punched it on with a little too much force. While it woke itself up, I jammed the thumb drive in. I took my coffee from him and looked pointedly at the stool in front of the computer, giving him a "good boy" when he sat.

Leaning around him, I danced my finger over the track pad to open up her files.

"Melodie was not your fault."

Talon tensed. Years of practice at avoiding this topic at all costs meant he was very good at not showing any reaction to the name.

His eyes roamed over the dozens of files in the folder.

"What is this?"

I clicked the first one open for them.

"Melodie had checked herself out, signed an AMA, from a residential treatment program a week before meeting you. She was diagnosed with bipolar disorder at twelve. She had stopped taking meds."

His eyes raced across the screen, using his finger to scroll up and down on her medical records.

I pushed his hand away to open another document. This one was the intake form at New Oxford General emergency department. It showed Melodie being brought in, severe lacerations to her forearms and mentioned NOPD arresting the young alpha for trashing the waiting room.

"You know this happened, that they never pressed charges against you, but you don't know about this."

I pulled up the psychologists' evaluation form from eight months later. She'd left that treatment program too, hooked up with another alpha, and ended up attempting suicide again.

"How did you..."

I closed that and opened another - the committal documents I'd had Judge Exitor sign.

"You had temporary guardianship over her?" His finger trailed across my name typed into the document.

I then showed him 4 years of monthly receipts from Gold Haven, an inpatient and rehab facility. Super posh. It was where all the celebrities had their nervous breakdowns.

I clicked into the last file and brought up a picture of her and her new husband.

"She went sliver pack," the designation you could choose that stated your intent to never join a pack, "married a beta last year. They just had their first kid."

Talon's hands shook as he wandered through the files, trying to make sense of it all.

"Why?"

"Because you loved her, you fucking asshole."

"I don't..."

I sighed, not believing I had to explain it all.

"You were wrecked the first two years we were together. Guilt ate you alive. I knew Melodie was the reason you didn't want to form a pack. Packs meant omegas."

"But..."

"So, I looked into it. Into her."

"This is confidential medical information." His brow creased.

"Yeah, so?"

"Jackson, that's a crime."

I barked out a laugh, then covered my mouth. Everyone was still asleep.

"When will you fucking understand that laws are meaningless when it comes to pack?"

He stared at the computer again. I wasn't sure if he was actually taking in any of the information.

"She was unwell when she met you. Not her fault, certainly not yours. And this was part of her pattern, part of her manic and depressive episodes. You didn't do this to her. You were were a kid when your aura presented. Your dominant nature and your aura developed at the same time."

He slumped on the counter, clicking documents open, seemingly at random.

"Melodie found you, fresh off her meds, at the height of a

manic episode. You were flush with power you didn't fully have a handle on. But you did not break her. She was already broken."

"Guardianship?"

"You think I could let someone you loved suffer when I could fix it with money and a round of golf? At that point, she wanted to get better, get treatment, but she didn't have the resources. Guardianship was the fastest way to do that."

"Why didn't you tell me?"

"Why would I, when you spiral just hearing the word omega?"

Hanging across his shoulders, I clicked back to her picture. It was from ReadMe, the social media app, on their six-month anniversary. She was probably pregnant in this pic, but it wasn't showing. She looked fantastic, in that boring, normal person way. Her hair was shorter, she wasn't gaunt anymore, and she looked truly happy. I wrapped my arms around him as he stroked her face on the screen.

"Talon, you are a good person. The best person." I whispered in his ears, pressing my lips to his neck. "You're a careful and considerate alpha and Dom. *You* did not push her to the brink of death. *You* didn't ruin her life. The guilt you're carrying does nothing but harm *you*."

He nuzzled me back. I could have him purring if I wanted. He turned his head to find my lips for a kiss.

"Do you know how many laws you broke here?"

"Do you have any idea how many laws I would break for you? For the pack?"

I turned his head away and bit his neck, just hard enough so I could see the marks for a few hours. His moan vibrated into my lips.

"No biting at the table." Luther said, patting my shoulder as he headed right for the coffee pot.

I closed all the open tabs and yanked the thumb drive. I put it in his back pocket with a light spank.

THIRTY-NINE

CROSS

They all had only gotten halfway into their coffee. I was only fashionably late. No one but Luther was ever up this early. Dawn was barely pinking up the sky.

They hadn't woken me up. Not with their voices, at least. I doubted anyone slept well last night. Except maybe Jackson. He was still in the same clothes he wore yesterday, looking rumpled but bright eyed. The fucker.

"So," Jackson said, hopping up on to the counter, "let's go hunting." His grin was wicked. His attitude was unphased, like last night didn't happen.

"Hunting what?" Luther asked. He'd been standing in front of the open fridge for the past 5 minutes.

"Ugh, choices, choices. The betas that tried to fuck us? The cop that's trying to fuck us? Ruin Winters?"

"Which is the real threat?"

"Now," Jackson said, pointing a finger gun at Luther, "that is an excellent question."

"What's this?" Talon asked, holding up a manila envelope.

"Duo brought it." I said. Taking my first sip. Talon must have made it, not Jackson. Talon's coffee was for shit. It needed more sugar.

Luther and Jackson debated the merits of dividing and conquering. I slumped on the counter. It would take more than one bad cup of coffee to get me through the day.

I hadn't slept. Spent the entire night staring at my ceiling thinking about her. I should have checked on her after putting her in the bath. I didn't trust myself to do that, though.

Talon ripped the envelope open absently and shook the contents into his palm. A white glossy photo toppled out and floated to the ground. He took two steps away, flipping through the pages, and stopped dead.

I bent and picked up the photo. I turned it over just as Talon's aura flashed white hot.

The realization knocked my knees out. I didn't have to read the "R. Frost" in the bottom corner to know it was Ruby.

It was just her naked back, her creamy skin streaked with angry red welts, a few deeper. Too many to count. They were healing and scabbed.

Blood would have flowed down her exquisite skin.

TALON

My mind was still reeling with the whole Melodie thing that I had to scan the first page several times before it actually registered.

The first page was a cover sheet with Ruby's basic information. Birth, parents, date of perfuming and registration.

The third page was a statement from one of the clinic doctors.

During the routine medical examination prior to the administration of the shot, lacerations and contusions....

.　.　.

Then followed a list of every mark found on her body. It carried on to the next page.

My aura burst, stopping my heart.

I turned back to the kitchen. Cross was on the floor, fixated on the glossy photo in his hands. Luther and Jackson both were wide eyed, coffee cups halfway to their mouths.

"What?" Jackson asked.

I shot a look toward Ruby's bedroom. Not here. I couldn't show them this, where she could feel the aftermath.

Cross got to his feet shakily. The fear and dread he couldn't keep to himself was slowly morphing to rage.

"Talon?" Jackson said, looking between us with growing concern.

"Outside." Cross snagged the stack of papers from me, then headed for the mudroom.

I caught up to Cross at the fire pit. He had at least scanned the first few pages. He handed me the photo and caught my elbow as I staggered. Cross sank into his Adirondack chair.

"What?" Jackson said as he and Luther jogged to catch up. I looked down at Luther's feet. He hadn't even bothered with shoes.

I froze, staring at Jackson, my breath coming hard and short. I couldn't tell him. I couldn't be the one.

He made a grab for the picture. I snatched it away. "Don't."

Luther pried it out of my fingers, covering his mouth in horror. Jackson snagged it from him. He was silent. For too long.

"Jacks," I stepped towards him, reaching for him. He backed away from my touch.

"What the fuck is this? Someone needs to explain what's happening right now?"

"Cross tried to pull her file. It was sealed." I explained how I asked Duo to get it for me. If a file was sealed, there was no digital version of it. It only existed on paper and was stored in the archives. Unusual, yes, but not completely unheard of. To access those files, you actually had to go there in person. Duo had someone he was blackmailing in the Valentine Division just for this reason. Because they dealt with society elites, they had unfettered and unmonitored access to the archives. Duo had come up here to drop this off.

"And?"

Cross had finished reading for the time being. The stack of papers resting on his knee.

"Cross?" Jackson asked.

I kept an eye on Luther. If the news about his sister Havoc hadn't killed him, this might... There might not be any way to come back from this.

"She has a history of abuse. Severe. And I don't think it's stopped."

"That's in the file?" I asked.

"No." He curled the paper in his hands like he wanted to eradicate its existence from the universe.

"Either give me the goddamn file or explain, Cross."

"She perfumed just before her 18th birthday. During one of the medical exams, they found extensive evidence of abuse."

"What does extensive mean?"

"Jacks..."

"Shut the fuck up, Talon. I am not a baby."

He spun his wheels in silence, the moment stretching till he reached a breaking point. He snatched the photo from Luther. I watched him run a finger across her back in the photo, like he could erase even the memory of the marks.

He clenched his teeth and cracked his neck, wrestling with the effort to keep the pack bonds shut and his aura to himself.

"She was still a minor. She was not from a pack family, so the

Institute had little recourse when her foster mother checked her out of the Institute before she came of age."

"And then?"

"There was some investigation."

"Jesus Christ, Cross. Just fucking say it."

"She was in Berry Creek."

Jackson squeezed his eyes shut and rubbed his temples. We all knew that only meant bad things. It wasn't safe to drive through Berry Creek if you weren't a beta. It was not uncommon to be run out of town or worse, if your aura presented there.

"OK." Jackson was taking slow, deep breaths. "What do you mean you don't think it's stopped?"

Cross got to his feet and stepped over Luther, who was lying on his back in the grass, like the spinning of the world and gravity was too much to deal with.

"Tell me you haven't seen the red flags," he said.

I took his seat and picked up the file, not really reading, just scanning words here and there.

"What do you mean?"

"The personality shifts?"

Jackson blinked at Cross, not comprehending.

"She gets spooked and it's like she turns on another identity. More confident, flirty..." Cross spoke gently.

"It's been a few stressful days. She's with strangers." Jackson's voice pleaded.

"She flinches. Like she expects to get hit."

"That's..."

"Our first night here, I left her alone for a bit. I found her in a closet, in a space too small for her. When I asked her about it, when I asked if she was nesting, she lied and said nesting was wrong."

"Nesting is what?" Jackson asked, the words not computing.

"She's an omega who doesn't know what it means to be an omega. Our scents hit her like a drug, like she's never been around alphas before. She didn't understand why she was holding a gun on Duo. For fuck's sakes, Talon gave her a gun because she didn't think we could control ourselves." Cross was ticking the events off on his fingers.

"She's been sleeping on the floor. She won't touch the bed." I was not successful keeping the growl out of my voice.

"She…" Luther's voice was rough.

He dug his fists into his eyes like wiping away a memory. Giving up the fight with his aura, he loosed his grip and something beyond rage oozed out. I had never felt anything like it.

"She has bruises across her stomach, one right here. Deep purple." He ran his palm along his side. A kidney punch. Deep purple means recent."

Jackson bolted for the house. Cross didn't let him get more than a half-dozen steps.

"What are you going to do? Strip her naked and demand answers?"

He pushed off Cross. They both staggered a few paces.

Jackson stilled, he went icy. He covered his mouth, horror filling his eyes as he turned to me.

"Talon," he said around panting breaths. "Oh god. What if… spoons…" He bent double, hands on his knees.

"Spoons?" I wanted to reach out to him, take him into my arms, soothe both of us, but I couldn't.

He paced in circles, arms covering his head like that would keep the bad things away.

"I found her in the kitchen. Last night. Eating ice cream with her fingers." His pacing became frantic as the words tumbled out of him. "When I asked her why, she… she said 'there are spoons?'" The pace of his speech picked up to match the circles he was carving into the grass, his anxiety spiking as he worked something out, "I thought it was odd, like, of course, we have spoons. Who doesn't have spoons? So, I got one and fed her some ice cream. Then," he covered his face with his hands, "oh god, then I asked if I could kiss her. She said no. Cool, fine, that's great. We barely know each other, right? So, I just ate more ice cream with her. But she, she panicked, like I'd be mad at her for saying no."

He took a step toward me and stopped short.

"What if... oh god, what if she was... what if they... Talon? She said 'omegas don't say no.' What if she was..." he broke, unable to say the word.

LUTHER

The blue sky was all around me. It was that watery, weak color of blue. Cool, with touches of pink at the edges from the sunrise. Not a summer afternoon blue. Not the blue of playgrounds and barbeques.

I breathed in that blue and let it take over my aura.

I didn't need a file to tell me what I had already figured out. I huffed out a laugh no one heard. It takes a trauma survivor to know a trauma survivor. I think I knew before I saw the marks on her body. This file, that picture was unnecessary proof.

"What if she was..."

I closed my eyes. The sound of Jackson's heart breaking rattled my teeth. I had already figured that part out, too. But not until after I'd slept with her.

Talon was calming Jackson down, rationalizing with him. I let the words flow over me. I had already decided what I was going to do.

There was no fucking way I could tell them about Ruin Winters now. I'd have to figure out how to solve that problem all on my own.

There was a tap on my shoulder. I flashed my eyes open to see

Cross crouching next to me. He was twirling a blade of grass in his hands.

We were silent for a long while. There really wasn't anything to say when the woman you lo... I huffed out another silent laugh and shook my head... loved, had been raped and abused, there's only one thing to say...

Let's go kill them all.

CROSS

Jackson's agitated pacing had pulled him and Talon further from the fire pit. Talon was holding on to Jackson by the neck, his thumb rubbing Jackson's cheek while he fell apart.

I had asshole parents, with drug and mental health problems, and more kids than they had ever wanted. I had the shit kicked out of me countless times. And that was not the kind of abuse that was outlined in that file.

It was the kind of abuse that Luther saw. The systematic breaking of a person, a child, for no real reason other than it could be done.

And she was still being abused. I was sure of it. And it was happening because she was an omega.

I tapped Luther on the shoulder, pulling him out of his own version of hell. A sad smile played about his lips.

His hand connected with my foot, curling around the top of it. I put my palm on his chest. I took a deep breath. For once Luther was bringing me down. His presence in the pack bonds was intense, but kind of soothing, like the sound of chainsaws could be soothing.

I knew two things for sure in that moment.

I still would not take her as an omega.

And a lot of people would be very dead soon.

JACKSON

Omegas don't say no.

She had said it so softly.

I had jumped right over it, racing to get her lips on me. It was such a ridiculous statement, I'd convinced myself I hadn't heard it.

Talon had accused me... In the living room, before the attack... He'd accused me of using my aura on her. Getting her to comply, to come with me, dominating her.

Oh god, what if I had?

Omegas don't say no.

What happened to her to make her say that? Instantly, images of rough hands digging into her soft skin flooded my brain.

Talon caught me by the neck, squeezing just enough to get my attention. He put his forehead to mine.

"What if I..." I couldn't even say it out loud.

What if she was only here because it was what I wanted? What if I was making her do this? What if I was just another man that made her do things?

Do what things? What did they make her do?

The thought instantly spiked a growl deep in my chest.

Talon shook me, his fingers tightening around my neck.

"We're not doing that. We're not going there. Stay with the facts on the page."

I nodded. But I knew it would be useless. Until I knew everything, my brain would invent it, fill in the horrible details.

I broke Talon's hold and stepped a few paces away. I didn't want to be soothed and stroked and hear him whisper "it's going to be OK, baby," in my ear. It wasn't OK.

My lungs burned like there was no air here, just toxic fumes wafting up from our collective simmering rage.

"We have work to do," Talon announced.

Yes, the fuck we did. We had have to figure out who'd put hands on her and then rip them all off.

"We need to make one last shot at finding Ruin Winters before a bounty gets announced."

"Fuck Ruin Winters. Are you serious right now? You want to go into the office and act like it's a normal workday?"

"It *is* a normal workday." Talon picked up the stacks of papers and stuck the photo in between the pages. He sat in the chair and put his ankle on his knee.

"Our omega…" disbelief had my brain shorting out.

"The betas are the threat." Cross said evenly, "The NOPD thing is political, not life threatening."

"Have you run down the partial plate on the van?"

"Are you fucking with me? You want to play Sherlock Holmes right now?"

"She was in our living room when they attacked us. That is the imminent threat to her life right now."

Fuck Talon. He had a point.

"The van is registered to a contracting business in the Gritch. Reported stolen a month ago."

"Who do we know down there we can lean on for information? Arsenal?"

"Nah, his nose is so squeaky clean right now it sparkles. Connie Brick maybe. Her girls are everywhere."

"She's got NOPD clientele too. Take Jackson, and swing by and see Vex too. See if you can encourage her memory."

"I'm not leaving…" Talon cut me off.

"Ruby…" he paused to rearrange his words, tapping the reports on his knees. "All we know is that she has a history of childhood abuse. And she is not the one who told us."

Fuck. We shouldn't even know this much. Women generally found it distasteful when their love interests ran background checks on them.

"We have way too much experience with abuse survivors." He pitched his voice low. It had a rough edge to it. "We can't steam-roll her. Going off half-cocked is going to cause harm."

"Talon!" A high-pitched panicked voice floated over the field between us and the cabin.

We watched Ruby fly around the corner of the house. The t-shirt she was wearing came almost to her knees. She rocked to a stop, put her hands in her hair like she was going to tear it out, and spun around twice. Then she caught sight of us, a little way from the house. I was surprised we weren't all knocked flat by the power of her smile.

And then it crumbled. We watched her sink into herself, like her thoughts were taking her to some place of horror. A blink later, she stepped into that coy persona, playing with a lock of her hair, angling her shoulders to look approachable and soft.

"See what I mean?" Cross said.

"She's fawning," Talon added. God damn it. Now that we knew, it was so fucking clear.

I put a hand on Cross' waist as I slid by him and jogged to Ruby. Up close, her smile was less charming, still pretty, but I could see it for the shield it was now.

I kissed her temple and turned her back to the house, draping an arm lightly over her shoulder.

"Sorry about that," I jerked my head toward the fire pit, "We had a work thing come up and we didn't want to wake you talking about it."

Ruby twisted to look back at the rest of the pack as I walked her back into the cabin.

"Did you sleep well? I'm glad you moved to the bed. What the fuck was I thinking, making you sleep on the floor? Let's go make some coffee. Talon made the first pot and his coffee is for shit."

I babbled moronically, needing to take up all the space with

317

nonsense words, so my brain wouldn't linger on what ifs, and the marks on her body.

TALON

Ruby woke up alone, got scared, and then screamed for me.

Fuck.

There's a part of you I can't fill.

When Jackson said that last night, it felt like an accusation. As I laid next to Ruby, I knew it for what it was - a truth I could never voice myself. It didn't matter if Ruby could fill that for me. I couldn't be what she needed.

I tapped the file on my thigh, flipping through it absently, trying to not absorb its contents.

Cross shook out his hair and stared at the house. He blew out a breath, testing to see if he was composed enough to go back inside.

"Leave the file for me. I'll find them. I'll find them all."

I nodded. We didn't need a pack meeting, didn't need to take a vote to know we were going to erase everyone connected to this file. He shoved his hands in his pockets and made his way back to the house.

Luther was still lying on his back, looking up at the sky.

"Luther." I said when I knew Cross was out of ear shot.

He didn't respond. There was the initial medical report on her, a mental evaluation, her aptitude test results. There was a notation that she hadn't graduated high school and there were no homeschooling reports found for her.

"Luther." I said again, looking up. "You doing OK?"

He sat up. "She's..." He started but didn't finish.

"What?" I eyed him.

He felt OK. Better than OK, actually. When the mess with Havoc went down, he was radioactive. There was something he wanted to say but couldn't quite find the words for. I wasn't going to push him today. I just needed for him to stay in one piece until we figured out what came next. We had betas to hunt, a terrorist to find and a scent matched omega to avenge.

"You sleep last night?" I asked.

He stood and shook his head.

"Go eat something and get some sleep. This," I tapped the file, "isn't going anywhere."

He nodded and walked back to the house.

I turned the next page in the file. It was an arkologist report. Standard bullshit about potential damage that abuse in early aura formation can cause. A mention that late perfuming could be due to childhood trauma and the death of her mother.

I flipped to the last page and froze.

It was a police report detailing the incident that killed Opal Frost and orphaned her six-year-old daughter. Large portions of it were redacted, ugly, black lines marred half the page. It didn't matter. I knew what it said. I had the original in my safe. I thought I had destroyed all copies of it. Tearing this page out of the file, I folded it neatly and put it in my pocket. I'd destroy this one too.

We had a lot of contacts. We knew someone in every organization that dealt with abuse and trafficking.

I ruined every omega that came into my life. Every single one. All the proof Jackson showed me about Melodie, it didn't change the truth.

FORTY

CROSS

Jackson was being happy. On purpose. And it was getting on my last nerve. There was literally nothing to be happy about, yet here he was pumping the pack bonds full of sunshine and daisies.

He'd been on his phone since we left Connie's. The asshole was probably watching porn or something.

I let go of the steering wheel to flex my fists a few times. The tension was starting to make my joints ache.

I stopped too fast at the next light. My old ratty leather coat slid off the seat from the sudden stop. I rolled my eyes and snagged it off the floor, punching it down into the seat between us. The irony was not lost on me. Jackson wore my old jacket when he had to look gritty enough in the Gritch District. My former self was a costume he wore.

"Oh," Jackson said. "Turn left here."

I clicked the turn signal on before even questioning why I was turning. Jackson always got his way.

"We should get waffles. BetaButter's is at the Opera House."

"You want me to go fetch you waffles?"

"No," Jackson said, not looking up from his phone, "I want you to fetch Ruby waffles."

All the tension was back as her name left his lips.

The reports left out a ton of information, but the shit we waded through on a daily basis made reading between the lines very easy. Having a person in your life with that kind of history...

We were stopped at a light which let me close my eyes for a long second.

We were not making her pack. Luther was enough for us to handle. We didn't need two trauma survivors. My dance card was full. We'd get her safe, get her in a program and send her on her merry way. We didn't need an omega.

"You know nothing is going to happen to her, right?" Jackson said.

"We have no idea what her situation is. And this current threat? She wouldn't even be in danger if you didn't drag..."

He grabbed my chin and forced me to look at him.

"Look me dead in the eye and tell me one thing you think Ruby could possibly do that would make any of your brothers want to kill her."

My control of the pack bonds cracked, rage seeped out and filled the car. It pushed Jackson back like it had a physical presence.

We sat at the light while it changed, car horns blowing all around us.

"Besides, it's not like we have a rogue in the pack. There's nothing that's going to shatter us."

Jackson sat there, completely unphased by the dagger he'd just stabbed into my heart.

"We're not making her pack." Telling him to fuck off wasn't going to piss him off at this point. We told Jackson to fuck off on the daily. I squeezed my fists again. I looked up at the street sign to figure out exactly where we were. I could dump Jackson out of the car and make him walk home.

My words weren't even registering on him. The pathological optimist.

"You fucking ruthless little slut, you are not going to bully us into this."

"I have never bullied you into anything. I'm just right all the time."

"Oh right, like you didn't lie, cheat, and steal your way into Talon's pants."

Jackson shrugged.

"Jackson, you poisoned someone."

"Oh c'mon. If you can't complete an obstacle course with a little tummy ache, should you really be in the GPRE? He was in my way, and then he wasn't."

"You're the one who wanted the cabin."

"Cross," Jackson put his phone down, "look me in the eye on that one too and tell me the cabin isn't your favorite place?"

Fucker. It was.

I ground my teeth together, winding up for this one. "When you made…"

"Nope," Jackson cut me off with a smug wag of his finger, "You are absolutely not going to drag us into the pity party story." He shifted his voice to a mocking deep growl. *"You only made me pack because you felt sorry for me.* That's fucking nonsense and you know it."

"An omega will…"

"Be fucking perfect." Jackson looked out the window like he'd only just noticed the traffic swerving around us, blaring their horns. "Fucking drive the car. What the hell is wrong with you?"

My jaw hung open. The little prick was pouring salt in my trauma like we were discussing which waffles to get?

"Oh, that's right, it's a 'truck' not a 'car,' so sorry." He added snotty air quotes.

"Don't you see..." I started.

"No, Cross, that's the problem. I do see. I've seen it from the beginning. I have seen *you* from the first. And I see through all the bullshit you put out."

I slammed the car, no truck, into gear and was very careful with the amount of pressure I put on the gas.

"I see how much you crave Luther. Crave the pack. I see that the only time you let yourself be loved is when one of us is hurt. Because in your mind, if we're already hurt, you can't hurt us more."

"What the fuck did you just say to me?" Traffic was heavier here. It was getting increasingly difficult to swallow the nonsense coming out of Jackson and drive the car. Fuck. Truck. Jackson even bullied my vocab.

"I wanted you from the first day I met you."

Ah ha! I knew it. I opened my mouth to tell him I knew this was all about sex.

"And fuck me," he threw his head back against the headrest, "I wish it was as simple as just wanting your dick in my mouth."

Am I blushing? Jackson Serrano is making me fucking blush now?

"Just picture it. You and me in that alleyway, you with that fucking tiny little gun, right after you just tried to rob me. Ugh." He made the chef kiss gesture. "We have to get Talon to change the gun play rules."

I laughed. I couldn't help it. Only Jackson could manipulate my emotional state like this.

"You just did it because..."

"Because I wanted Talon? Use that shiny IQ of yours for a second."

"What the fuck does that mean?"

"I am a ruthless slut. You are 100% correct on that front." He sighed heavily like he was explaining, yet again, to a toddler why you can't stick your finger in a light socket. "The second my aura presented, I became independently wealthy. Inheritances and trust funds galore. I'm from a family and pack that has wings of libraries named after us. And," he lolled his head toward me. "I'm fucking hot. You don't think I had people asking me to bite them, bond them, every goddamn day?"

"You're such an arrogant prick."

"I know! Doesn't matter because it's all true. I could have bonded any douche at the country club to make a pack with Talon. And I didn't. Why? Because I fucking wanted you, you fucking dickhead."

I got real interested in adjusting the rear-view mirror.

"Oh, yeah, that's right. Uncomfortable isn't it? In your world, it isn't possible for someone to want you like that. Want your soul entwined in theirs?"

"Pack bonds don't let you mind read," I muttered under my breath.

"Your first pack lead wanted a thug to throw at people. Your first omega wanted a boy from the wrong side of the tracks to hang off her arm until being poor wasn't funny anymore. I wanted you."

And I wanted out of this fucking car. God damnit. It was a truck, not a car.

"The moment I met you, I knew you were mine. And I have no shame that I capitalized on the opportunity when it came."

I took some shallow breaths. Why did he have to bring this up while I was driving? The realization crashed through me. He waited to have this conversation when we were in the car, so I couldn't get away. I should have volunteered to stay with Ruby and spent the day torturing myself with what I couldn't have.

"What happened was a tragedy. One that you did not create,

Cross. Between your trauma and Talon with the Melodie thing. Fuck, Luther and his sister would be enough for us to handle."

I stared at Jackson. I couldn't believe he just said "Melodie" out loud. Talon never once talked about it with me. Jackson was the one that told me.

"OK. Fair points, and what do all those issues have in common? An omega."

Jackson sighed heavily, like I was too dumb to breathe the same air as him.

"Cross, I knew the second I met you that you were mine. Just like I knew Ruby was mine. Same with Talon. Same with Luther."

"I will never agree to an omega."

"Oh, turn here. BetaButter's is parked at the Opera House."

"I'm serious, Jackson."

"My guy, what are you doing? You missed the turn. We're going to have to circle around the block now."

"Jackson. Are you even listening to me?"

"Asshole, *you* are not listening to me. I said you are mine every bit as much as she is. Fight that if you want. Lie to yourself about that. It doesn't fucking change the truth. The proof is in the scent match, buddy."

"Stella was a scent match." I mumbled as I ran the yellow at the next intersection. Fucking Jackson.

"Dude. You have to turn for waffles." He pointed out the window, looking at me like I just fell off the turnip truck.

"Fine. Fuck you and your waffles," I said as I made the turn to circle the block to go get fucking waffles.

JACKSON

The white van in the left lane next to us must have lost its muffler, the sound was ungodly. I tried to crack my neck. That noise was exactly how the pack bond felt right now.

I needed a nap. When we were all tired and cranky, the pack bonds were amped up, and it was worse when we were apart. And it would not calm down until we all were together again. I had the pack bonds wide open, torturing Cross with the truth he refused to see.

Whatever. If he was determined to have his own pity party, he would just have to suffer through feeling what I was feeling on top of Talon's cranky pants. And we were in his car so he couldn't get away, so that was fun.

I tilted my head and tapped my phone to my lips. If I thought about it, the bonds stayed wire tight until we touched each other.

It wasn't like this with other packs. I had asked, even spoken to an arkologist about it once. She surmised that the dangerous nature of our jobs could be a contributing factor. She didn't come right out and say it, but Cross was probably the real reason.

We'd formed the pack immediately after Cross' first pack shattered, like 8 hours later. The body of his poor omega wasn't even cold. His aura was unstable. Talon wasn't entirely sure he wouldn't untether, and we'd lose Cross all together. We were told to wait. I refused.

I looked over at Cross behind the wheel. He was working extra hard to keep his body posture pissed off. If he would just give in…

I leaned forward and looked at the guy in the passenger seat of the van.

"Hey," I tapped Cross with my phone, "That guy look familiar?"

Just as Cross turned to look, the light changed, and the van punched into the intersection with a tire squeal.

"A42." The partial plate of the van that attacked the house.

"Fuckers."

Cross and I both pulled seatbelts across our chests. I slammed my phone in my back pocket as Cross concentrated on following the van. I pulled two handguns out of the glove box, cleared them and checked they were loaded. Cross leaned forward so I could reach across and behind him to stick extra magazines in his back left pocket. I tucked the weapon in his waistband and fluffed his shirt out around it.

We cut a corner tight, forcing me to put a hand to the dash as I checked my own weapon.

I turned completely around to look out the back. Rush hour was just starting. There were too many people on the street. Pedestrians and vehicles.

"I could take out the tires." I rolled down the window. Cross knew I could make the shot, even while moving. The risk assessment would be about collateral damage.

"Let's tail them for a bit." He slowed to let another car, a beater, with mismatched fenders, overtake us to put another car between us.

The van made a wide left turn at the next light. The junker in front of us was slow on the get up. I blinked in disbelief.

"You've got to be kidding me." I pointed at the driver. Long dark hair, big black sunglasses. I squinted, black lips?

"No fucking way that's Ruin Winters." Thank god Cross saw what I saw. Yes, a lot of women had dark hair, and black lipstick was trending. But what are the fucking chances?

We were stopped at a red light. This stretch of the shopping district was littered with short, one-way streets. It was meant to encourage foot traffic. The street dead ended with the Opera House, and its courtyard, where they held a lot of outdoor concerts. They could easily block off the side streets and turn the entire area into a block party.

"We could take them right now."

"Too many people. If they run, people will get hurt." Cross was right. If we wanted to kill Ruin Winters, I could do it. I had incendiary rounds in the glove box. I could blow the whole fucking van up. But we weren't trying to kill her. We wanted to help her.

With squealing tires, the van accelerated through the red light we were stopped at, and was going to blow past the next. Cross cursed and pulled around the junker, but had to wait for traffic to clear to give chase.

They blew past the next red, speed increasing.

"No." I whispered.

There was a sea of people in the courtyard of the Opera House. Must be an event or something. Hundreds of people. The van was not slowing.

"Fuck."

Cross barreled through the intersection, breaks screamed, cars skidded around us. The van was not making any effort to stop. I ripped the seat belt off and popped out the window. Cross hooked an arm around my leg to steady me. I steadied my gun arm on the top of the truck.

Before I could get a shot off, the van plowed into the crowd. Bodies flew through the air. The van bounced a few times as it ran over people.

Cross slammed on the brakes, yanking me back into the truck. It was eerily silent, dead silent for three breaths, then the screaming started.

The doors of the van popped open and two figures poured out.

"I got Winters," I said, flying out of the car. I could hear Cross behind me, hear his boots pound the pavement, fading as he tracked the other assailant.

I locked onto the black head bobbing through the crowd. The panic would hit any second, then it would be chaos. The crowd still didn't know what had happened. I pulled on my aura to gain on Winters.

She veered left behind the gift shop pavilion. I went right. I could cut her off with the speed my aura could give me. I pulled my gun out, holding it low, tight to my thigh. The people in the crowd began to shift from "milling" to "surging" and the knowledge of the tragedy spread.

No black hair. Where the fuck was she? I began back tracking through the crowd, fighting now to move forward. A few people started running, more followed. A skinny guy with dirty brown hair all mussed, panting, bumped into me. I sent him flying back a few places with a blow.

How the fuck could she have just disappeared? People started panicking now. A girl fell. People were tripping, trying to step over her. This was going to turn into a trample event. She was trying to scramble up, using the garbage for balance. I bent, roughly grabbed her arm to get her on her feet.

The trash can caught my attention. Right on top, there was a black wig, black glasses.

Fuck me. She could be anywhere now. She could be anyone. Sirens started wailing in the distance.

I staggered when Cross ripped into the pack bonds. Oh, he was pissed. Not hurt... but not OK.

The tide of people was pushing me away from where I needed to be, where Cross was. I managed to get to the street. Cars were stopped, engines idling as people ran to provide aid. A half a dozen men lifted the van up from one side to pull out someone trapped underneath.

If Cross was running down a beta, they couldn't have gotten far. Where? Where would I run if I just killed dozens of people?

I ran back along Smith Street. This was the old part of the city. There was a shared alley, just wide enough for a garbage truck, between this block and the next. I grabbed the edge of the old brick building to swing myself around the corner.

Cross was on his back, knees bent, hands up with his gun dangling from an index finger. Two of NOPD's finest stood over him, guns trained on him. Cross saw me, they didn't. Fucking cops.

Cross acknowledged me with a flick of his head, indignation flowing out of him. Then his potty mouth got going.

"No, you fucking limp dick turd, you put your fucking pea shooter down. Do you actually know how to use that fucking thing or do you just use it jack off to pictures of your mama with it?"

Good one. That was a nice distraction. Gave me the cover for a modified Krav Maga disarm tactic every rookie in the academy learned. NOPD recruits did not get similar training. Pity.

I popped the magazine out of Cop #1's gun and tossed it with a clank down the alley before Cop #2 thought to change his aim.

"GPRE. Stand the fuck down." I had my hand on my gun, but I didn't pull it.

#1 and #2 traded glances, unsure of what to do.

"What the fuck do you not understand about a being outranked?" I pointed between us.

"Orders are…" #1 started.

"Yeah, your new orders are to holster your weapon and walk away."

"He matches the description…"

"Do I have to give you till the count of three, like a toddler?"

Cop #2 narrowed his eyes at me. "Commander Treyfor said…"

Cross, tapping into his aura, lunged from a prone position and snatched the weapon away from the other cop, skidding it down the alley to join its mate. He dusted himself off.

"Nice doing business with you." I said, giving the dumbfucks a jaunty salute.

I had my hand on Cross' back and we jogged out of the alley and back to his truck. It was absolute chaos. Ambulances were screaming to a stop, people were running. Cross' truck, still running, was now in the way.

We got in and he backed it down the street. It was slow going. The further you got from the Opera House, the more shock sank in. People were just milling about, filling the street.

When the street was finally clear enough, Cross u-turned and sped out of the shopping district. He pulled over after a couple of miles and put the truck in park. We just sat there and breathed, letting the shock roll through us.

I looked over my shoulder. Cross did too. I wondered if we should go back, help or something. We were not first responders. That's not what we were trained for.

Killing Ruin Winters was what we were trained for.

FORTY-ONE

LUTHER

"Hey."

Talon kicked my foot and pulled me out of my thoughts that were just circling and going nowhere. I had been sitting out by the fire pit for the last hour.

"Going for a run?" He crouched down next to me.

I looked down. I was in sweats, my favorite running shoes. Running wouldn't solve this problem.

"Have they checked in?"

He shook his head. Something had happened, but we didn't know what, not exactly. It was life threatening and upsetting on a scale we've never really felt in the bonds before.

"Have you talked to her yet?" I asked. We were still reeling from reading her file.

They were, anyway. It wasn't a shock for me. I was sitting out here, avoiding Ruby and trying to figure a way out of this.

"Pleasant coffee conversation. That's all."

I nodded. I tilted my head back, a small smile touching my lips.

"They're on their way home. Must be close, too."

Talon stood and stretched. "How do you know that?"

"Jackson always gets horny when he gets close to home. You don't feel it?"

"Jackson's always horny." Talon laughed and turned towards the cabin.

I followed with a groan, rubbing my side. My hand lingered on the bruise, like comforting mine could comfort hers.

I kicked off my sneakers in the mudroom and pulled my t-shirt off, tossing it in the washer. I pulled one of Cross' black t-shirts out of the folded stack on the dryer. His scent still lingered on it.

Ruby stood in the kitchen, a glass of water halfway to her mouth. I watched a half dozen different emotions flash across her face, the last one being panic.

"We have to talk," I said softly. Talon's footsteps just hit the top of the stairs, so we'd have some privacy.

She smiled weakly, crossed the kitchen to put the glass in the sink and turned to leave.

I caught her by the arm and pulled her into me. A desperate desire flared between us.

"Ruin," I whispered, fingers trailing down her face.

She tried to step away. I pulled her closer.

"We have to tell them." My voice was barely a whisper.

Her lips, rosy pink, not black, rounded into a "no" but she didn't have enough breath to actually make a sound.

"I know. I know it all." My fingers trailed down her back and she shivered. "I know about the Reset. I know about your foster father, Mason Forthright. I know what they did to you."

"They'll kill you." It was just a simple statement of fact.

"We'll kill them first."

She searched my face. She wanted to believe that. With all her heart. I knew the kind of danger hope like that could be.

Talon's footfalls thundered down the stairs. Ruby pulled from me, like a naughty teenager stealing a kiss. I reached for her, but she darted away from me.

"You see the message from Duo?" Talon called out from the living room, searching for something. He found the remote and clicked the TV on.

"That's right Rodrick. The crowd was several thousand strong, many had been camped out overnight to be first in line to buy tickets for Perfume and the Alphabetas when tragedy struck. As of now, three are confirmed dead, that number is expected to rise. Hold on a second... There's..." The reporter held the microphone away from his body as someone stepped into the frame, whispered in his ear and then handed him a tablet.

"Yes, um, I..." visibly shaken, the reporter gathered himself and read from the tablet. "Perfume, daughter of Sparkle, the famed duchess, and front man for the Alphabetas has issued a statement..." He scanned the tablet again. "Zenith, lead guitarist for the band was killed in the attack..."

The images on the screen pulled us all into the living room. People running, screaming, bodies on the ground. Cell phone footage spliced together in a chaotic mess.

For the next few moments, we were mesmerized by the carnage. Video images looped from different angles of a van plowing into a crowd. My arm crept around Ruby, I felt her stiffen when we both saw it. She stepped toward the screen, like she needed to get closer to believe it. I tightened my arms around her.

The beta from the warehouse. The one that also attacked the house. Ruby knew who it was.

"My god," Talon breathed.

Talon and I both shot a look towards the door when we heard Cross' truck come up the drive. Moments later, they clattered into the cabin, not even bothering to take their boots off in the mudroom.

"You were there." Talon flicked a glance between the screen and Jackson's stricken face, putting the pieces together.

They crashed together in a proof-of-life hug and the pack bonds immediately eased. I stretched across the island counter, extending my fist to Cross for a fist bump. I needed to touch him, but we weren't the hugging type. My other hand stayed around Ruby's waist, bringing her into our pack ritual.

Jackson snagged me by the back of the neck, his fingers digging in, the pack bonds driving him to affirm our connection. Ruby was caught between us. More gently, he ran his hand up Ruby's arm. I felt fear pulse through her. Jackson tilted her head up, misreading the source of the emotion.

"We're fine." He whispered, touching his lips to her forehead briefly, before stepping away.

"What happened?" Talon asked the obvious question.

Jackson ran both hands through his hair, moving to stand right in front of the TV to take in the footage.

"It was Ruin Winters."

RUBY

Red and blue lights flashed on Jackson's face from the TV. His face was sharp, just as beautiful, but defined and determined.

I could feel them, all of them, all around me. I could see their connections, their... bonds... living and real between them. It was like it was its own creature. Like a dragon or a lion, combining to make something else, something more when they were all together.

Cross was talking now. Running hands through his hair, taming it, like he'd tamed himself, binding it all up to be acceptable. He had chased Bennett. I saw Bennett in a flash on the video. And Billy, in a black wig. They were there. They did this. I did this.

Talon pulled up the hem of Cross' shirt to see if Bennett's foot made a mark when he'd kicked Cross. I wanted my fingers there with Talon's, my touch making it better, too. They slid guns and extra magazines out of his clothes and piled them on the counter.

I wanted Talon's fingertips on me, telling me what to do, making sense of this.

Luther tried to pull me back. But there was no pulling me out of this. This was not mine. What they had... what they shared. Not mine. Ever. Not now. Not after...

They were all drawn back to the TV. As a unit, a family. Pack.

The words flowed through me, taking away every possibility, every promise delivered in fingertips and whispers.

"As commissioner of New Oxford Police Department, in cooperation with The Gold Pack and Rogue Enforcement Agency, with the sanction of the Alpha Omega Institute, we can now confirm that the Reset and Ruin Winters have claimed responsibility for this horrific act of terrorism on our city, our people. A one million dollar bounty will be issued on the capture or death of Ruin Winters and her associates. We would like to assure all our citizens that this act, and its perpetrators, will not go unpunished and we will bring the full force of the law to bring justice and order."

Luther reached a hand out for me and found nothing but empty space. Each word that bled from the screen pushed me back to the other side of the room. His eyes were wild. He knew the truth, too. There was too much death in the space between us now. There was nothing now.

"Luther?" He turned his head at the sound of Talon's voice, but he still held me with his gaze.

"The whole city is going to hunt her now."

"Good. I know we had our theories, but this just proves we were wrong," Jackson gritted.

Good. I closed my eyes, hearing that word fall from Jackson's lips. *Good.* I nodded to myself. It was good for them to get rid of me. I just hoped Jackson would never know.

They started talking plans, strategies, on how they'd capture and kill me. More words creating more space.

A phone rang in the distance. Talon patted his pockets, then took the stairs two at a time with curses under his breath.

"That fucking bitch. Do you see this? That kid is, what, twelve?" Jackson was biting his nail, talking to the TV.

"I really don't get it. A couple months ago, she was talking about girls puking in the bathroom. Now this? It doesn't make sense." Cross joined him at the TV.

Talon appeared on the stairs. His face white, hands shaking. They all turned. Except Jackson. He backed away. He knew whatever it was that had hit Talon was coming for him.

"Jacks…"

"What?" Jackson asked, his voice small, unsure.

"Jonquil. She was there."

"Jonnie? Jackson's sister?" Cross' eyes darted back to the screen, like he could find her in the crowd and save her.

"No. She wasn't going until later. She had to work. Someone was saving her a spot in line."

"Mitexi called. He's not with the fire department anymore, but he was on scene…"

"You're fucking lying. She wasn't supposed to be there."

"Jacks… I'm so…"

Jackson lashed out and punched away from Talon's comforting grasp.

He scrunched his face up and balled his fists. And they all felt it. Cross reached out to the wall, holding himself up with shaking fingertips. Talon went whiter, if that was even possible. Luther stared at me. He knew. He was caught between Jackson's pain and my past.

"I'll kill her. I'll kill her myself."

Luther took a step toward me. I put a hand up to stop him.

"I'll fucking rip that bitch's head off."

Jackson spun around like he could find a way out of this, like there was an exit and he just had to find it. He grabbed for me, desperate for the pain to stop. He sank to his knees, wrapping his arms around my middle, resting his head on my stomach.

"I'll fucking dark bond her myself. Sink my teeth into her. Make her pay every day for the rest of her life."

Luther held my eyes while Jackson, my mate, my... love... planned my death. Talon pulled him from the floor with soft words and gentle touches. His ragged breath was the only sound in the room.

I couldn't take it. I couldn't see his pain. I couldn't see him destroyed by Ruin Winters. By me. By everything I'd done.

A tear slid down my cheek.

I... I could end this. I could give Jackson his vengeance.

I could give him Ruin Winters.

I took a step forward. "I..." only air came out, no sound.

"Don't." Luther's aura hit me before the word did. His aura, his essence, him full of fear, pain, desperation.

I nodded at him. *It will hurt less this way, I promise.*

"I am..."

Energy popped in the room, with sound and force coming from Luther.

"I'm a rogue."

FORTY-TWO

LUTHER

It was the only thing I had. It didn't make sense to admit it now. What was left of my logical brain knew that. Anything to stop the words "Ruin Winters" from coming out of her mouth.

I threw myself on the only grenade I had. Maybe they'd think this latest tragedy was one too many, and I wouldn't be able to hide it anymore. It didn't fucking matter. Me being a rogue would keep them all occupied until Ruby came to her senses and we had time to figure this out.

"A what?" Jackson panted in the sudden shift of energy. I let control of my aura slip. The tight hold I had for years began to evaporate with the fear of losing Ruby.

"My god," Jackson's eyes scanned me, like he was a seer, like he could physically see auras rather than feel them. He looked at Talon and his face fell. He knew this was not news to Talon. "Since when?"

"Six." I sounded like a little kid again. Jackson slumped to the arm of the couch, wiping a shaking hand across his mouth.

"Six." I watched the realization flash across his face. He'd know what a six-year-old rogue would mean. "Fuck."

All his anger suddenly collapsed. Jackson, born into pack life, hearing the stories, raised on the lore, would know. He would have heard the boogey man stories of a kid going rogue. A cautionary tale to keep all the other little boys in line.

"Ruby figured it out. She could feel it, sense it. Omega." I didn't know what the fuck I was saying. It didn't matter. I just had to stop her from sharing her truth.

I stepped to her, put my hand in hers. So she'd know, so she'd know I was taking the hit for her. So she'd know we'd figure this out.

"Don't. Touch. My. Omega."

Each word from Cross was quiet, icy, deadly. His aura didn't explode, but simmered, hit the boiling point and then swamped the whole room in choking fury and pain. Ruby and I both looked down at where we were joined. Cross was locked on to us.

"Step the fuck away from her."

His eyes were glassy, like he wasn't completely here.

"Cross, that's not Stella." Talon's movement to come between us halted with a bloodcurdling growl from Cross.

Stella. I closed my eyes. I was fucking dumb. How could I fucking forget that? How could I have sprung this on Cross like that?

Cross' aura felt like it was cracking, a chunk of it sucked into the past where his omega was killed by a rogue.

"Cross." Talon put all the authority he had as pack lead into his voice. It should have been a bucket of ice water on his rage. I moved Ruby behind me to protect her.

With the next breath, Cross had his gun in his hand. His whole body shaking with the effort to pull the trigger. He couldn't. We were bonded together. We were pack, brothers. The laws that ruled alphas didn't allow brothers to kill each other. It was physically impossible. And as a rogue, those were laws that didn't touch me. I was bonded to Cross, parts of our souls lashed together, forever. But I could take his life if I wanted. I had more power and that's what made me, made all rogues, a threat.

He threw the gun away with a frustrated howl.

He launched himself at me. His hands at my throat. The force of our collision knocked Ruby off her feet. I barely noticed Jackson grabbing for her and Talon trying to pull us apart.

"I'm sorry. I'm so sorry," I repeated over and over, my voice getting more hoarse with each word.

"You killed her. You'll kill her again."

"I couldn't. I love her. You love her."

"I can't kill you." His eyes were wild and blank. "But you can. You can kill anyone. You'll hurt her, take her from me again. Take them from me again."

"I couldn't."

"You're a rogue. Rogues can do anything. They have no conscience. Nothing stops them. That's why we kill them."

"Cross." My breath was ragged and harsh, my head going fuzzy with lack of air. "I love you." squeezed out.

Rage bellowed from him like that was the biggest insult. "I trusted... I loved..."

"Please," her voice was small and soft but powerful. Cross' breath staggered. Ruby had wedged herself between us, her hands around Cross' neck.

"Cross."

A sob broke in him before the pain jacked him up again.

"He'll kill you. I can't lose you again."

She held his face, curling herself around his body, and sunk her teeth into his neck.

Waves of peace and soothing omega energy consumed the room. Cross' knee gave out. Staggering, I held him up, held them up.

CROSS

She was in me.

My pulse jumped to meet hers.

Her teeth broke me.

Split wide and filled with her.

My fingers slipped from Luther's neck to get lost in her hair. I cradled her like precious gems. Orange blossoms and cream splashed my senses. The colors of summer burning out the blackness that overtook my vision, pushing everything away. The past, the present, the pack. Until it was just her.

Her omega aura wrapped around me. She was light, weightless, like she was made to be there. Always.

She slid her legs from around me, bringing us both back to earth. A whimper when she pulled her teeth from me.

Red stained her lips. Staining both our lips now as she pressed into me. Her tongue in my mouth, mixing the tastes of citrus and blood. Her kiss claimed me as much as the bite.

"Luther's pack," she breathed into me, her lips moving against mine.

I breathed deep, wanting more of her in me. Hints of smoke and cut grass clung to her.

He clung to her.

A snarl rumbled in my chest. She was everything I ever wanted and nothing I deserved.

Him too.

Orange and smoke stung my eyes.

I forced her and the promise of forgiveness that lingered on her lips away from me.

I lifted my head and Luther was there, reaching for her.

I shoved her back, away from me. She stumbled right into Luther's arms.

It was happening all over again.

Rogues were uncontrollable. They could not be contained. They could not be stopped. Except by a bullet.

My neck throbbed. Her teeth in me felt so good, so right. I touched her bite. My fingers came away wet and red. It was my blood this time, it would be hers next. Her blood was all over my hands. Again.

"Cross." Talon's voice sounded far off, almost alien.

He knew. He knew from the start Luther was a rogue.

Jackson looked as rocked as I felt.

"Nothing's going to happen to her, right, Jackson? Fuck you."

I closed my eyes and let my fingertips guide me around the island counter into the kitchen.

"No, let him go, let him burn this off," Jackson said to my back. "Omega bites are healing, just let him…"

I punched my way out the mudroom door without bothering to listen to whatever Jackson was spewing.

Not bothering with a tidy K-turn, I made a big sweeping turn across the front field to get the fuck away from my pack. And my omega's aura.

FORTY-THREE

JACKSON

"I thought it was an urban legend."

"What?" Luther said, exhaustion dripping from him.

"A kid going rogue and wiping out a playground."

"Jackson!" The admonishment in Talon's voice was cutting.

"Sorry. Sorry." I put up placating hands.

I had been lying flat on my back for at least the last hour. Probably more. I felt like I had run a marathon. I couldn't calm my breathing or my heart rate.

Talon had built a fire in the pit, just to have something to do. It was almost full dark now. We had all said we needed some space. Ruby went to her room. Talon and Luther and I gravitated out here. We couldn't, in fact, be alone after all.

"Makes sense now," I said.

"What does?" Luther asked from one of the Adirondack chairs. He'd been exceptionally quiet since Cross left.

"It never made sense that Lhevus would take you in. I could never figure out that part."

"Jackson, could we not pick this apart right now?" Talon said.

"Why the fuck didn't you tell me?"

Talon just stared into the fire. Luther leaned his head back and squeezed his eyes shut tight. I propped myself up on one elbow.

"No, seriously, why didn't you tell me?"

Luther tilted his head back even further to look right up at the darkening sky.

"What did you say about that uncle that went rogue? 'He put a bullet through his head. I would have too if I found out I was a rogue?' Something like that?"

"Fuck." I slumped back down on my back and blew out a shaky breath. "I'm a fucking asshole."

"Don't worry about it," Luther muttered.

"No. This is important." I sat up and raked my fingers through my hair. "I was raised by traditionalists. Basically, raised to be a bigoted asshole, too. It's just more convenient for me and the rest of society to lay all our problems on 'dangerous rogues' and gold pack omegas."

I stood up and poked the fire, getting one last good burst of heat out of it before it would start to die down.

"I mean, not all rogues are monsters, right? There was that guy we helped relocate down south two, three years ago. Oh! And Ebony Starless. He's out and loud and proud as a rogue. It's the main draw for him in all his movies, right? The two of you could start like the Rogue Preservation Society or something."

"Jackson?"

"Yeah, Luther?"

"Shut the fuck up."

I snorted and warmed my hands in front of the fire.

"We should go make Ruby some food," Talon groaned as he got out of his chair and walked back to the cabin.

"I don't think she's eating enough," I agreed.

"I…" Luther started hesitantly, "I never wanted to lie about it. It… It just got too hard to say after a while."

"Yeah, suffering alone and causing yourself psychological and auratic trauma these last few months was a waaaaay better option."

"Jackson, I just…"

"Look, I created the situation where it was impossible for you to tell me. I'm in the wrong here. Let's just not do that anymore." I offered him a hand to pull him out of his chair. He looked at it like it would bite him.

I stared pointedly at my hand until he used it to hoist himself up.

"You're really OK with this?"

"When will the three of you learn? Pack is pack. Nothing else matters."

"Cross…"

"Will come around." I stretched up and hooked Luther around the neck to walk back to the house. It was awkward as hell due to our height difference.

"You sure about…"

"Yes. He'll be back by morning or we'll go get him."

Luther peeled my arm off his shoulder and threw his over mine. Way more comfortable. We both needed some physical touch.

"I can't keep it to myself any longer. Since you know, we're telling secrets and all."

"What?" Luther asked.

"Ruby biting Cross was fucking hot, right?"

"For fuck's sake, Jackson." Luther did his best to hold back a laugh.

"Fuckboy is how I deal with my trauma, OK? I've had a rough night."

FORTY-FOUR

TALON

I raked my hands through my hair to get it to lie flat and give me a minute to settle myself. I was running this pack into the dirt. Duo was right. I had to get my shit together.

I hung my head and forced my breathing to slow.

Cross pulling a gun on Luther was the last thing I thought I'd ever have to deal with. Jackson was the hothead in this pack. Not Cross.

And the sight of Ruby wrapped around Cross. Her teeth in his neck. Him cradling her gently... There was a ridiculous spark of jealousy at wanting her teeth in me. Of course, that got immediately swallowed up by the euphoria they were pumping out, but still.

She asked to be alone. I didn't think she had a clue about what happened. She acted on pure instinct to... to what? To protect Luther from Cross. To protect Cross from himself.

Omega bites created a connection. Not a lasting pack bond. When an omega bit you, as an alpha, it was like mainlining their aura and all its soothing properties. Or so I'd heard.

Ruby claimed Cross with that bite. I wasn't sure Ruby or Cross were aware of that.

I ran my hand up the doorjamb of her room, needing a little bit of clarity before walking in.

Her room.

I barked a silent laugh to myself. When had I assigned her a room in my head?

Fuck.

We had an omega now. She'd claimed the whole damn pack with that bite.

I knocked twice. There was no response.

"Ruby?" I pushed the door open a crack to stick my head in. Then I pushed it wide.

She wasn't here.

The sleeping bag was folded neatly at the end of the bed. Bathroom door wide. I flicked on all the lights, as if that would show where she was hiding.

Cross had said something about the closet, hadn't he? The small walk-in was empty. Spare pillows and blankets along the top shelf that was it.

I pulled the shower curtain back. Nothing. The linen closet didn't have a door now. I ducked to peer in the bottom. Empty. I even pulled open the little doors under the vanity. Doubtful she could fit, but I checked anyway.

She was not in this room.

I now had two members of my pack in the wind.

Unease creeped into my very soul.

"Hey, what's up?" Jackson popped his head into the room. Maybe drawn by my emotions.

"She's not here."

Jackson disappeared from the doorway. I heard him relay that to Luther and then their soft calls for her.

"Jonnie's car is gone." Luther said as I came back to the great room.

"We would have heard that." I rubbed my hand across my face to get my brain to work.

"We'd hear shit. It's electric."

Cross had been gone for hours and hours. Did Ruby follow him? How would that be possible?

"Would she have gone after Cross?" Luther asked, reading my mind.

Jackson flew up the stairs to our bedroom, two at a time. He was back 30 seconds later with a lockbox, panic making his movements sharp and decisive.

He dumped the contents out on the island counter. Thumb drives in all colors spilled across the top. He picked one, seemingly at random, and jabbed it into Cross' laptop.

Luther and I both leaned in to confirm what we were seeing on the screen.

"Did you clone Cross' phone?" I drew my brows together in disbelief.

"Of course, I fucking did."

"Hold up. Are you spying on Cross?" Luther turned the computer toward him with a finger. Jackson turned it back and kept clicking on the trackpad.

"No." He was biting his lip in concentration. "I don't care what's on the phone. I've never looked at it before. But you're damn right. I'm going to have a way to track you, track all of you in an emergency."

"You little control freak."

"OK. This is the last cell tower ping. Let me pop the coordinates into a map."

He cut and pasted the text into a map. We all leaned in to watch it zero in on a tract of green space.

"Greenlawn Cemetery?" Jackson read out the location.

"It's where Stella and his pack lead are buried." I rubbed my chest at a phantom ache. Cross hadn't gone to the funeral, but he of course knew where they were buried.

"He's been there for..." Jackson flipped back through some lines of code on the screen, "maybe 4 hours."

"So, he went right there?" Makes sense.

Jackson leaned over and pulled another thumb drive, and jammed that one in next.

"Did you clone Ruby's phone, too?" Luther asked, pulling out a stool to sit.

"Yeah, about that."

There was something in his tone that was mighty suspicious.

"Remember a while back, we got that lead on Riot? That he was meeting with a GPRE analyst?" Jackson continued as he went about sorting through different windows of data. "That's when I met Ruby."

"Wait, what?"

"I was jacked up on heavy scent blockers. Walked right past her. Caught her scent. Knew instantly."

"That was like weeks and weeks ago." Luther said.

Jackson didn't respond.

"Have you been stalking her this whole time?"

"What did you expect, that I'd meet my scent match and not do anything about it?"

"Why didn't you tell me?" I asked, oddly hurt by this revelation.

"Oh no, you don't get to be angry at me for not delivering information in a timely fashion." He turned toward me while pointing at Luther. "You held on to this little nugget for 8 years."

I winced. He had a point.

"Fuck, wrong window." Jackson muttered.

"Wait, what's that?" The word "whore" jumped out of the screen at me.

"Her texts." He was about to click it closed, but I batted his hand away and maximized the window.

I pulled the screen toward me as a stream of filth poured across the screen. Jackson elbowed me to make room for him, too.

> Scrub yourself down before you get back, your rank stench is everywhere.

> We'll stick you in the kennel for two months this time

> You want the Crimson Bullet treatment?

> Nester whore.

"What the fuck is this?"

"OK." Luther snatched the computer away to get our attention. "You're going to have to listen to the whole story before flying off the handle."

"Luther?"

He took a deep breath and pulled the computer out of my grabby hands.

"She's Ruin Winters."

My brain absolutely could not comprehend those words. Luther wanted to look away from me, I knew it, but he held steady until he was sure I actually heard what he said.

Jackson stood, spinning off the stool he was sitting on. He started and stopped, asking about a dozen different questions.

"Remember I said I caught a woman in the warehouse explosion? I had a concussion, so I thought it was all fake. It was Ruin Winters, black hair, black lips. I scent matched to her. I knew it instantly."

"A pack can't have two scent matches. I scent matched to Ruby a month before that, at least. Once you scent match, it locks in. You don't get another, unless she dies."

I watched the realization creep across Jackson's face, ending in a look of horror. If Jackson scent matched to Ruby two months ago, that match would be locked in. Any omega we recognized after that would have to be the same person.

"She killed…"

"No." Luther shook his head. "She was here with us. She wasn't driving the van. You said you found a black wig and glasses, right?"

Jackson was pacing in tight circles, his arms covering his head as he worked through his thoughts and feelings. They ping-ponged through the pack bonds in a chaotic mess.

"When she showed up here, I didn't exactly remember what happened at the warehouse. Then all the red flags that Cross mentioned. That incident in the kitchen?" He jutted his chin towards the room. "She repeated something I said in the warehouse. So, I knew for a fact then."

"Why the fuck didn't you say anything then, that we had a terrorist in our house?"

Luther put his elbows on the counter and picked at his thumbnail.

"Because you were already in love with her. I… I couldn't break your heart." He said the last part on a rushing exhale. "And she's not a terrorist. This isn't her."

"How do you know that?" I pulled the computer over again and I scrolled to her latest text. "*Get the fuck back here.*" It was attached to a quick video of a guy face down on the ground.

"Lhevus."

"Luther. I can't pull teeth in this conversation. I don't have it in me. You gotta give it all to me." I said, putting my elbows on the counter.

Luther nodded. He straightened and put his back against the counter and crossed his arms. He kept his eyes on the floor.

"Right after Havoc perfumed, before he forced her to go gold pack, Mason Forthright kept showing up. He's the unofficial leader of the Reset, right? Talking about this reeducation program he was starting. Manchurian candidate stuff to turn omegas against the Institute. He wanted Havoc. I forgot all about it."

Jackson finally settled, propping himself up on the edge of the couch. His emotions were still shifting all over the place.

"After I figured out the warehouse thing, I confronted her. She denied it, of course."

"That's what you were talking about in her bedroom?"

Luther nodded. Jackson was biting a nail.

"Then when we were having sex..."

Both Jackson and I were on our feet now. Luther winced. He probably did not want that tidbit out.

"You... You had sex? With Ruby?"

"Look, that's when I put it all together..."

"You had..."

"Jackson, let him get the whole story out." We could process that later.

"She... She practically bullied me into it, alright, Jackson? A dubcon scene right out of one of your romance novels." He rubbed his eyes, pinching the bridge of his nose. "She was going on and on that being around so many auras would put her into heat and she had to have sex to stop it."

"That's not..."

"I know that's not how it works. But that's in Reset propaganda. That's how *they* think it works."

Jackson put his back to a wall and slid all the way to the ground, not trusting the couch or gravity to hold him up. I was battling nausea. It was a lie they told omegas unfortunate enough to be born in Berry Creek. Most of them probably believed it. It gave them unfettered access to omegas to have sex with.

"Just think about this for a second," Luther said, putting up one hand, "think about all the vile shit we pick up in Reset propaganda." He held up his other hand. "Now think about all the weird shit we've noticed about Ruby. The bed. Food. Flinching. If you feed an omega enough of that Reset shit, Ruin Winters is going to come out the other side." He mashed his two hands together.

"Luther, that's a stretch." I said, grinding my teeth. His math had to be wrong on this.

"Is it? Her body is covered in fresh bruises and old scars." Luther's voice soft, pain and regret pitching it low.

Jackson started banging his head against the wall. I leaned next to Jackson and pressed my leg into his shoulder. He put his head on my thigh, loosely curled his arm around my leg, resting his hand on the top of my foot. He blew out a tense breath.

"That's when I knew. When I put it all together. They were…" he swallowed audibly, "beating her into this."

Jackson was taking short, shallow breaths again. "Now the whole world wants her dead." He covered his mouth in horror. "I said *I* would kill her myself."

We all zoned out for a minute. A bunch of minutes. The implications of the picture Luther was painting. She was seventeen when she perfumed. Ruby and Luther were the same age. At right about the same time, Luther was on the streets, getting away from his foster father. And Ruby was just beginning…

I focused on the looping video on the computer. I couldn't go there in my thoughts. Not right now. The video was shaky and dark. One flash of white practically glowed in contrast to the rest of the shot. A spot right at the nape of the neck. Just below the collar of the jacket on the dead guy.

It drew me in like a tractor beam. I stepped out of his hold on my leg and frantically tapped until I got it to go full screen. It was hard to make out, but it definitely looked like the letter A, done in a graffiti style text. The anarchist patch young hooligans in the punk scene like to plaster everywhere.

"No."

Cross' beat up leather coat that Jackson sometimes wore had that patch right at the nape of the neck.

"Tell me this is not Cross."

Luther and Jackson were instantly at my side, Jackson ripping the computer from me. He pulled up the metadata information on the image. It would have geolocation tags.

"Cross." Jackson breathed as he punched in the coordinates in a map and it zeroed in on the cemetery where Cross was.

"How?"

"I was wearing that jacket the day I met Ruby. Met her for real. In the mall. Shit. That's how the betas found us. A tracker or something in the coat?"

Jackson batted my hands away as he frantically opened and closed different windows. Jackson was good with computers. Not as good as Cross, but good enough for this, apparently.

"The last ping on her phone was 40 minutes ago, here…"

She was in Berry Creek.

Without a word, we all bolted from the living room. We'd be in full battle rattle in 3 minutes.

FORTY-FIVE

CROSS

The jacket was tight across the shoulders. Couldn't quite zip it up either. The leather cracked in places. One of the snap buttons had some rust. It smelled like Jackson.

I hopped the last fence one handed. This place should have better security. Or not. It wasn't like the residents were going to be walking out. Maybe grave robbing wasn't all the rage with young hooligans these days.

The glass bottle tinked ominously when I tripped and caught myself on a headstone. I held it up to the decorative lamp post that lined the footpath. No cracks. I was good.

I took a swig, the amber liquid trickling down my chin. I swiped at it with the back of my hand, shaking off the excess moisture. I already smelled like whiskey. Didn't matter if it got all over me.

I was a walking god damn cliche tonight. Strolling a grave-yard, half drunk, bottle of booze in one hand, a decade old journal in the other, looking for my dead mate's grave.

I had gone to our house in the city to get away from my traitorous brothers, to get away from her scent, only to be surrounded by theirs. We'd had people come in and rip out the carpets and throw out the couches. The bedrooms didn't get doused when the fire suppression system kicked in, so the house wasn't a total loss. But it was bare and cold. Empty. More like a memory of a home than a home.

The jacket was tossed on the kitchen table with other items the workmen decided to save. I grabbed it, the journal, and a bottle on the way out.

This journal was only half full. Details of the funeral were on the last page I had written on. I couldn't bear to open it again after carefully copying down the information.

I had only bought the thing the year before, when Stella found us. I couldn't make sense of what was happening, writing it down helped. I hadn't written a lot, but I took it everywhere with me. It fit perfectly in the inside pocket of this jacket. Stella had bought me the jacket. She even said she liked the anarchy patch - "it added character."

She was lying.

She lied about everything.

She was 27 when she met us. I was 19. David and Roy were only a few years older. I had been couch surfing and stealing cars for a good year when I met David. I left home just before my 18th birthday because I couldn't stand to watch my dad beat on my mom for the affair she'd had that resulted in me. Surprise! There's only one way for beta mom and a beta dad to produce an alpha son, and it didn't involve the beta dad.

David saw himself as a smooth criminal. Off to set the world on fire with his gangster empire. He was too dumb for that though, but he was smart enough at least to find a smart kid and a straight up thug to pack up with. As pathetic as it was, I thought he was my golden ticket.

And Roy? Roy was just mean. He liked the power he had over

people. I didn't know what possessed the universe to make him an alpha. They really should make it a law that you can't join a pack until your frontal lobe is fully developed. We were just young and dumb. David saw us as tools, not brothers.

Then we met Stella out at one of the nice bars in the Gritch. She was playing tourist with a girlfriend, slumming it with the peasants. David got fucked in the head when Stella's strawberry scent latched on to us. He wooed her by saying she smelled like strawberry lip gloss and going all caveman on her, fucked her in the women's room and bit her the next day.

Stella was an abject lesson in being careful what you wished for.

It was hot in the beginning. She was practically ancient for an omega to not be bonded into a pack. She was holding out for a scent match. But when poverty became chronic rather than trendy, she regretted letting David bite her. And she didn't want a bite from me or Roy. That was the mind fuck of it. She wanted to be scent matched, but she didn't actually want her scent matches.

She insisted on keeping her job. Roy became increasingly paranoid and controlling. They'd fight, then she'd climb on my cock and make sure David heard it. She'd never let Roy touch her except during a heat cycle. I didn't know if he cared.

Those scent match bonds were powerful, but didn't make you a good person or a good partner. Not automatically. This fucking journal turned into a teenage girl's lament with pages of "why doesn't she love me?" Stella wanted the omega dream of a rich pack, balls and galas, a gaggle of hot men on her arm falling over her, fucking her, and bringing her pretty things. What she got were three broke, dumb kids who were only good at the fucking part of the job.

It wasn't enough for her.

It didn't matter. I still followed her like a puppy, doing whatever I could to make her happy. I drove her to a girlfriend's house one day. She said it was a reunion of her Institute class. A sleep-over. She was gone for five days. That was my clue. But I kept it to myself.

I should have done something. I should have gotten her safe. I should have gone ape shit and ripped her out of there. I shouldn't have let her come home to David all blissed out, post-heat, with the scent of other alphas all over her. The second I figured out she was going through heat with other alphas, I should have done something.

I still didn't know what happened exactly or what was said. But I felt it. Her anger and disgust seeped from her carefully constructed walls. It felt like a normal fight at first, and then David's aura exploded. The rage was so intense, I could taste it. Her anger turned to fear, the primal kind. The kind of fear you only get when you know your life is going to end. Then nothing but pain from her that faded with each heartbeat. Eerie quiet bled into our shared emotional space before the bonds shattered and the world ripped apart. It knocked me unconscious in the grocery store.

Days later, Talon explained to me what had happened. David had gone rogue, shot Stella, and put her in the freezer in a sad attempt to hide the body. Our pack bonds shattered, leaving me shattered. When David appeared in the doorway to the garage, I fired a gun without even thinking about it. I was able to kill him, proof we were no longer pack. I never found out where Roy was when it all happened, how he reacted, what he felt. I never saw him again.

I felt like shit for that for the longest time. I just left him out in the cold. Our connection was broken, and it was like I threw him away with the trash.

Talon and Jackson showed up in the chaos. I had known them for a while. Liked them. Did anything they asked me to. I needed the money they could pay me. And... Fucking Jackson. He was a goddamn drug. He gave you a taste of friendship and you couldn't not want more.

It was Talon who took Stella's dead body out of my arms, the gun I used to kill David still in my hands. Jackson sat with me in the shower for hours as I disintegrated. Your aura was able to just flake away, untether, no longer coalesce around you to keep you sane. Jackson refused to let that happen. Talon offered a pack bond later that night. I couldn't say no. The pain of floating away like stardust was too great.

I put my whiskey bottle on top of her gravestone. Jackson paid for the funeral. He bought me a truck, all new clothes, computers, everything. I couldn't go back into that house. I couldn't stand anything that carried their scents. All I had was this fucking jacket and the journal. The jacket hung on a hook by the back door until Jackson started wearing it.

I sat right on her grave, my back to the stone. The alcohol did a moderate job at numbing my emotions. It didn't touch Ruby's. They were crystal clear and chimed through me. I touched the bite mark on my neck.

That was what mates were supposed to feel like. Entwined and connected. She put her teeth in me to stop me from hurting someone I loved.

I rested my head back on the stone and opened up to Ruby's emotions, made possible by the bite on my neck. She was worried, scared, confused. It felt awful, more so because I knew I was the cause of it. I couldn't tap into the pack right now. I couldn't bring myself to know what they were feeling.

Jackson always said pack was pack. Anything could be forgiven. This though? Hiding the fact Luther was a rogue?

Putting a gun in Luther's face? Could that be forgiven, too?

I squeezed my eyes shut and fished in my pocket for cigarettes and a lighter. My head started to pound like I was going to jump right over the buzzy drunk part and get straight to the hangover.

Flipping the journal open, I tore out the first page. I snapped it open and caught a whiff of sweet butane. The flame ate up a corner of the page, devouring it too fast to even want to catch a word or two before the flames took it.

The burning paper was not at all comforting like Luther's wood smoke scent. I tore another page out to watch its ashes float on the soft breeze.

I leaned over and smashed out my cigarette on David's headstone. It horrified me when I learned they were buried side by side. Something felt wrong about putting her next to her murderer.

I lit up another page, held onto it until pain bit my fingers.

This entire book was a quest to figure out why she couldn't love me. How could a scent match go wrong like that? I only had books and movies to go on. I didn't know any other scent matched packs.

The next journal I bought was all about Jackson and what the fuck possessed him to push Talon to make us a pack. I never understood it.

I sighed. I never *wanted* to understand it.

The book after that was Luther.

I'd been breathing my last breaths when this big blond kid had come out of nowhere with a cheery "hey, need some help?" when we got pinned down on a job gone bad. He stuck his finger in the hole in my chest to keep me from bleeding out. His aura created a bubble around us that did more to protect us than the handful of bullets Jackson had left.

I never understood why he did that, either.

Reaching up for the bottle I'd left on the headstone, I gave myself a disgusted snort. The next journal would be Ruby's.

I took a drink and let myself wallow in Ruby's increasing anxiety. It was better than feeling my own emotions. I took out my phone. Swiped to our group chat. Maybe I could have Jackson tell her I was fine, that I just needed some time. She shouldn't be wasting this kind of energy on me.

Fuck. I could just let her in, let her feel that for herself. Touching the bite mark, I let her in, just a little, just enough so she could feel me. Relief crashed into her, chased by confusion. This wasn't a pack bond but it was similar enough. That sense of comfort omegas could pump out, seeped into me. It tightened my chest because it felt so good, and I didn't deserve that.

The bottle was halfway to my mouth when I heard metal scraping on stone. Not an alpha, no aura to speak of. A beta security guard most like. I rolled my eyes. The perfect cap to this night would be Talon bailing me out of jail for trespassing in a god damn cemetery.

"Well, that's convenient. Kind of cuts out the middleman." He was average height, average build, average everything. He was backlit so I couldn't see his face. I turned my head slightly. He had a buddy behind me. Two buddies.

"I ain't dealing nothing you want here tonight, man." I draped an arm over my knee to look as casual as possible.

"We thought the tracker was dead, then it pings to a cemetery."

Tracker? What the fuck?

"Too bad we can't mess up Serrano's pretty face now. I was looking forward to beating information out of him." That came from Buddy #1 over my shoulder.

"Do you just want to get on with your villain monologue and get to the fucking point?"

"You must be sucking dick of some really important people. Not even our plant in the Institute could find you."

"Find me?"

"All he could find was a mention of Cross Stirling being in the Serrano pack. It was easy to get to Jackson."

"Look, can you just cut to the fucking chase here? I've had a rough night."

"Oh, sure buddy," he reached into his waistband. I got to my knees to lunge for him. "Roy says hi."

The neon yellow of a taser flashed in his hand. Three pops of propellant and the biting sting of voltage hitting me in the thigh, back, and chest. Pain exploded in the back of my head with a dull thud.

A spike of soul-crushing fear from Ruby was the last thing I felt.

RUBY

"Don't hit her in the face. We don't have time for editing." Mason said, snapping his fingers in Billy's face to drive the point home. His hair perfectly combed, his double-breasted suit jacket hanging open. "If you ruin this shot, Billy, you'll never see the outside of a kennel."

Ruin. I had ruined everything.

Bennett let go of my shoulder and pushed me back, so hard I tripped and landed on my butt. I heard the make-up pallet crack in my hand. The mirror had split, but the highlight powders would still be useable. Someone would find a way to punish me for this, too.

Jackson's sister. I had killed her. She was dead because of me. And Luther? Why had he said that? And Cross...

I touched my lips, they still tingled from biting Cross. My teeth in his neck was ... *right.* Then I could *feel* him. He was angry, hurt. Sadness seeped into my bones from him, and then it was like he turned the volume down. Why had I done that?

I didn't understand any of this.

I had paced that little bedroom trying to figure it all out. I hadn't wanted to touch my phone since Jackson gave it back to me, but I needed to know what they were doing. I stared at all the messages. They just washed over me.

The sudden pain from Cross was blinding. Then the text message. I knew it was Cross. I knew they had him. I had to get him back. For them.

I stole the little electric car in the driveway and drove like I was in a trance. I hadn't driven a car since I was seventeen. Ruby would panic about this, but not Ruin. Ruin could do anything. I left the car in the woods outside of Maypole and walked the rest of the way.

"Get the fuck up," Bennett said, tearing apart a plastic shopping bag. He threw black jeans, a shirt, and a jacket at me. The Ruin costume.

As I changed, the room emptied. None of them looked at me, too busy with their own tasks. Bennett checked the two guns on the table, like he had forgotten which one was the good one and which one was the bad one. He slid in an empty magazine and handed the bad gun to me.

There was a commotion down the hall. My breath caught when I heard Cross' laugh. I closed my eyes as he flooded back to me. He was hurt, pissed off, but there was something new in his emotions. I touched my lips again, smudging the black lipstick. He felt light, like he had cut weight off and was floating.

Bennett poked his head out into the hall to eavesdrop greedily on the conversation. I looked at the gun in my hand and the one on the table. I switched the two, tucking the loaded weapon, the good gun, behind my back.

He fumbled through a box of equipment and pulled out a mic pack. He put his hands on me like I was a doll, attaching the battery pack to the back of my bra, threading the wire under my shirt. Bennett touched me like he had rights to me. Anger flared in me. I was theirs. Not his.

He pushed me out the door. A van was parked on the lawn.

Everyone was skittering about. Mason Forthright was here, they all wanted to look busy to impress him.

Billy and Bennett had me in the middle of the lawn, checking my mic, making sure the levels were right. Their hands were rough inside my clothes, tugging at my bra in the back to make sure it wouldn't show.

"I don't believe it for a second." Billy spat out. "They held you captive, and you just managed to escape?"

"Lying whore. I bet you fucked your way out." Bennett roughly pulled down my jacket to put my clothes back in place.

He had said he loved me once. He was the lying whore. I knew what love actually felt like now.

I turned on all of Ruin Winters' best venomous charm.

"Oh, is the little beta upset because his little beta cock could never do the job?" A fake sympathy pout rounded my black lips.

If Bennett had an aura, it would have vibrated the air with his fury. He pinched my shoulder and punched me in the stomach. No holding back because I was a girl, either. I crumpled to the ground, on my hands and knees, taking his kick as the word *whore* rained down on me.

I picked my head up.

Cross was there and he filled my world.

FORTY-SIX

CROSS

The shock of the cold water had me choking and spitting. Pain screamed through my head. I had to force one eye closed. It lessened the pain and put a cap on the double vision.

I touched the back of my head, fingers came away bloody. Nausea rose acidic in my mouth.

Poor Luther. He went through this twice in one week.

"That's gonna leave a mark." The voice was strained, almost like there was vocal cord damage.

I pushed back to sit against the wall, hoping it was solid enough to keep the room from spinning. I opened one eye and looked at whatever asshole had clocked me over the head and dragged me out of the cemetery.

"Roy?" He'd... aged. It had been nine years, but he looked well into his 40s. Deep wrinkles streaked his forehead. The frown lines were slashed into his cheeks. He crouched next to a bucket, dusting something off his New Oxford PD uniform.

"Brother." He said in greeting. It held no warmth, it was pure menace. Nothing blood, legal or metaphysical, made us brothers anymore.

"You couldn't just ring me up with a 'Yo, let's grab a drink and catch up?' You always were a douchebag." I barked out a laugh. I needed to lie down, being half vertical fucking sucked. I scraped my now damp hair back and ran a hand down my beard to release excess water.

"It's not like your number's been in the phone book. Talon has far too many contacts to let your information be public."

He stood and loomed over me. I think he needed the height advantage to feel superior. I took a deep breath. His burnt toast scent was nonexistent. Orange and cut grass jumped up to meet my nose. I grinned.

Someone ducked his head in the room. I narrowed my eyes at him. Fuck me. He was one of the betas that attacked the house. I reached for my phone in the jacket pocket. No jacket. No phone. Fuck. I didn't have any obvious connections to the pack on it. But if you were good, you'd find it. I looked the beta up and down. How good was he?

"Commander Treyfor, we doing this or not?"

"Treyfor?" I couldn't hold back the barking laughs.

Roy, my former pack mate, brother, a man I left for dead out of my own grief when our bonds shattered, was now a ranking commander of New Oxford PD. That's fucking great. Rage turned his face purple.

"NOPD really does let anyone join, huh?"

"You left me with nothing. You took my pack lead. You took my omega. You took my bond. I didn't even have a name."

"Stella never wanted us. She was cheating. David went rogue when he found out. Killed her. I killed him." I nodded at his dress blues. "You're PD now, you should have had access to that file."

"You enabled her. You could never say no to her. You put her in another alpha's arms."

"I didn't know," I shook my head wearily, "Not until she was already dying."

"And you didn't save her."

The guilt of that had been chasing me for years. Every day, it was like a knife in the gut. Talon had tried to talk to me about it. I even tried therapy once. To hear the accusation come out of Roy's mouth, the one I've been torturing myself with, broke me. But in a good way.

To hear him say it, blame me for killing her, hearing it sound as ridiculous as it really was, unlocked all that guilt. I closed my eyes and thought of her face. Her beautiful face, on the day I met Stella, radiant and flushed with excitement replaced the blood-stained one that had been haunting me.

I could let her go now. A smile broke across my face.

I opened my eyes just in time to see Roy's boot come at me. It connected with my stomach. But I caught it, twisted his leg into a knee lock and took him down to the ground. I pulled on my aura hard to overpower him. A snarl ground out of my clenched jaw.

Blinding pain split me in two, sending me to the ground, my whole body twitching. The beta stood over me while Roy collected himself. Electricity snapping off the cattle prod in his hand. I just breathed for a bit.

"So, you've got two choices," Roy said, standing over me, a string of spit lazily dropping from his mouth. "You either get to watch while I kill your pack in front of you, so I get to watch your aura shatter this time."

I got up on one elbow. Just the fact that I wasn't going to stay down got him all sorts of jittery.

"Or you do a little job for us." I looked from him to the beta armed with the cattle prod. They didn't have to say it, whatever it was, I was not going to walk out of that alive.

"Get up." He limply kicked me in the thigh.

I got to one knee and had to take a break to breathe through the pain. Once on my feet, I cracked my neck with some wild hope that it would clear my vision. Roy was trying to stare me down, stroking his chin like some comic book villain.

"I'm actually kind of curious about which you'll choose. Do you want to feel all the pain, or are you going to force your pack to take it again?"

I'd find a third option.

The beta motioned me out of the room and bullied me down the hall with the cattle prod. Intense light poured in the door at the end of the dingy hall. Given how the light was stabbing pain into my brain, it was really going to suck stepping outside.

The light blinded me for a few moments. I shielded my eyes. The lawn was littered with flood lights, making it as bright as day.

The only thing I was aware of was someone shouting "whore" and some dull thuds. They kept me moving across the lawn. I picked my head up, blinking away the pain feverishly.

There was a woman, dressed all in black, matching black hair crawling across the ground. A beta kicked her in the ribs, another stood next to her, a delighted smirk on his face. She retched, but didn't crumple. Didn't even scream. She clawed herself to standing, head down, unsteady, wiping her mouth with the back of her hand.

She picked her head up and stared right at me. Fierce determination in her eyes.

Ruby.

Ruby dressed up like Ruin Winters.

My heart stopped.

I took in the whole scene. I knew this place. We had raided it once on a trafficking sting. There was a white van, all its doors open. A dozen betas, all armed, littered the idyllic yard. Kennel cages off the right. Suspected HQ for the Reset.

And Ruin Winters standing in the middle of it all. Beaten, but not fully broken.

I put all the pieces together. The emotions coming off of Ruby led the way. Chunks were still missing, but I'd sort out the finer details when this was over and I came back to kill everyone.

Ruby was a foster kid in Berry Creek. She perfumed, and they tortured compliance out of her. Her issues with nesting. The flinching. The fawning. *Omegas can't say no. I won't be bad.* We figured out she had been abused. But this?

They orchestrated this. They created Ruin Winters and put Ruby in it like a costume. They took a defenseless, needy girl and hurt her so badly for so long, she'd do anything to make it stop.

It was stopping. Right now.

My aura flared hot. It ramped up like a rogue's, like David's, like Luther's.

I looked around at the betas. With my training on a good day? I could take out three of them before anyone even thought to raise a weapon. If I burned out my aura, I might be able to take them all. And with my omega standing there? My mate? I had endless sources of rage to fuel me.

Ruby felt it, felt my rage soar in the bond she'd created through her bite. Her eyes went wide and shook her head once. I had to be tactical about this. A rogue could go berserk and level the entire house. I'd need a hint of a plan, at least.

"So this is how we're going to do the shot." Mason Forthright stepped out of the house. Of fucking course. The name was on her paperwork as foster father. I had skipped right over it, glossing over the fine details in her file. "We're going to pan across the field and then push in on the van."

I turned and looked at the van, trying to figure out how it was going to star in this little number.

"Then we'll track Ruin Winters across the lawn, have her show off the truck…"

"I swear to fucking god, the nester whore had better remember her lines this time. We don't have time for cue cards."

I bit back a growl at the slur.

"Then she'll do the bit about "even the elite members of the GPRE want to see the Institute fall"," he said in a falsetto, "and we'll push in on him in the driver's seat."

"We'll edit in rubble from the institute in post-production." Another beta added helpfully.

Rubble? Institute? My god. It was a truck bomb. And they expected me to drive it.

Well, that was my third option right there.

The beta standing next to Ruby grabbed her by the back of the coat, shook her, and pushed her forward a few steps. I turned back to Ruby wearing Ruin Winters' look. It was so obvious now. It was all there. I'd just been too wrapped up in my own melodrama to see it.

I had watched countless hours of Ruin footage. Ruby picked up Ruin's body language and affect whenever she was stressed, confused, scared. The tilt of her head, the roll of her shoulder. The heavy makeup changed the angles of her face, making Ruin look more chiseled. But the flat look in Ruin's eyes was Ruby's when she was backed into the corner that first night. Ruin wore the same dead look when... they made her do porn.

I couldn't hold back the growls now.

Ruby felt it, probably in her bones. Ruby looked around frantically, and reached out through our bond. I could feel her on the edges of my awareness. The fear was there, but so was that quiet strength that omegas could have. She was giving that to me now. The strength to be smart and do this right.

I touched the bite mark on my neck. Her bite.

I cocked my head. There was something else. Something was pushing to get to me. Us.

Luther.

I had a sudden vision of Luther, tearing across grass, ripping someone in half, literally, just pulling a body apart with his hands. And then it was gone. I shook my head to clear my vision.

I grinned.

"Cross." Ruby's voice was soft and solid.

"Yeah?" They all heard us, but they were used to ignoring the omega they'd turned into a doll and tool.

"Fuck you." She didn't smile, but fire blazed in her eyes and in her aura. The pack's love language.

"Fuck you, too."

She shook her arm quietly to get my attention. There was a gun in her hand.

"Run."

She lifted her arm and shot the beta standing next to her in the head.

Before the body hit the ground, I had her in my arms, tackled behind the van.

Luther's aura, in all its rogue terror, burst across the lawn. The distinctive sound of MP5 automatic rounds crackled among the screams. The flood lights illuminating this section of the yard went dark as Jackson shot them out.

"Don't you ever fucking put your life on the line for me again." I held Ruby's face roughly, relief and rage swirling in me.

"You're mine. They can't have you."

Bullets hit the van above us. I had to get us moving in case the van blew. They did not seem like careful demolition experts, so the thing was probably unstable. I hauled Ruby up by the jacket, tucked her under me as we broke from cover.

I ducked to pick up a gun off a dead body. It was an AR, modified stock, extended magazine. Fucking awkward to use one handed.

I didn't need accuracy. Jackson would have that covered.

The pack had me. Had my back. Always had.

I could feel them clear as a bell now. Jackson, all this ruthlessness naked and exposed. Talon, calculating, precise, fearless. And Luther, a hot mess of pure alpha.

A beta running for me dropped. A tidy hole in his forehead. The exit wound probably took out the back of his head. Jackson was good like that.

Talon's SUV was maybe a hundred yard sprint away, left running next to the kennels.

Sizzling pain exploded in my thigh, taking me to the ground, putting sparkles in my vision. He *(wait, who? The beta with his brains blown out?)* hit me again with the cattle prod in the chest before running down Ruby.

I struggled to my feet, no breath in my lungs, my vision going dark. I crashed to one knee. The zap from the cattle prod must have hit a nerve. I couldn't feel my left leg from the hip down.

That beta had Ruby down on her back, hands around her throat.

I tore into my aura, pulled on everything it could give me. I didn't care if it killed me.

A single gunshot. It was slightly muffled, not the usual crisp clean crack. Everything stopped for one horrified second.

And then he started screaming.

Ruby scrambled to push him off of her. He curled on his side, gripping his crotch. Ruby staggered to her feet like she was drunk. Her midsection and her thighs were soaked in his blood.

She wiped at her mouth with the back of her hand, the one that still held the gun. Black lipstick smeared across her face.

I picked the AK up off the ground. The patter of gunfire had slowed. There were screams and moans here and there.

Ruby was transfixed. Staring at the man she'd almost killed on the ground, writhing.

I touched her elbow, I wasn't sure what was getting through to her. She leaned into my touch, but shifted her gaze. I slid my hand around her waist to pull her away, but she wouldn't budge.

"You have a choice to make Darlin'," I extended my arm with an AK, aiming it right at the beta's head. He had no color left in him. "He'll be dead before help can get to him. But he'll suffer." She'd shot him in the groin. Fucking perfect. But he would bleed out.

"Or I could kill him now."

"Ruby. Help." The dead man screamed from the ground.

A roar from Luther brought her head up. That made the decision for her. She staggered away. I fisted her jacket to keep her upright.

A black-clad figure jogged toward us. I knew it was Jackson before he ripped the ski mask off, leaving his perfect hair a mess.

He grabbed her by the back of the neck and flashed her a dazzling smile. He roughly kissed her, then reached for me and did the same. He flashed his eyes to Ruby and then back at me. I nodded. She was in shock, and mostly unharmed.

"Talon's going to need a minute to bring Luther down." He turned and jogged back, stopping just long enough to grab a body and drag it away by the arm.

I had her by the waist, moving us back toward the van, limping but making it work? When her feet got reluctant, I kicked over a milk crate that held sound equipment and pushed her down gently by the shoulder until she was sitting. I'd rather put her in the SUV, but I couldn't bear to have her that far away from me.

Leaning down, I grabbed the next body on the lawn by the wrist and staggered when the arm came away from the body. It was torn clean off from the shoulder.

Well, that was going to haunt my fucking dreams, that Luther had access to enough power to rip an arm off. I bent to grab the guy by the shirt.

It was Roy. His face frozen in his final moments of pain and horror. I closed my eyes and dropped my hold on the pack bonds, letting them in, letting them fill me.

They were the pack I was always destined for. Ruby's bite throbbed on my neck, making my teeth ache to be in her.

Jackson and I made quick work of piling all the bodies and any other evidence we could snag into the van. He pulled the van right to the front steps of the porch.

I crouched in front of Ruby, gently pinching her chin to turn her face toward me. Her eyes were flat and dark. I watched them slowly fill with tears.

"We have to go. Do you need me to carry you?"

She shook her head, but couldn't quite get to her feet. I hooked my arm around her upper back, my fingers in her armpit to get her up. Jackson fell in alongside us, shifting his MP5 to his back. He jogged ahead of us to open the back door of the SUV.

Talon was holding Luther up against the side of the vehicle. They both turned as we approached. Ruby stiffened and then practically launched herself at Luther.

Luther jerked back and put up a hand. "I can't... I need... Not yet."

Ruby crumbled. Her breathing got tight, her lip trembled. Luther reached out and touched shaking fingers to her lips. They both sighed, like that amount of contact would be enough.

He climbed into the far back, contorting his big body to get around the seats. Ruby was a statue. Talon flashed a look at me and nodded. We didn't have time to baby her through this. They were quick and efficient, killing everyone on site, but this was Berry Creek. We'd be outnumbered if someone sent out an alarm. I picked Ruby up and climbed in with her, setting her down behind the driver's seat.

Jackson slammed the rear door shut and walked around to get behind the wheel, stuffing his long rifle awkwardly next to him. I should be driving. All of us hated when Jackson drove. I didn't trust the concussion I was probably sporting to get Ruby home safe. Dirt and grass kicked up as we peeled out.

Jackson stopped us probably a hundred and fifty yards from the house, the SUV angled across the dirt driveway. Talon handed him something from the glove box, an incendiary round. Jackson got out, rested his elbows on the hood of the vehicle, sighted his rifle. The wave of sound from the explosion hit us like a brick wall. Ruby pressed herself up against the window, watching the fireball shoot up hundreds of feet in the air.

TALON

Jackson was the absolutely wrong person to be driving right now. He was not careful like Cross. We were clocking over a 100mph down back country roads with blind turns. That truck bomb cratered the house. We couldn't be seen here.

I turned back to look at my pack. Luther was curled in a ball in the back seat, trying to settle his aura and not let it overwhelm the pack bonds. Ruby was staring out the back, like she could still see the house. Cross was darting his attention between Ruby and Luther. He leaned into Ruby to pull the handgun from her.

A growl erupted from her. She skittered back, wedging herself on the floor behind the driver's seat. Cross had his hands up, like he had touched a hot stove. She had the gun in a two handed grip, finger on the trigger, aimed at his midsection.

Awkwardly, I turned in the passenger seat and steadied myself with one hand on the seat behind me. I wanted to fill her field of vision but not encroach on her too far.

"Ruby," I said her name with pack lead authority behind it.

"I want you to take your finger off the trigger." I choose my words carefully. I didn't know how she would respond to an outright order to obey right now. I hoped she would respond to my desires, though.

She looked at the gun in her hands, her eyes narrowing, like this was hard work and she had to concentrate. She licked her lips, smeared with that black shit, and slowly eased her finger off the trigger.

"Good little omega." She took one slow blink. "Eyes up at me again. Good. Cross is going to put the safety on. You can hold on to the gun, but we need to be safe." I held her with my eyes as Cross gently tipped her hands down, pointing the gun at the floor, flicked the safety and unchambered the live round.

"We have a little bit of a drive. What's going to make you feel safe right now?"

She darted forward, on her knees, and put her head in my lap. Reflexively, I pet her head, smoothing her hair out. She violently shook her head. I snatched my hands back and balled them into fists. She didn't want to be touched. She could have all the control right now.

FORTY-SEVEN

TALON

Jackson pulled right up to the mudroom door. We all tried to help Ruby out of the car, but she shied away from our touch. We corralled her into the kitchen. She looked around like it was her first time here and let the gun slip from her fingers. It made a metallic thud when it hit the tile.

She tore through the house to her room, dragging us all in her wake. Ruby balled the bright blue sleeping bag in her arms and turned toward the bathroom, seeming to notice us standing in the doorway for the first time.

She looked at Cross, darted her eyes to the bathroom and back again. Chewing on her lip and bouncing from foot to foot, she made a choice and slipped into the bathroom. Cross closed his eyes, muttering fuck under his breath.

I peered around the door into the bathroom, yanking the door wider when I didn't see her. The room wasn't big enough to lose a person, even a tiny omega. I finally noticed the bright blue leaking out of the closet. Crouching down, all I could see of Ruby was an index finger grasping the sleeping bag to her.

All omegas needed to nest. It was a biological drive. A nest could be as simple as cozy blankets and pillows. A pillow fort. Duo's nest was a tent. They could be super elaborate. Jackson's birth pack had a whole house that was essentially a communal nest.

There was something very unnatural, very wrong about seeing our omega in a closet like this.

I straightened and nodded for everyone to take this out into the hall.

Cross looked furious. "I'm not leaving her in there," he said in a hiss. I caught him by the arm before he made it two steps to the bathroom.

"Now." I said with some pack lead juju behind it. Cross snapped his arm out of mine and stormed out of the room and down the hall.

I left her door open. A closed door would be way too much of a barrier between us right now. I wouldn't be able to stand it.

"You can't leave her in a closet," Cross said.

"This is not about your comfort level, it's about what makes her feel safe."

"I'll fucking go make her a nest."

I stopped Jackson with a look. "We need to bring the energy and hormones in here down. This is hard on Luther too."

Jackson and Cross traded glances and made a visible effort to take it down a notch.

"Go shower, take off your kit, stow your weapons."

I snagged Cross by the waist as he blew past me to his room. He scowled.

I put my hand on his face and pulled his eyelid down.

"You get clocked?"

"Yeah. Tased too. It's fine."

I pulled his head down. There was a pretty good gash that was crusted over.

"Luther, go with Cross and make sure this wound gets taken care of."

Cross opened his mouth to protest, but shut it when he saw my look. I nudged Luther to get him moving. I didn't really want either one of them alone right now. Cross had been beaten unconscious by his former pack brother, and Luther had killed a dozen people by ripping them in half. We were all going to need fucking therapy after this.

I hit the stairs to our bedroom. I could already hear the water running. I sighed. I needed to fall apart in Jackson's arms before I could figure out what to do.

FORTY-EIGHT

RUBY

Half Ruin. Half Ruby.

I tilted my head, so did Ruin in the mirror.

Ruin's black lips covered mine.

There was a tiny bar of soap wrapped in crinkly paper. I held it to my nose. It smelled like flowers, not grass or whiskey. I picked it up. It had words on it I didn't understand. I rubbed it on Ruin's lips. Scrubbed them in a fury now.

All the white towels were smudged with black. Smudged with her. With Ruin.

She ruined everything.

I stuffed them in the trash. They'd put me in the kennel for that.

They.

They didn't exist anymore. Gone. That explosion took every bit of them. They only lived in my head now.

I reached out and touched the shower curtain. There were two, a plastic one, and a flowy one, leashed together on sliding hooks. It matched the towels. I stepped out into the dimmer light of the bedroom.

I pulled the corners straight. There were too many pillows. What do you do with all the pillows? I ran my hands up and down where Talon laid the other night.

He belonged here. In a place with two shower curtains and soap you can't understand.

Everything seemed made of glass. If I breathed too hard, it would all shatter. I tucked my fingers under my arms, hugging myself. Couldn't touch anything else and ruin that, too.

I could hear them out there. Feel them. Most of all, Cross. He was a calm wall around me, if only he could get between me and Ruin.

They drew me down the hall. Cross was slumped with his head in his hands over his computer. Talon and Luther sat side by side on the floor with their backs against the wall. Jackson was stretched out on his back, his head on Talon's leg.

None of them wore shoes.

I looked down at the boots they'd made me put on. Ruin's boots. Black and shiny.

Would I get in trouble for this, too? Wearing shoes in the house?

Nothing made sense here.

Then Jackson saw me and scrambled to his feet. He took a jerky step forward but stopped.

I nodded. They didn't want to touch me either. I'd ruin them, too.

I already had ruined them. Cross hated Luther for being a rogue. They'd hurt Cross. I'd killed Jackson's sister. And they'd just murdered a whole yard full of people.

"I want to go home." I had to whisper it so I didn't break anything else.

"You're welcome to stay here." Talon said very carefully.

"I want to go."

Space and time stretched between us. He would say no. Keep me here. Just like they said.

"Alright."

Jackson took a step forward, but Talon spun to block his path. They had a whole silent conversation.

"Cross, will you drive us?"

I kept my head down. I couldn't look at any of them.

TALON

I closed down the pack bonds. I couldn't really deal with the feeling of betrayal they were all pumping out. Ruby was already standing by the SUV.

She had slept for 12 hours. We had not.

We spent the day monitoring the news about the attack at the Opera House. The death toll sat at 6, countless more injured. News trickled in about Jackson's sister. She was in critical condition. Out of surgery but real information was spotty. His birth pack was causing a scene. She was in a beta room, not a pack suite. The dads were up in arms at the treatment.

Initial reports rolled in on GPRE channels in about a suspected truck bomb explosion in Berry Creek. From the tone of the chatter, it didn't seem like it would be investigated too heavily. I'd have to meet with Duo and figure out if we could spin this in our favor. Having it look like the Reset was incompetent and blew themselves up would probably work for all involved parties.

Ruby asking to leave was a shock. Their anger on top of everything else was pushing me to a limit.

I pulled on socks and my boots in the mudroom, avoiding making eye contact with my pack brothers who huddled in the tiny space.

"You... You can't seriously... Talon, you can't do this," Jackson's voice shook.

"She's ours," Luther said softly.

"Cross, tell him. She's pack. He can't make her leave."

"I'm not making her. She asked to go home," I said, trying to keep the defeated tone to myself.

"That doesn't fucking matter."

I walked out of the house without a look back. It mattered. It was the only thing that mattered right now.

CROSS

The 40 minute drive back into the city was one of the most painful things I had ever done. Worse than letting go of Stella's dead body. Ruby sat in the back, her head down, with only an occasional glance out the window. The only thing she said during the entire trip was to rattle off her address.

I could feel her all around my edges. Her bite throbbed on my neck still. She was flat and numb. Not an unexpected response after what happened.

Talon was unreadable. His posture seemed relaxed. He had the pack bonds on lock down.

This was wrong, and he knew it.

A day ago, we had all said we didn't want an omega. Well, three of us anyway. That had all changed. We didn't have to have a pack meeting about it.

We had debriefed what happened. The betas at the cemetery, using my skull as T- Ball practice. Commander Roy Treyfor. They told me how Luther put the pieces together. Thank god for Jackson's obsession about the pack. I didn't think I could have gotten both Ruby and me out of there alone.

That was the thing. Pack meant you never had to be alone. Yet, here I was, driving Ruby away from us. Literally.

I parked illegally in front of her building. It wasn't a bad part of town. Relatively safe and tons of shopping within walking distance.

Talon got out without a word and held the door for Ruby. She punched in the code at the door. And we waited patiently for the elevator, my sense of dread growing as we waited for the numbers to count down, returning the elevator to the first floor.

She froze in front of her door. She seemed stuck, unable to move forward. All I got from her were muted emotions. I jammed my hands in my pockets to prevent myself from snatching her up and taking her out of here. Her trance finally broke, and she punched her code, 4434, into the keypad. This was an older building. These kinds of locks were not secure.

"Ruby." She whirled at the sound of Talon's voice. She held onto the doorknob behind her back like she was guarding it.

Talon shifted his weight backwards, putting more space between them.

"You've been through a lot. I don't think you should be alone, but I respect your request."

The two of them were waging a silent battle. Not against each other, but themselves, each denying what their own instincts were screaming at them to do.

"I..." Talon blew out a breath and gathered himself. "We...," He tried again. "As an omega, you've scent matched to our pack. That's not fate. There's no law that says you have to do anything about it. You can reject it and walk away. You have all the power here. It is your choice to join our pack or reject us." He thought for a second and clarified. "I want... We want you as part of the pack. But the choice is completely yours."

I watched confusion wash over her face, like Talon was speaking a foreign language. And then Ruby was replaced with Ruin Winters right before my eyes. A dazzling smile, batting her eyes, a pretty pout. She didn't trust us. She didn't trust anyone except Ruin Winters to protect her.

Talon saw it, too. Even though he had the pack bonds shut, I could feel his anger simmering.

"Ruby." His voice was sharp and harsh like a whip crack. "I need you to say it, that you understand that this is your choice. You have the power here."

She lifted her chin, making an effort to hold on to Ruin.

"I understand." She said in the most unconvincing voice ever.

She turned the knob behind her back and cracked her door open just wide enough for her to slip through.

Talon turned on a heel, punched the stairwell door, flying down the five flights of stairs. He stopped at the bottom, not for me to catch up, but for him to catch his breath.

"What the fuck are we doing?" I stepped around him and blocked his way out of the stairwell. He looked back up the stairs, like he could see Ruby from here.

"I want you to stay here. Jackson and I will drop off your truck. I don't..."

"What the fuck are we doing?" I repeated.

"Giving her a choice."

FORTY-NINE

CROSS

Talon stalked out of the elevator.

He had been here for a couple of hours last night, so I could catch some sleep in my truck and recharge my tablet. He had the envelope I had couriered over in one hand, Chinese take-out in the other, and was wrapped up tight in a bad attitude. He handed me both items.

"NOPD give you any trouble when you flashed your ID?" I asked.

"I can't believe her neighbors called the cops," Talon said with a look over his shoulder at the doors lining the hall.

"She's been doing demolition in there for a solid two hours." We both stared at the door. I had been on the verge of breaking it down myself when a neighbor poked their head out into the hall and I practically bit it off.

"Whatever you are doing here is not working, man," I said.

Talon stepped past me and knocked on the door. He frowned when no answer came.

"Ruby, I would like you to open the door." Talon was choosing his words carefully. It was odd. His hand hovered over the keypad. We had both memorized her code, but neither of us wanted to break in unless we had to.

The lock scraped, and the door opened a few inches.

Talon skated his eyes up and down her, frowning.

"Can we come in?" Ruby slowly backed up into the room, hiding something behind her back.

The room was a disaster.

TALON

Her hair was matted. Her face was dirty. She was still wearing the blood-stained clothes they had put her in at Berry Creek, boots and all.

I turned my head to take in the room. There was a toppled folding table with computer equipment, ring lights, mic stands littered across the living room floor. The flimsy closet doors were hacked open, like she had clawed through them with her bare hands. Bits of cheap splintered wood were everywhere. There were piles of rags on the floor. One pale pastel, another black with splashes of bright red and hot pink here and there.

She was holding a pair of scissors in one hand, a gauzy white blouse trailed on the floor from her other hand.

"Ruby, what have you been doing here?" I tried to keep my tone neutral, so I didn't sound like I was scolding a child.

She took in the room like she was seeing it for the first time. She looked at her hands and the pile of fabric scraps on the floor. Her eyes shot wide with panic. She backed up, hiding the scissors behind her back.

I grabbed her gently by the upper arm and tilted her head up to meet my eyes. I heard the scissors slip from her fingers and make a dull thud on the floor. She was terrified.

I stroked her face, hoping the touch, if nothing else, would get through. Her eyes fluttered, and she turned her face into my palm.

"I want you to go take a shower. Wash your hair, brush your teeth. Put on clean clothes." She nodded slowly and backed into the other room. I didn't move until I heard the water running.

I covered my mouth, not trusting I wouldn't scream. Cross stepped into the tiny kitchenette area and began pulling open cabinets. I moved to one of the shattered doors and flicked the padlock that had been screwed into the frame.

Cross was rapidly opening and closing drawers and cabinets. He stopped, put his hands on the counter, and exhaled slowly.

"They're empty," he said to the floor. "There's no plates, pots, pans, silverware. There's nothing here. No food either."

I crouched, sorting through one of the piles of rags. Black knit fabric, black denim, all cut up into ragged bits. Pops of colored lace and the remains of an underwire bra were mixed into the debris.

"This isn't a home, this is a prison camp."

Bile rose in my throat.

"Talon…" the edge of rage in Cross' voice was deadly sharp.

"I know. I fucked up."

I shouldn't have left her here alone. At the very least, I should have stepped one fucking foot inside her apartment.

"Fuck you, man." Cross pulled out his phone and tapped furiously. "There's a SmartMart a couple of blocks from here. I'm going to get her some basics."

The water shut off. Indecision plagued me. I couldn't leave her here, but I couldn't compel her to come with me. I needed the pack to find its strength again before we took whatever the next step was.

I'd spent the day chest deep in political bullshit at the GPRE. I'd given Duo the basics on what happened, light on the details, so he was armed with just enough information. We were trying to sow seeds of speculation that Ruin Winters had died in the explosion. He had no fucking clue if it would work.

Meanwhile Jackson and Luther were trying to hold each other together. Their attempts were questionable at best. The constant pinging from Jackson's phone was too much for him, but he wouldn't mute it or turn it off. Luther was still on a razor's edge. Instability in the pack was not helping. The two of them were splitting their time between doing buddy runs through the woods and burning shit in the fire pit. And Jackson hated to run, so he was super pissy.

Ruby appeared in the doorway, water dripping from her hair, wrapped in a towel. My mouth went dry at the sight of blue-black finger marks on her upper arms. She danced from foot to foot, working up her courage.

"I..." her eyes darted back to the piles of shredded fabric on the floor, "I don't have any clothes."

I tamped down a growl before it could erupt and peeled off my jacket. I was too angry, angry at myself to let my fingers shake when I undid the buttons of my flannel. I draped it across her shoulders, kneeling to do up the buttons once she had slid her arms in.

"Cross is going to go do some shopping for you." I didn't even bother to look at him as his pissed off stomps trailed out of the apartment and down the hall.

I picked up one of the folding tables and shook two folding chairs out of the debris. I unpacked the Chinese food, thanking the gods there were forks, sticking one in the pint of fried rice.

"Come have a seat and eat some food." I held the chair out for her. She nervously sat down and pulled the take-out container to her lap.

"Have you been sleeping?"

She shrugged, digging the fork into the rice, but just moving chunks of veggies around. I touched her knee, hoping contact would ground her. If she was pack, if she was mine, I'd be better at judging what she needed.

"Eat," I said, tapping the white box.

She was stalling out and retreating within herself. I needed to keep her moving forward, not back. She took a forkful, then another. Tears welled in her eyes, and she was shaking more and more with each bite. The container slipped from her fingers and hit the floor.

She flew back, knocking over the chair, slamming both hands over her mouth, before bolting for the bathroom. She was huddled over the toilet, heaving up the tiny bits of food she'd just eaten. I cradled her in my arms, pulling her hair out of her face. I made shushing sounds until the heaving stopped and the shaking started.

"That's all they would give me some days." I squeezed my eyes shut when her whispered words landed on me. "And if I threw up..." I pulled her into me, folded her into my lap, when the sobbing started.

I sat with her on the bathroom floor, rocking her as her sobs quieted and the shaking stilled. Somehow, I managed to get my phone out of my back pocket to text Cross to pick up a sleeping bag and pastina from Mama Gina's. I made little circles on her shoulder with my fingertips. I could hold her like this forever. And fuck them for making me have to hold her like this.

At the sound of the lock punching open announcing Cross' return, Ruby bolted upright, furiously rubbing at her tear-stained face. I stood with her in my arms and sat her down on the counter. I picked up a towel from the floor, hoping it wasn't filthy, and ran it under cool water. I held her face gently in my hands, dabbing a corner across her cheeks. She was beautiful, even wrecked as she was. Cross wouldn't care about tears. But she cared.

"Better?" I asked.

She nodded and tried a weak smile. I kissed her forehead and led her out of the bathroom.

Cross had set the Italian food on the table and was unpacking kitchen items. He brought over a plate, a real plate, with a fork and knife and a glass of water. I opened the containers of food for her and put a small amount of the pastina, tiny star pasta, some lasagna and some penne with red sauce on her plate.

I held out a fork full of pastina for her. "It's just pasta with butter and cheese." She opened her mouth tentatively and took the bite. I laid the fork down on her plate and nodded for her to keep eating. Cross puttered around, putting things away as Ruby shoveled food into her mouth.

I squeezed her knee and joined Cross in doing a quick cleanup. He was shooting daggers out of his eyeballs at me every chance he got.

When the room was presentable, at least not a hazard anymore, I leaned against the wall and crossed my arms and watched Cross pull the tags off a small crowbar he must have bought. He wedged it into the padlocks that were drilled into the fridge and pried them off. He did all the padlocks on all the doors too, even though she had already broken through them. I pulled the sleeping bag out of its sleeve and snapped it open on the bed, unzipping it and flipping a corner down, hoping it would be inviting.

I rubbed my head. A dull throb had started an hour ago. I pulled my jacket back on. Cross glared at me, the courier envelope in his hands.

He pulled the chair out next to Ruby and sat. She gulped the last bit of food and wiped the back of her hand across her mouth.

I could feel what Cross was feeling, dread, determination, anger. He took a breath that tasted of courage.

"You know they took compromising photos of... Ruin

Winters. Video too. I managed to break into the server where they were storing them and deleted them all."

Ruby's eyes went wide and her nostrils flared with her ragged breaths.

"They were selling them. So, I can't erase every picture that exists." He ripped open the envelope and shook out its contents. He placed a plastic credit card on the table in front of her. "I hacked into their bank account and transferred all the funds through several shell companies to this account. It can never be traced to you. They will never come looking for it."

"Isn't... Isn't that a crime?"

I stifled a smile. That was an odd worry for the girl to have right now.

"Yes," Cross said simply. "Talon is going to make me leave you here. Whatever happens, this," he tapped the card, "will let you be comfortable for a long time."

Cross stood. Ruby grabbed his pant legs in her fist.

"Don't," she licked her lips and looked up at him with desperation, "don't tell Luther. Or Jackson. Please."

He nodded once and stepped away. If I didn't do this now, I would never be able to leave. I zipped up my light jacket, not because I was cold, but it gave my hands something to do so I wouldn't sweep her up in my arms and carry her out of here.

"Ruby, I'd like you to do something for me." I jammed my hands into my pockets and clamped down on my aura and the pack bonds, hoping that this landed like a request and not an order from an alpha. "The choice is still all yours. Whenever you want to make it. I'd like you to wake up every day, shower, wash your hair and eat at least twice a day. I want you to get out of this apartment and go for a long walk every day, too. Can you do that for me?"

She nodded, unsure of herself.

"Can you use your voice, Ruby? Will you do this for me?"

"Yes," she whispered, biting her lip.

"Cross will be in the hallway. If you need help, ask for it. Alright?"

She nodded and looked down briefly, before her eyes flashed wide and she corrected herself with a verbal "yes".

Without another word, I stepped into the hall and flew down the stairs. Cross hauled me back by my jacket and threw me into the wall when we got to the bottom landing.

"What the fuck are you doing, Talon? How can you leave her alone like that?"

I sunk down on the bottom step and put my aching head in my hands.

"I don't have a choice."

"The fuck you do."

Cross paced like a caged animal in the stairwell. If I had the energy, I might be matching him step for step.

"This is how it started with Melodie," I said, hanging my head. "I don't know where Dom ends and alpha begins, alright?"

I pulled myself off the stairs and interrupted Cross' little circuit to slump against the wall.

"We got into a fight. I was out of control, all hormones and aura. She said she'd kill herself if I left. I told her to go do that. And she did."

I was pretty sure Jackson had told him about Melodie, but I don't know what he'd said. I was a coward and never wanted to pull up the image of finding my first love in a bathtub full of her blood, so I never talked about it.

"I honestly don't know if Ruby is agreeing to things because she wants to or if she's just obeying. Cross, I don't know where the line is any more and I..."

Cross switched places with me and sat on the stairs.

"I don't know if she has the capacity for free will and I can't help her find it. She just spent, what? A decade with a cult that controlled everything she did? And then what? Her scent match pack sweeps her up and love bombs her? What if in 5 years she wakes up and realizes it was all coerced and she never got a chance to make a choice about what she wanted her life to look like?

"I don't know if I can do this," Cross said to the floor, rubbing the back of his head. I had to remind myself he was still recovering from a blow to the head.

"You have to. I can't be here to influence her. Luther needs a little bit of self-care right now. And Jackson…" I sighed. "Jackson has his own morality when it comes to the pack and things that he wants. I don't know if I can trust him not to take the easy road."

Cross stood and ripped the elastic out of his hair, scraping his fingers through it to tighten it again.

"I fucking hate you right now," he muttered.

"I don't care, so long as we do right by her."

He bounded up the steps two at a time.

FIFTY

RUBY

The sleeping bag was a slippery mass crumpled up in my arms. My eyes were stinging, they were dry and burning. I looked back over my shoulder at the bed. I held my breath and twisted the doorknob before the door defeated me, too.

Cross was sitting on the floor right across from my door. His laptop propped on one leg, a paper coffee cup in his hand. He looked up at me and smiled. It almost made me fall down.

"What do you need, Darlin'?" His voice was rough, like he had been talking too much.

I looked back over my shoulder. I didn't even know how to explain the problem.

"Um," I wrangled the sleeping bag in my arms, "I, uh... Talon said I couldn't..." I couldn't do this. I shook my head and took a step back.

Cross shifted to his knees and caught the back of my leg in his palm, stopping my retreat. He made slow soft strokes up and down my calf, like petting a scared animal. That's what I was after all.

"Go slow. I got all the time in the world for you."

My eyes began to slide closed. I felt myself weave on my feet. I needed sleep, but...

"I'm not allowed..." I swallowed and tried again. "I can't sleep on the floor. Talon said so. But I... The bed... He... His bed..." I bit my lip and shook my head. I ran out of words.

He looked past me into the apartment. He didn't say anything for a long while, but he never stopped stroking my leg.

"Well, my lap isn't the floor or the bed."

"What?"

He let go of me and an ache bloomed, already missing his touch. He closed his laptop and moved his coffee and messenger bag out of the way. He sat back against the wall, hitched his jeans up, crossed his legs, and held a hand out to me.

He waited for me to make a choice. I put my hand in his and he pulled me to the floor and settled me in his lap. He brought up one knee for me to lean against and arranged my legs over his.

"Not the bed, not the floor," He whispered, and he pulled the sleeping bag out of my fingers. He arranged it around me, tucking me in.

I sat frozen and stiff. No one had ever touched me like this before. Except Talon this morning. I nuzzled into the shirt that carried Talon's ocean pine. It mixed with Cross' whiskey cherries like they were made to go together. Biting my lip, I tentatively put my head on his shoulder. His chest rose and fell, creating a rhythm of ocean waves.

I reached a finger out and touched the bite mark I had given Cross. I didn't know why I'd done that. It felt like the only thing to do at the time. I couldn't stand him being mad at Luther because of me. I was nothing, they were everything.

A deep rumbling started in his chest as my eyes closed. Maybe that's what the ocean sounded like, too. I had never seen the ocean. Maybe they would take me one day.

FIFTY-ONE

RUBY

I smoothed the sweater down and looked at myself in the mirror. My hair was still damp from my shower. The jeans were a little tight, and the sweater was a little too big. It was deep blue and had a wide neckline.

Ruin would never wear anything like this.

Neither would Ruby.

Cross had left two shopping bags of clothes. And he thought of everything. Underwear, a sports bra, socks and a pair of high-top sneakers.

I adjusted the neckline of the sweater. If it wasn't sitting just right, it would show a bruise.

I reached for the blue box that held my vitamins. I didn't know what day of the week it was, but the last "S" compartment was the only one that had four pills in them. I dug under the sink for extra bottles to restock a week's supply. I filled the little boxes with three of the pills, but one was always hard to open. Bennett always had to do it for me.

I frowned.

I carried the pill box carefully into the other room, being sure not to jostle it and send pills raining to the floor. The last time I did that, Bennett said…

I squeezed my eyes shut and tried very hard not to hear him calling me a dumb whore. Cross was sitting on one of the folding chairs, his ankle on his knee. He had showered, too. That is, after he ran to the store to buy a shower curtain.

"Could you open this for me?" I asked, handing him the bottle and carefully putting the pillbox on the table. I sat to lace up my sneakers.

"What are these?"

"Vitamins. I skipped a bunch of days, so I have to make sure to take them."

He shook out a handful and they made little clicking sounds as he dropped one in each compartment.

"Vitamins?" He asked.

"Mm hmm."

"How long have you been taking these vitamins?" He asked, staring into the box.

I shrugged.

He closed his eyes, leaning forward and resting his arms on his knees, the box of pills in his hands. He blew out a breath, sat up, and ran his fingers through his hair. Closing all the compartments except for one, he tipped the contents out into his hand and put them on the table between us. He sorted through them and singled one out.

"This," he said with a sharp exhale, "is an over-the-counter birth control. It's very common, very safe. Everyone takes it."

My brow wrinkled at the pills.

"This one, Milprofenteen" he pulled out the little pink one, "is also birth control. It was pulled from the market due to unexpectedly high rates of infertility. They only give it to gold pack omegas."

Birth control?

"This is a scent blocker. Very safe, very common, you can get it in gas stations. It only usually is good for a couple of hours, though."

We both looked at the last pill. It was a capsule, half red, half clear, with little beads inside.

"This last one is an illegal drug. Outlawed 10 years ago, maybe more. It came out of a failed medical program. We find it a lot on the job. There's a big black market trade for it."

"Wh... what does it do?"

"It's a heat blocker. Its side effects can be mild when you're taking it, but if you stop cold turkey, it can lead to psychotic episodes and intense painful heats."

I stared at the pills. I didn't know how long I had been taking them. Always, I guessed. Cross' voice had been completely neutral, so I didn't know if this was good or bad. I didn't know what it meant. Or what I should do.

I scooped the pills into my hand and popped them in my mouth. My hands shook on the glass of water as I tried to choke them down. There was too much new, too much that was scary. I couldn't think about more bad things right now.

I stood and covered my ears to protect them from the screaming inside my head. Cross reached for me, his fingertips grazing my arm. I stepped out of his reach and smoothed my hair down.

"I have to go for a walk."

Shower. Wash hair. Food. Walk.

Four things. I could do four things. Two of them were already done.

Cross bent down to tie his boots. I picked up the bank card he had given me. It had a fake company name on it. Citrus Holdings, LLC. I put it in my back pocket. I didn't have a purse anymore. Or a phone. I didn't have anything.

He held the door open for me and pushed the button for the elevator. He held every door open for me.

I walked down the street with no direction in mind. I didn't have any place to go. And Cross refused to lead the way. He stayed just a step behind me. Some part of my brain told me that I should probably go to the spa I worked at. That I used to work at. Did it make me a bad person if I just never showed back up? I stopped to ask Cross.

I shook my head and kept walking.

Kids on skateboards shot by us. I jumped out of the way, losing my footing off the edge of the curb. Cross caught me by the waist before I could twist an ankle. His fingers lingered on me, sending tingles all the way to my toes.

We were now in front of the shoe store that was right across from the Leaf and Bean. Where I'd met Jackson that second time. I'd stood right there, right next to those red pumps, when everything changed. The same girl was in the shop. She was arranging a silk scarf that was tied in a pretty bow on a green leather handbag.

She had given me a card. It was gone now, with my bag and everything else.

My hand paused on the shop door without pulling it open. I turned and looked up at Cross. He was already reaching around me to get the door.

"Could you, maybe, if it's OK, stay out here?"

He quickly scanned the shop, and smiled. There was something hollow in his smile. "Of course, Darlin'."

My breath felt shaky as I stepped into the store and pretended to look at the red shoes. I didn't want to interrupt her. I didn't really know what I was doing here.

I looked out toward the coffee shop. This is dumb. I should just go.

"Can I help you?" I turned toward her. She had her dark brown hair pulled into a high pony, bangs that just touched her eyelashes and perfectly applied cat eyeliner.

I opened my mouth and closed it. I didn't know what to say.

"You were in here the other day, weren't you? You were real nervous about meeting someone across the street."

"I um…" I tucked my hair behind my ear, trying not to cry all of a sudden. "You, um, you gave me a card."

"I did." She touched my elbow and immediately I felt less nervous. I still wanted to cry, though.

"I think I might need some help," I said it so softly, I didn't know if she heard me. She flicked a nervous, angry glance outside. She was looking at Cross, who was leaning against the glass, on his phone.

"Not him." I blurted. "He's… Not him."

"OK. Are you in immediate danger?" She put an arm around my back as she pulled me deeper into the shop. I shook my head.

She held open the employee's only door for me. There was a tiny table with two red plastic chairs and a counter with a fridge and microwave. A set of lockers lined one wall and storage shelves with dusty looking boxes was on the other..

"I'm a volunteer intake coordinator with Lucy's House. I'm not a counselor, but I can help you figure out what kind of services you might qualify for."

I sat down and picked at my nails in my lap. My manicure still looked good. I thought about the card in my pocket. I'd have to pay for them myself now.

"Can you tell me what's wrong?"

Where to start with that fucking question? *Oh yeah, I'm Ruin Winters, the terrorist, criminal, who just killed a bunch of people.*

And I've been ab... My breath caught, gagging on the words. I tried to swallow, but my mouth was too dry.

"I'm from Berry Creek."

Her eyes went wide. She got up and got her phone out of the locker and immediately placed a call.

FIFTY-TWO

RUBY

The dull sound of metal clanking against metal was soft, but it filled the entire apartment. I had spent hours in the shoe store with Dove, that was the shop girl's name and Emily, a counselor for Lucy's House. We just talked. No, we didn't actually do a lot of talking. They talked.

I didn't understand some of their questions, and I just couldn't seem to put things in the right order. Everything was jumbled up in my head. Dove kept her hand on me almost the whole time. She was an omega. I didn't know that we could do that, that we could make someone feel warm, peaceful, and safe. They sent me home with a stack of papers and appointments to come to their office.

There was a huge box in the hall when we got back. Cross said it was a futon. Not the floor or the bed. He was putting it together while I tried to eat the salad he bought for me. The plastic bowl sat on my lap and I just pushed brightly colored vegetables around.

The blue pill box on the table stared at me like it was a threat.

I nudged one of the papers over to cover it so I didn't have to see it.

Cross pulled the futon into couch mode and tested it out. It met with his approval and with some clicking noises it folded flat into a bed. He stretched new sheets across the wide expanse.

"I think I broke it." I muttered.

"Broke what, love?"

I blinked rapidly at hearing that word come out of his mouth. He crouched next to me when I didn't answer and waited.

"The computer. Do you think it still works?" I nodded at the mess of equipment that was in a messy pile on the floor. I had thrown it all to the ground. I knew I had done that. But I didn't remember doing it.

"You can use my laptop." He grabbed his bag that was by the door and put his laptop on the table.

"Don't you need it for work or something?" I lined up a cucumber, a carrot slice and a green snap pea in a straight line in my salad bowl.

"I have a tablet I can work on if I need to."

I moved the veggies into a triangle shape. I sat up and looked around the apartment suddenly. I couldn't remember if I had even seen a pen in this place. There were some forms to fill out, and I needed to make a list.

"I need a pen and some paper," I said absently, picking through the salad to find a fourth veggie to make a square.

Cross sat and pulled his bag over. It was boxy and leather and stood up all by itself. It looked like it was old. There were scuff marks and a gash on one side. He pulled out his leather journal and put a fat black pen between his teeth. The one I saw him use the first night we were at the cabin. He flipped the journal open and tore out about a dozen pages that he tucked into his bag.

The journal and pen sat like an accusation on the table. I agreed, I wasn't good enough for them.

"I think I need to be alone for a little bit."

Only once the door closed softly behind Cross did I open the journal. I thought I might cry, and I didn't want him to see that. The paper was shockingly white. I scribbled the word "help" at the top of the page before I convinced myself I'd ruin this, too.

Choices.

Pack.

I wrote those next.

As if that's all the pen needed to get started, three whole pages filled themselves with wobbly words.

I pressed the start button on the computer. It was new and fancy and started right up. Not at all like the equipment Bennett...

I opened up a browser tab and tried to remember what the word was.

Milteen?

Melproton?

Milprofan?

FIFTY-THREE

CROSS

Luther: did she get you another latte?

Jackson: You put her in that?

Jackson: You are not allowed to dress our omega anymore.

Luther: have u figured out her favorite food?

Jackson: I got the sleeping bag you asked for. We need more pillows. Aurabuddies?

Luther: wtf is an Aurabuddie?

Jackson: You know, those stuffed animals, unicorns, narwhals and shit in different aura colors that you can put a scented heart in?

Luther: narwhal?

Cross: Sea Unicorn.

Luther: the fuck? maybe too cute? Body pillow???

> Jackson: Check.

> Luther: He's been watching Pimp my Nest nonstop.

> Jackson: shut the fuck up, you love it too. Faux fur is super on trend right now.

I sent a pic of her sitting in a salon chair talking with the stylist.

> Jackson: JFC

> Jackson: what is she having done?

> Jackson: Cross?

> Jackson: Don't leave me like this.

> Jackson: I swear to god Cross, if you don't send a pic the second she's out of that chair, I will make her nest so small, your gigantic head will never be able to fit in it.

I laughed and tucked the phone in my back pocket. I had been sending them pics throughout the day. Candid shots of meaningless things. Guilt bit at me. She didn't know I was doing it. She'd been used so much. Her image had been used so much. None of the pics were of her, really. The t-shirt and jeans she had laid out on the bed while she showered. A pic of the matcha latte she bought me. How she lined up veggies on her plate when she was pretending she was eating.

They weren't doing great. Neither of them, nor Talon. The second I sent them a pic of a dandelion dangling from her fingers that she picked on our first walk, the emotions they were pumping through the pack bonds shifted and eased. They needed connection even if it was just digital.

I leaned my head back on the glass when the realization hit me. I was punishing Talon by not sharing these little moments with him. Maybe we were all punishing him just a little, and it wasn't fair.

I was standing outside another business, leaning against the glass, so she could see me. It was a little ritual she was developing. It was equal parts adorable and heart breaking.

We'd be walking along, she'd stop suddenly, I'd feel a flurry of nerves and determination war in her. Then she'd gather some courage to go into a shop but ask me if I didn't mind waiting outside. It was like she had to prove it to herself that she could do it, whatever it was, on her own.

Yesterday, I watched her through the window as she ordered at the cafe. She slid that bank card from her back pocket and came out with two drinks and a giant bag of pastries. She handed me one of the drinks, saying it was supposed to taste like Luther. I had no idea how a matcha latte was supposed to taste like Luther, but it was the best fucking thing I'd ever put in my mouth. Because she bought it for me.

I got a sick sense of satisfaction that she used the money, their money, to buy me food. They had used her, tortured her, turned her into a sex toy and now she was feeding me treats that reminded her of my brother with the profits of what they'd done to her. Everything alpha in me roared with glee and fury.

My head was down, I was deep into my phone, monitoring message boards affiliated with the Reset. Apparently, we took out a good portion of their top ranks. I left a few anonymous comments suggesting that Ruin Winters was dead in the explosion. That rumor was taking off like wildfire.

The toes of her Converse appeared in my field of vision. I looked up at her and my heart fucking stopped.

I had been being careful not to touch her unless she invited it first, but my fingers couldn't hold back now. They traced a perfectly messy curl that fell in front of her eye. I traced a fingertip along her jaw. "Ruby," I said in an astonished, panting breath. She could bring me right to my knees.

Her hair was maybe a little shorter and dyed a vibrant, rich, cherry red. It made her look fierce, like a goddess of fire.

"Is it OK?"

I grabbed for her hand and put it to my chest. "Do you feel my heart pounding? That's what you do to me."

Don't be an ass and mention your dick right now. You can't pull off fuckboy like Jackson can.

Desire flared in her eyes for only a second before she pulled her hand away. A sassy smile touched her lips. She took a few steps back, pulling me in her wake. A little shopping bag swung from her hand.

That was Sexy Ruby. Not the fake sultry of Ruin Winters she could slide into like a costume.

I followed behind her, panting like the dog I was.

I watched her watch her reflection in all the windows we passed. She gave herself shy smiles and little hair flips. Heads turned like she was a duchess with alphas in tuxes on her arm.

She slowed, stopped, stared down at the bag in her hand. And she crumpled. I could feel a sense of panic rising off of her.

"Do you have a phone? I don't have one anymore," she asked, making a visible effort to not hyperventilate.

Instantly, I slipped my phone out of my back pocket, handing it to her.

"How... How do I call Talon?"

I drew her down an alley, my hand lightly touching her back so we'd be out of foot traffic and away from street noise.

I brought up Talon's contact and tapped the call button. She held the phone to her ear with closed eyes, discomfort of some flavor scrunching up her eyebrows.

"Look, I'm sorry. I fucked up. I've already begged." Talon's voice was low, but I could make it out.

She didn't immediately answer.

"It's me. Ruby."

"Hi." He shifted his voice. It softened, but held a note of concern. And hope.

"Um, I... I dyed my hair."

"That's great."

She rubbed her forehead with the back of her hand like it hurt, the shopping bag still in her grasp. I nudged it away with a fingertip so it wouldn't hit her face.

"You..." She looked down at the bag in her hand again. "The stylist gave me special shampoo. Instructions on how to wash it."

I could feel her struggle. It about ripped my guts out to see her shining and now all twisted up.

"It's a special dye. She said not to wash it more than once a week. Longer if you can."

"OK." Neither Talon nor I were getting the significance of this. This was a serious problem. She understood that, but not how to explain it. Or how to ask for help.

She licked her lips and blew out some shaky breaths.

"You told... You said I had to wake up and take a shower and wash my hair every day."

A distinct *fuck me* emotion came through the pack bonds from Talon. My head hung with the realization.

This was exactly what he meant when he said he couldn't tell where the line was anymore.

I could practically see him sink into his easy chair in his office and scratch his eyebrow with a thumb. It was his tell that he'd fucked up and was thinking about how to fix it.

"So, I..." he paused, second guessing every word that was about to come out of his mouth. "I trust you to make smart choices about your own wellbeing. In this instance, you're capable of following the advice of an expert or my... request. What do you think is appropriate?"

Alright, that was an oddly empowering way to handle this problem.

"I... I think I should follow her instructions."

When Talon told her to take a shower, eat, go for a walk, I didn't think anything of it at the time. I noticed the shift in her, that it gave her a sense of ease, something to focus on. It didn't occur to me that she'd view it as operating instructions.

There are people who function better with structure and routine. And that isn't necessarily connected to the natural submissive and responsive tendencies of omegas. Luther liked structure and ritual. He kept his gear a certain way. He hated mess in the kitchen. No one went into his room. He preferred that when we ate together, it was at the table, not the TV.

It was a fucking trauma response for Luther.

Ruby was programmed to obey by a cult that hated omegas. What must it do to the psyche of an omega to be beaten into submission and punished for what you couldn't help being?

All this, everything from the last few days, was her trying to figure out how to simply exist with no foundation to her life anymore. We'd literally blown it up. She was untethered, floating in space with only hair washing instructions to keep her grounded.

"OK. That's what you should do."

The silence stretched between them. Her anxiety dipped but built rapidly. She reached out, caught my sleeve, and fisted it. I reached for her to put a soothing hand on her shoulder. She sidestepped and shied away, but didn't let go of my shirt. She wanted strength, not comfort.

"What will happen when you don't like it?" She rested her forehead on my arm, waiting for a blow.

My heart broke into a billion little pieces. Yet again. It was the "when" not "if" line. I didn't need to have a mystical bond with Talon to know he was gutted, too.

"Do you like it? Does it make you feel sexy? Pretty? Powerful?" She nodded, but didn't say anything.

"Ruby?" She needed a prompt to say yes.

She rubbed her cheek on my sleeve, taking deep breaths. She was using my scent to get through this conversation. I clenched my jaw. It was taking everything I had not to sweep her into my arms and obliterate anything that caused her discomfort. If all she would take from me was my scent, I'd strip it from my body for her. She could use me however she needed.

"What makes me feel good is you feeling strong and powerful, however that looks for you." Talon said carefully. After a long moment, he added, "If I truly hated it, I would keep it to myself."

That was a real answer for her - an answer that was tangible and practical. Something she could understand. "I like how it makes you feel" was far too conceptual for most people. Even me. It wasn't until I was in a pack, in Talon's pack, that I could actually experience another person's joy like it was my own. Ruby was light-years away from that right now and without pack bonds, without being able to feel another person's emotions to know its truth. A thinly veiled "I'd lie to you" was an answer she could live with because it wasn't "I'd beat you".

"OK."

Another long silence swept between them. Ruby was coming out of her spiral, finding a way to trust what Talon said.

"I'd like to see it."

"See what?"

"Your hair."

"Oh."

Ruby straightened, picking up her head, most of the forehead wrinkles had smoothed out. She darted a quick glance at me. It was the first time she looked at me since getting on the phone.

"Talon?"

"Yes, Ruby?"

"Am I in trouble?"

"No." Talon said quick and simple. No fluff with that. There was no "don't be silly" or "what could you possibly be in trouble for". She needed direct and simple.

"If you don't need anything else, can you give the phone to Cross?"

She immediately handed it to me.

"Yeah?"

"You OK?"

"No."

He hung up on that. Direct and simple was the new vibe he was rocking.

"Can I carry that for you?" I pointed at the bag. She needed to know I wasn't going to dwell on the conversation she let me be a part of. She held the bag out to me.

I took a step down the alley to get her in motion. She smoothed out my sleeve.

And then she put her hand in mine and I just about died.

FIFTY-FOUR

CROSS

I was sitting in the hall again, absently trying to fit a waste management plant into my SimCity layout. She had asked for some privacy, and this was the only place to go. I didn't mind at all. I'd sit here all day just for that moment when she'd crack the door open at 2am and ask to sit in my lap or zip her into a sleeping bag.

I checked my watch. It was still early for her to want to go for a walk. The door popped open like she knew I was thinking about her. Which was honestly stupid. I hadn't stopped thinking about her.

I couldn't hold back the smile that blazed across my face. She was simply stunning. Her red hair put color in her face, made her lips seem fuller, her cheekbones sharper. The contrast with her eyes made her look almost unreal. She was wearing a simple light blue long-sleeve t-shirt and dark blue jeans.

Jackson was right. I should not be in charge of dressing our omega.

She had my leather journal, and a stack of papers clutched to her chest. The amount of satisfaction I got from seeing her fingers clutched around my journal was obscene. Indecent. Borderline immoral.

"I would like to go see the pack," She said slowly and deliberately.

The drive took a good forty minutes without traffic. I made it in 25. Normally, I'd be more careful with something this precious in the truck with me, but I couldn't keep my foot off the gas.

She was quiet on the drive. I didn't push small talk. Occasionally, I'd catch her lips moving out of the corner of my eye. She was rehearsing. Giving herself a pep talk, maybe. Her emotions stayed pretty even. Tension and uncertainty coiled around her, but she wasn't spiraling.

I parked next to Talon's SUV and got out of the car. She was staring straight ahead. I came around to her side and opened her door. It wasn't until I leaned across her to unclick the seatbelt that she got moving again, flashing me a weak smile.

I unlaced my boots and kicked them off in the mudroom. Ruby stalled out by the door, scanning the giant boots and shoes that littered the space. She looked up at me. There wasn't fear or dread in her, that awful feeling she got when she thought she did something wrong knowing punishment was coming. This was genuinely a thing she didn't understand and wanted to figure out.

"Is this a rule?" she whispered, like she only trusted me to tell her the answer. "To take your shoes off?" She was trying to figure out the rules of a new environment, one she saw herself having to navigate.

"No. It's stressful for Luther when there are muddy footprints on the kitchen floor. We care about Luther, so this is a simple thing we do for him." The context here was important for her to understand.

"Oh, OK." She brightened, a smile lighting her face, as she pulled the bows on her laces. She was doing something for

Luther, to improve his life, and that felt right for her. I put my fingertips on the wall to steady myself, as I fell off the cliff for her a little harder.

They were all on their feet when I stepped into the kitchen.

"Play it fucking cool." I said in a loud whisper, pointing a finger directly at Jackson. He had a throw blanket draped over his shoulders, desperate hope, and some lust on his gorgeous fuckboy face.

Ruby appearing in the kitchen sent a shock wave through the pack bonds. I smirked. Jackson was going to have to sit down before he fell down. She was hugging the journal and papers tight to her chest so she didn't nervously touch her hair.

She walked around the island counter into the great room like she'd bought just enough courage and she had to spend it fast. Talon sank back down onto the couch and pulled Jackson down with him.

FIFTY-FIVE

TALON

She was breathtaking. In choosing a new hair color, she was claiming a new identity. Not Ruin Winters, and not Ruby Frost. The old Ruby Frost. I sat, not trusting I wouldn't lunge for her, and put my teeth in her skin. I pulled Jackson down next to me, needing him to hold me back, hold me together.

Luther had been lying on the floor. He did that when he was unsettled, like having full contact with the earth was necessary to not break apart. He sank back down, hugging his knees like a puppy at her feet.

She took a deep breath and shivered. Our scents were so thick in the air, she could probably taste it. She had documents pressed to her chest, part armor, part resource.

"Talon said," she tucked a lock of that gorgeous hair behind her ear, "that joining the pack was my choice."

A collective heart attack flew through the pack bonds.

"I..." she lifted her chin and jostled the papers in her arm, "want to join the pack." Her voice wasn't uncertain, but the words were uncomfortable in her mouth, like she was speaking an alien language and wanted to get it right. "But, I have some conditions." That last bit cut off the explosion that was on the verge of erupting in our collective emotional state.

Jackson dug his fingers into my thigh, his breath shaking with dread, maybe? Like there was something she'd request that we wouldn't tear the world apart to give her?

"I need my own room," she said in a rush. "I... I need some place that's just mine."

She looked at each of us to judge our reactions to her being so bold. Whatever she found was enough to get her to the next part.

"I think I need..." She licked her lips, flicking her eyes to the empty kitchen, "I want to have a job. I don't think I can be a stay-at-home omega. I don't know how to do any of that stuff... I don't know how to be a real omega... and figuring that out... learning how to... being responsible for..." All the words were coming out in a rush. She got frustrated with herself, course corrected, and continued. "There's too much that's new, that I don't understand. And it freaks me out a little."

She was god damn beautiful, fighting so fiercely for herself. She was drawing a line in the sand and making a declaration about the future she wanted. In the face of the abuse she suffered, the pressure of society to be a proper omega, she was claiming her own space.

Ruby cleared her throat. Maybe she didn't think she'd get this far in the conversation. She looked down at the stack of papers in her arms, and spoke the next part to them, not us.

"I think I need therapy. But Ruin... I've done bad things that I should pay for. But I don't know what to tell people."

I looked at Cross. He leaned against the wall, as stunned as I was.

"And, I can't... Well, I might not..." Her breath shifted to fast and hard. She dropped to her knees and spread the papers out on the floor in front of her. The sudden movement made us all jump. She frantically shuffled them, flipping through pages in the journal. Jackson shot me a nervous look. Luther shifted to one knee, prepared to destroy an unseen foe.

She stood, having found the right page in the journal. She used one finger to lead the way, reading out the words she couldn't find on her own.

"'Milprofenteen,' or however the fuck you pronounce that jumble of letters, 'was pulled from the market after initial test subjects showed a marked increase of infertility, upwards of 43%, after completion of the trial. At the time of publication, it is unknown if that factor would resolve without further medical and therapeutic intervention.'"

Luther and Jackson rounded on me with confused, worried looks. Cross had told me about the drugs they forced on her. I did not tell them. They had sense enough to keep their questions to themselves right now and not make it harder for her.

She flipped a page or two in her journal, hunting for more words to make this easier.

"I don't want to be a mom." She hugged the book to her and picked at the corners of the pages. "So, if that's why you want an omega…"

She was quickly losing steam, like she'd expended all the courage in her bank account.

Oh, c'mon, baby girl. You can do it.

She sniffed and blew out a hard, sharp breath.

"Oh, one more thing…" She flipped the journal back open, slid the pen off the cover and made three check marks. She read silently for a second, her lips moving. She looked up, shifting her weight from foot to foot.

"Um, because of the drugs they gave me," Ruby looked down at her notebook again, missing the absolute fury that poured out of Jackson when he put it all together. I dug my fingers into his thigh to tell him we could be angry later.

"Well, see, I've never been through heat. Not really. And all my life, they told me heat kills omegas." Tears pooled in her eyes. She was rushing to rip this bandaid off. "I think it's a lie. It was all lies. I think. I don't know what's true. I'm really scared about heat and I need help." She ended on a sob.

"Yes," I said clearly, loudly, no hesitation.

"Um," the tiny word short-circuited her brain like it was the last thing she expected to hear, "yes to... to which part?" Her face slid from despair to confusion.

"To all of it."

She put her hand on her hip, not believing it would be that simple.

"This is a lot," she jostled the journal. "I'm a lot. And this is... bossy. Omegas aren't supposed to be bossy."

"Yes."

"I'm a criminal. A terrorist. I shot someone in the head that night." She pointed to herself for emphasis.

"The answer is still yes."

She continued, her body posture getting a little more aggressive to convince me "yes" was the wrong answer.

"I killed someone that night."

"Yes."

"I'm going to be a terrible omega. I don't know how any of this works." She made an offhand gesture toward the kitchen.

I shrugged. "Still yes."

She narrowed her eyes at me, a challenge burning in her red hot, like her hair, readying herself to throw down her trump card, the thing that would blow this all up.

"I shot Bennett in the dick."

Cross snorted. Luther put a fist to his mouth to keep in a bark of laughter.

"I don't know, Talon, *that*," Jackson held up a finger, "kind of makes it a "fuck yes" in my book."

"Since shooting assholes in the dick is not a hard limit, is there anything worse than that, that you think we are going to say no to?"

"No." Her tone was total disgruntled and petulant teenager.

"For fuck's sake, will someone say she's pack so I can hug her?"

"Ruby?" I raised an eyebrow at her.

"I'm pack?" Her voice raised into a whiny questioning lilt at the end.

"That was a question. Not a statement, little omega."

"I'm pack."

Jackson gave her about a half a second before he had her in his arms, the hug taking her off her feet. She held my gaze for one second longer before dissolving into Jackson.

But it wasn't until Luther put tentative fingers to her back that she broke, giving into uncontrollable sobs.

"Ruby," I bent down and wiped a tear from her cheek, "I don't hate your hair."

She threw both arms around my neck, pulling me down into Luther's lap with her.

JACKSON

We were all in a puddle right in the middle of the floor. That post-breakdown-crying-jag exhaustion hit us all. Luther had his head on Ruby's stomach when it let out a roar. He sat up sharply, concern lining his face, his hands on her hips making circles with his thumbs to solve the problem of Ruby's empty stomach.

"Pancakes. You need pancakes." He dug her out of the pile of alpha limbs that covered the little omega and lifted her to her feet. He took her gently by the hand to lead her into the kitchen.

"Maybe waffles?" Ruby contributed, thinking it was a helpful statement.

Luther staggered but didn't say anything. I snorted. Talon punched me in the arm. Luther, inexplicably, had become very anti-waffle recently.

"Maybe German pancakes?" Luther said, pulling her toward the fridge.

"What's a German pancake?"

"Oh, they're kind of custardy in the center and crispy on the edges. Cross is boring and only likes buttermilk. They are sometimes called Dutch Babies."

They continued to discuss the intricacies of pancakes. These would be good pancakes.

"Three things. First, what the fuck have you two been doing these past few days? That is a whole new person, and I'm not talking about the hair." I flopped onto Cross' back, forcing an *oof* from him. I kept my voice just above a whisper.

"Which brings me to Number two. With that hair? How the fuck am I going to sit across from her at dinner and not fuck her right on the table between salad and the main course?"

"Jackson, shh." Talon hushed me.

"And third..." I didn't even know how to put that into words. Rage and pain boiled out of me in rhythm with harsh breaths, trying to keep in the scream. Cross rolled underneath me, hooking a leg around mine. Talon grabbed me by the throat.

"Together." He growled low into my ear. "Together is how we're going to get through this. OK?"

Cross grabbed a fist of my hair and pulled our foreheads together. He threw the bonds open and finally let us in, really in. Something clattered in the kitchen as Luther felt it, too.

I put my teeth on the mark Ruby left on his neck, until he nodded his head, acknowledging that together, all of us, was how we would get through this.

"Oh. Fourth, please tell me we are going to go kill the rest of them, right? Anyone who so much as rolled their eyes at her?"

"Abso-fucking-lutely" Cross said.

Ruby's delighted giggles poured out of the kitchen as she broke eggs and made a mess with Luther. I didn't even need a pack bond for that to feel fucking fantastic.

FIFTY-SIX

RUBY

I buried my face in the poofy fabric. It didn't smell like anything. It didn't smell like them.

Their scents had been so thick all night. It had been almost like a physical thing. Like I was being constantly hugged, touched; sandalwood, cherry and smoke and pine, all like a million fingertips holding me together. It made me feel safe... and horny.

But the bedroom only smelled like me.

I had been staring at the door for... I didn't know how long. It was dark, it was night. Everyone was asleep. I had tried knocking, tried turning the doorknob, but I couldn't make myself do it.

Now that he was home, what if he didn't want me at all? Now that he was back with his pack... maybe I was just a job, a thing to take care of. Since he'd brought me back, maybe I was too much to deal with. And he knew about the pictures. He'd never want me after that.

I was stuck. I couldn't open his door. I couldn't go back to the bedroom. My bedroom.

The door flew open, freezing me in place. His hair was down, all pulled to one side. He wasn't wearing a shirt. Cozy plaid pants clung to his hips. His body was like a canvas. Little ink drawings splashed across his chest.

He was angry. I had woken him up. I should have just stayed in my room. I backed away. The hall started spinning.

Cherries and whiskey swamped me, I moaned. I closed my eyes and tried to breathe deep, but I couldn't get my lungs to work.

"Hey, hey, hey."

Cross grabbed me by the elbows when my legs buckled, pulling me a few steps into his room. He closed the door, but opened it wide again, kicking a book in front of it so it would stay open.

"What's wrong?"

I hefted the crumpled mass of the sleeping bag to show him. But he didn't understand.

"It's broken." My voice sounded somehow not like me.

"Baby, how's it broken?" Cross tugged at a bit of the fabric.

Once I started, words just tumbled out.

"It doesn't smell like anything. It doesn't work. It can't be my bedroom. It's too big. It shouldn't be mine. The bed is just angry. You were supposed to say no. You shouldn't have said yes. Now I have a bedroom with a bed I don't know how to use and it doesn't smell like anything. You were supposed to say no. I had it written down. All the reasons. The big ones anyway."

I struggled to get enough air in, like the words took up all the space in the spinning room.

"Can you stand, whoops, I guess not." Cross said as I crumpled to the floor, my legs following my lungs, deciding not to work too. He followed me down, his hands making sure I didn't land hard.

I tried to gather up the sleeping bag into a neat pile, but it wouldn't behave. It slithered and slipped and escaped when I tried to hold on too hard. That was exactly what was happening in my head, too.

"Anything else?" He was sitting next to me, not touching me. He had one knee up, his forearm resting on top.

I nodded, keeping my head down. I couldn't look at him. I couldn't be horny right now too, knowing he didn't want me. I wanted to tell him that. I wanted to yell and scream, demand all the things my body was telling me that I wanted. But I couldn't.

"I feel dumb," I said to the sleeping bag. "This shouldn't be that hard."

Cross was silent for a long time before saying, "That's a lot of big feelings."

I closed my eyes. The room was spinning again.

"Let's figure out a solution to the immediate problem. You need to sleep. You're so tired you can't stand up. How do you want to solve that problem?"

"I tried. It doesn't work."

"There are other places to sleep besides the bed in your room."

"I'm not allowed to sleep on the floor."

"Darlin', that's not the only solution. There's the couch. You could sleep in the pack bed. I could wake Talon and Jackson up and you could sleep with them…"

"They'd be mad." I whispered.

"They wouldn't."

"They'll think I'm dumb."

"They won't."

I shook my head.

"You can sleep in my bed. I'll sleep on the couch if you want."

Another head shake. He ducked his head, so I was forced to meet his eyes.

"You are doing so good, talking about your feelings and about what you need and want. It feels hard. But it's not dumb. There are no wrong answers."

My hands crept up to cover my ears. Everything was spinning in there. I couldn't. I just couldn't say it. I couldn't just say that I wanted him all around me, his scent, his body. I needed him in me. He didn't want me. He'd seen the pictures. He knew what I'd done.

"Hey," he lightly stroked a hand covering my ear, "you're spinning again. Can you come back to me?"

I jumped at his touch. It was like lightning through my body. I gathered up the sleeping bag tightly in my arms.

"Here…" I swallowed hard and licked my lips, "you…" the only words I could catch in my spinning head and get out.

"OK." He stood and pulled the sleeping bag from my arms. I made a sound like it hurt. He spread it on his bed and came back for me with a hand out to help me stand. All the air got stuck in my throat. He zipped me up and stretched next to me.

"Do you want to be the big spoon or the little spoon?"

"Spoon?"

He gave a little huffing laugh. "Here," he rolled away from me, but reached for a fist full of the sleeping bag, pulling me tight up against his back. "When you're on the outside, you're the big spoon. When we're like this, you're the little spoon…"

He rolled us both over and pulled me into his body, wrapping his arms around me. I slammed my hand over my mouth to hold in a moan. I squirmed to get away from him. It was too much. I didn't deserve to feel that good.

"OK. Big spoon it is." He rolled away from me. I snuggled up close to his back and rested my forehead between his shoulder blades. I clamped a hand over my mouth to keep from kissing the stars and moons that splashed across his back in black ink. I wanted to make a map of him, know all of the art on his body by touch.

Tears filled my eyes as his scent, sweet and stinging, wrapped around me, knowing this was all I would have of him.

LUTHER

Her bright red hair spilled across her face and tumbled onto the pillow. Soft, even breaths puffed up a lock of it in an easy rhythm that my aura jumped to match.

Since the raid, since blowing my aura and going full rogue, killing everything in sight, my aura had been revving out of control, just how Moxie described it. It was the first time in a long time, since the news about Havoc, that I felt truly scared. But now at Ruby's side, it felt manageable.

I had been watching her sleep for hours. Her dreams played across her face. I could see when the bad guys came in the wrinkles between her eyes. And when the good guys got them by victory curling her lips into a smile.

Staying focused on her sleeping face, the present moment, gave me more peace than I'd had in a long time. The only other thing I let myself think about was making pancakes with her. She didn't even know you could make tiny baby pancakes you could eat with your fingers.

Ruby's eyes fluttered open. She must have ended on a good guy dream.

"Luther." She was surprised but not disappointed. She snuggled into my arms, putting her head on my chest. I let out a gasp as my aura flatlined and receded into the background. Like a normal fucking person.

"I thought I was in Cross' room," she said, taking a deep breath. A sigh left her.

"You are. We didn't want you to wake up alone."

Last night was apparently a little rough. Cross told us she was almost in a full-blown panic attack by the time she knocked on his door at 4am.

We started to put the whole picture together, filling in gaping holes in the story. Talon surmised that she was made to sleep on the floor and was forbidden to nest. I balled my hand into a fist, the hand that wasn't touching her. Just the thought of punishing an omega for nesting threatened the little bit of peace I was clinging on to.

Talon had to kick Jackson out of the house to go for a walk this morning. He was pumping so much frustrated rage into the pack bonds. His aura was like sandpaper, making Cross close up and pushing me to the edge. Jackson's normal baseline was unhinged happiness. Having him flood our shared connection with the exact emotions we all struggled to wedge into tiny little mental boxes was upsetting by itself. We were upset that Jackson was upset, which made him more upset, and so on. Pack bonds sucked ass sometimes.

We'd have to figure out a nest situation and get her comfortable enough to sleep through the night. Or the blue smudges under her eyes might become permanent.

"Where is everyone?" Her voice sounded content, like this was a question she asked every day. A smile split my face so wide it hurt.

"They had stuff to take care of in the city, so you're stuck with me."

Jackson was at the hospital with his birth pack. Talon was with Duo trying to pull off some super spy shit. Cross was retrieving the computer equipment from Ruby's apartment. His murderous glee at tearing the Reset's digital world apart was frightening. Nah, not frightening. Fucking exciting.

And then she purred. She was fucking purring, the soft rumble vibrating against my chest. The pure alpha pleasure that I had my omega on my chest purring was going to stay with me forever.

FIFTY-SEVEN

RUBY

It was a dance, and I was in the way.

I felt like I had slept the whole day, but I was still tired. Every time I woke up, Luther said "hi" like he had been waiting for me. I'd ask him where everyone was. He'd ask if I was hungry. Then I'd put my head on his chest to listen to him purr. Alphas really did purr. I thought that was a myth, too. I'd fall back asleep, and we'd do it all over again.

They were all back now and putting out food. They all seemed to have a specific job. Jackson was filling water glasses. Cross was putting a huge white plate in front of all the chairs. They moved around each other like a dance they had practiced.

Their conversation was light but hard to pay attention to. They all knew what they were doing, what was going to happen next. But I didn't.

I jumped when Luther touched my back and eased me toward the table. Tingles shot through my body, I suddenly wanted his touch everywhere. I bit my lip, hoping no one would notice.

Bennett always said he could tell when I was wet. And he was just a beta.

I sat as he started unpacking silver metal containers with plastic lids. I looked down at my plate. There was a knife, a fork, a spoon, a cloth napkin. Jackson pulled his napkin out, snapped it open, and put it on his lap. Talon didn't touch his. I edged the fork to the center of my napkin, unsure of what to do with it. I squeezed my legs together. Thinking of forks was better than thinking of sex.

Luther was watching me out of the corner of his eye as he opened more food containers. Everyone was taking huge spoonfuls of different dishes. Italian? Was this Italian food? There was pasta but other things too. He nudged his plate over and started taking a scoop of every food that was on the table.

He took a deep breath. "Food is surprisingly complicated." He scooted his chair closer to me and sat, "when the people who are supposed to love you use food as a weapon."

He was trying to gather some stringy green vegetables on a big spoon to move to his plate. He had to use his fingers.

"I used to throw up a lot as a kid. Lhevus, my dad…"

"Lhevus Saint? He's a legend." I turned, mouth opened.

"He really was not." Luther snorted, "If I threw up, I was wasting food. So, he'd make me sit at the table and watch my sister eat. He'd precisely measure out the food on her plate. If I wanted to eat, I'd have to take food from her. So, I didn't eat. She caught on and would try to only eat half of everything. But he'd force her to eat every last bite. She would sit there, silently crying, knowing I wouldn't eat that day."

I took a quick glance around the table. They were all quiet. Luther finally got some of those green veggies on the spoon, holding them in place with his fingertips to make the journey to his plate. He wiped his fingers on the napkin and put it over his knee. I slid the square of fabric out from under my fork and did the same.

"I was kicked out when I was about sixteen. Instant ramen was a fancy dinner. Then when I joined the pack…" he flashed a look toward Jackson. "Food is different when you have money. You can go to the grocery store and buy whatever you want and not have to check your bank account first. When you're poor, you just get bread. When you're rich, you get handmade artisanal sourdough with imported flour from a bakery made fresh that day."

"That's a thing?" I asked.

"Yeah, and it's fucking delicious."

Jackson caught my eye. He wasn't eating, just twirled his empty fork over his plate.

"And then there's all the restaurants. I'd stay up late at night reading menus and looking up words online. I didn't know what the fuck a balsamic glaze was. And half the places we went to, the menus weren't even in English."

He chuckled when he sat back down and took a sip of water. Cross had a beer. Jackson had a soda. Talon and Luther just had water. I stared at my glass before taking a sip. I didn't even know what I liked to drink.

"One of the first nights I was in their house, I sat in the bath for an hour trying to read the soap bottles. They were all in French."

"Me too." I said, astonished. "That was French?"

Jackson sat back in his chair and rubbed his eyes like his head hurt.

"Anyway, food is complicated when people use it to fuck with you. You develop all these coping mechanisms that turn into habits and then you can never shake those habits. The hardest one to shake is wasting food. Especially when trying something new. If you don't like it, then you either have to waste it, or force yourself to eat it. There's a..." he cleared his throat, "a lot of shame tied up in it, too. So, you just don't try anything new."

"Luther," Jackson said, his face serious and intense.

"Don't, man."

"I'm sorry."

"You didn't ask to be born rich and not be able to survive without 9 kinds of ice cream in the freezer." Luther said with a smirk.

"I'm sorry," he said again, a smile twitching his lips.

"Forgiven, a long time ago, man. Get over it," Luther said with an eye roll. Luther slid a glance toward me. "It doesn't have to be that hard this time."

Luther edged his plate toward me again and picked up his fork, taking a deep breath. "Anyway, if there's something you want to try and you get that twisted up feeling that you're going to get in trouble, just have a bite off mine."

Talon choked on a sip of water. They all looked at Luther with shocked faces.

"OK," I said tentatively, feeling like I was making some kind of mistake.

"Can I steal fries off your plate now, too?" Jackson asked with a raised eyebrow.

Luther immediately tensed up and fidgeted with his silverware. "No. Just Ruby. OK?"

"Fucking perfect." Jackson beamed.

"This," Luther pointed to something on his plate, "is broccoli rabe, sauteed in garlic and oil. It can sometimes be a little bitter, but it's really good."

Luther took me on a tour of all the things on his plate. We had our heads together talking softly, while the rest of the pack talked about the city council. I was relieved that we weren't the center of attention anymore.

"Luther?" I said softly.

"Yeah?"

I didn't know how to say all the things I was feeling. It was all jumbled up, so I just leaned over, kissed the back of his hand that was resting on the table between us. He took a shuddering breath and slipped his hand under the table to rest on my knee. I had to work hard to keep my breathing slow. I took another sip of ice water, hoping that would cool things off. It didn't.

I tried a few things but mostly focused on a big spoonful of the little star pasta. We spent the rest of dinner that way, his thumb making little circles on my knee. I knew that conversation was hard for him, too.

I stole glances at the men around the table. They were all so different, but when they were together like this, it was comfortable and... fucking sexy. I looked down at my plate, lining up these tiny tomatoes, and little balls of cheese into a straight row. I tucked hair behind my ear, oddly nervous all of a sudden. I didn't think it was appropriate to be this horny at dinner. Part of me wanted to push Luther's hand off my knee. Part of me wanted to grab his hand and put it where I needed it.

Their scents were all soft and mingled with each other, overpowering the garlic and herb aroma coming from dinner.

"OK," Jackson stretched and put his napkin on the table. "I think we should have a new pack rule. Whatever Ruby wants and asks for, she gets. Immediately."

I snorted a big laugh and covered my mouth.

"What? I'm serious." Jackson grinned at me.

"That's not how it works." I said, taking another tiny bite of pasta.

"Oh, and how does it work, know-it-all?" Jackson was leaning into the table, something sparkling in his eye. I looked down at my plate. That look was dangerous.

"You just don't get anything you ask for," I muttered, pushing around a tomato.

"Try me."

I rolled my eyes. *"Anything?"* I mocked him, "It's not like you can sit at the dinner table and say "Can I have an orgasm please?"" My hand shot to my mouth, realizing I said that aloud. Everyone was staring at Jackson, not me.

"Do it." His smile was blazing, his aura filled the room with cracking energy. "I dare you."

"Fine," I said in my best snotty teenager voice, tossing my fork to the table, "Jackson, can I have an orgasm, please?" And rolled my eyes.

I screamed in surprise when he yanked my chair back from the table three feet. He lifted me with one arm under my knees, another behind my back. I looked back at the table as Jackson strode out of the room. Talon was rubbing his eyes. Cross was covering a smile.

"Wait, Jackson. What are you…" I squeaked when he jostled me hard. We were already halfway down the hall. "You can't. Alphas don't…" He gave me another light toss, a yelp cut off my words. He stopped at the other door in Cross' hallway. My eyes got huge. The pack bedroom.

He put his nose in my neck and took a deep breath, groaning.

"Say no, and I put you down immediately and you can go have dessert like a good girl."

I should say no. I should demand to be put down. I should run screaming. My body was on fire. I had two heartbeats, one pounding in my chest, the other between my legs. Jackson's eyes searched me. They were deep brown and endless. This close, I could see little gold flakes. Everywhere he touched me burned. I looked nervously back down the hall. This… this was my pack. This was my life now. There was no one coming to drag me back there. They were all dead.

I looked at the door to the pack bedroom. I had never been in here. For all my life, packs were evil, dangerous, a billion other words used to make me afraid. I could run from what they were offering me. Turn away from the *anything* Jackson promised me. Or I could...

I held my breath and turned the doorknob and pushed the door open.

A feral grin broke across his face. He kicked it closed behind us. I didn't have time to notice anything about the room as he tossed me on the bed. I landed with a little bounce. Jackson put a delicate index finger on each knee and pushed them wide, to prowl up my body until he had one hand by each shoulder. His body hovered an inch from mine. He bit his lip. I almost came right then.

"You, little omega, have a lot to learn about alphas."

"But they said..." He covered my mouth with his whole hand to stop any other words from coming out. I stared at him in shock. He ran his tongue along his teeth, like he was considering how to devour me. He flopped down next to me, bouncing the bed again, leaning back on one elbow. I looked down at my body, confused as to why he wasn't covering me with his anymore.

"So," he said casually, flipping hair out of his eyes, "I want us to play a game."

"A.. I'm sorry, what?"

"A game." He tilted his head back to look at the ceiling, tapping his bottom lip like he was lost in thought. "I want you to pretend like you were dropped off on an alien planet."

My mouth moved like I was formulating a question, but nothing came out.

"Yup. An alien planet. I know, this is a brilliant idea, but it gets better. So, you get dropped off on this beautiful alien planet. It's all alphas, all omegas. But you, little astronaut, you don't know anything about anything."

I sat up. "Jackson, what the..." He covered my mouth again.

"You don't know anything, and you have to discover it all, like an explorer. You have to experience everything, taste everything, *twice*, and discover it all for yourself, and find out what's true."

I moved his hand away from my mouth, but I didn't say anything, trying to understand.

He gasped. "We'll get you a notebook, like a proper astronaut scientist. Oh my god, a clipboard, sexy glasses. *A lab coat.*" He groaned and tossed his head back.

"Jackson, you're not making any sense."

He looked at me, intense and serious.

"I want you to pretend that no one has told you a thing about how alphas and omegas are supposed to be. No one has ever told you what a nest is, or heat, or auras. So, that when you have a bad thought like "alphas are scary", or "nests are bad", you can be like "I'm a sexy astronaut scientist, is that true? Let me check my notebook"."

I looked at him like he'd gone off his rocker. "Jackson, that's..."

"Fucking genius! I know! But here's the rule," he counted out three fingers, "everything is sexy. Everything is exciting. Nothing is scary."

"That's not going to work."

"How do you know? Have you played this game before?"

I laid back and looked up at the ceiling. My mind was scarily blank.

"It's not that easy." I whispered.

"But what if it was that easy sometimes? Just sometimes?" He tilted my face towards his. Love and devotion painted his face, making him even more beautiful. "Just sometimes, Ruby?" He whispered.

Fear burst like popcorn in my stomach. I covered it with my hands. I closed my eyes. I could pretend, right? His fingers traced my lower lip. I could pretend. I was good at pretending.

"OK." I said on a trembling breath.

"Perfect." His groan pulled a giggle from me. "OK, so first lesson..."

He rolled back between my legs. This time, he touched me everywhere. His body made contact with mine in a million places at once.

"Pleasure is an omega's birthright," he growled into my ear. His hard cock against me, thin fabric the only thing separating us. I arched my back, moaning.

"It's what you were made for. It's what you deserve." Jackson's lips skated over my neck and face. "And alphas were made to give omegas pleasure."

I reached for his lips, wanting his tongue in my mouth, but he kept them from me, just out of reach.

"Giving you pleasure is what *we* need. When you're happy and satisfied, it fills us in a way nothing else can." His lips whispered against mine, my moans turning to grunts of frustration.

"Can I make you come, Ruby?"

"Can I tell you a secret first?"

"Please," he said with a little moan.

"I never have," my breath coming faster with sudden nervousness, "an orgasm, not a real one, before, you know, Luther."

He shivered head to toe, dropping his head into my neck.

"That is the fucking sexiest thing I have ever heard in my god damn life."

"Really?"

He perked up. "Was it good?" he asked, wrinkling his nose in that cute way of his. I smiled huge, bit my lip and nodded.

"Ugh. I can't stand it. How did he... No, don't tell me. I want to discover all the ways Ruby likes to come myself. I'll make a list. Put it on the fridge. You can rate it. Five stars. Like a restaurant review."

My rolling laughter cut off sharply when he had my leggings

off in three quick tugs. He sank his teeth gently into my knee to get my attention. Without a word, he demanded eye contact.

He slid his hands under my parted thighs and yanked me to him an inch or two by the hips, making me yelp. Heart pounding, I levered myself up on my elbows to see what he would do next. One long, slow lick had my eyes fluttering shut in bliss. He moaned, and I gasped, throwing my head back. He rubbed his tongue slowly across my clit with light pressure, increasing it with each pass.

"Jackson." His name left me without a sound as his tongue stole all my breath.

Then there was sudden intense pressure on my clit. His name tore out of me on a scream this time. I grabbed a fistful of his hair, torn between wanting to get away from the intensity he was rocking through my body, and wanting more of it until I split in half.

When the crashing waves slowed, he blew cool air on me like I was on fire, setting off another shock wave of pleasure through my body.

He picked his head up and kissed the inside of my forearm, my hands still in his hair. Gulping air, I looked down at him. The look of smug satisfaction almost made me come again.

"I... didn't know," I said between panting breaths, "it could happen that fast."

"Oh, fuck me, Ruby."

I raised my eyebrow and grinned. I could pretend to be an explorer. With Jackson, I could be *anything* he wanted me to be.

"More?"

"Fuck yes!" He climbed up my body again, kissing me deeply. "I want to watch you come this time."

He stretched out beside me again, pressing his palm to my pubic bone, curling his fingers to stroke me up and down. It wasn't that he wasn't being gentle, he was just getting right to it.

"Isn't there supposed to be like foreplay or something?"

"Don't you worry, little astronaut, I'll get around to tying you down and slowly teasing you for hours, but that is not what you need right now."

He rolled my clit between his fingers, the sensation so sharp and intense, I snapped my knees shut. He pinned my leg down with his. He changed the pressure, just using his fingertips now, lightly, barely touching me. I grabbed his wrist.

"You said you wouldn't tease."

"Oh, right, got distracted. Sorry. You make the best noises." Jackson grabbed my hand and curled all but my index finger down, his hand covering mine completely. Then he slid our two fingers into me. My hand in his, he fucked me slowly until my moans turned to a grunt of frustration.

He brought our joined hands to his mouth, leaving me empty and aching.

"You taste amazing," he whispered before sucking my finger into his mouth, his tongue moving against my fingertip.

Strong flickering pressure on my clit while he sucked my finger had me throwing my head back as the sudden orgasm broke across me. He released my leg so I could pump my hips into his hand, reaching for every last bit of pleasure I could.

Jackson carefully brushed bangs out of my eyes. He was smug and satisfied, smiling like he won the jackpot in a game show.

"Now, say it."

"Say what?" I barely had enough breath to push out words.

"I would like you to say "Jackson was right'."

"About what?"

"That you can have anything you want."

I tried to hide a smirk behind a fake pout and rolled my eyes. "Fine. You were right."

"OK. So, we'll need a notebook, probably some highlighters. Oh, those little sticky gold stars."

Jackson yanked me off the bed by my waist and put me on my feet. He was on his knees, sitting back on his feet, holding my panties out for me to step into. Unsteady, I put a hand on his shoulder.

He slid them up my legs, taking time to adjust the elastic. He ran a knuckle up and down the triangle of fabric in the front making my thighs tremble.

"God, you're soaking these panties." He slid them down my legs so quickly, I didn't have time to apologize for my slick. "I'm keeping them."

"Jackson, alphas don't..." I tried to snatch them back, but he shoved them in his back pocket.

"Are we playing the game or not?"

"Fine. Why would you need a pair of my panties?"

He shook out my leggings for me to step into.

"Oh. Great question. Thank you for asking. I'm going to wrap them around Talon's cock and jerk him off until he comes in my mouth."

Not a single word made it to my mouth. Jackson stood and tugged at my waistband to smooth out a wrinkle.

"You know, I am not sure which is sexier. Taking you out of your clothes or putting you back into them. We'll have to run some tests. We need ice cream. Apparently, I have nine different kinds." He bit his lip and pulled me by the hand down the hall.

Jackson left me in the center of the kitchen, about to die of embarrassment while he hunted in the freezer. I asked for an orgasm at the dinner table... Oh my god, they heard me screaming Jackson's name. My cheeks flamed red.

Cross slid his hand around my stomach to move me a step forward so he could pass by. His hand lingered on me, his body warm behind me. And then he stepped around me to put something in the pantry. Talon side stepped me too, with plates in his hand, leaving a drive-by kiss on my cheek. He put them in the sink where Luther was washing up.

Jackson handed me a pint of ice cream and a spoon and lifted me to sit on the counter. His smile was still huge, smug and satisfied. They all wore pretty satisfied grins, actually.

"I'm taking out the trash," he said, sticking a spoon into the ice cream.

I ate a bite, trying to decide if this was weird or not weird. Weren't alphas supposed to be all possessive about sex? They all seemed to be delighted that Jackson made me come and then gave me ice cream. I worked on freeing a huge chunk of chocolate. If we were playing Jackson's dumb game... Did this *feel* weird? They didn't seem to be embarrassed or upset at all. And judging by the bulge in Talon's pants... I crunched down on the cold bit of chocolate before I started thinking about my panties wrapped around his cock.

I snagged Luther with a foot as he walked past me to put a dish away, offering him a spoon of ice cream. His smile was so sweet it melted me. He nestled between my legs, his hips making room for him to fit.

"You know," he said around the ice cream in his mouth, "I don't think I kissed you properly yet." His voice was soft and close to a purr.

My eyebrows wrinkled as I thought about that. I covered my mouth in shock when I realized I demanded sex from him and didn't kiss him. He eased my hand away, taking my face into his huge, gentle hands. His lips were tender and soft against mine. There was no desperation in this kiss, no frenzy. I relaxed into him, feeling my aura flow into the room. I would take a while to get used to feeling my aura do things. I pictured it reaching out and hugging Luther to me.

His soft moan brushed my lips too now. "I love you, Ruin," he whispered, so soft I might have imagined it. I smiled into his kiss.

He loved me as Ruin first, when he knew I was bad, the worst of the worst. If he could love Ruin...

Whenever one of his brothers passed by us, they rubbed his head or squeezed his shoulder. Maybe they were feeling more than I was from Luther. Our kiss lingered forever, well past the dishes being done. The TV murmured softly behind us. And we kissed and kissed.

Anything, Jackson had said. If I could ask for anything, this was what I'd ask for.

FIFTY-EIGHT

RUBY

There had to be a class on this or something. How did people just know where everything went? Did you line everything up by color or by type?

I was kneeling in the walk-in closet trying to figure out how to put away the two shopping bags of clothes Jackson bought me. There were two more that he was returning today because he said they weren't quite right.

I scooped up the pile of panties. Those, at least, I knew what to do with. I put them in the top drawer of the skinny dresser. They were an explosion of colors and texture. And different styles, too. So far, Jackson liked the pink cotton ones the best.

I picked up the black lace one. I would have thought he'd go for the skimpy, slutty kind. I wondered if they all had a preference. Maybe I should give each of my alphas a drawer so they could start their own collection of favorites?

My alphas... Would I ever going to get used to saying that?

I put my hands on my hips. Should I fold them? Did panties go in color order too? I closed my eyes and took a deep breath to push down the anxiety that was always in the background. *You don't have to push through.* Talon told me I didn't have to finish a task all at once. I could take breaks.

I downed the rest of my glass of water and brought it to the kitchen for a refill. My heart skipped a beat when I saw Cross in the kitchen. What panties would he like? Warmth crept into my face.

Cross was leaning his head on his forearms like he was holding up the fridge. I could feel his discomfort and his concern like wet clothes, heavy and clinging. I wanted to run to him, throw my arms around him. Bite him again.

He straightened and rubbed his face. His exhaled breath was hard. It almost had a texture to it, rough and jagged.

"Is everything OK?" I asked softly. I knew he didn't want me here. I'd be the last person he'd come to for comfort. I'd fallen asleep in his bed for the last few nights, but he was never there when I woke up. I looked upstairs, then remembered that everyone else was gone today.

He took a breath, settling himself. Just like he did when he had something true but bad to tell me. I looked down at the water glass in my hand. Right. I had come in here to put it in the sink. He was just like this when he told me about the pills and finding the pictures.

"I'm not doing great," he said. He had his back to the fridge. His legs kicked out in front of him almost casually.

I bit my lip to keep it from trembling.

"It's been really stressful. A lot has come up, memories, about my first pack, Stella. Roy is dead. I'm not upset about it and that upsets me."

I held the glass in both hands so I wouldn't drop it.

"Dealing with a lot of stress can bring an alpha closer to rut. And I don't want to deal with that right now."

My eyes went wide. *Rut.* Fear grabbed at my stomach. This, too, was all my fault. I really did ruin everyone.

"And lying in bed with you every night…"

I nodded. I was being selfish and dumb. He didn't want me and I kept forcing him to be near me.

"… being so close to you, and you not wanting me to touch you. I understand that and respect it. But as an alpha, having your omega in bed with you when she doesn't want you…"

"I'm sorry, what?"

"Ruby, it's perfectly understandable…"

"What did you just say?" My hands were shaking, I had to put the glass down or drop it.

"Darlin', I'm not saying this to pressure you or anything. It's natural, healthy even…"

"Cross, shut the fuck up for a second. What did you just say?"

"I know you need comfort and support, and if that's all you'll ever want from me…"

"I am so fucking dumb." I tilted my head back to look up at the ceiling, hoping that staring into the overhead lights would burn away the tears before they would fall. "I'm a fucking terrible astronaut scientist."

"An astronaut what?"

"I can't bear to have you touch me because I know you don't want me, not after finding… the porn." My voice broke on the last word. "Sometimes, late at night, I have this crazy thought that if you were wrapped around me, in me, everything would just make sense."

"I want you so bad every cell in my body hurts because I can't have you."

We crashed together in the middle of the kitchen. This wasn't Cross with his careful touches and gentle caresses. This was a Cross that was as needy as I was.

He had both hands in my hair, his lips bruising mine with a

desperation that tasted of drunken joy, boosting his cherry whiskey scent.

I grunted in frustration, my shaking fingers fumbling with his belt. He kept us connected with lips and tongue, putting just enough space between us to rip his belt free and give me access to his cock. I heard a button pop as he tore at my jeans. We shrugged them off together.

He pushed into me. I moaned into his mouth as his tongue and growl answered me. His fingers bit into my hips, like he wanted to slow us down, take his time. I didn't want careful, or gentle. I wanted to chase the desperation and the need. I slid my butt off the edge of the counter, wrapping my legs around him, held up by only his cock in me.

"Slow down," he groaned, breaking from my mouth just long enough to take us to the floor and put me on his cock. On his back, he had one foot flat on the floor to thrust himself up and into me.

Cross pushed me back, sending his cock deeper into me, and gathered up the edge of my shirt. I fought him, trying to pull it back down, tear the fabric from his fingers.

"Oh god," he breathed in horror when he won and got the shirt halfway up, "Ruby..." hurt and dread drowned the deep blue of his eyes as they took in my torso that was still covered in bruises. Blows I took because of him, for him. That I would take again and again.

I growled. I used all my body weight to pull his hand away from me and pin it to the floor. I wrapped my other hand around his throat and squeezed.

"No. Don't let them take this from me, too."

I grasped his wrist and brought it to my neck, moaning when he applied pressure. I held my breath as his fingers bit into my throat and hip. He pulled me toward him, off his cock until just the tip was in me, just to push me back down, so I could feel him fill me again and again.

A sharp electronic beep sounded. A satisfied grin split his face wide. An alpha grin.

Talon appeared in the doorway to the mudroom. I froze, little skips of panic tracking across my skin. Talon tilted his head, let his eyes roam around the scene we were making on the kitchen floor, leaned a little to the left to get a better view.

Then he stepped to me, slid his hand in my hair and yanked my head back hard. My breath stopped in my chest. He put his lips to my ear.

"You're doing such a good job, little omega," he bit my earlobe, "fucking my brother like this." He used the tone that made me hot, wet and trembling. No one else in the pack could affect me like that. He kissed me, tugging harder on my hair. His tongue moved in me, as Cross thrust his hips. Both of them. In me.

Talon let go and stepped over and around us. My head swam. I was woozy, disoriented. Cross grabbed my chin, pulling me down to him again. His thumb traced my bottom lip.

"You have a job to finish, omega."

He pushed his thumb into my mouth. My eyes rolled back in my head as I slipped closer to falling off the edge. Cross withdrew his finger. I made a greedy sound, forcing more of his thumb into my mouth.

Cross growled low and leaned forward, pressing a finger into my ass. I rocked back into him, needing to be as full of him as possible. I started to come.

And then everything began to make sense.

FIFTY-NINE

RUBY

I chased down a fluttering cut-out of a chair, upsetting all my careful stacks. Stretching for the colored markers Cross lent me, I held down each stack with a matching marker, hoping that would keep them in place. The magazines all looked like swiss cheese now.

Jackson had brought stacks and stacks of catalogs back from his birth pack house. He had been spending a lot of time there and I knew he was hiding it from me.

I fanned my shirt to get some air moving around my face. I was hot all the time now. They said that would probably happen when I stopped taking the drugs. We had tapered off, hoping that would lessen the intensity of the side effects. I had a heat spike yesterday. It wasn't too bad, just some cramping, and I was hornier than I had ever been in my life.

I was trying hard not to think too much about heat. I was, of course, still taking birth control, the safe one, not the illegal one. I was pretty sure I didn't want to have kids, but I was trying hard not to think about that one, too.

I sighed and picked up the sequined pillow that I had cut out. Jackson had circled it with a red marker. He said it reminded him of my eyes, with blues and greens mixing together.

I frowned at it. It wasn't cooperating. One of the corners had red marker on it. Picking up the scissors, I couldn't decide which was worse, leaving the red mark on it, or cutting off a corner. And then where did I put it? Should it go on the blue page? Or the green page?

I'd had my first therapy appointment, and we spent almost the whole time talking about colors. I had a minor freak out that I didn't know what my favorite color was. No. It was a major freak out. Making collages was not what I thought therapy homework would be about. I was cutting out different nesting products, sorting them by color, and then trying to assign a "feeling word" to them. The therapist even gave me a dictionary of words to describe emotions.

I discovered black was not my favorite color. Black made me feel "antsy" and Jackson said that was the wrong vibe for a nest.

The chair I had just cut out looked comfy. It was shaped like a giant egg. I squinted at it. I couldn't quite tell if the inside of the egg was red or a rich brown. There was only one other brown cut out, a poop emoji pillow. It made me laugh, but I didn't think it was suitable for a proper nest.

Talon made me jump when he crouched down next to me. He drew circles on my shoulder with a light touch, looking at all the bits of paper spread out on the floor. I was officially not allowed to ask him anymore if I was in trouble for making a mess. That was after I got a cutout of a pirate themed sleeping bag stuck to the floor. It was based on one of Prey Nightingale's movies. Luther was a fan of hers. I sobbed for an hour and Talon had to use *that* tone with me to get me to stop.

"Have you decided what green is yet?" he asked, letting me lean into his touch.

"Um. "Minty?" I don't know. It's the only word I can think of, but *minty* really isn't an emotion, is it?"

"Hm. If you told me you were feeling minty, I'd believe it."

I leaned my head on his knee. Things had gotten a lot better this week. Sleeping was still a problem, but we were working on it.

"C'mon, I have something to show you." He slid his finger in my hair and gently pulled my head back, giving me a kiss on the nose.

I followed him up to his bedroom. There was now a plain gray blanket at the foot of their bed. I sort of stole the pale blue fuzzy one. I was determined to sleep alone the whole night in my own room, but I needed a "cheat code" as Cross called it. I usually slept in one of Cross' flannels or Luther's t-shirt if it was too hot, with my face mushed in the blue blanket. I now had four sleeping bags. They gave them to me the other day, telling me they had each slept in a different one for a few nights so it would carry their scents. I hadn't been successful sleeping alone yet, but I was determined.

Talon pulled me gently by the hand in front of the full-length mirror. It was on the back of their closet door. I suddenly got really interested in the contents of their closet so I didn't have to ponder the reflection in the mirror.

"What did you want to show me?"

He slid his hand around my waist, pressing into my back. I smiled and closed my eyes, settling into him, breathing deep, pulling his fresh ocean in, so he was all around me. I was getting used to them touching me all the time. I was still jumpy occasionally, but it was a work in progress. *I* was a work in progress.

"You." Talon whispered in my ear.

"What do you mean?"

"Open your eyes, little omega." He had that tone in his voice, the one I couldn't resist, didn't want to resist. There were moments with Talon where I could just empty my head and just follow where he led me.

He tilted my chin toward the mirror. He was standing behind me, tall and a little scraggly looking today. He hadn't shaved and his hair was messy, like Jackson had been running his fingers through it. His sleeves were rolled up. He had a tattoo on his inner forearm of an arrow. I loved tracing it. Cross' too, he had so many more to marvel at.

"Look at you." I watched his mouth move in the reflection. "You're so stunning. Your hair is a perfect match for how fierce you are."

I tensed to step away, looking at myself was uncomfortable.

"Nah uhh," Talon whispered in my ear, curling his fingers around my throat. A moan escaped from me. "Oh, and that sound. You make the best noises. That little "mmm" when you eat ice cream. The gasp when I slide a finger in you."

I watched myself bite my lip and squeeze my thighs together.

"I want you to see how beautiful you are. Can you see it, little omega?"

I twisted to look into his face, not the reflection.

"You're mine," he purred into my ear, "do you think I would have anything that wasn't beautiful?"

I turned back to look in the mirror, lacing my fingers into his that were splayed across my stomach.

"Tell me one thing, one thing you find beautiful."

He squeezed my neck just hard enough to chase away the thoughts other people put in my head. I didn't want them and their poison. I didn't want anything ruining something that belonged to Talon.

"Tell me I belong to you," I said in a raspy breath.

"You belong to me, little omega, now and forever." His growl went straight to my core.

"My lips are beautiful."

"Are they? Tell me."

"They're round and soft. A nice shade of pink."

I leaned into his hand around my throat, making the grasp tighter when black smudges, a phantom of *her* lips threatened to appear.

"Jackson says he loves seeing them around his cock," I whispered. Jackson loved them. I could love anything Jackson loved.

"I love seeing them around Jackson's cock, too. You know what else I love about them?"

"What?"

"They say the most astonishing things. They give life to your heart and your soul."

I sank deeper into his arms, hoping he'd never let me go.

"Ruby Frost, do you want to join my pack?"

My heart thundered in my chest.

"Yes. Please."

He let go and spun me to face him. Talon traced my bottom lip with his thumb. He brought my right wrist to his lips, placing a soft kiss right where my pulse was pounding.

"You'll be ours, now and forever," He said, kissing each fingertip. "Do you want to be mine?"

I closed my eyes as my head swam.

"Yes. Now and forever."

He sunk his teeth into my wrist. Sharp, blinding pain burst through me, melting almost instantly into intense tingling pleasure. Talon pressed me against him, his fingers digging into my lower back as a growl rumbled out of him.

I gasped as Talon slid his teeth out of me, his tongue catching a drop of blood before it ran down my arm.

"This bite," he said, licking the wound. "This bite is for me. It makes you mine. I want you to be able to see it every day and know who you belong to." He licked my neck, nipping lightly at the flesh. "Jackson will bite you here, making you ours."

He kissed my wrist again. It was red, my skin broken in places, little beads of blood dancing on my skin. It seemed to almost glow.

"This one's for you and me. I love you, Ruby."

My kiss was fierce and desperate. My "I love you" was muffled on his tongue.

A wave of shock and surprise blew out from my very center and exploded into the room. I fell out of Talon's arms and spun to find its source.

Shock... Surprise... Delight... A racing feeling... And lust? I looked down my body and turned my hands over, like I could see all those emotions pouring out of me... But they weren't mine. OK, maybe some of the lust. But these were not my emotions... They were...

"Pack." Talon said with complete satisfaction on his face.

"This is... them?"

Talon nodded.

"They're not even here." I said in wonder.

"Now, I think we should give them a little gift." He held me by the throat and walked me back a few paces until my knees bumped on the bed.

"A gift?"

He pushed me back with gentle pressure on my neck, his lips brushing mine.

"I want you to make yourself come for them, so they can feel it."

"They'll feel it?"

"Can you do that, little omega? Make yourself come for your pack?"

Nervousness fluttered my tummy suddenly. Talon's eyes danced. A surprised smile lighting up his face.

"You've never done that before." He said, delighted. "Jackson's going to die when I tell him."

I snorted. Cross teased Jackson that he was developing a "discovery fetish". He really was keeping a list on the fridge of all the ways he made me come.

"Touch yourself, Ruby. For them."

I stroked my middle finger up and down tentatively, my slick already heavy. I twirled a finger tip around my clit until I moaned and arched my back. Then I was flooded with a wave of different things all at once. A flash of confusion, surprise, lust.

I looked to Talon for confirmation, my eyes wide. He grinned and nodded. That was my pack, my alphas, responding to what I was feeling. I increased the pressure, using two fingers to make my circles. When pure lust and nothing else bounced back to me through the bonds, I made faster circles.

"Use two hands, omega. Put two fingers inside yourself."

My hands flew to obey. Fingers pushed in easily, coated with slick. I groaned, feeling the promise of being filled, stretched.

"Faster, omega." A growl was creeping into Talon's voice.

My hips rocked against my fingers, plunging into me. I put my foot up on the edge of the bed for more leverage.

"Oh, don't come yet, little omega. Let them enjoy this a little more."

"More." The plea followed grunts of frustration.

"What did we talk about?" He turned my face towards him. His brown eyes, always dark and deep, sent a wave of tingles through me. "If you can ask for it, you can have it."

"Three fingers, please?" Talon raised an eyebrow. I gasped and corrected myself to use complete sentences. "Can I fuck myself with three fingers, please?"

"Better. Yes." He said simply.

A constant stream of "mmm" flowed out of me when I added a finger.

"Can you come for your alphas, Ruby?"

I came instantly, the intensity exploding off my fingertips, rippling through my whole body, tensing every muscle. I came again, grinding into my palm when I felt them feel me. Eventually, Talon pulled my hands away.

He pulled me to sitting and curled his body around me. Over and over, he kissed my wrist until I remembered how to breathe.

SIXTY

RUBY

I hugged the wall, walking down the stairs on very shaky legs. There was no railing, and I didn't want to spend my first day as a pack member in the emergency room. The house was quiet with just the two of us. Talon said the rest of the pack would be home any minute.

The pack. *My* pack. *My* alphas.

I just got to the bottom of the stairs when I heard the faint beeping. The next second, Luther was in the kitchen. He had a hand to his chest like he needed extra pressure to keep his heart in his body. His eyes were wide, the short fuzz of his blond hair caught the bright kitchen light, creating a halo. My angel.

"You're so beautiful." The words choked out of me.

I couldn't see his aura, not really, but I felt him. His emotions and energy became almost tangible in the space between us. Now that I'd seen him, seen what he was feeling, he became distinct from the jumble of other people's emotions that coursed through me. His emotions were soft and fuzzy, like running your palm over his buzz cut hair. But it would flash into sharp, spiky static for a heartbeat.

We closed the space between us. Shaking fingers grazed my shoulder. He touched the outlines of my body like he wasn't sure I was real. A dream that stole into his life, given a body. He touched me everywhere, confirming for himself where my emotions ended and I began.

Luther was tracing the lines in my palm when Cross flew into the room and crushed me in his arms. My toes lost contact with the earth. His arms were so tight around me we both struggled for breath, and lost, dizziness pulling us to the floor.

Luther shot a hand out to catch us, but he got tangled up in our battle with gravity. Cross fisted Luther's shirt. He needed another touchpoint as an anchor. Winding my legs around him, Cross pulled me into his lap. Luther slid his hand off me, to give us space maybe, but I clutched at his arm and wouldn't let go.

"Ruby!" Jackson was shouting even before he made it through the mudroom. His emotions reached me first. He was sparkling sunshine, making me feel like I had to shade my eyes.

Cross shifted me in his lap to share, as Jackson skidded to his knees across the floor. He grabbed my face to kiss me. Jackson turned my head to the left, then the right. His sunshine clouded over suddenly, leaving me feeling chilled. He roughly grabbed my hair, checking the back of my neck, his fingers rough like he was looking for lost keys.

Jackson's excited panting breath turned horrified. He scrambled back, a hand over his mouth.

"Talon, what did you do?" Tears welling in his eyes.

LUTHER

Jackson back peddled away from us, from our omega like she was cursed. His emotions always flowed freely in the pack bonds.

Devastation flooded us all now, making our omega cringe and cover her ears.

I wanted to pull her to me, shield her from this. Cross dropped his hold on my shirt to wrap her in unbreakable arms. She would do better in Cross' arms than mine.

"Jackson, calm down." Talon said, jumping down the rest of the stairs where he had been sitting, watching over us.

"Why..." he scrambled back further until his back hit the wall, "Whatever I did, I'm sorry. Don't do this to me."

"Jacks, listen..."

"She's mine. You can't take her, you can't take them away from me."

Talon crouched, reaching for Jackson. He stiff armed Talon, knocking him to his butt.

"Jacks, let me explain."

Tears welled as he connected with me, Cross, his hopelessness clawing at my throat. "It's not real. He didn't bite her. She's not ours."

Cross and I traded a confused look. Ruby wiggled free enough to turn in Cross' arms and show Jackson the bite mark on her wrist that practically glowed.

He lunged for Talon, utter desperation demanding that his physical body take some kind of action. Talon used Jackson's momentum to flip him on his stomach, pinning him to the floor.

"A pack lead bite can create a bond. But it's not real. It will fade."

Guttural panting breaths came out of Jackson. He shifted his weight in an explosive move to force Talon off of him and switch their positions. Talon went with it, and with an extra flip, Jackson was right back where he started, face down on the floor. This time with his arm wrenched behind his back, Talon applied light pressure.

Ruby looked down at her arm. The bite was still red and angry looking. Raw, so fresh, blood welled in places. She looked at Jackson, panic overtook her with the next breath.

"It's not a claiming bite. He didn't claim her. Whatever I did, I'm sorry. I crossed a line."

Cross dug his fingers into my calf. The bond felt real. It was real. Had to be, right?

My aura surged, taking all the oxygen out of the room, fueled with Ruby's fear and Jackson's desperation.

"Listen to me. I did it for you..." Talon didn't get to finish the sentence before it went full contact.

Talon was cursing under his breath, trying to get Jackson into a submission hold. Jackson was better trained than all of us, but being emotionally out of whack made him sloppy. I couldn't tell what he was trying to do. Did he want to hurt Talon, get to Ruby, just have a tantrum?

"You didn't claim her. The bite has to be on the neck. We can't make her pack. She's not pack. Don't punish me like this," Jackson babbled while fighting to slip Talon's hold.

"Alpha!" Talon shouted with all the authority his pack lead status gave him. It sent both Ruby and Jackson over the edge.

Cross was now fighting to hold on to Ruby. All the intense emotions steamrolled her. I backed away from all of them, fighting to pull my aura back into shape. With all of us feeding off each other, an out-of-control rogue aura was the last thing we needed.

Talon finally got Jackson on his knees in a choke hold.

"Pack is pack, right? This is your pack. I did it for you." Talon said around grunts of effort to keep a hold on Jackson who was babbling apologies now.

"How much bribe money did you pay to get Cross' murder conviction overturned?"

"It doesn't fucking matter now if we can't have her." Jackson was still struggling, but his breathing was turning to sobs.

"What?" Cross asked

Jackson spit out "250" when Talon gave him a shake.

"Thousand dollars?" I said.

"And how many people are you currently blackmailing to keep Luther's paperwork hidden?"

Cross shot me a look. This was news to him, too.

"I know, I'm sorry. I don't know when to stop. I'm a terrible person, I've done terrible things. I don't deserve them, I know. But I can't be alone. You promised, Talon. Promised."

Talon wrenched Jackson's neck to the side and sank his teeth in. This wasn't a bonding bite, or a healing bite from an omega. If your pack lead bit you, it got your attention for sure. If your lover, mate did it?

Jackson's emotions froze and fell, like someone yanked his batteries. Ruby swooned in the sudden quiet.

"No, no, don't pass out, Ruby." Cross curled her into a ball, pushing her head down between her knees.

"Jackson, it's your bite that's going to claim her."

"Ruby." Her name left Jackson's lips on a sob. Ruby picked up her tear-streaked face as Cross resettled her in his arms.

"The wrist bite is for her, Jackson, so she can see it every day and know that we love her."

"But she won't be pack." He finally sagged in Talon's arm, defeated and hopeless.

Talon let Jackson go and put his arms around him in a more gentle and loving way. He stroked Jackson's neck. The bite would bruise, leave a mark, but it didn't break the skin.

"You're going to bite Ruby right here. It's your bite that's going to claim her for the rest of the world to see."

"What?"

"I created the bond, but you're going to make her pack."

"I don't understand."

"*You* are what makes us a pack, you little sunshine

psychopath. You claimed each of us. I just made it official. Ruby is going to wear your claiming bite on her neck for the rest of her life. I'm just pack lead. *You* make us a real pack."

Jackson put his face in his hands, silent sobs shaking him as relief and hope crept into the space around us. I put my hand to my chest, like I could reach in and reposition my heart.

"Just so we are all fucking clear on what happened here," Talon said, his voice somewhere between annoyed and amused. "My bite on Ruby's wrist creates a pack bond. Ruby is pack. To make it official, to register it, there has to be a claiming bite on the omegas neck. Anyone in the pack can give her that bite. I want Jackson to do it."

"You fucking drama queen," I said, laughter burning my chest.

"He was entitled to a nervous breakdown at some point just to make us appreciate the happy bullshit he's normally pumping out," Cross said, wiping sweat from his brow, his hands still shaking.

Jackson rubbed his nose with the back of his hand, then sat up on his knees. "I'm sorry,"

"For which part? The bribery? The blackmail? The stalking? You've poisoned at least one person that I know of. And I know you have photos of the Mayor with someone else's wife." Talon was trying really hard to keep a serious face, a smirk threatening the corners of his mouth.

"No, I would do all that shit again. I got a little out of control here."

"And you think I'm the mentally unstable one?" Ruby said to her arm as she rubbed a thumb over the bite mark.

I tried to cover up a bark of laughter with a cough. Cross joined in, so did Talon. Jackson smiled, but I didn't think he had enough steam for a laugh.

Jackson crawled over to Ruby to look at his mate's teeth on his omega's wrist. The bite mark went almost all the way around, given how tiny her wrist was. He cupped her face and traced a finger down her neck. She mirrored his touch, her fingers outlining the mark Talon gave him. She tilted her head back, giving Jackson access to her neck.

"Do you mind if we wait until heat? It's tradition."

Ruby nodded before flinging herself into his arms.

"I think we all need a nap now," said Cross, stretching and getting to his feet. He gave Jackson his hand. He kept Ruby tucked in against his side. I stood too and cracked my neck. My aura was simmering down, but not quite back to the new peaceful neutral I was getting used to.

Ruby held out her hand toward me and wiggled her fingers. I took it and kissed her knuckles, my aura instantly retreated. She gasped and pulled me closer to her, feeling my relief.

"And Talon's had a big day, biting Ruby out of the blue and then fucking her." Jackson kissed Ruby on the nose.

Talon dug Ruby out of our arms, and kissed her lightly.

"Oh, I didn't fuck her. I had her masturbate and come for her alphas."

It was at that point that Jackson passed out.

SIXTY-ONE

RUBY

"What the fuck is a narwal?"

"Ask Luther." He ripped the stuffed animal out of my arms and tossed it away from us.

"I don't know about this, Jackson," I said, throwing off the blanket and wiping sweat from my forehead. I'd been having heat spikes all day and bouncing between sweating and freezing, I was on edge, too. Last night I cried because there was parsley in my tiny star pasta. When Talon suggested I'd feel better if I tried to nest, I called him a fuckwad. That's when I had put myself into time-out.

My problem was I just didn't know what made me feel better. There was like this wall of scrambled up emotions that I couldn't break through to even begin to figure out what I wanted. The rule was that I was not to stuff myself into tiny spaces. Cross had apologized for our first night at the cabin and explained that seeing an omega like that had caused a flashback to finding Stella, his first omega, almost dead. Nests were supposed to be calming and comforting, but I just had far too much anxiety about them still.

"You don't have to make any decision. Just think about it."

"Talon won't like it. I'm not supposed to sleep on the floor." I didn't want to admit it, but I was feeling relaxed and cozy.

"If being on top of the bed is a problem, maybe under it is the solution."

"I don't think normal omegas nest under their beds." I reached up and touched the wood slats above my head. The bed was really tall, so there was a lot of space. It could work. I chewed on my lip, uncertain if my alphas would like it. They kept telling me that their opinion didn't matter when it comes to nests. But it did. It just did.

I yelped when Jackson jerked me out from under the bed by my ankles.

"Come try these on." The bed was piled high with shopping bags.

They had emptied my apartment last week. I didn't want anything from that place. I didn't own a single thing to wear. Cross had tried to take me shopping, and it was a disaster. I had tried on five different pairs of jeans, they were all different sizes and none of them fit. I locked myself in a dressing room and cried for an hour. They had to call security for a pissed off alpha that was biting the heads off anyone who came close to the dressing rooms.

That was when Jackson appointed himself my personal shopper. Every time he went into the city, he came back with a truckload of fashion finds. He returned most of it, insisting it wasn't the right color or fit. And when I liked something, he bought it in every color. My walk-in closet was filling up. I had an alarmingly large collection of lingerie that kept growing every day.

I shimmied out of my leggings as Jackson shook out a skirt for me to step into. He zipped it up and moved me in front of the mirror.

"The color is shit," he said, fluffing up the pale pink fabric, "but the drape might be exactly what I need."

"Need? Are you planning on wearing this?" I smiled.

"Not my size. We need enough fabric to keep covered, but not so much that it's bulky."

He stood next to me and watched himself in the mirror. His body mostly covered his hand skating up my thigh, the skirt hid the rest. The silky fabric fell into place almost completely, hiding his fingers tracing the outline of my lace panties at the V between my legs.

"See? With this skirt, I can have my fingers in you while we stand in line for waffles and no one will know."

"Jackson!" I smacked his shoulder. His fingers dipped under the lace edge of my panties, finding me already wet. I closed my eyes and made little "mmm" sounds, enjoying the light touch.

I doubled over when a violent cramp hit, the intense pain taking my breath away. Jackson eased me back up so I could breathe.

"Heat spike?" He asked softly, running soothing palms up and down my arms.

I nodded, groaning. They had been getting worse and worse. The doctor warned us this wouldn't be a normal heat, that the heat spikes could be intense and painful. I hoped this wasn't normal. I was scared enough from all the... *brainwashing*... I didn't think I could go through this a few times a year.

"I'll take care of it," Jackson said, wrinkling his nose in that cute way of his. "Open, say ahhhh."

"What?" I said around a pant when a fresh cramp hit. He put the hem of the skirt in my mouth and pushed my chin up to close my lips around it. "Jackson!" I practically barked at him around the thin fabric in my mouth.

"The least you could do is help. Being an alpha taking care of his omega is a tough job."

479

"Fuck you," I said, holding in a laugh.

"That's exactly what I'm trying to do and you're all yak, yak, yak."

He knelt in front of me. With the skirt out of the way, he snagged the edge of the panties with his teeth and dragged them a few inches down my hip. He had gotten them almost to my ankles when pain stabbed through me worse than before. I grabbed at my stomach, hunched over, my feet got caught in the panties as I staggered back.

A strong arm wrapped around my middle as Talon pressed into my back, catching me before I fell.

"How fucking hot is that? My little omega with her alpha on his knees." Talon growled in my ear, making both Jackson and I moan.

He pulled the edge of the skirt out of my mouth, gathering the fabric to me so it was out of the way. Talon's lips lingered on mine with a soft kiss as he settled himself behind me. I leaned into him as Jackson untangled my feet from the panties.

"Hold yourself open for your alpha so he can give you what you need. It is a tough job." I spread my legs wider, using both hands to ease my folds open for him. Jackson kissed the back of my hand before turning his attention to his task. Some of the cramping eased as soon as his tongue touched me. I let my head sink back into Talon's wide shoulder, enjoying the relief.

Jackson hit that spot with his tongue that always made me snap my legs closed. Talon kicked my legs wide again. He brought my wrist to his mouth, kissing and nipping at his healing bite mark, while Jackson pushed a finger inside me.

He grazed his teeth along my neck, teasing the spot where Jackson's bite mark would soon be, coaxing the skin there to be extra tender, extra sensitive. Jackson's fingers were almost lazy inside me. I rocked my hips, wanting more of him.

A dull ache started in my belly and radiated downward. It wasn't a sharp pain, but demanding and heavy. I squirmed in Talon's arms. Fisting Jackson's hair, wanting him to go faster, harder. Talon untangled my fingers and pinned my arm to my tummy. I thrashed my head against him, whimpering as the cramping got more intense.

On panting breaths I said, "I... want..."

"Oh no, omega, we are well past *wants* now. This is *need*. A needy little omega. Tell your alpha what you need." Talon's voice was dark and commanding in my ear.

Jackson looked up at me, his lips glistening with my slick.

"Alpha," I could barely get enough breath as he eased his finger out of me so slowly. His pupils went wide, a feral twinkle dancing in his eyes. He always reacted that way whenever I called him alpha. My head dipped and my eyes closed when Jackson pulled his finger all the way out. The aching became sharp, intense, needy, bringing tears to my eyes.

"Alpha, I need your knot."

Growling, Jackson got to his feet and scorched me with a kiss. He stepped back to strip off his shirt, and let the weight of his belt drop his pants to the floor. I bent my knees and curled my legs in toward my stomach, rubbing them together, desperate for relief of any kind.

Talon pulled Jackson to him by the neck. Their kiss burned through the bonds.

"I love tasting her on your lips. Be a good boy and give my omega your cock slowly?"

I felt Jackson's body shudder against me. I winced. The cramping was starting again. The feeling of being empty and desperate, needing to be filled, brought fear to the surface when the pain increased.

This was what scared me the most. *Knots.* All the pictures they showed me of mutilated girls, the stories, the reports.

"Astronaut remember?" Jackson cupped my face and kissed me softly.

"Omega, look at me." Talon tilted my head back to stare up at him. His arms held me tight, the pressure was comforting, not constricting. "Let go. You were made for this. Let your alphas give you what you need."

Talon changed his grip on me, one arm under my rib cage, the other snaked between our bodies, rubbing the tip of Jackson's cock on my clit. We moaned together, Jackson's fingers sinking into my shoulder. An emotion I nicknamed "pure alpha" burst out of Talon, it was smug and satisfied. It was a kind of pride that he could make his omega fall apart like this.

And I did fall. I came undone the second Jackson pushed into me, guided by Talon's strong fingers. All I got were two blissful thrusts before the desperate need had me digging nails into Jackson's back.

"You're doing so good, little omega. Can you tell how good you're making your alpha feel?" Talon said, the words of praise wrapping around my thoughts to push the fear out. "Surrender to your Alpha. Take his knot. I know you can do it."

Jackson nuzzled into my neck, short rocking strokes had his knot right there, pressing against me. Talon's words whispered in my ear, in time to his fingers stroking my clit. Jackson kissed me, his tongue now competing for attention.

He broke off the kiss suddenly. His eyes consumed me. I found love there, but a possessive devotion, something beyond simple love. He was mine, and he'd have me forever.

"I love you," Jackson said, his own need shaking him.

"Come now, omega," Talon growled in my ear.

I came undone, held up by my alphas. Pain, sweet and sharp, pushed the pleasure to new places, stealing all the air in my lungs, as Jackson's knot locked us together in a way that was more than physical.

Pleasure rippled all around me and wouldn't stop. The slightest movement took me over the edge again. When my head got too heavy to hold up, Jackson slid his fingers into my hair.

"I love you so much," I breathed, getting lost in his brown eyes, his aura, and this feeling of connection and fullness. They were right. They were right about everything. This was what I was made for.

We whispered "I love you" back and forth, as pleasure rocked between us. Jackson reached for Talon, their kiss bringing Talon into the space with us.

"Ruby, can I bite you and make you pack?" I could feel a thread of fear spool off Jackson, like he was scared I'd say no, and he'd lose me forever.

"Yes." I tilted my head back against Talon's shoulder, giving him my neck.

The bite was hard and fast. The pack bonds flared again, just like when Talon bit me. Now they were all there, my alphas, part of this moment with me and Jackson. Their approval and love flooded me, making me come again, feeling myself tighten around Jackson. He claimed me with his bite and his knot, but it was his heart that owned me.

He shuddered and crushed me to him, gasping my name as he came, causing wave after wave of delicious pleasure to spread out from my center. His orgasm pulled me along for more.

Jackson collapsed into my neck, every kiss he left on his bite mark made me tremble with bursts of sensation. Talon tipped my head towards him, brushing his lips softly against mine.

"I did it," I whispered. Talon was the only one I'd talked to about how scared of this moment I was.

"You are amazing." He kissed the tip of my nose, my forehead, my cheeks.

I felt Jackson's knot recede as he slipped from inside me. My gasp turned to a sob at the profound feeling of emptiness.

Fire flashed through my body, sweat instantly beading up on my brow. The pain immediately bounced back, but it had shifted from my stomach to my core. I groaned and doubled over, one hand covering my pussy that felt hot to the touch.

"What's wrong?" I whined.

"Nothing's wrong, little omega. This is heat and you have four alphas to take care of you."

SIXTY-TWO

JACKSON

My body was instantly doused in cold the second I slipped from her. I put a trembling hand to my mouth. I was not prepared for... that.

I was raised in a huge pack where every day an omega went on and on about the beauty and bliss of knots. The alphas would just smile and nod, often with shit-eating grins. I'd fucked enough omegas as a heat helper, necessary to deal with ruts since we didn't have an omega, to know it was good and primal, all around fun time.

I was not prepared to be stripped down to my very soul and be so completely... loved.

Since Talon's bite, they all kept the bonds open, greedy to experience Ruby in all the ways that they could. They were open and receptive and letting each other in now, too. That was great, but it meant I couldn't hide anymore. I had always kept the bonds open, filling it with dipshit happiness. It was genuine happiness, you couldn't easily fake that in pack bonds. It annoyed them, which was fun, but it also kept them from looking too closely. It was getting harder and harder to mask with carefree fuckboy.

The day I met Talon, he made me feel like I could be a better version of myself. Even at sixteen, I knew I was fundamentally not a good person, that I deserved to be alone and unloved. That was why I'd crushed everything that stood between us. Everything that threatened pack. I had been riding this wild high that if I could keep us all safe, then maybe I deserved their love.

And Ruby?

I did more than claim her with my knot and teeth, she let me claim myself, as an alpha.

I didn't know if I was strong enough to be loved by Ruby Frost.

A howl of pain snapped my thoughts. The doctor had warned us. Being on illegal heat blockers for so long was going to have consequences. We were all nervous about it for really different reasons.

Luther was super sensitive to shifts in Ruby's moods. She desperately needed a class in Pack Bonds 101 to learn how to modulate what she gave and received through the bonds. No one had ever taught Ruby how to work with her aura, either. I almost didn't want her to learn because it was doing Luther a world of good. He had stopped running so much and was putting weight back on. She would sit on his lap and they would get lost together, like they were sitting in each other's auras soaking up the goodness. Now that we knew Luther was a rogue, all the instability in his aura made sense. Just being next to Ruby was patching him up. And they were so fucking cute together, their heads together whispering about food or nothing at all. But that also meant if she got triggered by something, it would set Luther off instantly.

And that was Cross' biggest concern.

He had been with her after the explosion... after she shot one of her tormentors in the head and the other in the groin... as she began to clean off the filth the Reset had dipped her into. We all knew about the porn and we all pretended we didn't know about the porn. We knew about it before we even met Ruby Frost. And we were systematically destroying the digital lives of anyone who had purchased said porn. Ruby was light-years from a place where she could add "abuse" and "rape" to her vocabulary. Cross didn't want to trigger a flashback during sex, that something would be too hard or too fast for her and he'd add to her existing trauma.

My beloved Tal took that one step further. The whole sleeping on the floor debacle, the hair washing thing too, fucked him up and put a large dose of uncertainty into his brain. He was concerned that Ruby would do things just to please him that she was ultimately not ok with. They had a whole different landscape of trust that they had to build between them, and it would be slow going. He needed a level of nurturing control over her as much as she needed to be nurtured like that. A set back in that would be devastating for both of them.

And I, naturally, being a ruthless slut, was worried about the sex.

The pack had never had sex together. We had never all been in the same room when sex was happening. All packs handled sex differently, with or without an omega in the mix. Some were monogamous within their pack, some weren't. Some packs fucked like bunnies, some never touched each other even during heat, passing the omega from bedroom to bedroom when they got exhausted. I'd given Cross a booze fueled blow job years ago. It was hot as hell, but there never seemed to be an opportunity for a repeat performance. And there was a particular kind of tension simmering between Cross and Luther. It wasn't exactly sexual, but a painful need for intimacy. Sex was only one way to express that.

Heat, rut and sex could change a pack, alter the fabric that held it together. We all had reasons for being concerned about Ruby's heat. Her fear of knots and heat topped those lists.

I did it.

I heard Ruby whisper to Talon, both of them holding a note of pride and wonder in their voices. My chest sunk in with the weight of that. If I asked him directly if he orchestrated it so that my knot would be her first, he'd probably deny it. I didn't care about firsts, I cared about Ruby. But she might care. It might be important to her. And she chose me. That thought made my knot swell again.

Talon lifted a squirming, groaning Ruby into his arms and gave me a searching look that asked if I was OK. Not in the slightest, but I could deal with my precious mental health later.

"I... uh..." Ruby stuttered with astonishment. "I think I need someone to fuck me right now."

I looked down at my cock, ready to go again. I grabbed the sleeping bag off her bed, the one that held Luther's smokey cut grass scent, and followed them to the pack bedroom.

I was going to make this the best fucking heat ever.

SIXTY-THREE

RUBY

Talon put me down on the edge of the huge pack bed and I squirmed right off when a cramp hit me. I pulled my knees to my chest, stretching my t-shirt over them. Being curled up tight seemed to help.

"Hang tight," he said, "let me get the bed ready."

"Is this just a heat spike or..." Luther poked his head in. I groaned and toppled over, holding my pussy with both hands. "Oh. I'll go get..." and he disappeared from the doorway.

Jackson walked in, completely naked, with one of my sleeping bags in his arms.

"Thought she'd probably need a comfort blankie. Let me help with that." He tossed the sleeping bag in the walk-in, and grabbed a corner of the comforter. No, it was a *duvet*. Fucking French.

"Great. We're doing laundry now." I panted. Jackson gathered up the bedding and walked it to the closet.

I licked my lips. He was naked, tall and lean. His tan skin glistened in the low light. And he was hard. The knot at the base of his cock... it was so fucking good. A sob tightened my chest. It had all been lies. All of it. It wasn't dangerous or deadly. It was right and perfect. I had wasted so much time on fear, fearing who I was, what my body was capable of. I needed it. I needed more of him.

I tried to get my arms and legs to cooperate, to crawl across the floor to Jackson on his way back to the bed. Talon caught him by the arm, holding his face. Soft words passed between them that I couldn't hear over my groans. If they kissed right now, I was going to come everywhere.

"Why is it hot?" I pulled the neckline of my shirt out to wipe my face.

"Let's get you on the bed."

Talon put his arms around me to pick me up. I shrieked and backed away.

"It hurts?" Concern flashed across his face.

"Tingles." I said, eying him warily.

"Good tingles or bad tingles?"

"Undetermined."

He swooped me up and put me on the bed. I practically had a seizure. Little ribbons of pleasure shot through my body.

"Good tingles." I croaked out. I sat on my knees and curled myself into a ball, my forehead just brushing the mattress.

I felt the bed depress, and then Talon's hands on my upper arms dragging me over him. I squeezed my eyes tight as another cramp hit. He parted my legs to straddle him, positioning his cock. He pushed my hips back, just the tip entering me. I collapsed on his chest as the discomfort immediately receded. He rocked just slightly, seeming to know I needed a minute to catch my breath. His warm palms made big circles on my back.

"Everything OK?" I turned, hearing Cross at my left. He had three buttons of his flannel shirt undone and was working on the cuffs. The tattoo on his collar bone poked out. It was a dandelion on his shoulder, with the fluff blowing across his chest. I fucking loved it. Cross was art.

I growled and clawed my way to Cross.

"Ruby," and "Careful," Cross and Talon said at the same time.

I misjudged the edge of the bed. My sudden clumsy movement took Cross and me to the floor.

"Why do you and I always end up on the floor?" He said with a laugh.

My fingers wouldn't obey, failing me at getting a button undone. I tore at his shirt, two buttons popped, letting me put my mouth on Cross' skin.

"Why is everyone wearing so much fucking clothes?" I kissed and bit a path across Cross' collarbone.

"Darlin', you have to let me up if you want me to fix that problem for you." The smooth low tones of Cross' voice was gasoline, splashing fire through me. I frantically pulled at my t-shirt, burning up inside and out. Cross skated his fingers across my skin, freeing me from the shirt. I put my tongue in his mouth, desperate for more of him. He stood and lifted me off the floor, right onto Talon's cock.

I went rigid, balling my fists in Cross' torn shirt as I came with a burst of energy. He pulled my head back by the hair and traced a finger along Jackson's bite mark.

"Fuck." He panted out the words. "I just unlocked a new kink."

"What's that?" Talon chuckled.

"Putting my omega on my brother's cock." All my alphas groaned, lighting up the pack bonds with lust.

Something clattered to the floor, catching my attention.

"Luther!" I said like he was a meal and I was starving. Cross and Talon shared a snort of laughter as I crawled for Luther, groaning at the sudden emptiness between my legs.

"Oh, hey," was all he managed to get out before I attacked his mouth. He broke away to set down the bowl of ice he was carrying and popped a cube in between my lips. I moaned. It was the most refreshing thing that I had ever had. Luther tilted my head to place tender kisses all over Jackson's bite mark. I crunched the ice and swallowed it, his kisses burning all the way to my core.

"Luther, I love you, but stop being so fucking sweet and just fuck me."

"I love it when she talks dirty."

I snapped my head around just in time to see Jackson take Talon's cock into his mouth. I gasped and lunged for Jackson. Sharing Talon like this had become my new favorite thing. Actually, all of the sex was my new favorite thing.

"It's like she has heat ADHD." Luther said, laughing. The rest of them cracked up, too. All the humor was wiped away for me as pain poked me again.

"Why are there so many dicks in this room and none of them are in me?"

"You need to calm down." Talon said around a snort.

"Did you just tell me to calm down?" I said, batting at his hands and rolling away from him, curling on my side and bringing my knees to my chest. "I need dick and you're just fucking around."

"Technically, we're *not* fucking around."

"Jackson!" Both Talon and I snapped at the same time.

"For fuck's sake, someone fuck me right the fuck now!"

"Omega." Talon's voice had that edge to it that cut right through all the static in my head. I froze, panting. "You need to focus." Every syllable sent chills down my spine. My lungs emptied of air as every cell in my body responded to his direction.

Talon uncurled my body from its protective ball, parted my legs and filled me in one fluid movement. The shock of pleasure forced out all the little stabs of pain.

"Focus," he whispered again, turning my chin to look at him. "Focus on how good it feels to be filled like this." He had all his weight on me, ensuring I couldn't move. I had nothing to do but to feel the long, slow strokes of his cock moving in and out of me.

"Better?"

I nodded, little moans coming out of me every time he withdrew.

"You look unbelievably beautiful with Jackson's bite claiming you."

With that as a reminder, I could feel them all at the edges of my awareness, swirling around me, like millions of fingers caressing my soul. Need erased all memory of the cramping and discomfort, letting desire catch fire. A soft growl from Talon burned right through my core. I needed them.

"Show your alphas how you can take my knot."

Talon rolled us over in a sudden movement, leaving me dizzy on top of him, my head swimming.

"I got you," Cross' voice whispered in my ear. He kept me upright with a hand on the back of my neck.

I looked around the room to make it stop spinning. Luther was standing at the edge of the bed. He slipped his jeans off his hips. He was all sharp angles and muscles that carved out a V in his hips pointing right to his massive cock. His body was hard and sculpted, beautiful, like something that belonged in a museum. My mouth watered.

"Luther, come here, so she doesn't lunge for you." Cross squeezed my neck, keeping me in place. Talon grabbed my hip, thrusting up, reminding me to focus with a soft word.

Luther crawled across the bed, his smile brighter than the sun.

"Hi," he said, like he was so glad to see me. He did that all the time, saying 'hi' like I was a daily surprise in his life. He pressed his lips to mine in one of his tender kisses as Talon moved in me.

Luther trailed more kisses down my neck, shifting my bra strap out of the way.

"Off," I whined, shrugging my shoulder.

Luther unhooked my bra. Cross pulled it down my arms and tossed it away. Luther rubbed a hand across my rib cage, erasing the mark the underwire left with his fingertips. I groaned at the sensation of relief and shifted my hips, muffled by Luther's soft lips.

Cross turned my face toward him. His kiss was not soft. His tongue was aggressive and urgent in my mouth. They traded my lips back and forth, from Luther's softness to Cross' demands. They set a rhythm that my hips were called to obey. I clenched my fist deeper into Cross' shirt, using it for leverage.

A low rumble vibrated the air.

"She's growling," Jackson said, amused.

"Am not."

Jackson appeared in front of me, pointing a finger, then two, touching them to my bottom lip. He slid them slowly into my mouth. The growl was replaced with moans as Jackson fucked my mouth slowly. He withdrew his fingers to a chorus of frustrated grunts. He traced them down my neck and chest, all the way to my clit. I tried to clamp my legs shut at the sudden intensity, but Talon dug his fingers in my thighs.

"I think someone has gotten distracted." He said.

"What?"

"Weren't you told to do something?"

I looked between Cross and Luther, stumped. "What are you talking about?"

"Didn't your alpha tell you to show your pack how you can take his knot?" A collective groan went through all of us at Jackson's sexy purr. I wasn't the only one Jackson could unravel with a sentence.

"You want to be a good little omega, don't you?" Cross' whisper was rough with restrained desire.

"You need his knot." Luther said, rolling a nipple between his fingers.

"I can feel how much he's stretching you." Jackson slid his finger along where our bodies joined, where Talon's knot was pressing into me. Another finger was circling my clit. Luther's? Cross'? It didn't matter, it was just pack.

"Omega, take my knot for your alphas." Talon's voice went right to my core, pushing me over the edge. The intense stretching as I pushed myself on to my alpha's knot shattered me into a billion shivering pieces, stealing my breath.

"Fuck." Talon sat up and wrapped his arms around my back, pushing his cock even deeper into me.

Pleasure swirled in me and bounced off my alphas. I came and came, their lust and desire pouring through the pack bonds and into me. But it was more than lust. There was possession, satisfaction, pride, awe, and love. The emotion was so intense, I squirmed to get away. I could feel tears welling.

"Hey, hey," Talon gently took my face in his hands and searched my eyes. "Is this too much?"

"I..." gasping for air, a tear rolled down my cheek. "this is a lot of... love to feel."

Talon's smile was radiant. "I think it's something we're all going to have to get used to."

Cross kissed my cheek, soaking up the line of tears. Jackson grabbed Cross' chin and pulled him away. Something silently passed between them that I didn't understand. Cross took a sharp breath, his eyes fluttered shut when Jackson pressed their lips together, his tongue darting out to meet Cross'. Victory danced in Jackson's eyes when he broke away. Some sort of wall came down with that kiss. The energy in the bonds shifted.

"Now," Jackson said, his voice bright, "I think we're in a bit of a predicament."

I glanced nervously at Luther, who stopped kissing my shoulder to look up at Jackson, too.

"How ever shall we pass the time while we wait for Talon's knot to release you so I can watch my brothers fuck you?"

My eyes shot wide. Jackson winked and ducked his head, his tongue going right for my clit. I screamed as an orgasm ripped through me. Talon arched his back, his orgasm following quickly after mine.

"You are a ruthless slut," I said when I had enough breath to talk. Cross chuckled and Luther took my mouth with urgency now to match Cross.

I started making little panicked sounds when I felt Talon's knot shrink, instantly missing feeling stretched and so full. Hands grabbed my hips and pulled me off Talon's cock completely, making me whimper.

Luther rolled me onto my back. The round pack bed was the perfect height for Luther to stand and fuck me. He pushed my thighs wide and coated the tip of his cock with my slick. I moaned and arched my back, catching Jackson out of the corner of my eye, licking my slick off Talon's inner thighs.

"I fucking love tasting her on you." Jackson said, taking Talon in his mouth. I licked my lips and reached for Jackson.

"Darlin'," Cross slipped behind me, sitting me halfway up and supporting me, "I think you need to pay attention to Luther. He's about to slam his cock into you."

A huge grin split Luther's face as he did just that. It only took three strokes, his knot pounding into my clit before I was coming again. Cross was roughly cupping my breasts and pinching my nipples. I was still coming when Cross pulled me to the center of the bed, hiked my hips high, and entered me from behind. I collapsed on to my chest, rubbing my cheek into the soft sheets.

Jackson stretched out next to me and brushed hair out of my face. His deep brown eyes twinkled.

"I love watching you come."

I squeezed my eyes shut. Another orgasm was just beyond my reach.

"Keep your eyes open, omega." He pinched my chin, "Do you think we should add a whole new category to the list on the fridge just for knots?"

"Jackson, now is not the time..."

"Oh, no!" A horrified look spilled across Jackson's face. "If you're able to talk, you're not coming nearly enough. Let me fix that."

Jackson pulled me up by the shoulders. I placed my palms flat on the bed. Jackson pressed his tip to my lips, keeping perfectly still. Cross thrusting into me pushed Jackson's cock deeper into my mouth. He began to withdraw. My grunting protests must have changed his mind, he sank all the way into me. Being filled and stretched by two of my alphas sent me tumbling into another orgasm.

I decided right then and there, I was no longer afraid of heat.

SIXTY-FOUR

CROSS

Ruby was purring on my chest. I had no idea something so simple could be so completely wonderful. I drew lazy circles on her back, played with her hair, anything to keep the purring going.

She had been asleep for maybe four hours. Luther was getting some snacks to keep our energy up. Talon and Jackson were across the hall, catching some sleep in my bed. They didn't want to risk waking her up. She needed the rest.

It was day three of her heat cycle. We knew it was going to be intense, now that she was off the blockers. At the end of the first day, if she wasn't on a knot almost constantly, the cramping and discomfort would start up. That seemed to have backed off now, and she'd finally fallen into an exhausted sleep.

A fantasy wound through my head. I pictured fucking her so thoroughly, filling her so completely with my knot, that she would fall into a contented sleep with me still buried in her, keeping my cock warm all night. She'd wake up in the morning delighted and orgasming.

Filling her, stretching her body around me, satisfying her,

making her weak and trembling with desire, it all unlocked a new set of emotions in me. It was something deep and profound, purely alpha, awakening to its own need that could only be fulfilled by omega and pack.

Watching her take my brother's knots, feeling their bliss as they came in her, that was equally satisfying.

And fucking Jackson.

'The only time you let yourself be loved is when one of us is hurt.' The conversation in the truck, just before the attack, had been banging around in my head ever since. Jackson ripped all of that armor off when he put his lips on me while making our omega come on Talon's knot. He was right. He was right about everything. The asshole.

Ruby stirred in my arms. She took a deep breath and stretched.

"Where is everyone?" Her voice was full of contented sleep.

"Talon and Jackson are getting some sleep. Luther's getting food."

She sighed and snuggled back into me, throwing her leg over my hips. She picked her head up and looked down at our legs.

"Oh, you're wearing jammies?"

I laughed and kissed her on the forehead. "I got some sleep earlier, too. I was cold without you wrapped around me."

"Is it over?"

"Nah, Darlin', this is just a break."

"Was this..." she hesitated, looking up at me with concern crinkling her eyes, "normal?"

I would not lie to her. Not ever. But I didn't want her getting all twisted comparing herself to other omegas. I also didn't want to remind her of the abuse she'd suffered. Frankly, I didn't want to remind myself of it either.

"This is more intense than usual." I rubbed my thumb across her bottom lip. She kissed the pad of my thumb. "I think because you put off a true heat for so long, the discomfort is greater."

"So, next time I'll do better?"

"*This time*, isn't over, little omega, and it's been pretty fucking great."

She dipped her head, hiding a shy smile that made my dick hard. She stretched again.

"I think I need a shower. I feel sticky." She wrinkled her nose.

"You're probably covered in slick and cum." I chuckled. Her eyes darkened for a second. "It's fucking wonderful." I added, so she'd have no doubts about what we thought. "But we could do a shower. I'll look forward to making you all sticky again."

A blush seeped into her cheeks. She was leaning into her omega nature more and more. Watching her discover her needs and delight in them being fulfilled was the sexiest thing I'd ever experienced. I picked her up and carried her to the bathroom.

The room was completely tile with a shower big enough for three people and a deep tub. I always thought this bathroom, the entire room actually, was excessive, with its rainfall showerhead and two other handheld ones fixed to the wall. But Jackson insisted. It was another thing he was right about.

I put Ruby down and reached for the knob to get the hot water going. She collapsed with a yelp. I caught her too me, repositioned her so I had a better grip.

"I... uh, I don't think I can stand." She said, concerned.

"I got you, don't worry." I said, smirking.

"What? What's so funny?"

"It's an alpha thing, love. Knowing you fucked your omega so thoroughly she can't stand? Mmmm." I moaned.

I tested the water to see if it was warm enough before backing her under the spray, still holding her tight to me.

"Hey, you're getting your jammies wet."

"Doesn't matter." She shivered and sighed when the water hit her. She turned her face up, leaning back to enjoy the feel of the water raining softly on her, trusting that I held her tight.

"Oh my god, can I wash your hair?" We both jumped at the sudden appearance of Luther in the doorway. Ruby giggled and nodded. Luther put down the plates he was carrying on the floor. The only furniture in this room was the giant round pack bed. He stripped off his boxers and pushed Ruby's head under the spray..

"Luther has better sense than me to get naked first." I teased her when her eyes rounded at Luther's naked body.

"Oh, my special shampoo is in my…"

"This one?" Luther held up a bottle from a shelf on the wall. "Jackson stocked it with all your products."

He lathered his palms with the minty smelling shampoo and massaged it into her hair. She melted into his touch, a steady stream of 'mmm's' pouring out of her. Luther moved on to conditioner, running his fingers through her hair with a dopey smile on his face like this was the best treat of his life. Next was the big pink poofy sponge and the unscented body wash. None of us liked any fake scent on her skin.

He started with her fingertips and hands, paying each square of flesh devoted attention. Ruby's sighs turned into moans and the mews of frustration by the time he got to her stomach. Luther pressed into her back, and hooked her knee over his elbow to run the poof delicately between her legs. I still had her by the hips, keeping her wiggling to a minimum. Ruby finally grabbed the sponge and threw it to the floor, moving Luther's hand right between her legs.

Ruby's eyes flashed opened when she realized I was keeping her from grinding against Luther's hand. Her citrus scent rose in the humid air, filling the space with omega need.

"Alpha, I want your knot." Her voice was breathy.

"Which one?" I asked with a playful smirk.

"Both. Together."

Luther's head shot up, a little stunned, like he hadn't heard what he'd just heard.

"You feeling that empty and needy, omega?" I challenged. She nodded.

"Say it." Luther whispered hoarsely in her ear.

"I want both my alphas' knots in me. Now." She bit her lip like she was afraid she'd be denied.

I reached behind me to shut off the water while Luther grabbed a towel and roughly dried her hair. She giggled as the fluffy towel momentarily swallowed her.

"Let me give you a hand." Luther winked, then reached around Ruby to tug the now soaked pajama bottoms down my thighs.

"He's so helpful." I smirked down at Ruby, who snorted.

Luther stepped out of the bathroom to move the plates of snacks to the hall before climbing to the center of the bed. I spun Ruby in my arms, so her back was against me, and walked her into the bedroom. She giggled again and kicked her feet, her toes barely touched the floor.

I stopped at the edge of the bed, squeezing her tight against me.

"As Jackson would say, I think we have a bit of a predicament." I said. Ruby twisted her head to look up at me.

"What's wrong?" Concern flashed across her face.

"We just got you clean. Look at your alpha," I turned her face towards the bed, and bent to whisper loudly in her ear. "You see how big his knot is? You're going to need to be much more wet than this to take your alpha's knot."

I felt both their emotions stutter in the pack bonds. It was downright adorable how a faint blush touched their faces, like we hadn't just spent three days fucking her brains out.

Ruby struggled lightly in my arms to get to the bed. I held her back for an agonizing minute, denying both of them instant gratification, until she and Luther both started to pant. I crawled up the bed, with one arm still pinning her to me. Luther laid back, as I parted her knees and had her hover over his midsection. I pulled her upright, arching her back slightly, so he'd have the best view ever. He drew a finger through her slit like he was testing her wetness.

I bent her forward, her legs spread wide to straddle Luther, her palms on his shoulder, but her pussy no where near his cock. By the moans she made, Luther must have been rolling her nipples in his fingers, more gently than I would at this point. With my free hand, I stroked Luther's cock.

"Fuck," He threw his head back, biting his lip.

"What?" Ruby asked.

"Well, Luther? Tell her." I said.

"Cross is…" he grunted when I twisted my palm around his knot. "He's stroking my cock."

Ruby bucked against me. She hated being left out. I pulled her back just enough so that the tip grazed her entrance. She moaned in anticipation that quickly turned to frustration when that's all she got. I teased them both, rubbing the tip of Luther's cock on Ruby's clit, without enough pressure to satisfy. Luther took his frustration out on her mouth, kissing her roughly until they had to gasp for air.

I pulled her back onto his cock, just enough to open her, but not to fill her. They both shuddered beneath me. I eased my grip around her waist to let her rock her hips. Her 'mmm's' of delight faded when she couldn't get all the dick she wanted. She looked over her shoulder at me in confusion.

"Tell her, Luther."

"Fuck." He took her face in his hands and kissed her between words. "His hand is still wrapped around my dick." They were both being denied in different ways. Luther pumped his hips up, wanting more friction than I was giving him.

"You're still not wet enough, omega."

Luther reached between their bodies. He closed his eyes as his fingers explored mine on his cock. He pressed his thumb on her clit. She dropped her head to his chest, moaning. I repositioned myself, resting my cock between her cheeks. She kicked her head back with a gasp.

"You two are not nearly ready enough."

I rocked my hips, forcing Ruby's body to move on the few inches of cock I was allowing her.

"Don't come yet, little omega."

I felt Luther's hand still on her clit, backing off. I brushed the damp hair off the back of her neck, placing delicate kisses down her neck and spine. She shivered and ground herself against my hand, forcing a grunt out of Luther.

"I only want you to come when I give you my brother's knot and claim you with my bite."

They both froze as those words sunk in. Ruby started panting heavily, her emotions swirling. Luther stared at me, something raw and vulnerable in his eyes. I let go of his cock. My hand was drenched in her slick. I stroked my own cock, getting it wet.

I dragged her back by the hips, letting Luther's full length fill her. She groaned and trembled.

"No, no, Ruby don't come." Luther held her face, putting the force of his aura into his words. Not quite an alpha bark, but close. "Breathe. Just breathe."

I pushed her body forward quickly. She gasped with a sharp intake of air at the sudden emptiness.

"Don't chase it. Let go and just feel what your alpha is giving you." Luther's voice was intense and commanding. "Good girl. Surrender to it."

She collapsed on his chest and shifted her knees forward, opening herself more. She trembled, straining to do what her alpha said. Luther reached down and laced his fingers in mine on her hip. There were worlds of things we had never said to each other. There'd be time for that.

"Luther, please." Ruby picked her head up and said his name with a sob that was soaked in omega need.

"Ask your alpha to give you what you need."

She turned and looked at me over her shoulder, a "please" slipped out in a harsh whisper. He turned her face back to him and repeated himself slower with command in his voice.

"Alpha," she licked her lips, lost in a cloud of omega need, "please give me my alpha's knot."

I pulled her upright, her body weight sinking Luther's length deep into her. I pushed the tip of my cock just past the ring of muscles, until she whimpered, but no further.

My fingers circled her throat as Luther's dug into mine on her hip. I pushed her down on Luther's knot and sank my teeth into the nape of her neck. The bond between us flashed white hot with possession and love.

"Come for your alphas, Ruby." Luther groaned, feeling our connection burn.

The force of the pleasure rolling through her stole her breath. I held her still with my teeth, her blood dancing on my tongue. A feral edge tipped into Luther's eyes as I began to move in her with short, powerful strokes until my knot was pressed against her.

"You're so fucking beautiful," he said, to both of us. "Take Cross' knot." He groaned, straining to hold back his own orgasm.

Ruby grasped my forearms and then tipped herself forward, pushing herself against my knot. I let go of her neck to wrap my arm around her chest. My fingers dug into her breast. I bit down harder on her neck, and thrust into her, feeling her tight body take my knot into her, a growl bubbling up from my chest.

"Alpha!" she screamed, finding her voice.

"Fuck. Come Ruby. Harder." Luther arched his back as he released into her, pleasure so sharp he clenched his teeth. He pressed his thumb to her clit, not giving her a moment to recover, tipping her over the edge again, her body spasming around our knots deep within her.

"Cross," Luther said my name on a gasping whisper. I crushed my omega to me and filled her with my cum, my orgasm so intense it dimmed my vision.

Luther didn't let up, making Ruby come again and again, using her body, the connection through my bite to undo me completely.

I finally sagged forward, pulling my teeth from my omega. She collapsed into a quivering mess on Luther's chest. I licked at the rivulets of blood that had dripped down her spine, causing a final massive shudder to rock her body. Luther moaned, kissing the top of her head, his fingers circling the fresh claiming bite. I pressed my lips to her shoulder, Luther cupped the back of my head.

We all just breathed in a messy pile for a while, with Luther supporting both our bodies. When my knot receded enough, I slipped from her with a groan. She gasped, arching her back, coming again with the sudden movement and emptiness. Luther matching her with another orgasm, too. He grabbed my neck, crushing his lips to mine, letting me feel the last waves of their pleasure through his tongue in my mouth.

I curled alongside Luther, my head sharing space with Ruby's on his chest. Her breath had a little hitch to it, a distinctly satisfied omega noise. She struggled to pick up her head, so I held her chin for her. Her breath was ragged, but her blue-green eyes swirled with fire.

"You're mine now." Her declaration was met with growls from both Luther and I.

And growls from the bedroom doorway.

We all turned to see Talon leaning on the doorframe, his arms wrapped around Jackson, one hand on his hard cock. Satisfied alpha grins splitting their faces.

Jackson prowled across the bed, throwing himself into our pile of exhausted lust. He kissed each of us, his tongue playful yet demanding. He bent Ruby's head down to inspect her new bite mark. He pressed his lips to it, causing a full body shudder to rip through her. Luther moaned and bucked under her, his knot keeping them connected. Talon joined us, stretching on Luther's other side, propped up on an elbow. Ruby twisted her head to show him the mark to his proud purr.

"We leave you three alone for a minute and you do this?" Jackson said in mock outrage.

Ruby pushed herself up and looked down at her alphas. She should be wrecked, exhausted, spent. Her eyes danced over us, her lust simmering in the pack bonds.

"Well," she said thoughtfully to Jackson, "I needed dick. What was I supposed to do?"

We all lost it. Our laughter shook the pack bed.

"Luther," Jackson's voice was sharp, "hurry up and make your knot let go of her, so I can lick your cum out of her and fill her up again. Our omega needs dick." The two of them groaned when Ruby shuddered at Jackson's words.

"Fuck me." Luther gasped.

"Exactly my point." Jackson pulled Ruby up and circled her clit with a finger.

"We are not going to make it with two ruthless sluts, are we?" I said to Talon, who snorted.

Jackson dipped his head, bringing his lips to where Luther and Ruby were still joined.

"Jackson!" Ruby shouted in admonishment, just before he made her come again.

SIXTY-FIVE

RUBY

"No, it's 'shao' like in 'shower'." Luther corrected, adjusting the strap of his weapon so it laid flat against his neck.

"Shao... long... bao." I said the words slowly, wanting to get it right. "But how do you put soup in a dumpling?"

"Honestly, I have no idea. It's some kind of dark magic." Luther was trying to look relaxed, with a little chuckle in his voice. He was anything but relaxed.

I could tell now, I could feel it in our bond. Even though that connection was muted tonight, I could still feel a taste of his stress. He had a particular kind of tenseness that my other alphas didn't have. He was holding tight to his aura, years of practice at hiding the fact he was a rogue. He never really relaxed fully.

"Raviolis are a dumpling, too?" I asked, avoiding looking at the monitors.

"Yup. Every cuisine has a dumpling."

"And it's a whole restaurant just for dumplings?"

"Well, Kirriman's Noodle House is known for its noodles, obviously, but they have dim sum brunch on the weekends."

Luther was good at this. He was good at keeping my attention off of things that would send me out of control. He made everything logical and simple and in order. We were calling it 'the spins', when my thoughts would get all jumbled and whirl madly in my head. When I got that way, I couldn't talk or think straight. Luther could stop the spins before it even got started.

He wanted it to be a surprise, a pack outing at Kirriman's, so we were studying the menu. I wanted to be able to order for myself. Jackson's whole 'you can have anything you ask for' thing was harder than it seemed, especially when you didn't know what you liked.

The first time we went to dinner it was a disaster. The diner had a menu that was an inch thick and had everything from breakfast sandwiches to lobster. I panicked, pulled on my Ruin Winters costume, flirted with the server, and then burst into tears. Cross and Jackson growled at the server. Luther tucked me under his arm and ate his whole meal one-handed. Talon had ordered me waffles, but I couldn't eat anything. Luther made me tiny pancakes when we got home instead.

There was a clatter, then a thump from down the hall. I looked at the door. Luther looked at the monitors. He twisted off the cap of a water bottle and handed it to me. I took a sip as he brushed his knuckles down my cheek. It did nothing to remove the pasty feel from my mouth. I closed my eyes and leaned into his touch.

He towered over me as I sat in the rickety folding chair. He looked every bit the superhero angel from the first night we met. But now he was mine. For real.

"You don't have to do this," he whispered, palm cupping my face.

I nodded, not taking the exit he offered. They all had offered it. Closure was important, or so said my therapist. I doubt this was what she had in mind.

Luther eased my legs apart and knelt between them. He ran a thumb across my lower lip.

"Don't," I twisted my face away, "lipstick…"

He smiled, eyes lighting up, like that was the most ridiculous thing he had ever heard. He was so beautiful. I could lose myself in his hazel eyes long enough to find myself again. He pulled me down to him, pressing his lips against mine. There was another bump from the hallway. I rubbed his mouth with the cuff of my shirt. There were no lipstick smudges, though. Of course Jackson would buy me kiss proof lipstick.

I handed him back the water bottle. He stuffed it in a pocket on his thigh and offered his hand to pull me out of the chair. It was time. I didn't take it, and I avoided his attempt to hug me. That much touch was too confusing right now.

Luther stayed a half step behind me as we made our way down the hall, the click of my heels the only sound. His boots were silent.

We entered the room, and all I saw were my alphas. Cross was at a makeshift table with his laptop, headphones covering one ear. He turned his body toward us, but didn't stop working.

Talon's massive presence commanded the center of the room. Luther was the tallest, the biggest of my alphas, but Talon seemed huge right now. He was dressed all in black, a gun in a ready position across his stomach. 'Heckler and Koch MP5 submachine gun'. I corrected myself in my head, trying to remember what Talon said about it when he taught me how to fire it yesterday.

Jackson was crouched on the balls of his feet just outside of camera range. He tapped the business end of the cattle prod on the floor. He pivoted to look at me, giving me a head-to-toe assessment. His blank facial expression didn't change, so I couldn't tell what he was thinking. The bonds were no help, either. They were all carefully controlling our connection. It was disorienting to not feel them all so vibrantly.

Jackson stood and fiddled with the camera, moving the whole tripod setup out of the way. The blaze of the ring light was the only light in the room.

I took a deep breath and wanted to gag. The air was full of the scent of fear and fury, and piss, and burning hair. I closed my eyes to seek out my alphas' scents, desperate for the comfort of cut grass, and whiskey, and black pepper. Talon's sea salt and pine eventually wrapped around me and pushed out everything else.

I pulled back the metal chair that was placed next to the ring light to sit. On a whim, I turned it around, my legs wide to straddle it, sitting on it backwards, my arms resting casually on the top of the chair.

I watched his face as he stared at my shoes, red patent leather heels, and dragged his eyes up my legs, clad in skintight, deep indigo jeans. My shoes and off-the-shoulder top matched my red hair. He stopped at my widespread legs, disgust and desire twitching his facial features. Was he also remembering when he duct taped my legs together for three days to teach me not to sit like a slutty whore?

With effort, he pulled his eyes to my face. His lip curled in a snarl.

"You..." his words were cut off with a scream, as Jackson hit him with the cattle prod on the shin. His pants were rolled to the knee showing off dozens of red blistering marks.

"Father," I said in greeting. Only the girls, the young ones, could call him 'Father'. Everyone else in the group home called him 'Mr. Forthright'.

His double-breasted jacket hung open, hiding the ropes tying his hands to the legs of the chair. The fact he wasn't talking with his hands on camera would probably look a little weird, not that it would matter in the end. A big wet stain radiated out from his lap.

I took a deep breath. Jackson's peppery, woodsy scent joined Talon's. I woke up to their scents this morning. We must have been playing Twister in our sleep, their bodies had both been wrapped around me tightly. Jackson made just enough room between us to slide his fingers in me to make me come before I was fully awake. I fucking loved that.

I looked at my foster father and his disheveled state. 'Foster father' was generous. He did little more than stick kids in his house and collect government pay checks for our upkeep. I was never a favorite of his. I didn't even think he knew my name. And then I perfumed.

"You're going to get in your car and drive. There's enough gas in it to get you out of New Oxford." I pitched my voice low so it wouldn't crack. I had practiced a speech, outlining all the horrible things that should never have happened to a child. None of that mattered now. I just wanted him gone.

"Listen, whore..."

I tsked at him when his screams finally died down after another hit from the cattle prod.

"You're going to find a job at a gas station, get an apartment." I snapped my fingers at him to get his attention. "You are no longer Mason Forthright, leader of the Reset. You're just a beta with no prospects. Do you understand?"

He scoffed at me, so I continued.

"For the next 3,130 days, all you will do is go to work and sit in your apartment. If you create a social media account, we will know and take it from you. If you talk to another woman, we will know. If you contact anyone from Berry Creek, not that there are many left, we will know and put an end to it. If you sleep anywhere but on the floor, we will know."

Mason paused at that.

"You remember that, don't you, Father? How you made the girls earn the right to sleep in a bed?"

He let his eyes roam around the room, stopping on each of my alphas. Their reaction was what mattered to him, not mine.

"So, no bed for you for the next 3,130 days, until you find a way to earn it." I pouted, just like Ruin. Just like he taught me when he came up with the Ruin Winters idea.

I snapped my fingers at him again. Simmering hatred burned on his face. He had no idea what hate actually felt like.

"This is the thanks I get for taking you out of your dead mother's arms and giving you a home? Killed by knotters like them." He jutted his chin out.

A memory clawed its way out of my head. Boys bigger than me sitting on me, holding me by the hair. My mother screaming, being held back. Another boy, younger, blond curls messy across his forehead. His snarl that turned into a growl that split the playground in two. I shook my head to clear my vision.

Talon's aura burst into the room making me want to duck out of the way. Luther stepped to him, their shoulders just brushing. That was enough to bring Talon back down. I had insisted they not kill him. I was rethinking that now.

I nodded at Luther. He told me he'd try something like this. Mason would try to blame me, make me feel ungrateful, like I owed him thanks for the terrible things they'd done to me because he'd saved me. I licked my lips and continued.

"If you have more than one month's rent in a bank account, we will take that from you, too."

He snorted at that. Cross stood and held a tablet right in front of his face. He flipped through a dozen or so screen shots of different bank accounts, all showing zero balances as of this morning. The color drained from his face. His breath became ragged. Money was Mason's soft spot.

"You... you can't..."

"We did. All of it. We took all of it, Mason." I wanted there to be a sense of satisfaction at beating him finally. The fact that the money was the most upsetting part for him, left me feeling numb.

"So, do you understand?" I used the same tone he'd use with

us as children, "The corrective action is no bed, no bank, no girls for the next 3,130 days."

"Three thousand... what... what does that mean?"

"Oh, great question. Thank you for asking." Jackson snorted at my perky voice. "That's how many days it's been since I perfumed and you did... this to me."

"And... and then what?" I saw the twinkle of scheming hope brighten his eyes.

"The corrective action should match the misstep, right? A day for every day you took from me. That's when *my* punishment will end." I felt Talon behind me, his aura hot and sharp again. "That's when *their* punishment will begin." I gestured to the huge men around me.

Genuine fear seeped out of Mason now. Jackson stood and made a show of pulling out a giant knife from a sheath strapped to his thigh. He leaned into Mason, pinching his shoulder, cleanly slicing the ropes binding him to the chair. Mason rubbed his wrists, trying to get his breathing under control. Jackson tapped his cheek with the side of the blade and jerked his head toward the door.

Mason got to his feet, uncertain. He made a wide path around us.

"Let me walk you out, Father." My voice was dipped in acid, making him cringe.

His pace was slow at first, but he was practically running after a moment. We followed him out. I was flanked by my alphas, their growls no longer contained.

"Drive and don't ever look back. We'll be watching," I said to his back as he scrambled into the car and started it. Bits of gravel from the broken pavement kicked up as tires squealed.

Jackson put a hand on my hip and tried to pull me close. I shrugged him off and followed the car down the drive a few steps until I could no longer see the taillights. My breath came hard and fast, a sob trying to escape.

I turned to find Luther. His face was stone, but somehow still soft in the dim light that caught in fuzzy blond hair. He came to me and tilted my head up with a gentle finger, running his thumb across my bottom lip.

"We finish the job." The certainty in his eyes gave me something to hold on to.

He stepped back to pull on a helmet and zip up his leather jacket, repositioning his weapon so it would be hidden. Cross handed Jackson a thumb drive. He held it in his teeth while he zipped his own jacket up. Jackson reached for my hand and brought it to his lips, kissing the bite mark Talon had claimed me with. Cross pressed his lips to the top of my head before getting on one of the three dirt bikes.

They were going to follow Mason out of town and then get to work.

Jackson would deliver the thumb drive. I had spent all week editing a behind the scenes look at the making of the last Ruin Winters video. We had a lot of footage from the computer in my apartment. We only had to reshoot a handful of scenes to get the look I wanted. Cross had frantically added Mason's confessions tonight. Jackson was to deliver it to a contact he had who would leak it to the media.

Cross and Luther would be paying a visit to Berry Creek. There would be a tragic 'murder-suicide' event involving my foster mother and a few others that the news wouldn't cover and no one would care about tomorrow.

I watched them suit up and get on the bikes. Dirt bikes with no license plates or head lamps. Unidentifiable and disposable. Exactly what you wanted when you were off to deal out vengeance.

Jackson curled his fingers under the faceplate of Luther's

helmet and brought their heads together for a moment. I was too far away to hear whatever words passed between them. Luther nodded and hung his head before kicking the bike to life. He rode away without a look back. Jackson's hand lingered on Cross' back as they, too, shared a word. Cross pulled on his helmet and waited for Jackson before taking off together.

My hands crept up to cover my ears in the sudden silence, the rumble of the bikes eaten up by the darkness around me.

I spun to Talon. My alpha was tall, and lean, and deadly in the darkness.

"I don't feel any better." My words came out on panting breaths.

Talon wrapped his hand around my neck and pulled me to him, backing us up a few paces toward the car. His touch was gentle, but commanding. His fingertips danced on the claiming bites on my neck, sending a shiver through me.

"You're so brave, omega." He opened the bond between us, flooding me with a fierce, possessive love.

"Alpha." I closed my eyes and leaned into the grip around my throat. He threaded his other hand into my hair and pulled my head back. "Make me... make me feel something that's not this."

Talon growled low, vibrating the air between us, going right to my core.

"Is that what you need, omega? To be claimed again?"

I nodded, stretching my neck to feel his fingers digging in. My back bumped up against the SUV. His sea salt scent swirled all around me, making me feel drunk. He undid the button of my tight jeans and we worked together to get them off my hips and free one leg, the red heel falling to the dirt.

"Already wet for me, omega?" He pushed two fingers into me, making me grunt. "But this is not what you need. Is it? Tell me."

I ground myself into his hand, hooking my leg around his hip. "Knot me. Sir."

517

His eyes flashed with a feral intensity. I fumbled with his utility belt, letting gravity do most of the work to pull it off his hips. I reached into his pants and took him in both my hands. I whimpered when he withdrew his fingers from my body, only to moan when he pushed them into my mouth. I closed my eyes and greedily sucked his fingers.

"You need to be filled, don't you? Feeling empty, omega?" He pulled his fingers out of my mouth, ignoring my protests. He guided my legs around his hips and entered me in one smooth movement. My back went rigid as he ground his knot against me.

"Better?" He purred into my ear, his own breathing harsh. "Is this what you needed?"

I tried to buck against him, but he pinned me to the SUV.

"Knot." I panted.

He began to move, hard, deep thrusts, keeping me full and stretched. I buried my nose in his neck, wrapping my arms tight around him, wanting more of him. Wanting him to never let go. A high pitched grunt matched each thrust as his knot hit my clit.

Talon pushed me back, wrapping a hand round my throat, his finger pressing into both Jackson and Cross' bites.

"Tell me who you belong to, omega." I started to come at the growl in his voice.

"Pack!"

He put his teeth over Jackson's claiming bite, pushing his knot into me. A lick of pain at the sudden stretching intensified the waves of pleasure erupting from my core. My body tightened and pulsed around Talon's cock. He slid a hand between us, his thumb finding my clit with rough circles.

"Good little omega. Keep coming for me. Don't stop. Come harder, omega. You want my cum in you, don't you? Good girl."

His words flowed over me, only interrupted by his grunts and my screams. He thrust his tongue in my mouth as he came deep inside me, hot spurts causing more waves to crash through me.

Locked together, his knot still swollen and deep in me, he held me as I trembled. Talon covered Jackson's bite with soft touches of his lips. Each kiss sent a shock wave through my body.

I sagged in Talon's arms. Filled with my alpha, I knew that this was exactly what I was meant to be.

Omega.

Mate.

Loved.

EPILOGUE

LUTHER

I held the top of the door open, snagging the helmet out of her hands as Ruby ducked under my arm. I was super relaxed and horny as fuck, having had her wrapped around me on the back of my bike for the 30-minute ride.

She put up the collar of the leather coat, snuggling into it like armor. Jackson had just bought the jacket for her. She somehow managed to look badass and sophisticated at the same time. She nervously fluffed up her cherry red hair. I could feel she was concerned with how it looked after the helmet.

"You're so fucking hot," I whispered as I guided her to a large table in the back. She put a hand to her cheek. She was blushing.

The place was moderately crowded. There were only a few empty stools at the bar, but plenty of open tables. It was still early for it to fill up with locals and bikers.

I scanned the room. No betas in fatigues today. I suppressed a savage smile. Killing them all would top my lists for the rest of my life. There were a few people who'd skipped town right after the explosion, but Cross was keeping tabs on them. They'd have unfortunate accidents sometime soon.

The only thing out of place was an alpha who sat alone at a corner table, reading. A hard cover not a paperback. Who the fuck came to the Delta Lounge to read?

I pulled out a chair for her. Ruby scanned all of the TVs that hung close to the ceiling. The sound was down, and they were all on different channels. She looked at her watch. It was one of Jackson's designer ones that he had sized down for her. It was huge and overbearing on her tiny wrist. The other night as we cuddled on the couch, she confessed in a whisper that the watch felt like a hand wrapped around her wrist. With that and Talon's bite on her other wrist, it made her feel safe. Later, as she rode my cock, she told me in tiny gasping whispers that the feeling of being held down like that also turned her on.

I put a hand to my chest and took a deep breath as I sat. Ruby's citrus and cream scent rose off her and did absolutely nothing to bring my hormones down.

"They won't be late." I put my hand on her knee under the table and pulled the plastic sleeve containing the menu closer for us to both read.

The food here was surprisingly fantastic. There were about a dozen appetizers, burgers and a few sandwiches and specials written on a stained sticky note attached to the outside of the menu. We should have taken her somewhere like this rather than that diner. Too much choice was sometimes suffocating.

"Oh, he can fuck right the fuck off." Moxie said over her shoulder to someone in the kitchen as she kicked the swinging door open. She had three bottles of vodka in her arms. Her hair, her wig, was bright blue and cut at the chin to frame her face. It was pinned back on one side with electric pink flowers.

"Luther!" she said in a perky voice, smiling. Then she

frowned, her eyes darted between me and Ruby. "Can you step into the kitchen for a second and help me open a pickle jar?"

"A what?" Ruby narrowed her eyes and raised an eyebrow. I gave a quick glance around the room. "I'll be right back." I squeezed Ruby's thigh and got up from the table.

I followed Moxie back into the kitchen. She put the bottles down on the stainless steel counter and rounded on me and rained down a flurry of ineffective slaps.

"What the fuck, Mox!" I curled my shoulder away from her.

"You bring a girl here so I can read her aura? Without telling her I'm a... a..." she gave me an exaggerated wink instead of saying the word seer. "So I can tell you what's wrong with her? That's a shitty thing to do to the both of us."

"Hey!" Unimpressed with her own attack, she picked up bread rolls from a basket on the counter and threw them at me. "I brought my mate for drinks and to introduce you."

"Mate?" She paused, having exhausted the supply of rolls. She cocked her head, her brows slid together in confusion. "That's not what I'm..." Moxie stepped back to run her eyes up and down me again. "Mate? But you haven't bitten her?"

"She's bonded into the pack. That's what matters," I said hotly, rubbing the back of my neck.

"Oh for fuck's sakes, Luther, get over yourself and just bite her." She threw her hands up, and turned to reach for something on a high shelf.

"I..."

She thrust a pickle jar at me. I blinked at her. She gave me an 'Are you dense?' look. The top came off with a satisfying pop. She took the jar back, making sure the lid was loose but secure.

"I've been trying to open that for a month." Her eyes were a flat brown color, the contacts hiding the telltale red and white irises of a seer. "You're connected in ways you can't understand. Just bite her already."

She turned her back on me and headed for the walk-in fridge like that was the end of the conversation. I cracked my neck, my hand pausing on the door. I couldn't bite Ruby, not yet anyway. I just didn't feel... I scrubbed my face and pushed into the dining room.

My aura immediately flared. Ruby was on her feet, her back against the wall, her jacket unzipped and pulled off her shoulder to show off her bite marks. An alpha and a beta, young guys, in ripped jeans, one in an Alphabetas t-shirt, the other in a plain black hoodie were frozen with their hands up. They were being held back by the menacing presence of the book nerd alpha who commanded the center of the room.

"It's all good." The book nerd acknowledged me with an uptick of his head and a backward step. "We were just having a little grammar lesson. Reminded these two that 'no' was a complete sentence."

A growl rolled out of me and my aura pressed further into the room. Ruby stepped to my side, grabbed my wrist, and yanked my arm over her shoulder. She threaded her fingers through mine and pressed my palm to her breast, pushing my fingers down to squeeze. She was making a public claim, a sexually aggressive one.

And then she growled.

The pair turned on a heel and made for the door. They were stopped by the unmovable wall of Cross who had just entered the bar. His growl was subaudible, but even at a distance I could feel it in the pit of my stomach. They sidestepped Cross and practically tripped over themselves. Once the door shut behind them, Cross made his way over to us. The book nerd alpha gave him a nod and returned to his table.

The whole bar watched as Cross picked Ruby up into a hug, her feet left dangling from the height difference. She clamped her hand around mine harder, both of our fingers digging into her breast as Cross kissed her bite claimed neck.

"I want to fuck you right now," Cross rumbled into her ear. "But Moxie has a 'no sex in the bar' rule."

He rubbed his cheek against her, burying his face in her neck. My eyes shot wide. So did Ruby's. Her breath quickened. Cross had just scent marked her. It was the first time any of us had done that. Citrus and whiskey filled the space between us. Cross' hand joined mine over Ruby's breast, squeezing the back of my neck with his other hand.

As we took our seats, Ruby's aura seeped around us. It was calming but possessive in a distinctly omega way.

Heads turned back to the door when it creaked open for Jackson and Talon. All eyes were on Jackson and his movie star looks as he threaded his way to us through the haphazard collection of chairs and tables. He did not look like someone who would be a regular patron of a dive bar at the edge of town. Talon slid his hand into Ruby's fire-red hair, pulling her head back as Jackson traced the outlines of the claiming bite on her neck. They left no doubt as to who Ruby belonged to.

Jackson's brow crinkled. He dipped his head to Ruby's neck. His eyes popped wide when he realized Cross had scent marked her.

"Fuck me," he whispered, it barely audible.

"Have we ordered yet?" Talon asked, sitting on Ruby's other side.

Jackson was across from me. He was less unnerved than the rest of us about having his back to potential threats. Talon reached around Ruby to rub the back of my head. The touch was reassuring, reminding me that the pack was together and solid. My shoulders relaxed a little.

Moxie bustled out of the kitchen with a huge platter in her hands. She put down the plate in front of Ruby with two giant waffles, and two smaller bowls next to it. One of them piled high with whipped cream.

Ruby shot straight up with anxiety. "I... I didn't order this."

"I know," Moxie said in a big sister kind of way, "but it's what you need. Dylan, my cook, used to work for BetaButters. It's their recipe, but don't tell anyone. And dip it into the creme anglaise sauce and whipped cream. Trust me." She arranged the plates in front of Ruby for better dipping access.

"Ah, so," she put her hands on her hips and surveyed us. "An IPA for Cross. Milkshake for your mate. Congratulations, by the way." She nodded at Talon. "Orange soda for Luther. Jackson will have a..." she tapped her lip in thought for a second. "Mai Tai. No Cosmo. And Talon? Ugh. A root beer? Seriously?" She rolled her eyes and headed for the bar.

Ruby's eyes shot wide, and she turned to me.

"We'll explain Moxie later."

She looked down at the dishes on the table. She picked up a spoon and dipped it hesitantly into the bowl of creme anglaise.

"It's like pudding, but less pudding-y." I whispered to her. She took a taste, grinned, pulled it to her and took a big spoonful.

Jackson popped out of his chair and headed for the bar. He hoisted himself up so he could fish around for something on the other side. He came back and sat down with a metal bucket full of remote controls. He methodically clicked all the TVs to the Romeo Knight Show, which was just about to begin.

"Leighton said it would be in the B block, so after the second commercial break." He said, pounding the last remote against his palm to get it to work.

"Are we going to owe Romeo for this?" Talon asked.

"Nope. He doesn't know the source. But since Leighton is immune to my charms and I couldn't pay her in dick, we'll owe her a favor for sure."

The fork full of waffle stopped halfway to Ruby's mouth.

Jackson winked at her. She put her fork down, not knowing what to make of the comment.

Moments later, food came to the table. Moxie could match your drink order to your aura, but relied on past preferences for food. We were pretty basic with our bacon cheeseburgers and a giant order of onion rings.

I looked around at my pack. Jackson and Cross chatted about a possible job that was in the works. Mostly surveillance, nothing exciting. They both monitored the TVs. Talon had yanked Ruby's chair closer. He was undoubtedly whispering filthy things in her ear. The lucky bastard. She reached out a hand to steal a french fry off my plate. I snagged it and kissed her bite marked wrist, before feeding her a fry.

And I was stupid happy.

Jackson jumped, quickly wiping his fingers on a paper napkin before picking up two remotes to click the volume up.

Romeo Knight was perched on the edge of his couch. The omega usually had some celebrity or another on his weekly show. But he usually did one segment of "news." Just Romeo and his perfect hair going on and on about the issues of the day. It could be anything from zoning laws to animal rights. I held the suspicion that it was little more than his personal platform to unleash digital vengeance on people who pissed him off.

"We have an exclusive for you tonight. Some of this footage may be disturbing to our viewers at home." Romeo's stunning features were dour and serious tonight. It was a clue to his audience that some serious shit was going to happen.

Talon, Cross and Jackson were all riveted to the TV. Ruby watched the room. And I watched Ruby.

The video was her idea. She and Cross put it together with footage dug out of the computer in her apartment. She created a storyboard and a production list of shots that would have to be added. Cross had added Mason Forthright's confession clips in between torture sessions.

The video was pure propaganda, and Ruby was very good at it. The Institute should hire her on the spot.

It was also Ruby's idea to watch it in a bar with normal people. She wanted to see for herself if it was going to be successful. She needed to know if people would buy the villain origin story.

Ruby scanned the room, gauging reactions. At first no one paid attention really, but as Romeo got into the tale of Ruin Winters by Ruby Frost, the room quieted and then went dead silent. Ruby cleverly edited together different clips of Bennett and Billy degrading and abusing her in between takes. She was almost always in the same outfit, the dark turtleneck, black hair, the sunglasses and her luscious black lips. It made the editing almost seamless.

The entire world was now learning that Ruin Winters was an orphan, raised in a foster home in Berry Creek. Through words and fists, you saw Ruin's abuse firsthand.

"Billy, please, I don't want to do this anymore."

Ruby was biting her lip. With that line, several of the alphas in the room stood. It was an unconscious, protective move. The book nerd alpha closed his book and was on the edge of his seat. Ruby made Ruin just helpless enough to push everyone's sympathy buttons.

By the time we got to the final frames of the video, Ruby was biting her nails. A nervous tick I'd never seen from her before.

The camera raced across a charred lawn, smoke and fire in the background. A woman's foot came into frame and panned up her body lying on the ground. The last shot was blurry and jumpy. It captured Ruin Winters with blood trickling out of her black lips, her blank eyes staring up at nothing from behind broken sunglasses.

"Ruin Winters is dead." Romeo was back on screen looking shaken.

I scanned the people in the bar. They were all in different shades of horrified as Romeo continued to recap the video. Except for Moxie. She was staring right at Ruby, drumming her fingers on the bar.

The show went to commercial, and people returned to their drinks with hushed whispers to their neighbors. The mood turned from shocked to somber.

This job was complete now.

We all stood. Jackson peeled off some bills to pay the check. We grabbed our helmets and jackets. Talon ushered Ruby to the door. I waved at Moxie, who was frowning, and gave a nod to the book nerd.

In the parking lot, gravel crunched under our boots as we made our way to our vehicles. Talon held the door to the SUV for Ruby, but she pulled her helmet out of my hands and headed for my bike. Talon's eye twitched, but he didn't say anything. He hated having her on a bike, preferring she be cocooned in tons of steel.

I stilled her hands as she was wiggling the straps of the helmet out of the way, and tipped her chin up to look at me. I trailed my finger down her neck where Cross had marked her. I could feel Ruby's emotions through the bond. They were... complicated. It was like she was packing up her emotional house. Not suppressing things or stuffing them down, just putting them away.

Killing everyone who'd touched her was closure for us, the pack. Killing Ruin Winters, was closure for Ruby.

"Could we go to the beach one day?" She asked.

"The beach? I've never been."

She pulled her helmet on and fastened it under her chin. She stepped back so I could swing my leg over the bike. She got on behind me like a pro, sliding her hands around my stomach.

"Good. So, I'm not the only weirdo who has never been to the beach before. We'll go together."

I reached back and squeezed her thigh. My smile was wider than any ocean.

"Together."

WANT MORE?!

NOOOOO! Take it back! This isn't the end!

Didn't get enough of the happily ever after? Go to AmyNovaBooks.com

What's in it?

Nests. Problems with nests. Building nests. Nest trauma. Sex in nests, sex while shopping for nests, sex out of nests... but more specifically, oral knots, bondage, public play, primal play.

And remember to join my Facebook Group to chat about it!

WHAT'S NEXT IN THE POSONVERSE?

Leighton's story will be told by Olivia Lewin!

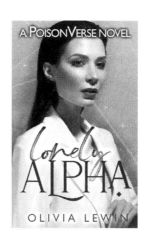

THE POISONVERSE

AMY NOVA'S NEXT POISONVERSE

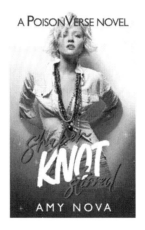

Pre Order Now.

Havoc Killed Her Alpha - *Marie Mackay*
Forget Me Knot - *Marie Mackay*
Pack of Lies - *Olivia Lewin*

Ruined Alphas - *Amy Nova*
Sweetheart - *Marie Mackay*
Lonely Alpha - *Olivia Lewin*
Shaken Knot Stirred - *Amy Nova*
And more to come...

ALSO BY ME!

Why Choose Vampire Romance

Accidental Vampire

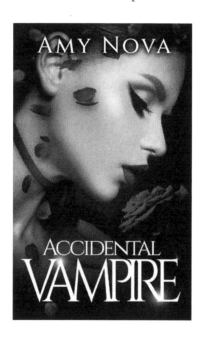

Printed in Poland
by Amazon Fulfillment
Poland Sp. z o.o., Wrocław